CAST OF CHARACTERS

KNIGHTS OF THE TRUE CROSS

RIN OKUMURA

Born of a human mother and Satan, the God of Demons, Rin Okumura has powers he can barely control. After Satan kills Father Fujimoto, Rin's foster father, Rin decides to become an Exorcist so he can someday defeat Satan. Now a first-year student at True Cross Academy and an Exwire at the Exorcism Cram School, he hopes to someday b... e a Knight. When he draws the ... manifests his infernal power in ... ames. The Order forbade him to ... he did anyway, and he is now ... y confinement.

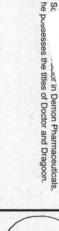

...URA

... ecome a doctor, he's a g... t student ever to be... e Exorcism Cram Sc... ctor in Demon Pharmaceuticals, he possesses the titles of Doctor and Dragoon.

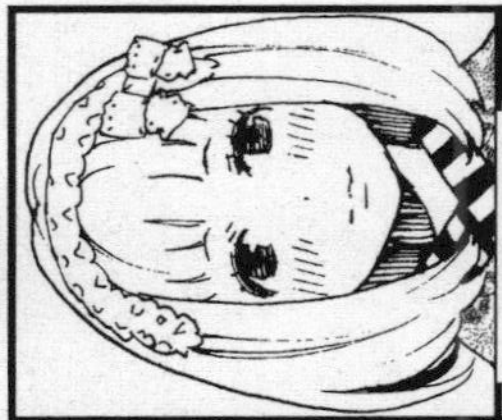

SHIEMI MORIYAMA

Daughter of the owner of Futsumaya, an Exorcist supply shop. Inspired by Rin and Yukio, she became an Exwire and hopes to someday become an Exorcist. She has the ability to become a Tamer and can summon a baby Greenman.

RYUJI SUGURO

Heir to the venerable Buddhist sect known as Myodha in Kyoto. He is an Exwire who hopes to become an Exorcist someday so he can reestablish his family's temple, which fell on hard times after the Blue Night. He wants to achieve the titles of Dragoon and Aria.

RENZO SHIMA

Once a pupil of Suguro's father and now Suguro's friend. He's an Exwire who wants to become an Aria. He has an easygoing personality and is totally girl-crazy.

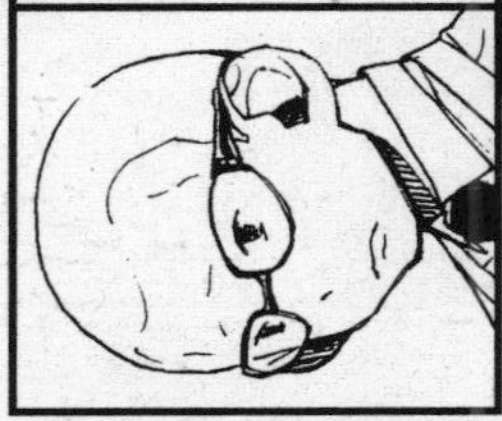

KONEKOMARU MIWA

Like Shima, he was once a pupil of Suguro's father and is now Suguro's friend. He's an Exwire who hopes to become an Exorcist someday. He is small in size and has a quiet and composed personality.

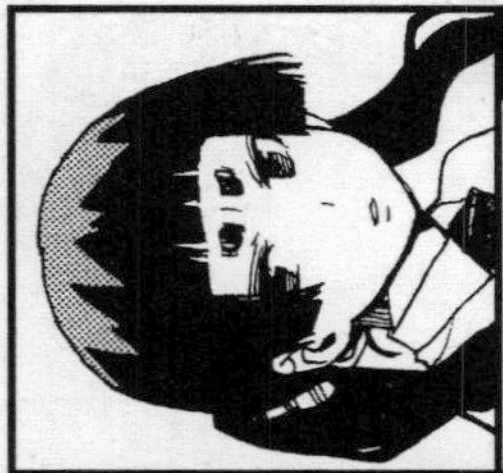

Izumo Kamiki

An Exwire with the blood of shrine maidens. She has the ability to become a Tamer and can summon two white foxes.

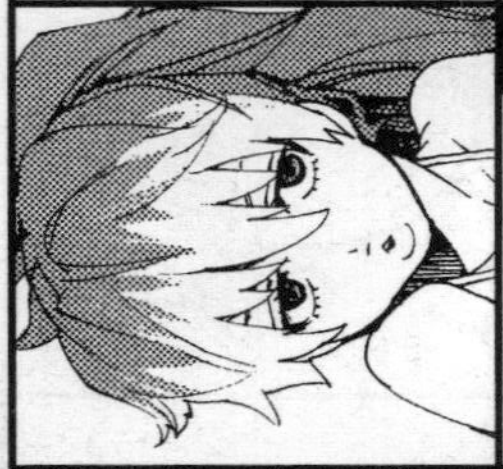

Shura Kirigakure

An upper-rank special investigator dispatched by Vatican Headquarters to True Cross Academy. A Senior Exorcist First Class who holds the titles of Knight, Tamer, Doctor and Aria.

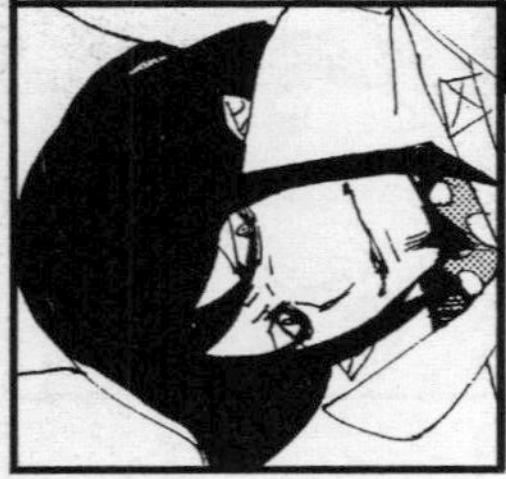

Mephisto Pheles

President of True Cross Academy and head of the Exorcism Cram School. He was Father Fujimoto's friend, and now he is Rin and Yukio's guardian. He plans to turn Rin into a weapon to use in the fight against Satan.

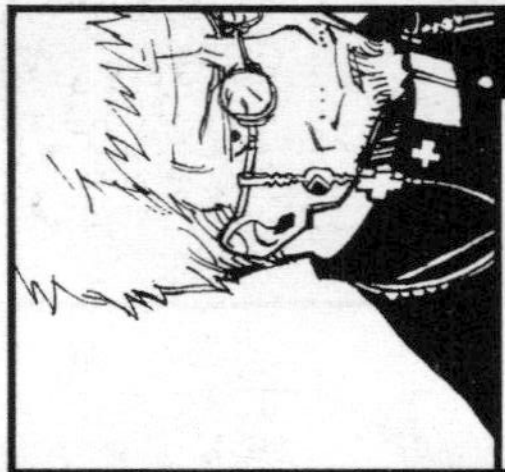

Shiro Fujimoto

The man who raised Rin and Yukio. He held the rank of Paladin and once taught Demon Pharmaceuticals. Satan possessed him and he gave his life defending Rin.

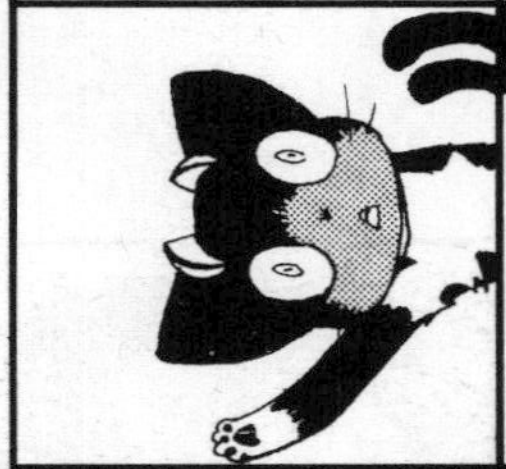

Kuro

A Cat Sídhe who was once Shiro's familiar. After Shiro's death, he began turning back into a demon. Rin saved him, and now the two are practically inseparable. His favorite drink is the catnip wine Shiro used to make.

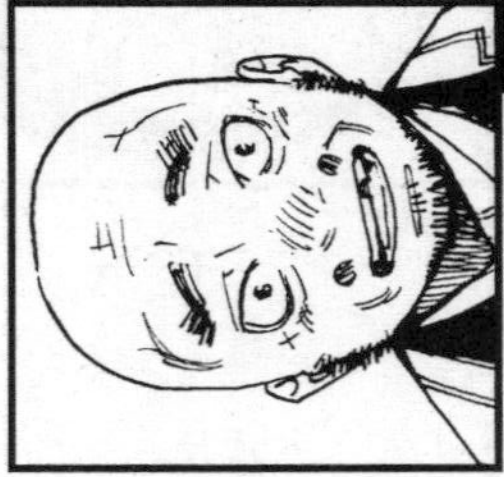

Tatsuma Suguro

Ryuji's father and the leader of Myodha. He doesn't appear to be doing anything to rebuild his temple. People consider him to be an immoral monk. He seems to be doing something in absolute secrecy…

TORAKO SUGURO

Ryuji's mother. She runs the Toraya Inn and secretly uses the proceeds from it to prop up the family temple.

YAOZO SHIMA

Renzo's father. A Senior Buddhist Exorcist First Class holding the classifications of Knight and Aria. In Myodha, he is an archpriest, one rank beneath Tatsuma.

JUZO SHIMA

Second son of the Shima family. A Senior Buddhist Exorcist Second Class holding the classifications of Knight and Aria. He looks cool and collected on the outside but is actually short-tempered.

KINZO SHIMA

The fourth son of the Shima family. An Intermediate Buddhist Exorcist Second Class holding the classifications of Knight and Aria. Like Juzo, he's always ready for a fight.

UWABAMI HOJO

A Senior Buddhist Exorcist First Class holding the classifications of Tamer and Aria. Like Yaozo, he is an archpriest and helps lead the Myodha sect.

MAMUSHI HOJO

An Intermediate Buddhist Exorcist First Class holding the classifications of Tamer and Aria. Todo took advantage of her worries about the future of Myodha and tricked her into cooperating with him.

⬡ DEMONS ⬡

SABUROTA TODO

Todo comes from an honorable family that has supplied the Order with Exorcists for generations. But now he has joined the demons and stolen the Left Eye of the Impure King from the academy. What is his goal now that he has both Eyes?

⬡ THE STORY SO FAR ⬡

UNKNOWN TO RIN OKUMURA, BOTH HUMAN AND DEMON BLOOD RUNS IN HIS VEINS. IN AN ARGUMENT WITH HIS FOSTER FATHER, FATHER FUJIMOTO, RIN LEARNS THAT SATAN IS HIS TRUE FATHER. SATAN SUDDENLY APPEARS AND TRIES TO DRAG RIN DOWN TO GEHENNA BECAUSE RIN HAS INHERITED HIS POWER. FATHER FUJIMOTO FIGHTS TO DEFEND RIN, BUT DIES IN THE PROCESS. RIN DECIDES TO BECOME AN EXORCIST SO HE CAN SOMEDAY DEFEAT SATAN AND BEGINS STUDYING AT THE EXORCISM CRAM SCHOOL UNDER THE INSTRUCTION OF HIS TWIN BROTHER YUKIO, WHO IS ALREADY AN EXORCIST.

HOWEVER, DURING SUMMER VACATION FOREST TRAINING, EVERYONE LEARNS THAT RIN IS THE SON OF SATAN, AND HE APPEARS AS EVIDENCE AT THE QUESTIONING OF MEPHISTO BY THE KNIGHTS OF THE TRUE CROSS. THE COURT LETS RIN GO ON CONDITION THAT HE PASS THE EXORCIST CERTIFICATION EXAM IN SIX MONTHS. UNDER THE SUPERVISION OF SHURA AND YUKIO, HE BEGINS LEARNING TO CONTROL HIS FLAME.

ON THE FIRST DAY OF TRAINING, SOMEONE STEALS THE LEFT EYE OF THE IMPURE KING FROM THE ACADEMY'S DEEP KEEP AND YUKIO GETS A PHONE CALL INFORMING HIM OF AN EMERGENCY SUMMONS. THE CULPRIT BEHIND THE CRISIS IS SABUROTA TODO, A FORMER TEACHER WHO HAS SINCE JOINED THE DEMONS...

◉ THE STORY SO FAR ◉

RIN AND THE OTHERS GO TO THE KYOTO FIELD OFFICE OF
THE KNIGHTS OF THE TRUE CROSS TO ASSIST IN THE DE-
FENSE OF THE RIGHT EYE OF THE IMPURE KING. WHEN
THEY ARRIVE, THEY LEARN THAT ALMOST HALF OF THE
COMBATANTS THERE BELONG TO A RELIGIOUS SECT NAMED
MYO-O DHARANI AND THEIR LEADER IS RYUJI'S FATHER,
THE HIGH PRIEST TATSUMA SUGURO.

TATSUMA FAILS TO ATTEND A MEETING OF THE MYODHA
FAMILY HEADS AND HIS BEHAVIOR DURING AN ATTACK ON
THE FIELD OFFICE WAS UNUSUAL, CAUSING SOME TO
BECOME SUSPICIOUS OF HIM.

THEN THE TRAITOR FINALLY REVEALS HERSELF!!

MAMUSHI HOJO OF THE HOJO BLOODLINE OF ARCHPRIESTS
COOPERATES WITH SABUROTA TODO IN STEALING THE
RIGHT EYE AND THE TWO DISAPPEAR. THEN RYUJI CON-
FRONTS HIS FATHER ABOUT HIS SUSPISCIOUS BEHAVIOR.
WHEN RIN INTERCEDES AND USES HIS FLAME—EXPRESSLY
FORBIDDEN BY THE ORDER—SHURA USES AN IMPRISON-
MENT SPELL TO INCAPACITATE HIM AND RIN ENDS UP
STEWING IN SOLITARY CONFINEMENT!!

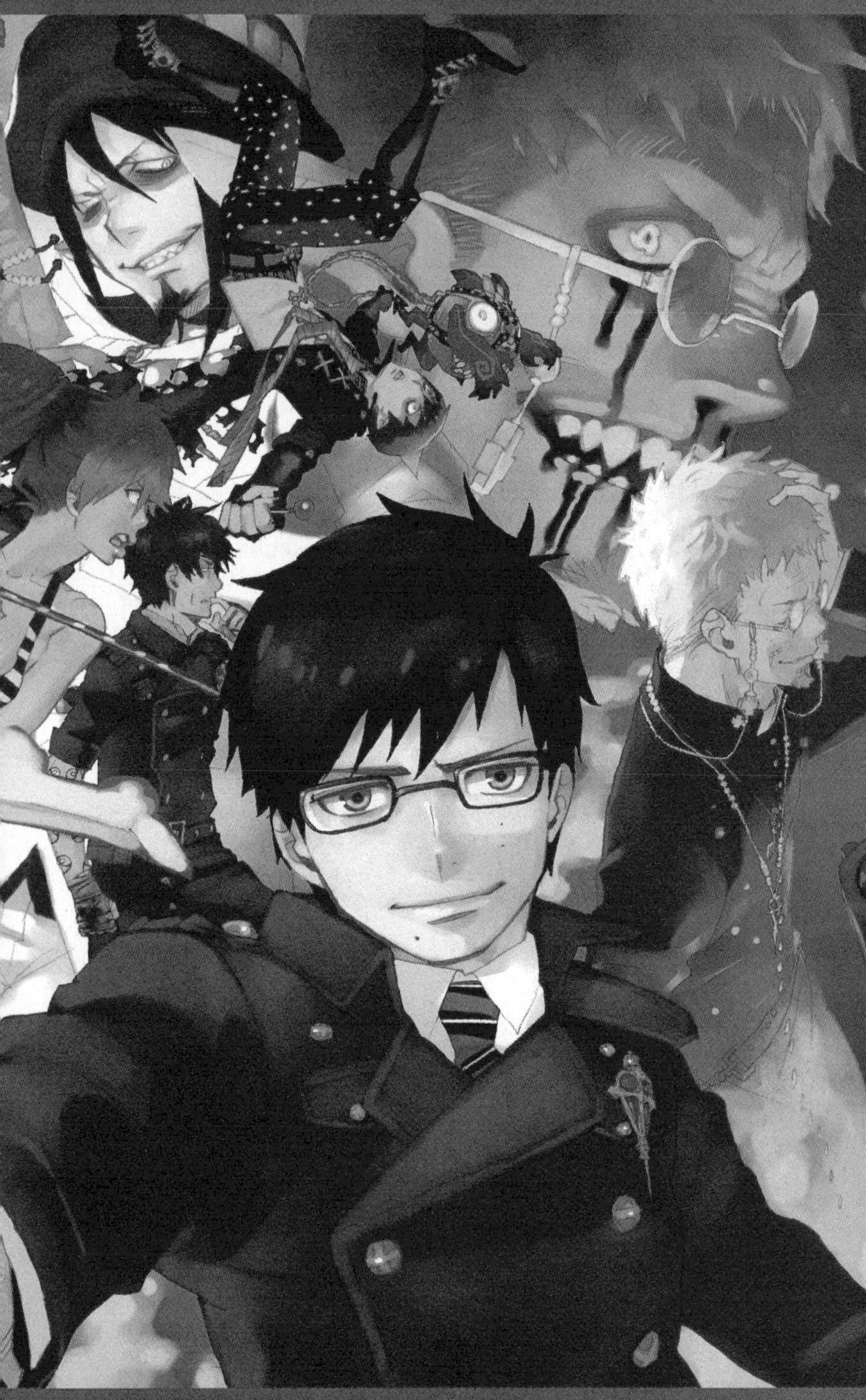

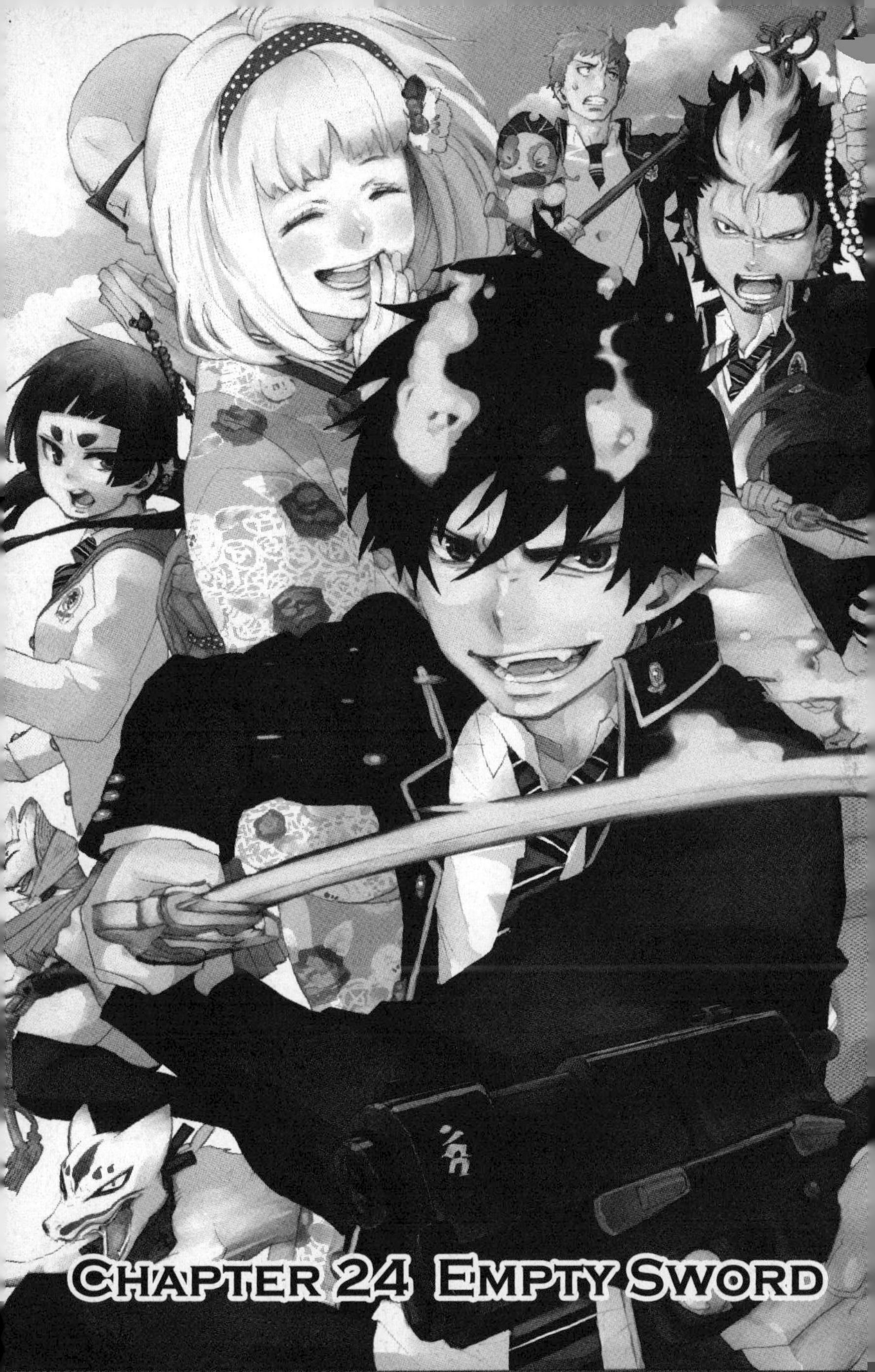

Chapter 24 Empty Sword

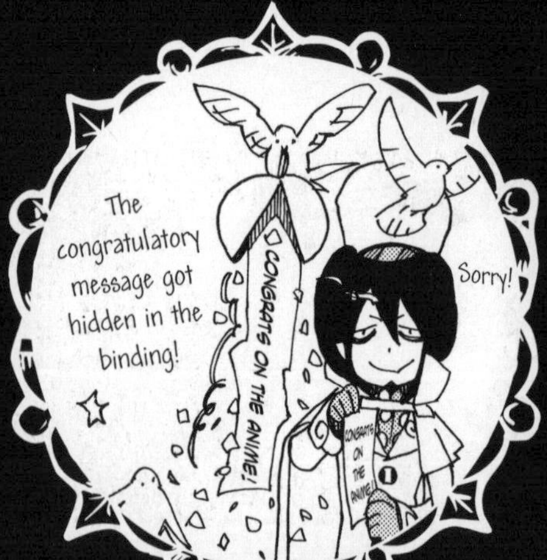
The congratulatory message got hidden in the binding!
Sorry!
CONGRATS ON THE ANIME!
CONGRATS ON THE ANIME!

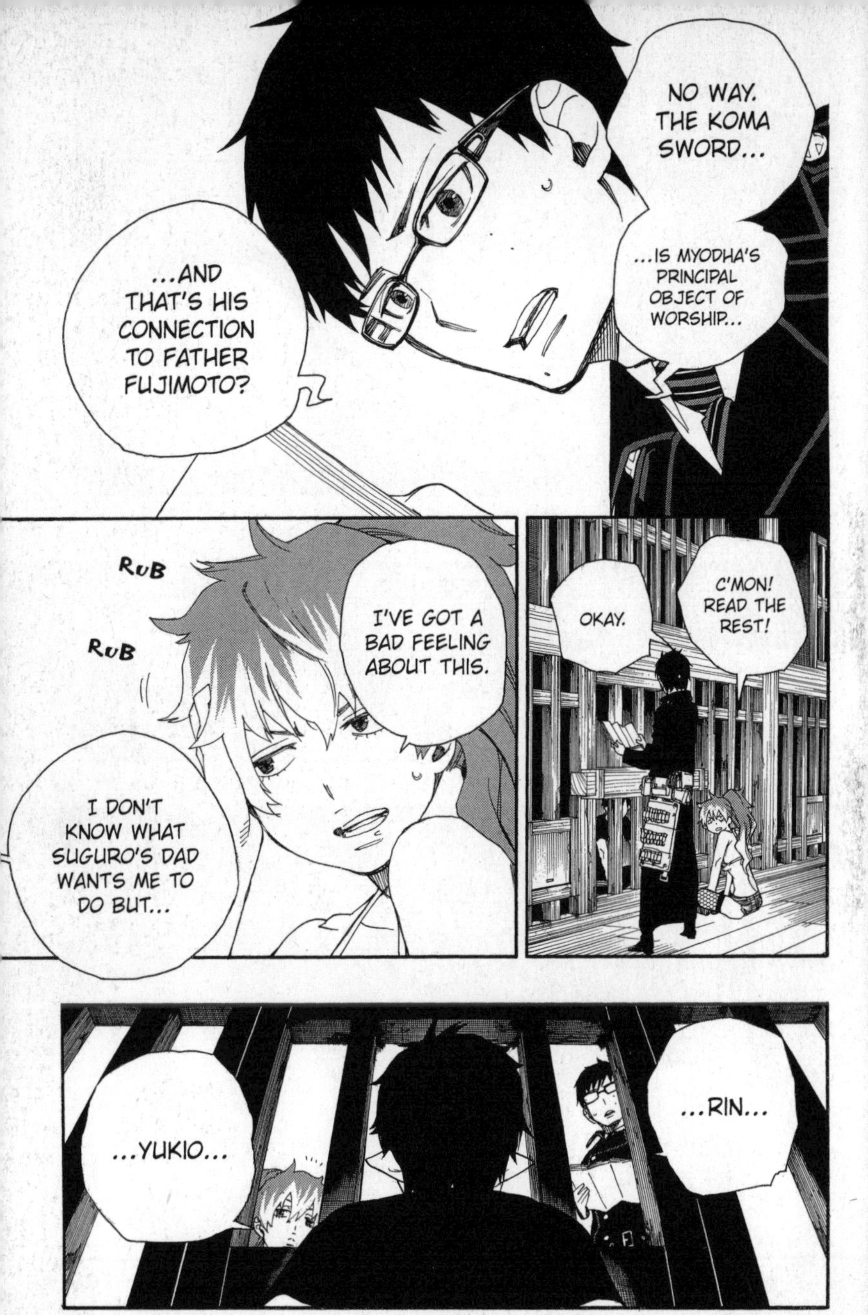
NO WAY. THE KOMA SWORD...
...IS MYODHA'S PRINCIPAL OBJECT OF WORSHIP...
...AND THAT'S HIS CONNECTION TO FATHER FUJIMOTO?
C'MON! READ THE REST!
OKAY.
I'VE GOT A BAD FEELING ABOUT THIS.
RUB
RUB
I DON'T KNOW WHAT SUGURO'S DAD WANTS ME TO DO BUT...
...RIN...
...YUKIO...

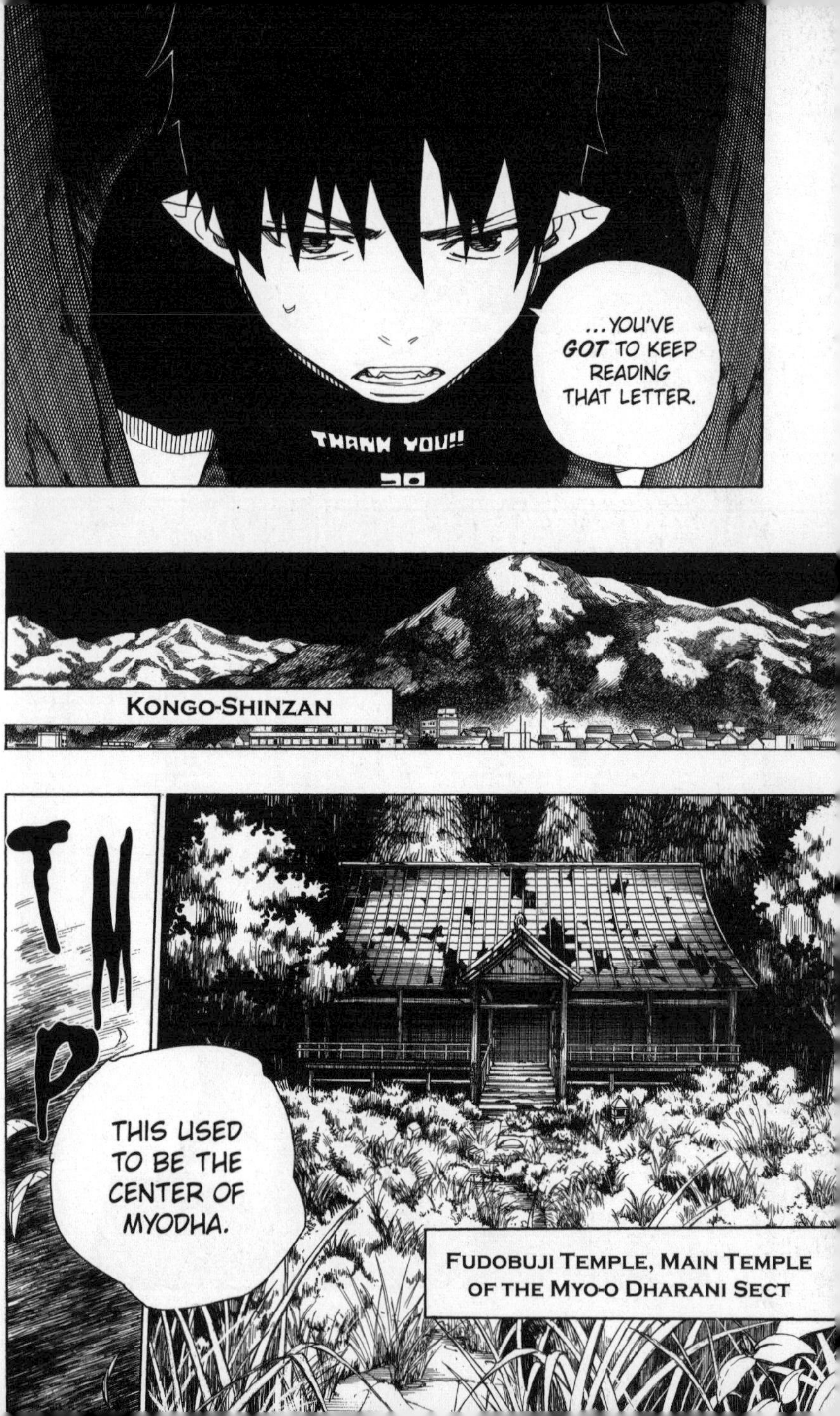
THANK YOU!!
...YOU'VE GOT TO KEEP READING THAT LETTER.
KONGO-SHINZAN
FUDOBUJI TEMPLE, MAIN TEMPLE OF THE MYO-O DHARANI SECT
TMP
THIS USED TO BE THE CENTER OF MYODHA.

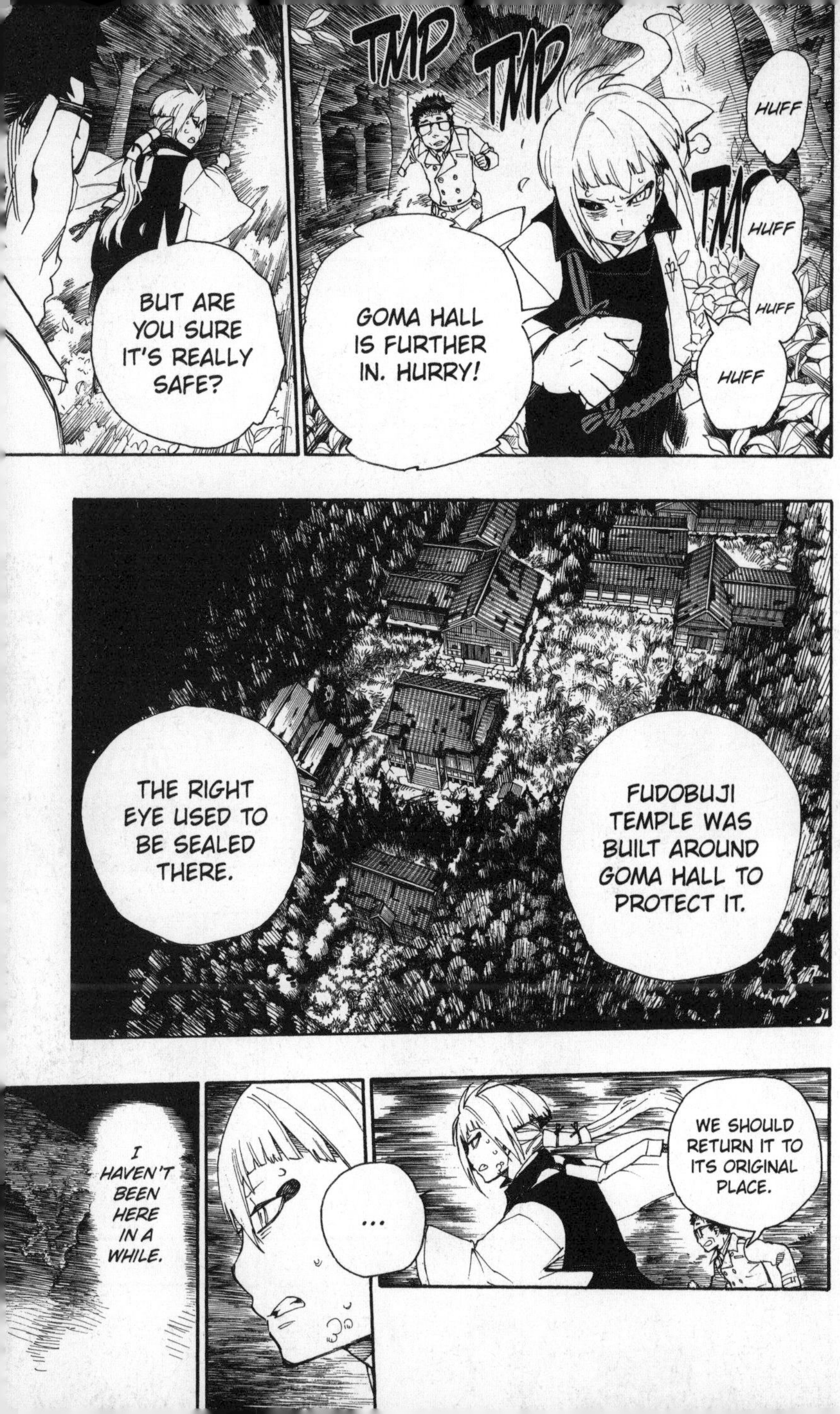
HUFF
TMP
TMP
TMP
HUFF
HUFF
HUFF
GOMA HALL IS FURTHER IN. HURRY!
BUT ARE YOU SURE IT'S REALLY SAFE?
FUDOBUJI TEMPLE WAS BUILT AROUND GOMA HALL TO PROTECT IT.
THE RIGHT EYE USED TO BE SEALED THERE.
WE SHOULD RETURN IT TO ITS ORIGINAL PLACE.
...
I HAVEN'T BEEN HERE IN A WHILE.

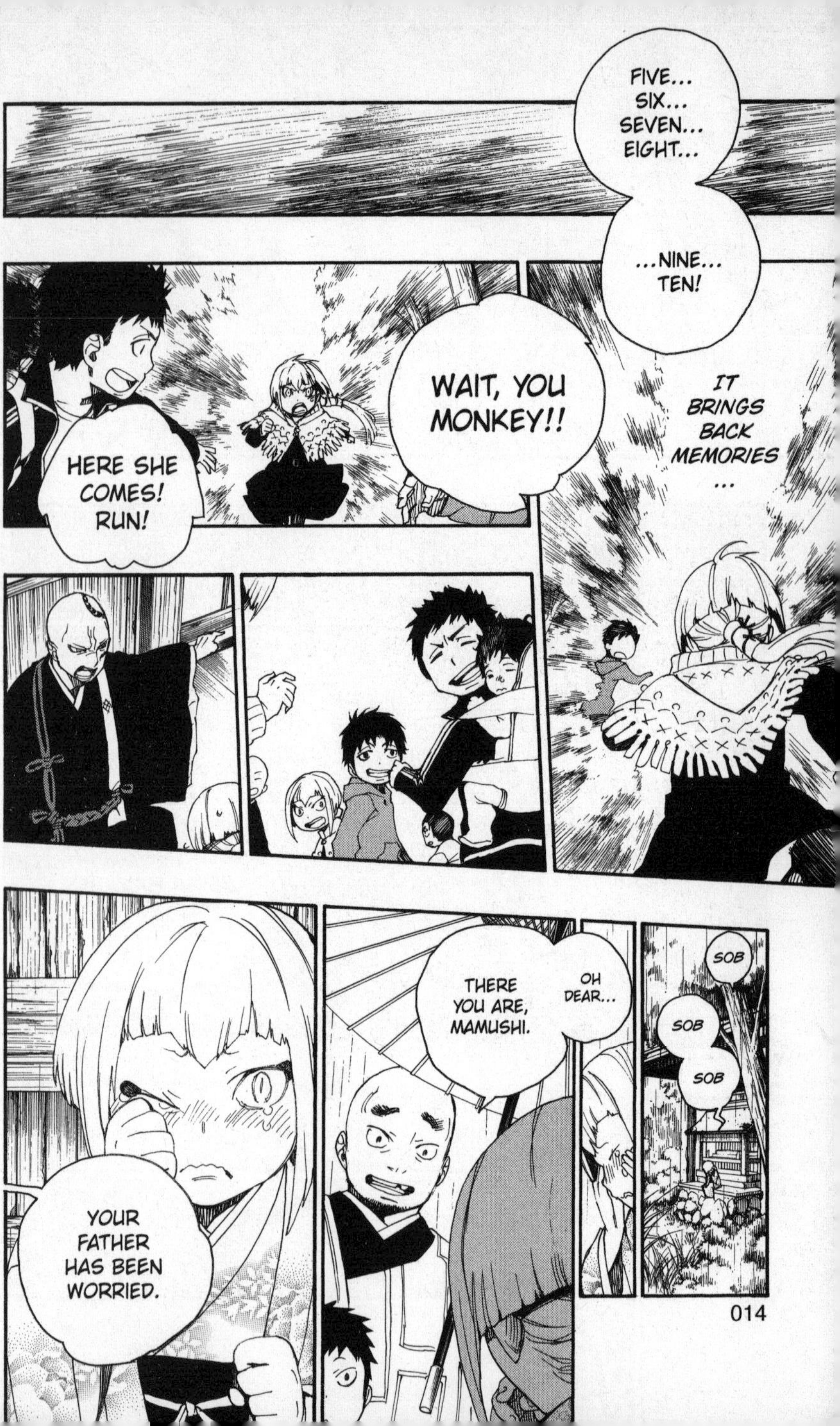
FIVE... SIX... SEVEN... EIGHT...
...NINE... TEN!
IT BRINGS BACK MEMORIES...
WAIT, YOU MONKEY!!
HERE SHE COMES! RUN!
SOB
SOB
SOB
OH DEAR...
THERE YOU ARE, MAMUSHI.
YOUR FATHER HAS BEEN WORRIED.

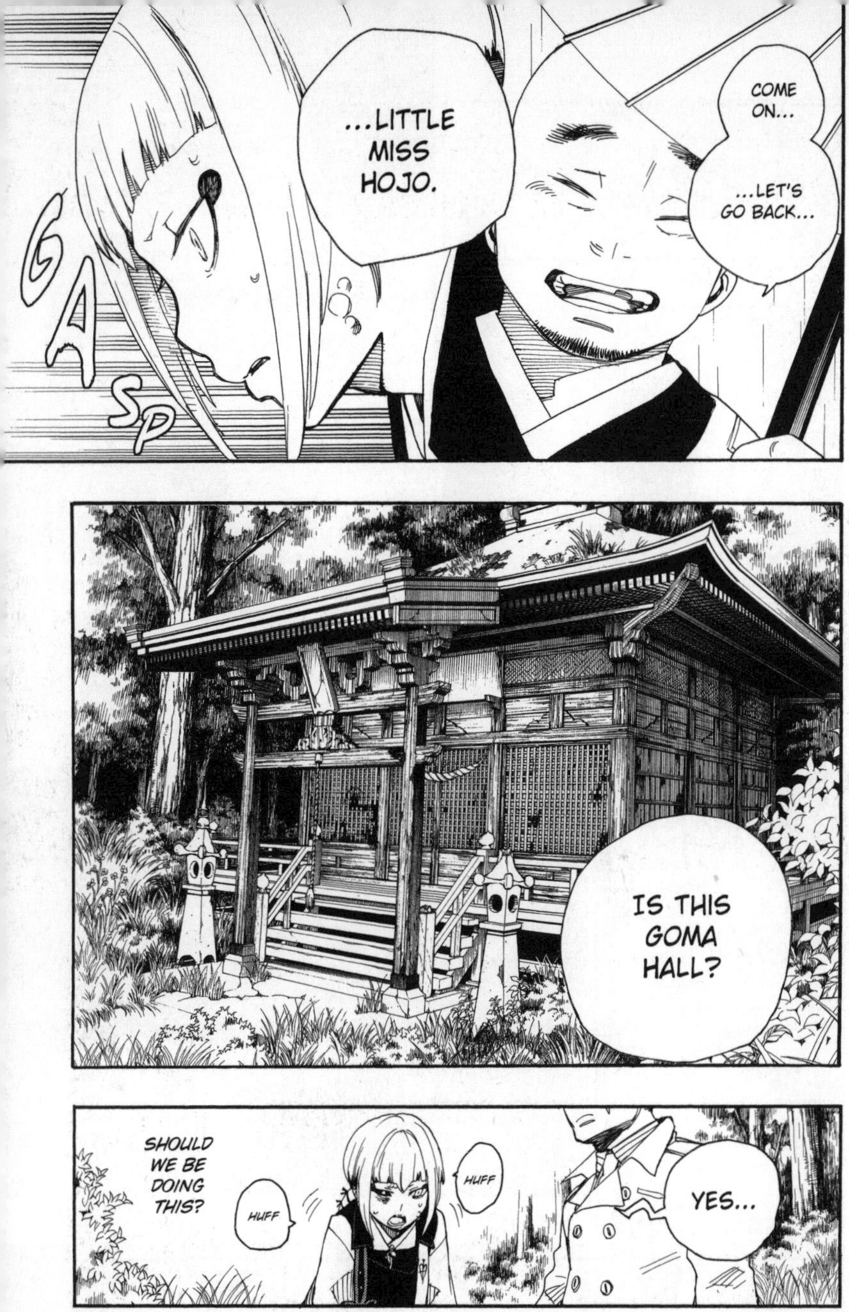
COME ON...
...LET'S GO BACK...
...LITTLE MISS HOJO.
GASP
IS THIS GOMA HALL?
YES...
HUFF
HUFF
SHOULD WE BE DOING THIS?

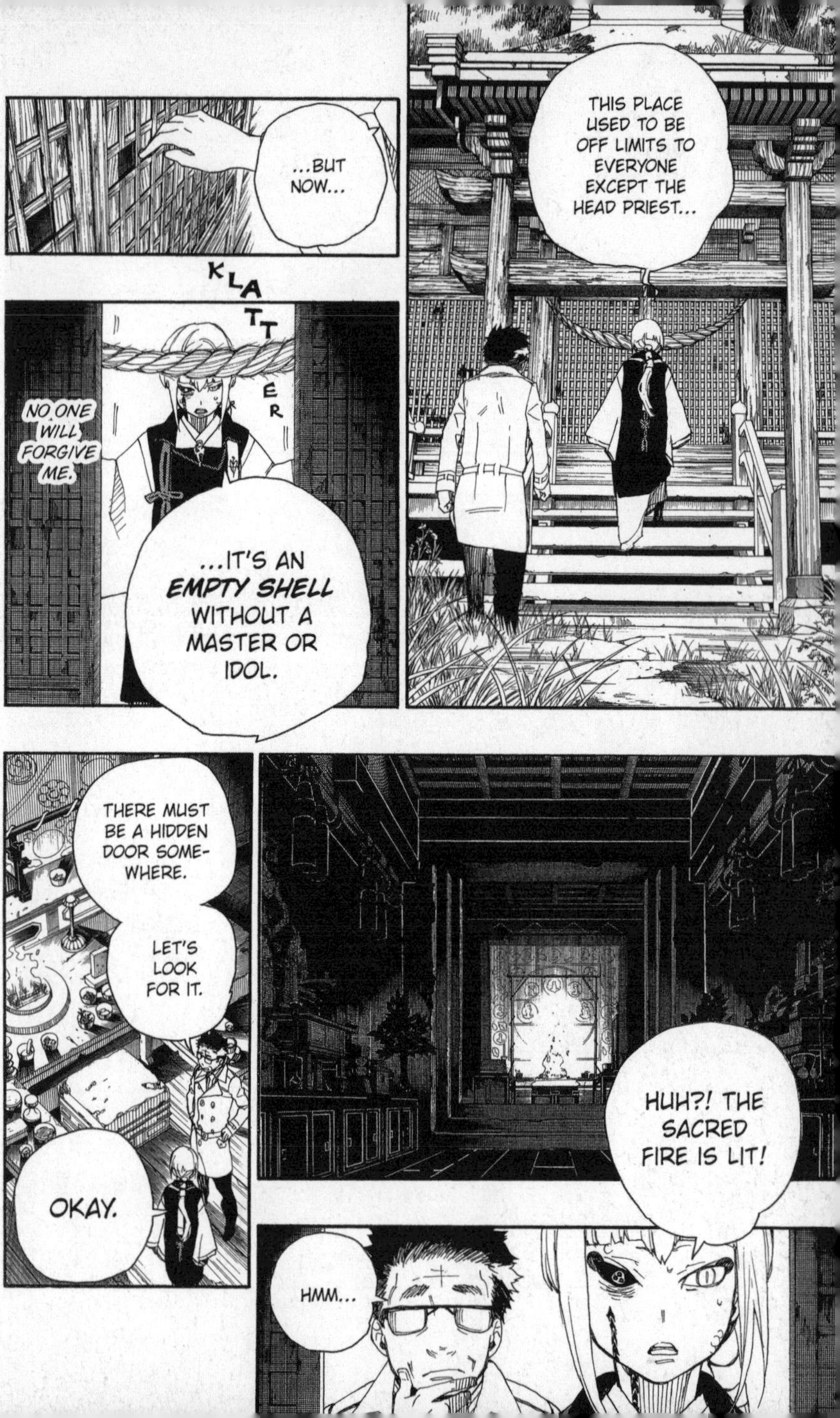
THIS PLACE USED TO BE OFF LIMITS TO EVERYONE EXCEPT THE HEAD PRIEST...
...BUT NOW...
KLATTER
NO ONE WILL FORGIVE ME.
...IT'S AN EMPTY SHELL WITHOUT A MASTER OR IDOL.
HUH?! THE SACRED FIRE IS LIT!
HMM...
THERE MUST BE A HIDDEN DOOR SOME-WHERE.
LET'S LOOK FOR IT.
OKAY.

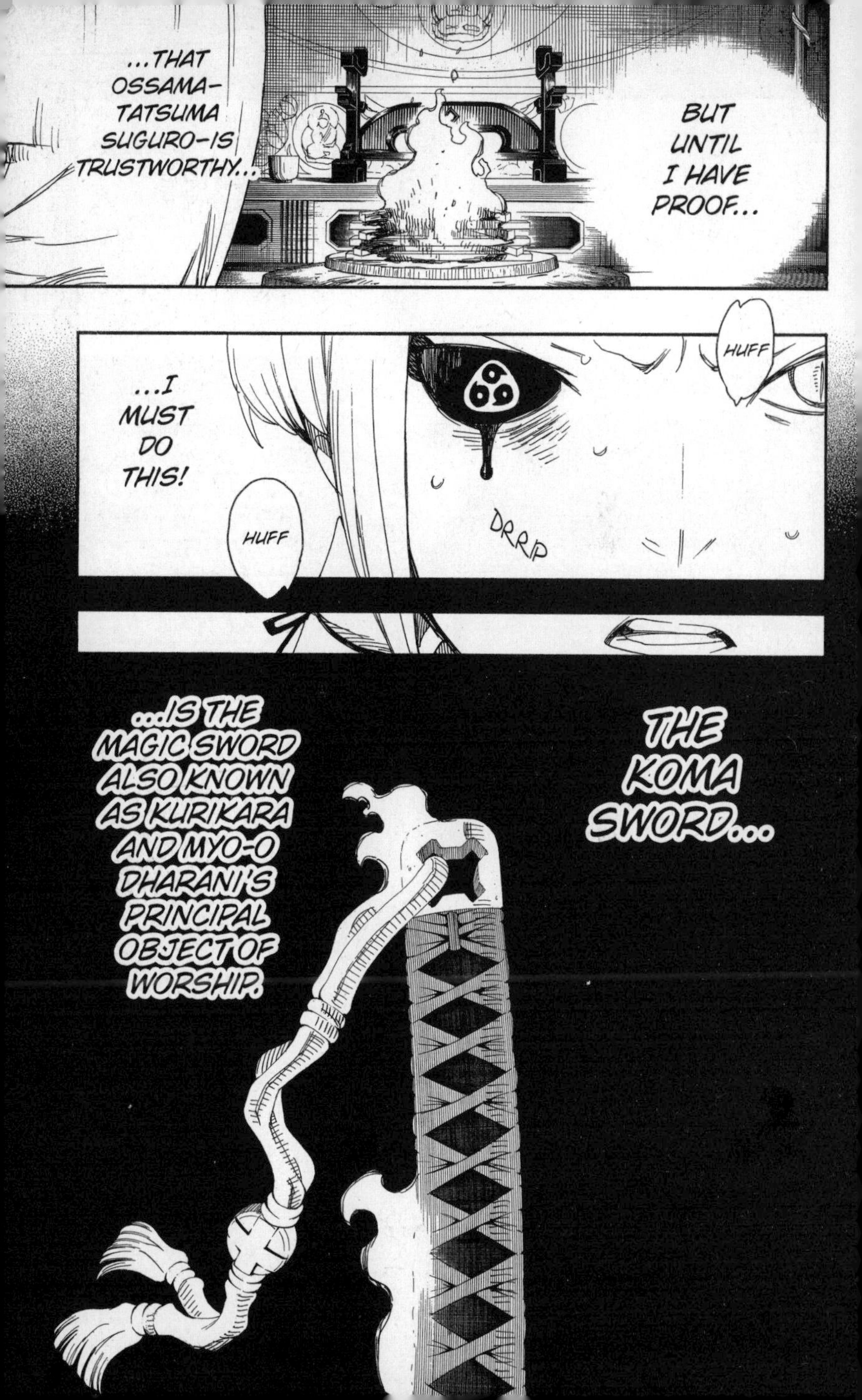
BUT UNTIL I HAVE PROOF...
...THAT OSSAMA-TATSUMA SUGURO-IS TRUSTWORTHY...
HUFF
...I MUST DO THIS!
DRRIP
HUFF
THE KOMA SWORD...
...IS THE MAGIC SWORD ALSO KNOWN AS KURIKARA AND MYO-O DHARANI'S PRINCIPAL OBJECT OF WORSHIP.

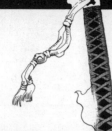

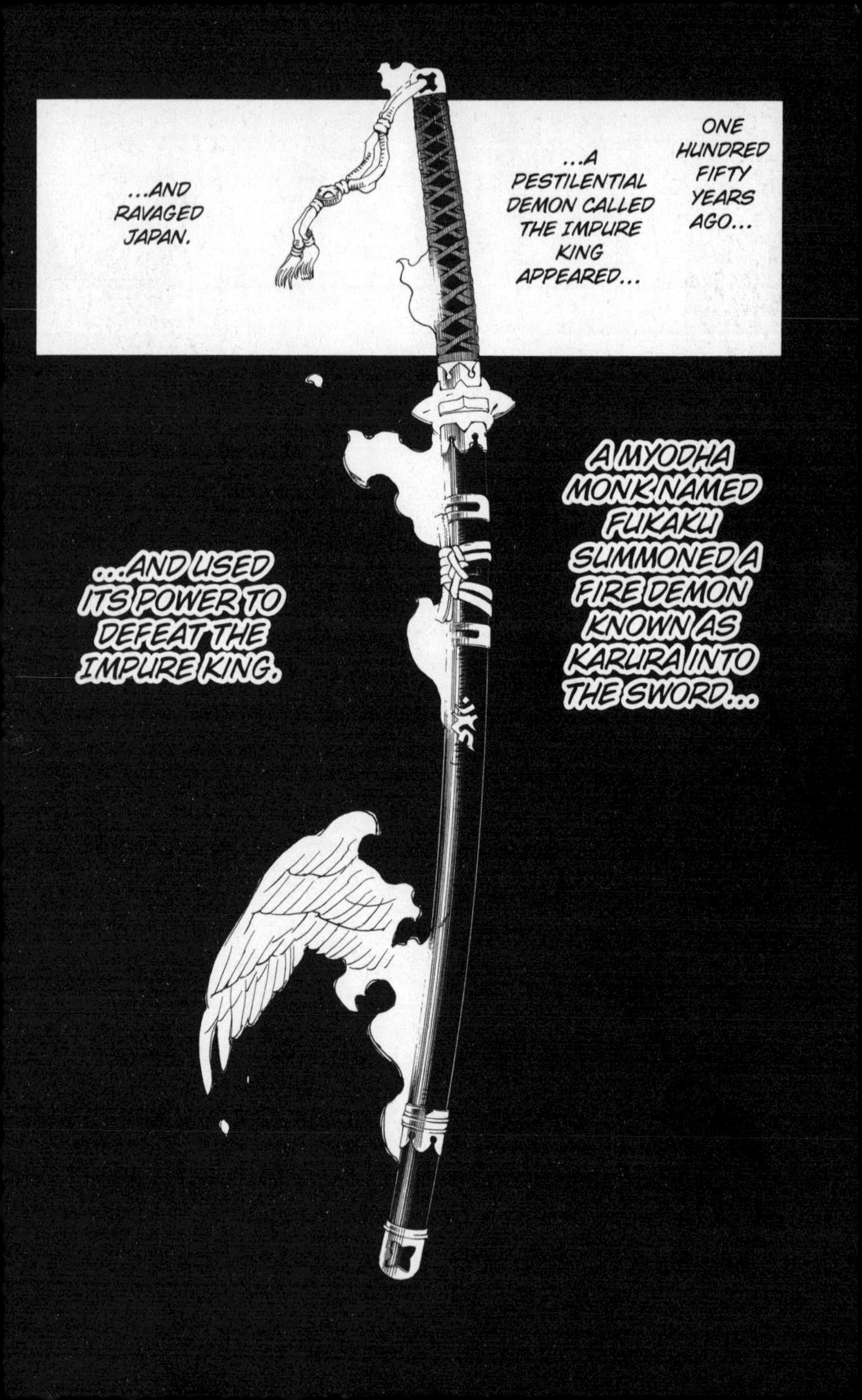

ONE HUNDRED FIFTY YEARS AGO...

...A PESTILENTIAL DEMON CALLED THE IMPURE KING APPEARED...

...AND RAVAGED JAPAN.

A MYODHA MONK NAMED FUKAKU SUMMONED A FIRE DEMON KNOWN AS KARURA INTO THE SWORD...

...AND USED ITS POWER TO DEFEAT THE IMPURE KING.

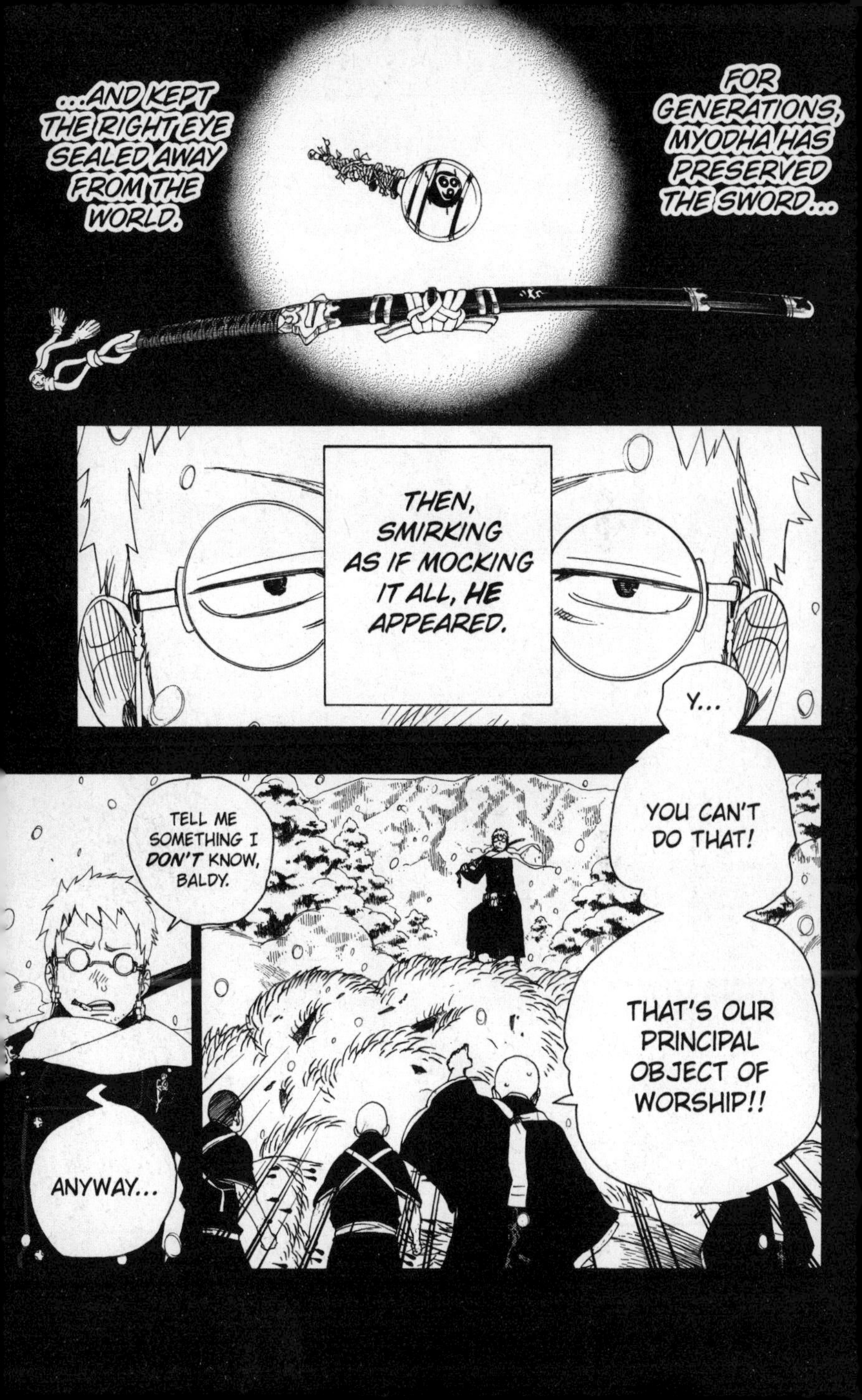
FOR GENERATIONS, MYODHA HAS PRESERVED THE SWORD...
...AND KEPT THE RIGHT EYE SEALED AWAY FROM THE WORLD.
THEN, SMIRKING AS IF MOCKING IT ALL, HE APPEARED.
Y...
YOU CAN'T DO THAT!
THAT'S OUR PRINCIPAL OBJECT OF WORSHIP!!
TELL ME SOMETHING I DON'T KNOW, BALDY.
ANYWAY...

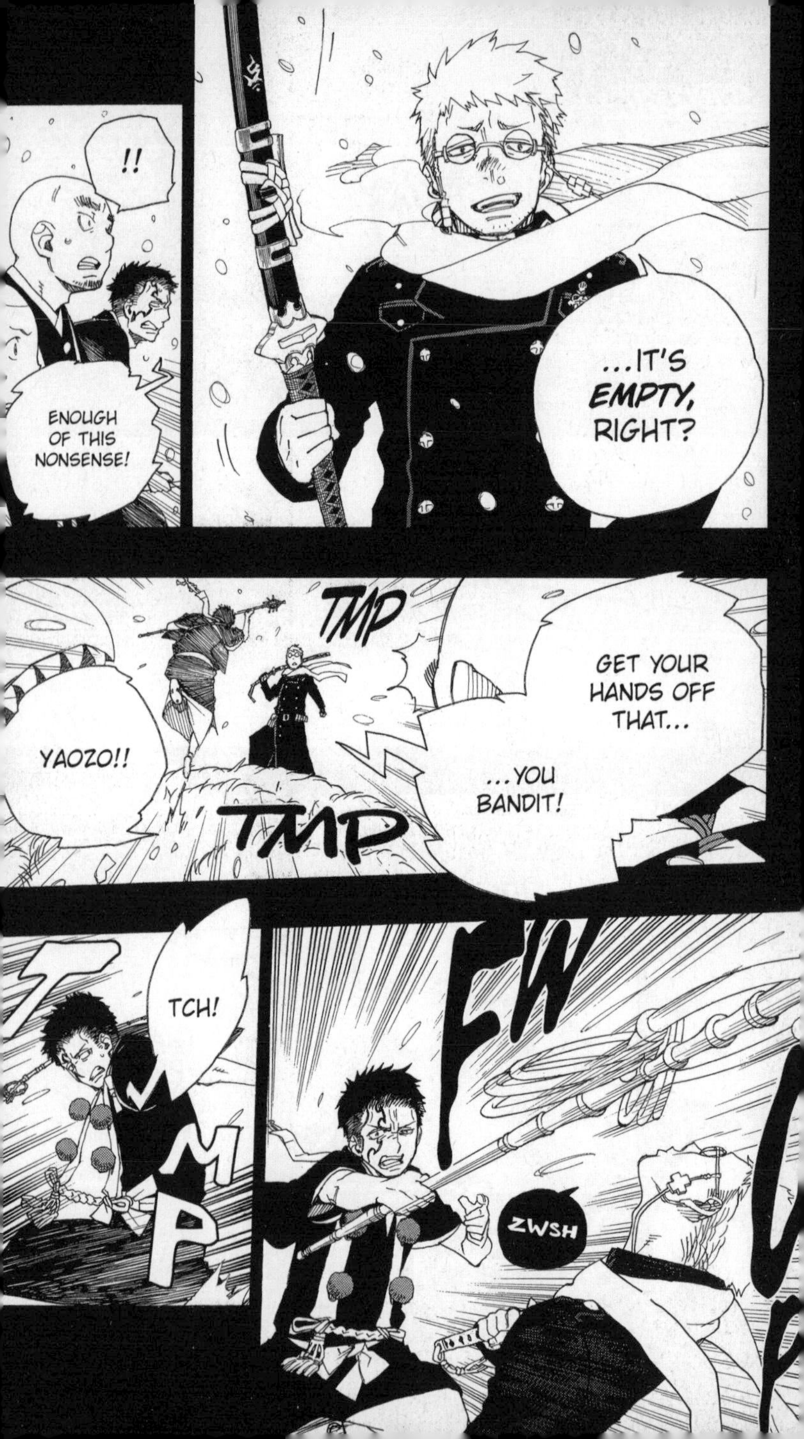
...IT'S EMPTY, RIGHT?
!!
ENOUGH OF THIS NONSENSE!
TMP
GET YOUR HANDS OFF THAT...
...YOU BANDIT!
TMP
YAOZO!!
FW
ZWSH
TCH!
TMP

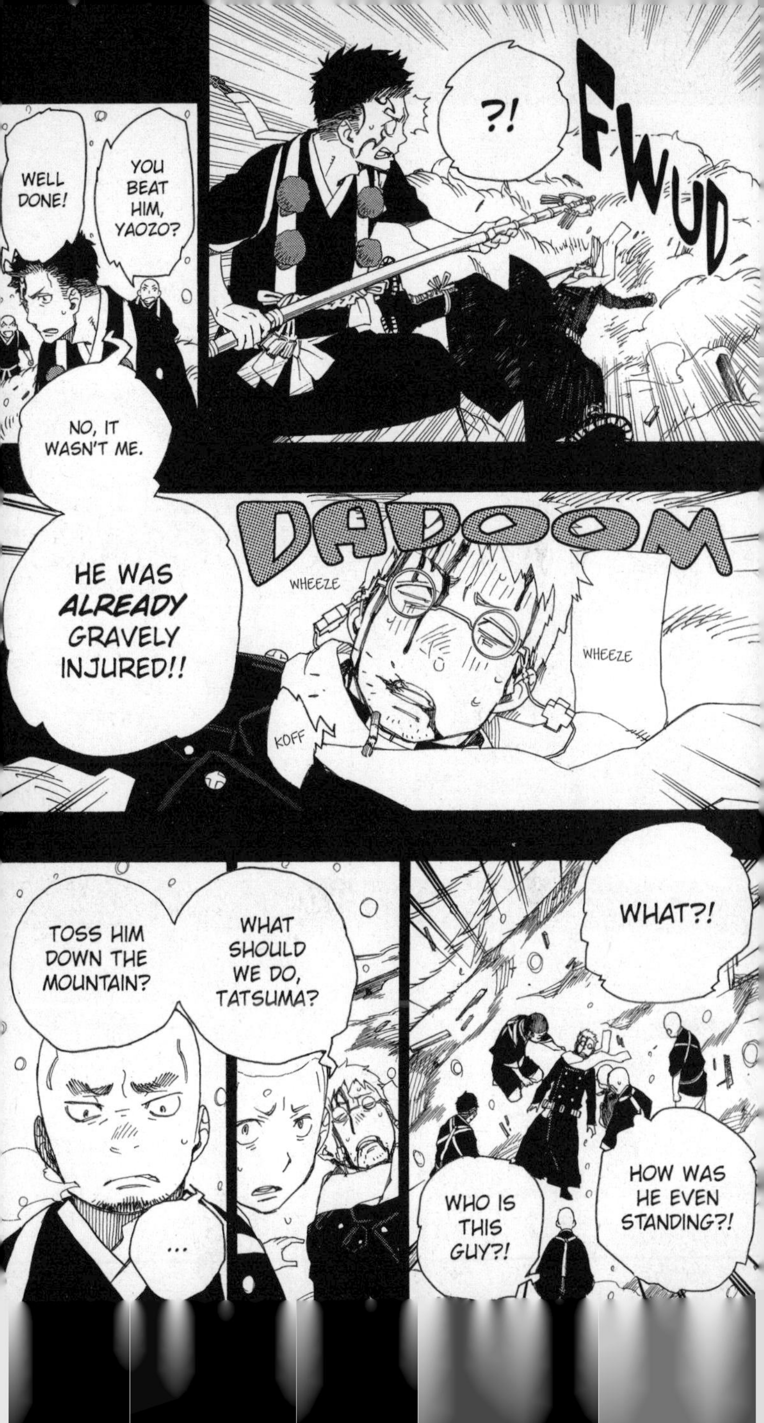
?!
FWUD
YOU BEAT HIM, YAOZO?
WELL DONE!
NO, IT WASN'T ME.
HE WAS ALREADY GRAVELY INJURED!!
DADOOM
WHEEZE
WHEEZE
KOFF
WHAT?!
HOW WAS HE EVEN STANDING?!
WHO IS THIS GUY?!
WHAT SHOULD WE DO, TATSUMA?
TOSS HIM DOWN THE MOUNTAIN?
...

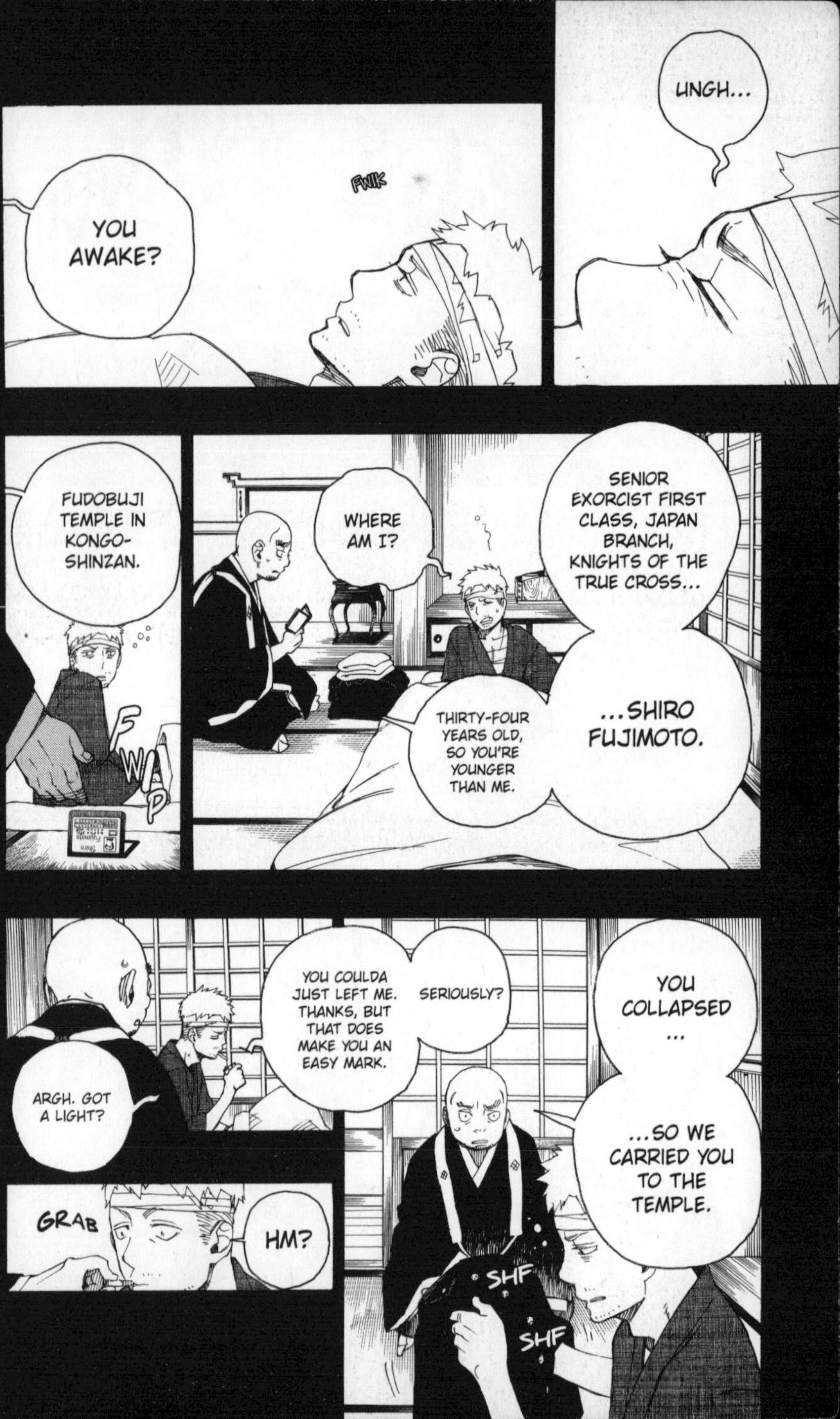
UNGH...
FWIK
YOU AWAKE?
SENIOR EXORCIST FIRST CLASS, JAPAN BRANCH, KNIGHTS OF THE TRUE CROSS...
...SHIRO FUJIMOTO.
THIRTY-FOUR YEARS OLD, SO YOU'RE YOUNGER THAN ME.
WHERE AM I?
FUDOBUJI TEMPLE IN KONGO-SHINZAN.
FWIP
YOU COLLAPSED...
...SO WE CARRIED YOU TO THE TEMPLE.
SHF
SHF
SERIOUSLY?
YOU COULDA JUST LEFT ME. THANKS, BUT THAT DOES MAKE YOU AN EASY MARK.
ARGH. GOT A LIGHT?
HM?
GRAB

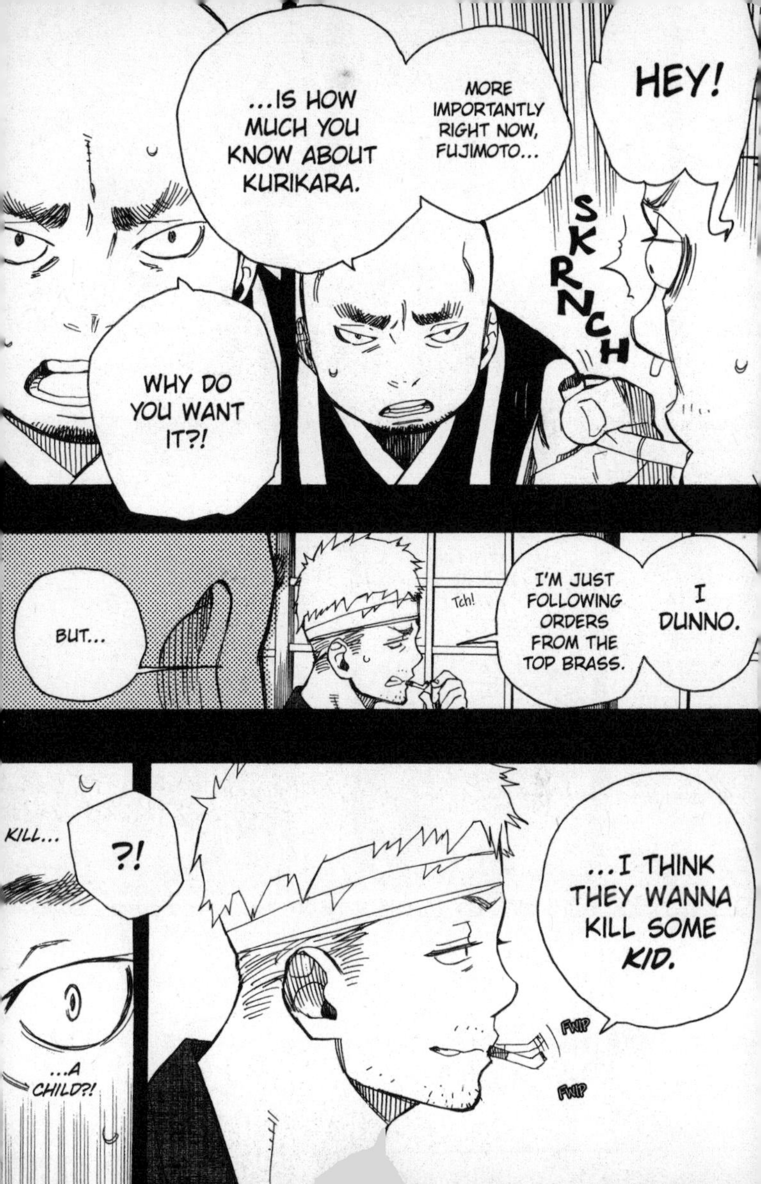
HEY!
MORE IMPORTANTLY RIGHT NOW, FUJIMOTO...
...IS HOW MUCH YOU KNOW ABOUT KURIKARA.
SKRNCH
WHY DO YOU WANT IT?!
I DUNNO.
I'M JUST FOLLOWING ORDERS FROM THE TOP BRASS.
Tch!
BUT...
...I THINK THEY WANNA KILL SOME KID.
FWIP
FWIP
?!
KILL...
...A CHILD?!

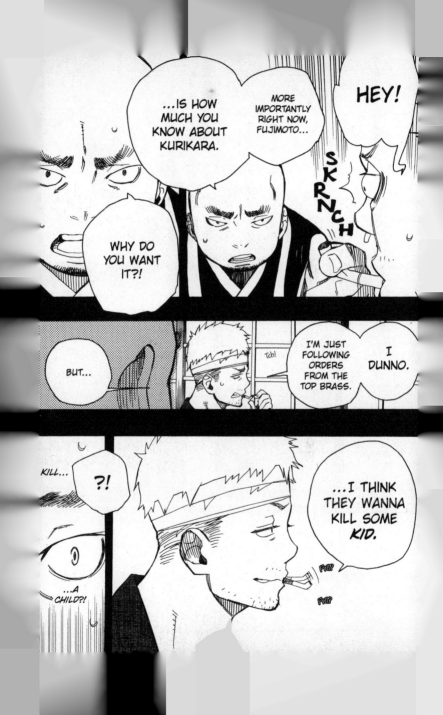

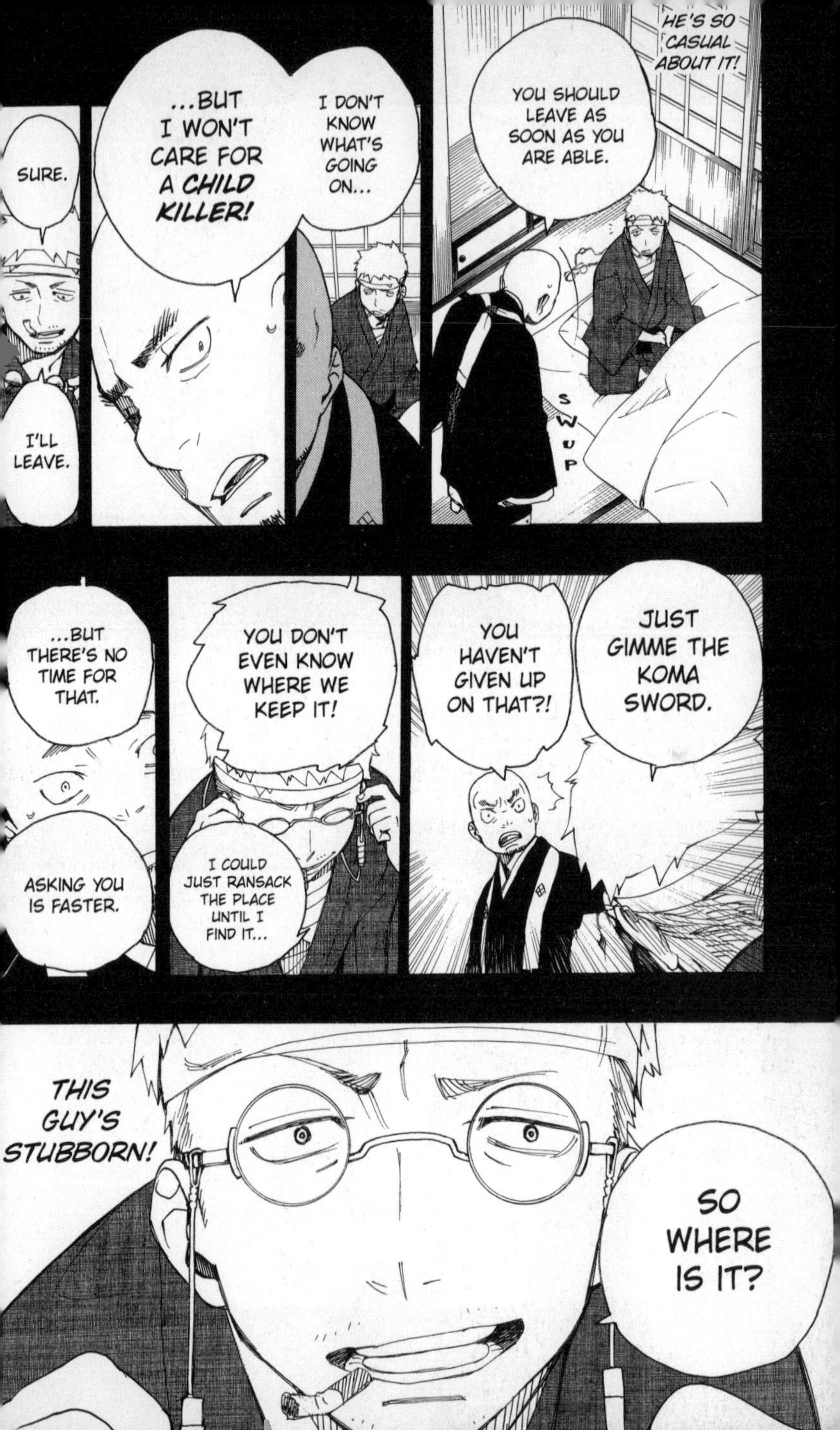
HE'S SO CASUAL ABOUT IT!
YOU SHOULD LEAVE AS SOON AS YOU ARE ABLE.
SWUP
I DON'T KNOW WHAT'S GOING ON...
...BUT I WON'T CARE FOR A CHILD KILLER!
SURE.
I'LL LEAVE.
JUST GIMME THE KOMA SWORD.
YOU HAVEN'T GIVEN UP ON THAT?!
YOU DON'T EVEN KNOW WHERE WE KEEP IT!
I COULD JUST RANSACK THE PLACE UNTIL I FIND IT...
...BUT THERE'S NO TIME FOR THAT.
ASKING YOU IS FASTER.
SO WHERE IS IT?
THIS GUY'S STUBBORN!

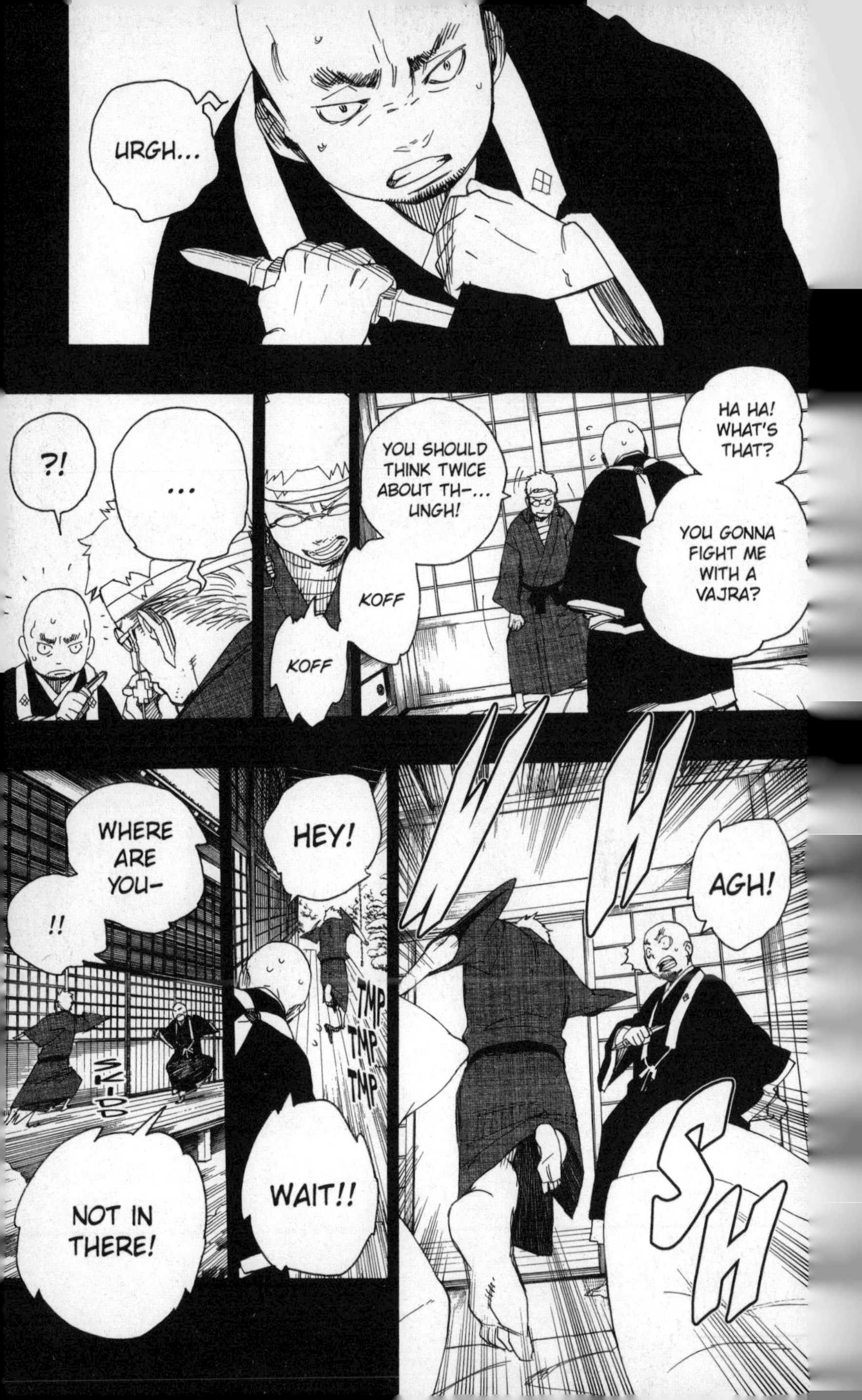
URGH...
HA HA! WHAT'S THAT?
YOU GONNA FIGHT ME WITH A VAJRA?
YOU SHOULD THINK TWICE ABOUT TH-... UNGH!
KOFF
KOFF
...
?!
AGH!
SH
HEY!
TMP TMP TMP
WAIT!!
WHERE ARE YOU-
!!
NOT IN THERE!

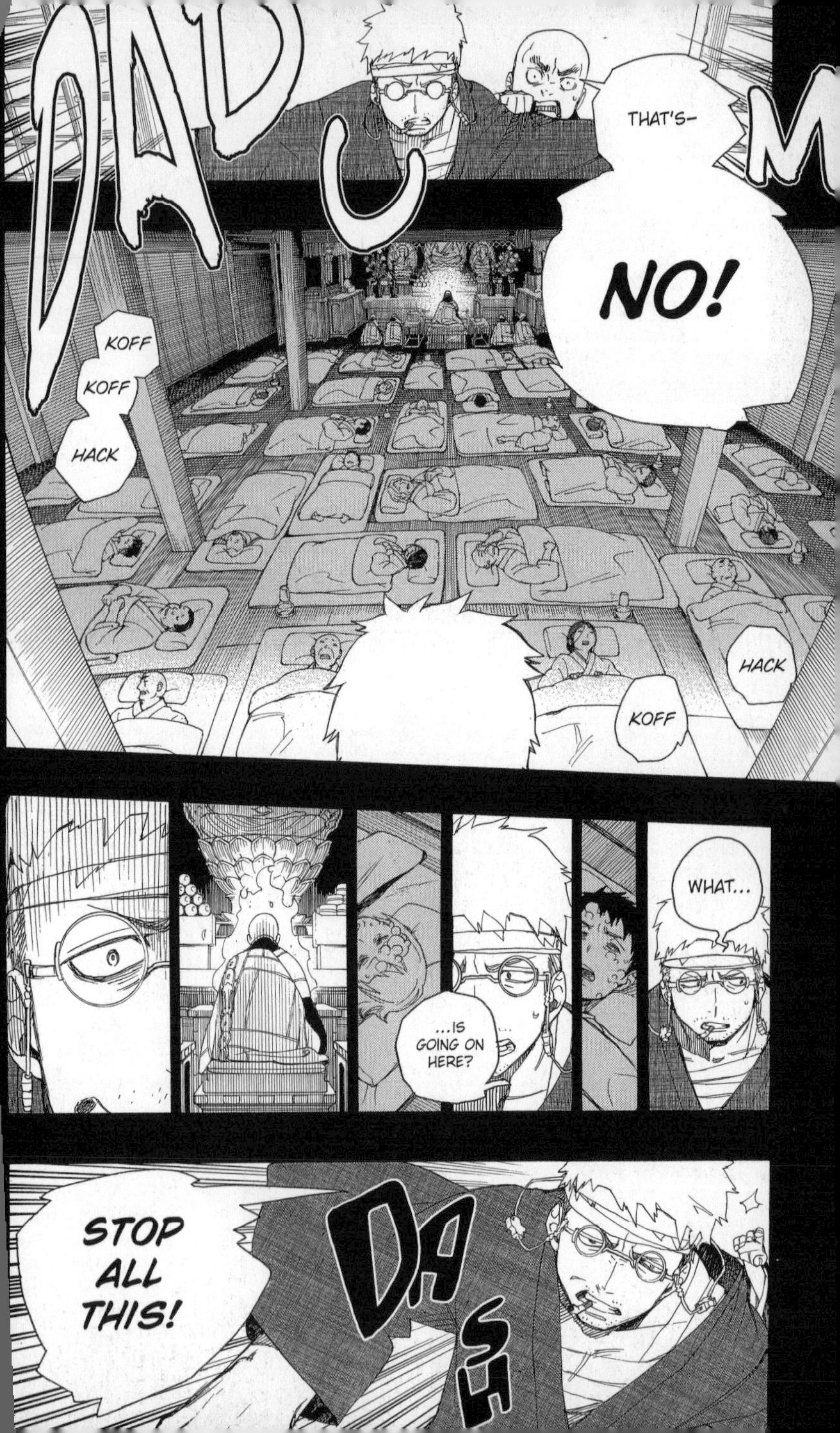
THAT'S—
NO!
HACK
KOFF
KOFF
KOFF
HACK
WHAT...
...IS GOING ON HERE?
DASH
STOP ALL THIS!

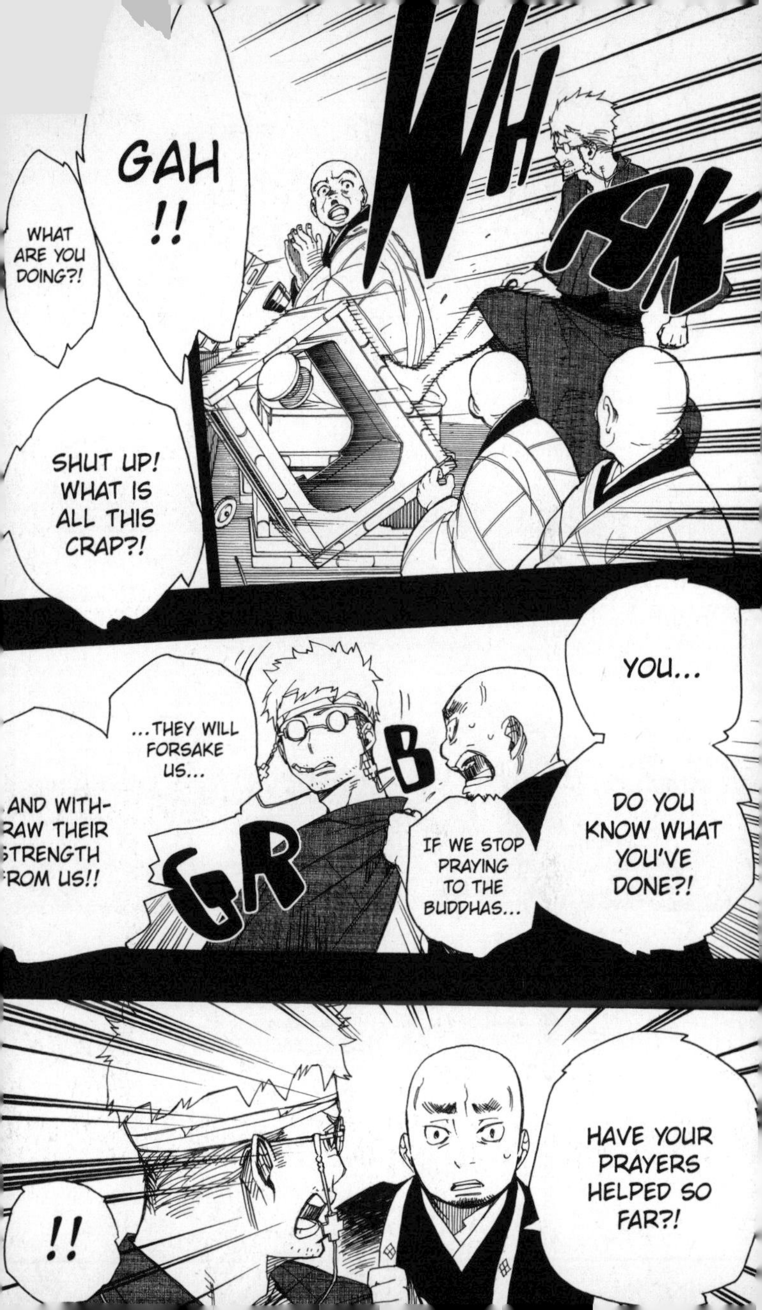
WHAK
GAH!!
WHAT ARE YOU DOING?!
SHUT UP! WHAT IS ALL THIS CRAP?!
YOU...
DO YOU KNOW WHAT YOU'VE DONE?!
B
GR
IF WE STOP PRAYING TO THE BUDDHAS...
...THEY WILL FORSAKE US...
AND WITH- RAW THEIR STRENGTH FROM US!!
HAVE YOUR PRAYERS HELPED SO FAR?!
!!

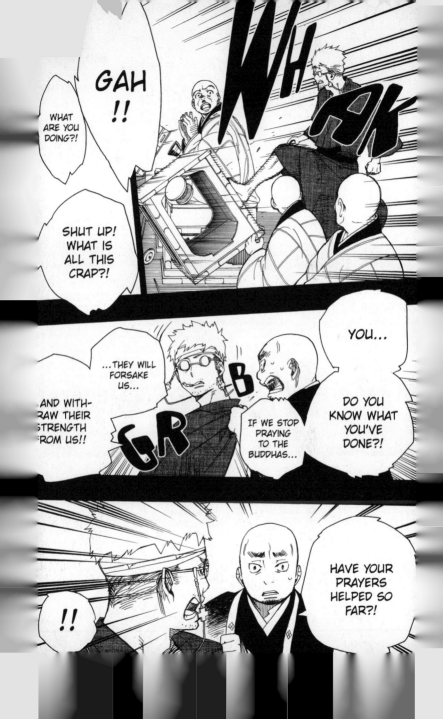

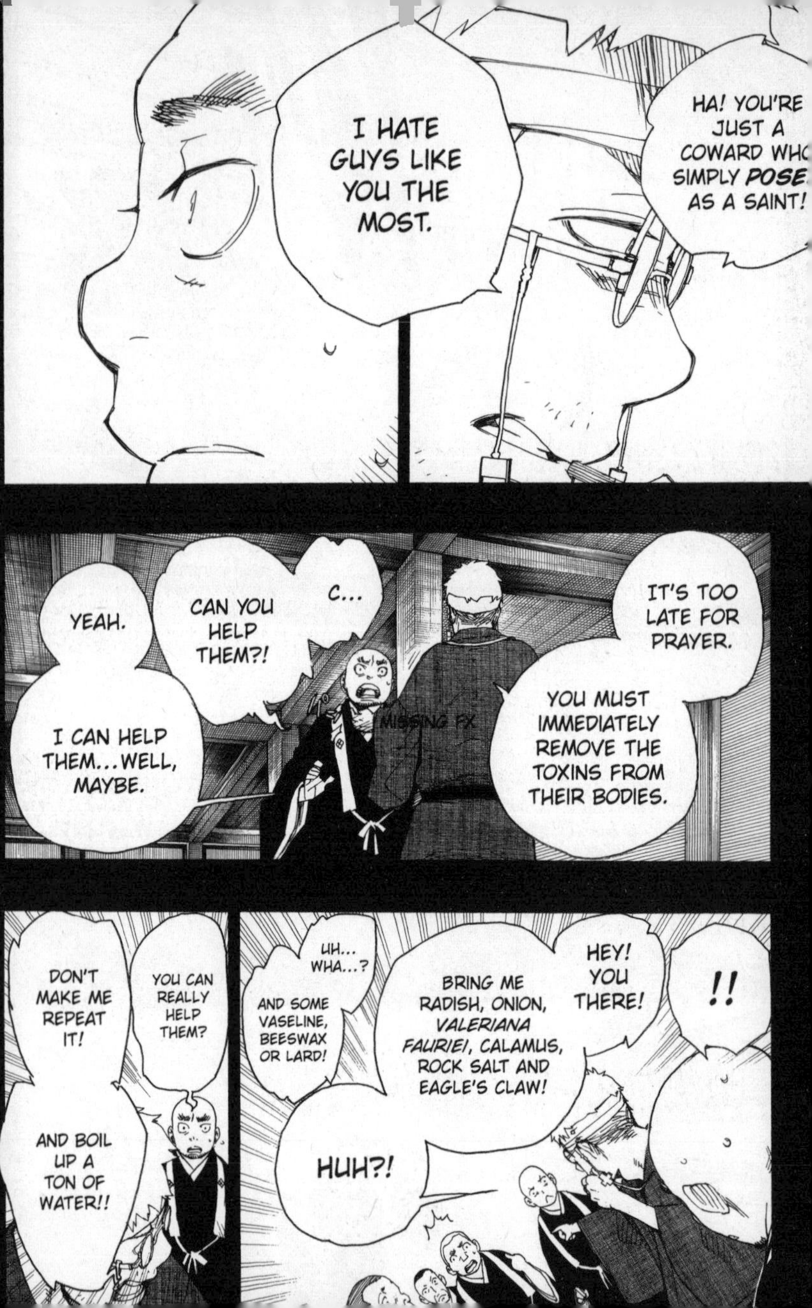
HA! YOU'RE JUST A COWARD WH SIMPLY *POSE* AS A SAINT!
I HATE GUYS LIKE YOU THE MOST.
IT'S TOO LATE FOR PRAYER.
YOU MUST IMMEDIATELY REMOVE THE TOXINS FROM THEIR BODIES.
MISSING FX
C...
CAN YOU HELP THEM?!
YEAH.
I CAN HELP THEM...WELL, MAYBE.
!!
HEY! YOU THERE!
BRING ME RADISH, ONION, *VALERIANA FAURIEI*, CALAMUS, ROCK SALT AND EAGLE'S CLAW!
UH... WHA...?
AND SOME VASELINE, BEESWAX OR LARD!
HUH?!
YOU CAN REALLY HELP THEM?
DON'T MAKE ME REPEAT IT!
AND BOIL UP A TON OF WATER!!

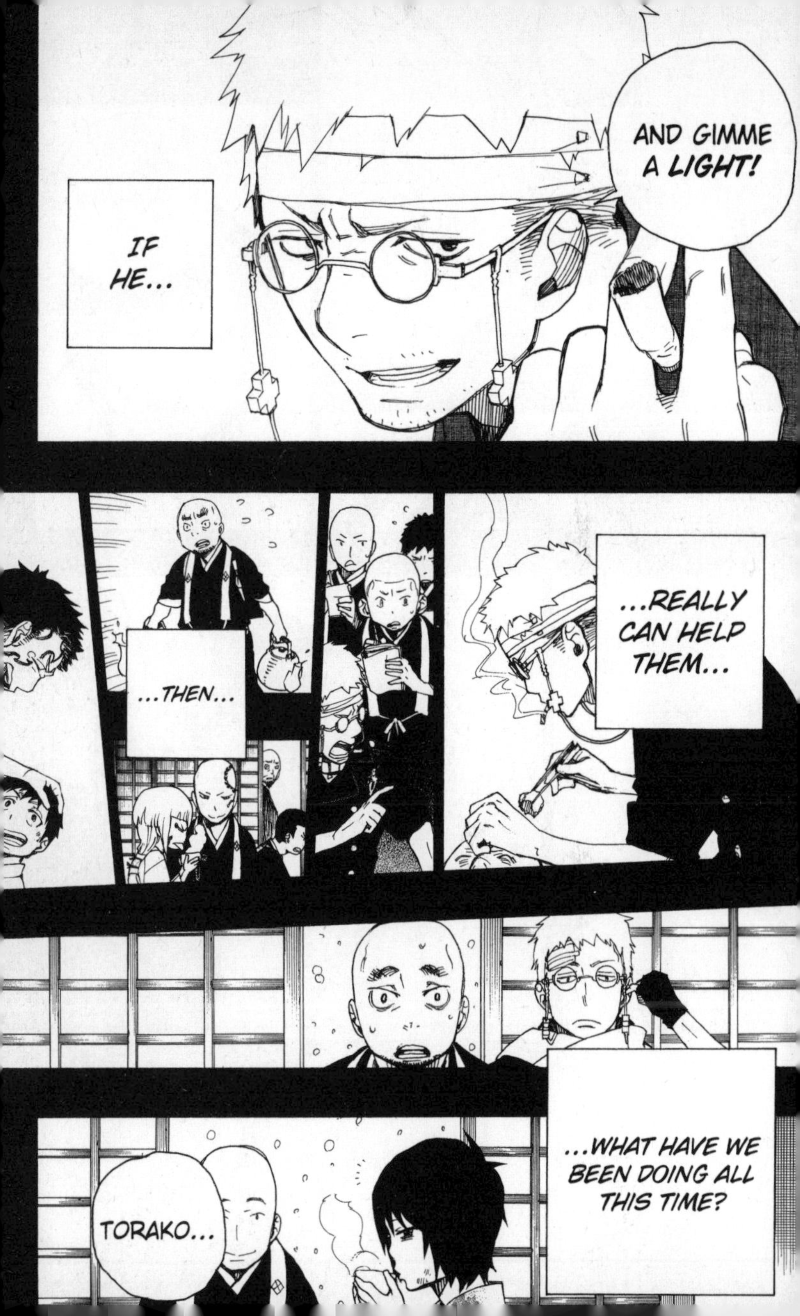
AND GIMME A LIGHT!
IF HE...
...REALLY CAN HELP THEM...
...THEN...
...WHAT HAVE WE BEEN DOING ALL THIS TIME?
TORAKO...

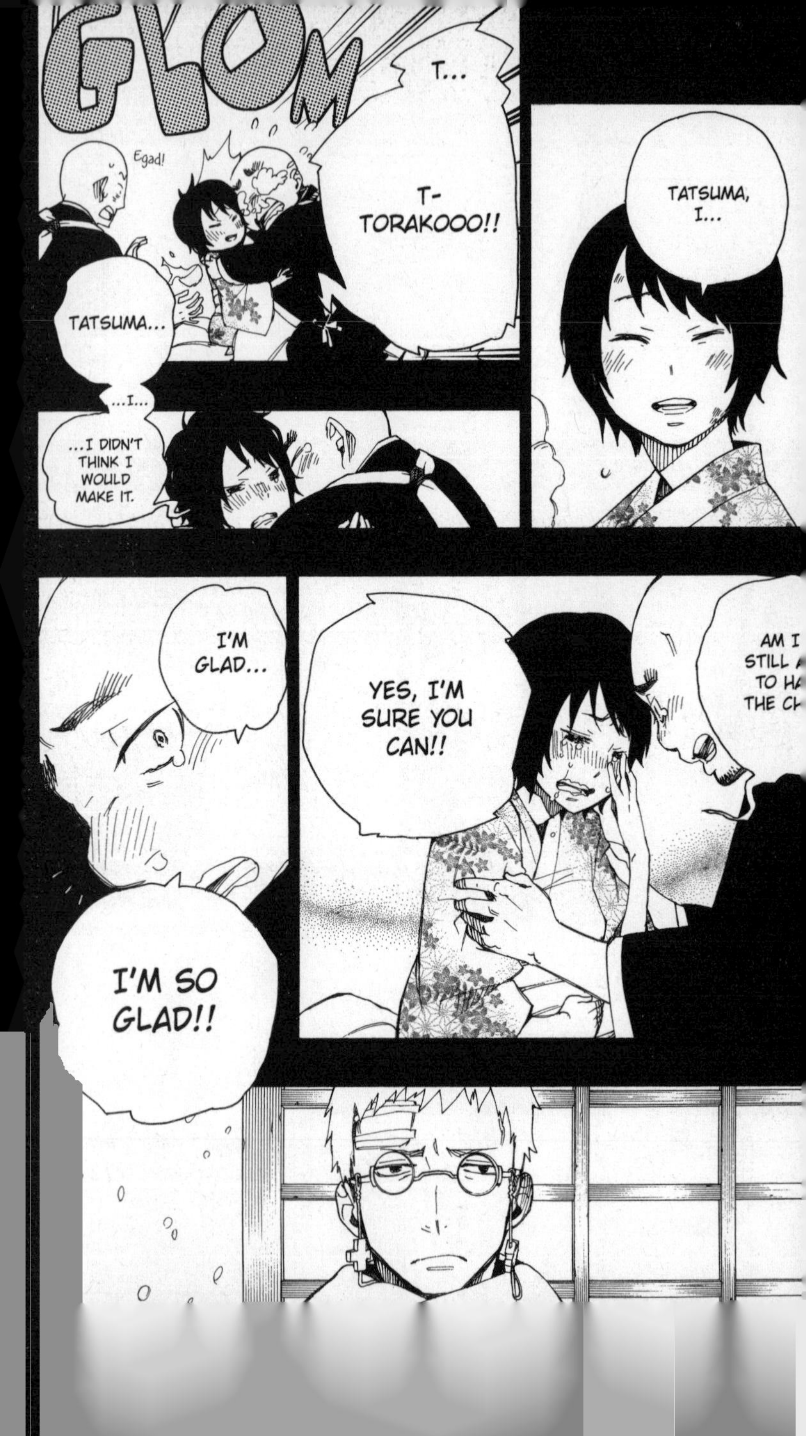
TATSUMA, I...
GLOM
T...
T-TORAKOOO!!
Egad!
TATSUMA...
...I...
...I DIDN'T THINK I WOULD MAKE IT.
AM I STILL A TO HA THE CH
YES, I'M SURE YOU CAN!!
I'M GLAD...
I'M SO GLAD!!

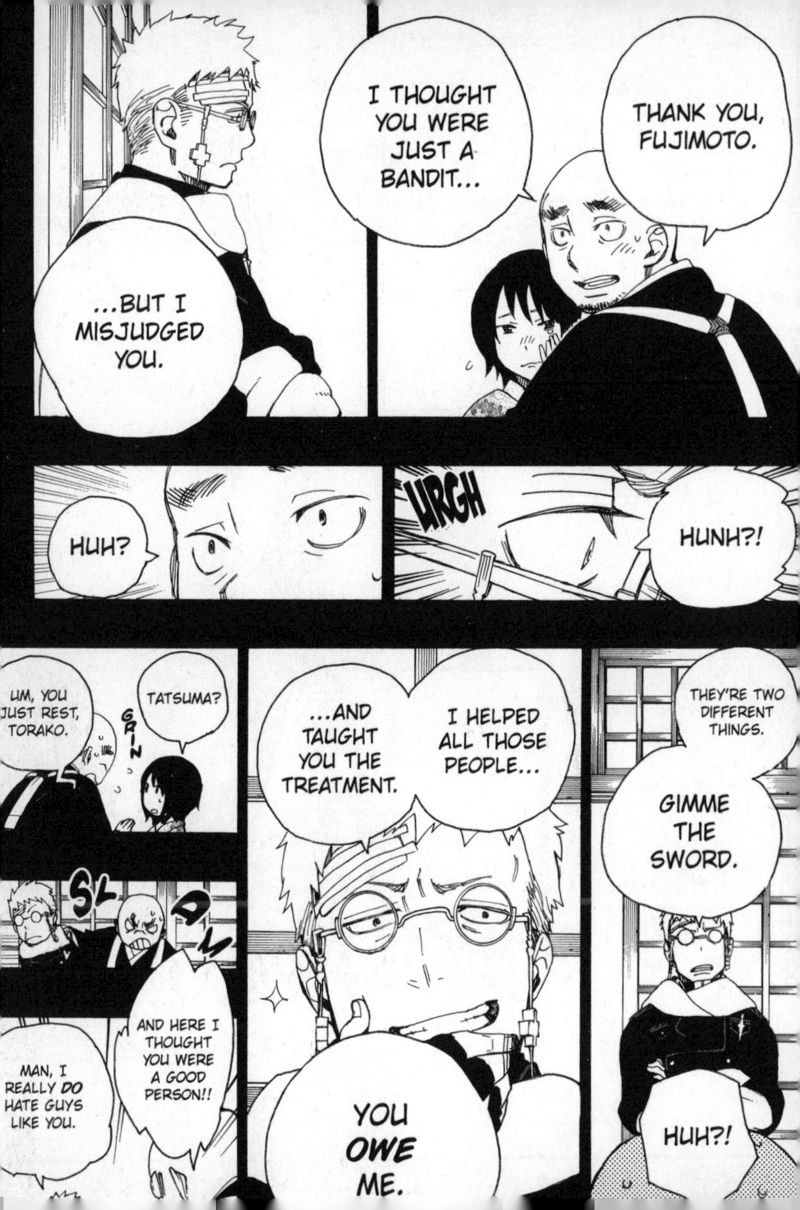
THANK YOU, FUJIMOTO.
I THOUGHT YOU WERE JUST A BANDIT...
...BUT I MISJUDGED YOU.
URGH
HUNH?!
HUH?
THEY'RE TWO DIFFERENT THINGS.
GIMME THE SWORD.
HUH?!
I HELPED ALL THOSE PEOPLE...
...AND TAUGHT YOU THE TREATMENT.
YOU OWE ME.
TATSUMA?
GRIN
UM, YOU JUST REST, TORAKO.
SLAM
AND HERE I THOUGHT YOU WERE A GOOD PERSON!!
MAN, I REALLY DO HATE GUYS LIKE YOU.

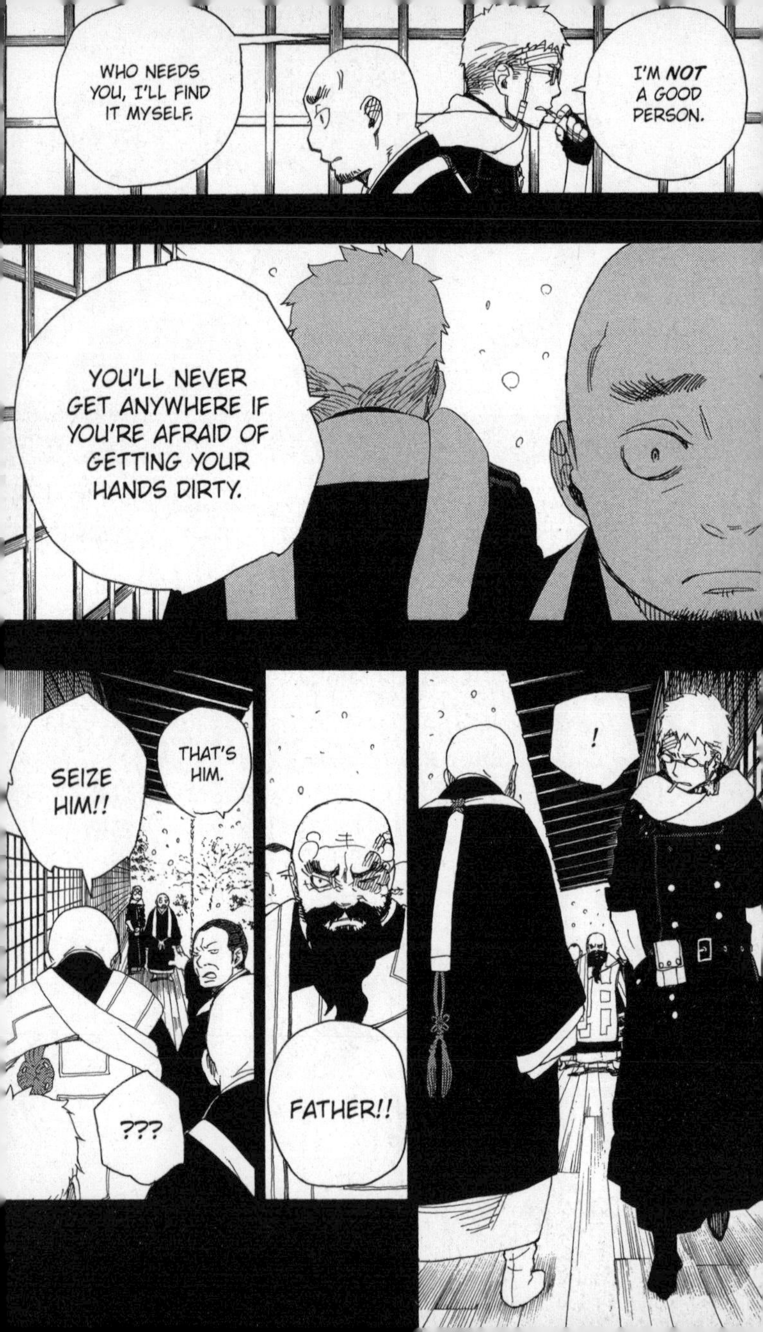
I'M *NOT* A GOOD PERSON.
WHO NEEDS YOU, I'LL FIND IT MYSELF.
YOU'LL NEVER GET ANYWHERE IF YOU'RE AFRAID OF GETTING YOUR HANDS DIRTY.
!
FATHER!!
THAT'S HIM.
SEIZE HIM!!
???

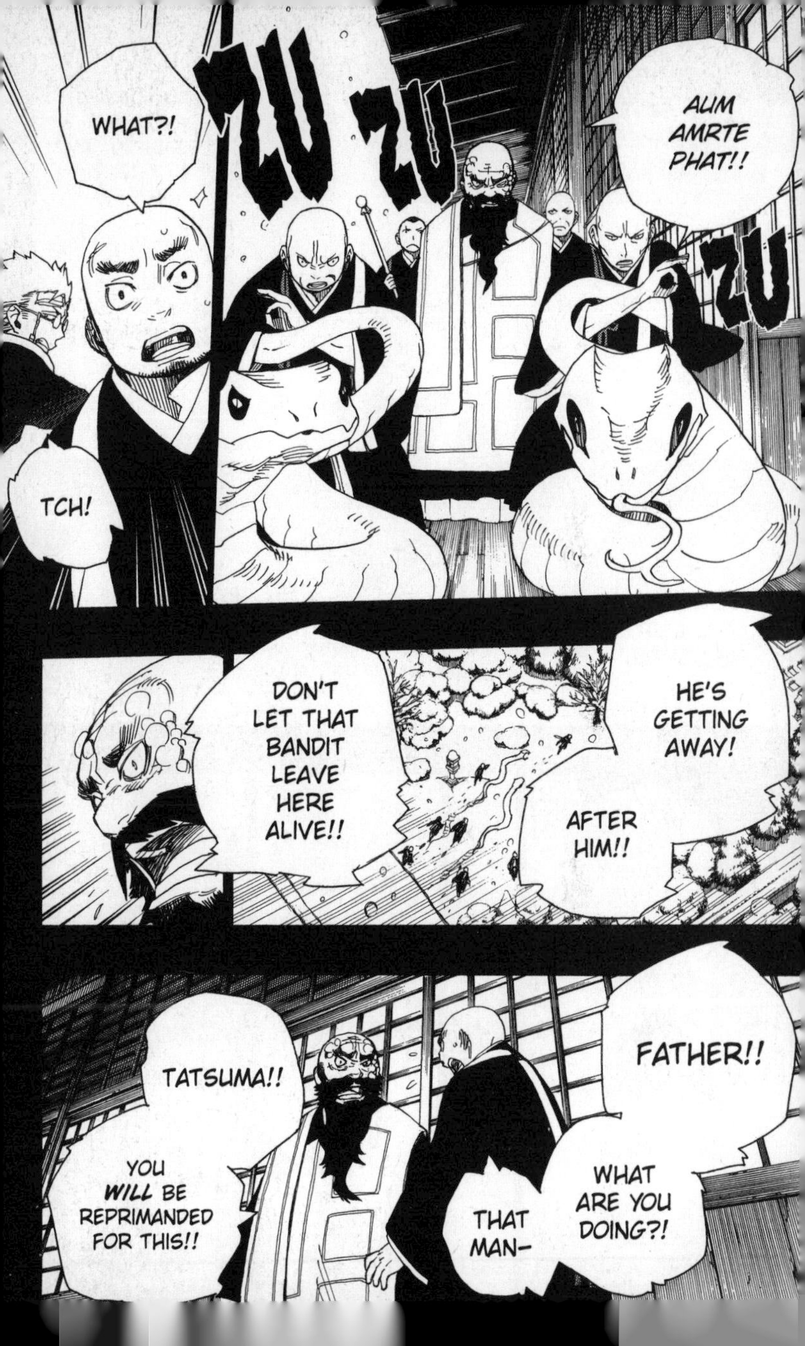
AUM AMRTE PHAT!!
ZU ZU
ZU
WHAT?!
TCH!
HE'S GETTING AWAY!
AFTER HIM!!
DON'T LET THAT BANDIT LEAVE HERE ALIVE!!
FATHER!!
WHAT ARE YOU DOING?!
THAT MAN-
TATSUMA!!
YOU WILL BE REPRIMANDED FOR THIS!!

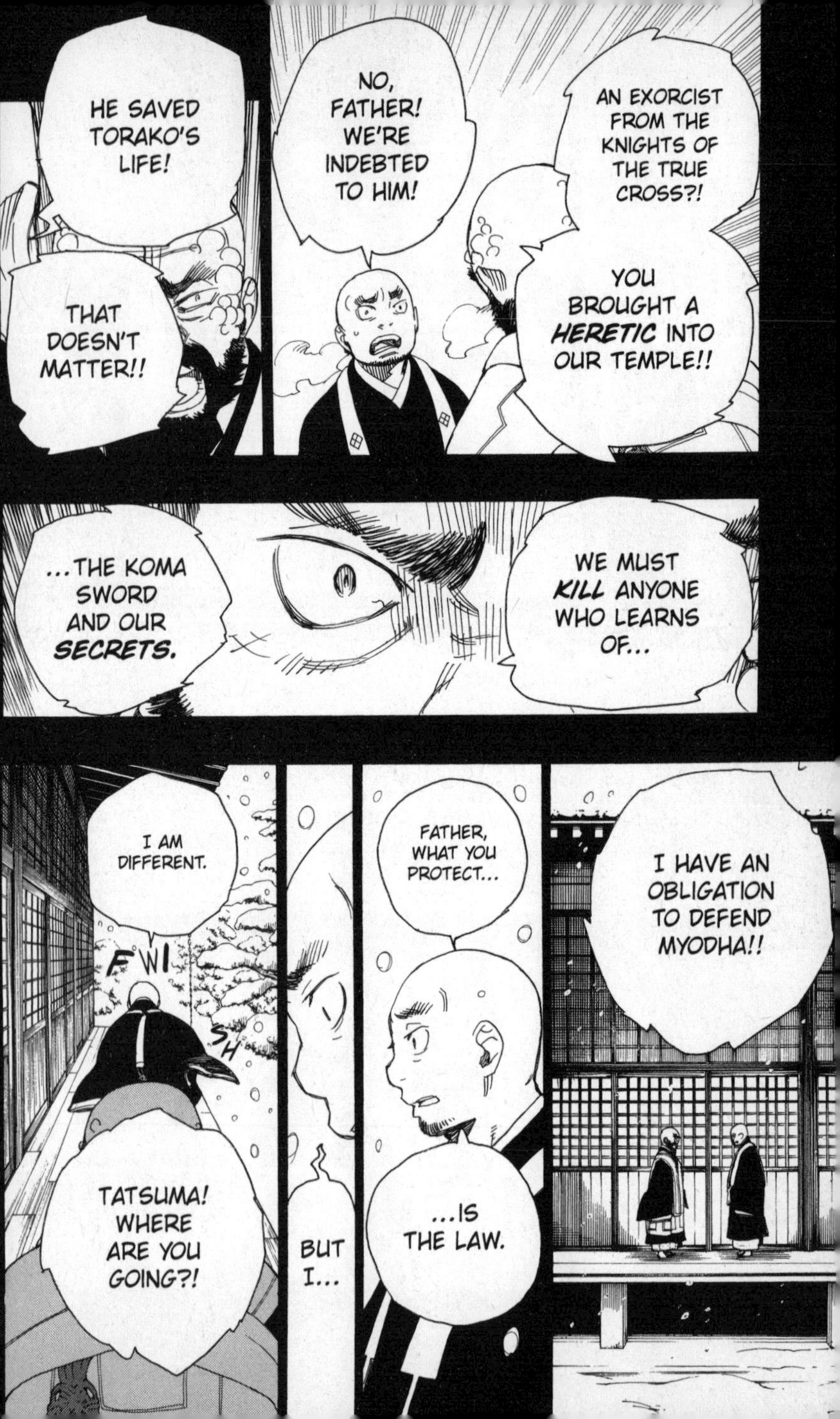
AN EXORCIST FROM THE KNIGHTS OF THE TRUE CROSS?!
YOU BROUGHT A *HERETIC* INTO OUR TEMPLE!!
NO, FATHER! WE'RE INDEBTED TO HIM!
HE SAVED TORAKO'S LIFE!
THAT DOESN'T MATTER!!
WE MUST *KILL* ANYONE WHO LEARNS OF...
...THE KOMA SWORD AND OUR *SECRETS.*
I HAVE AN OBLIGATION TO DEFEND MYODHA!!
FATHER, WHAT YOU PROTECT...
...IS THE LAW.
BUT I...
I AM DIFFERENT.
FWI
SH
TATSUMA! WHERE ARE YOU GOING?!

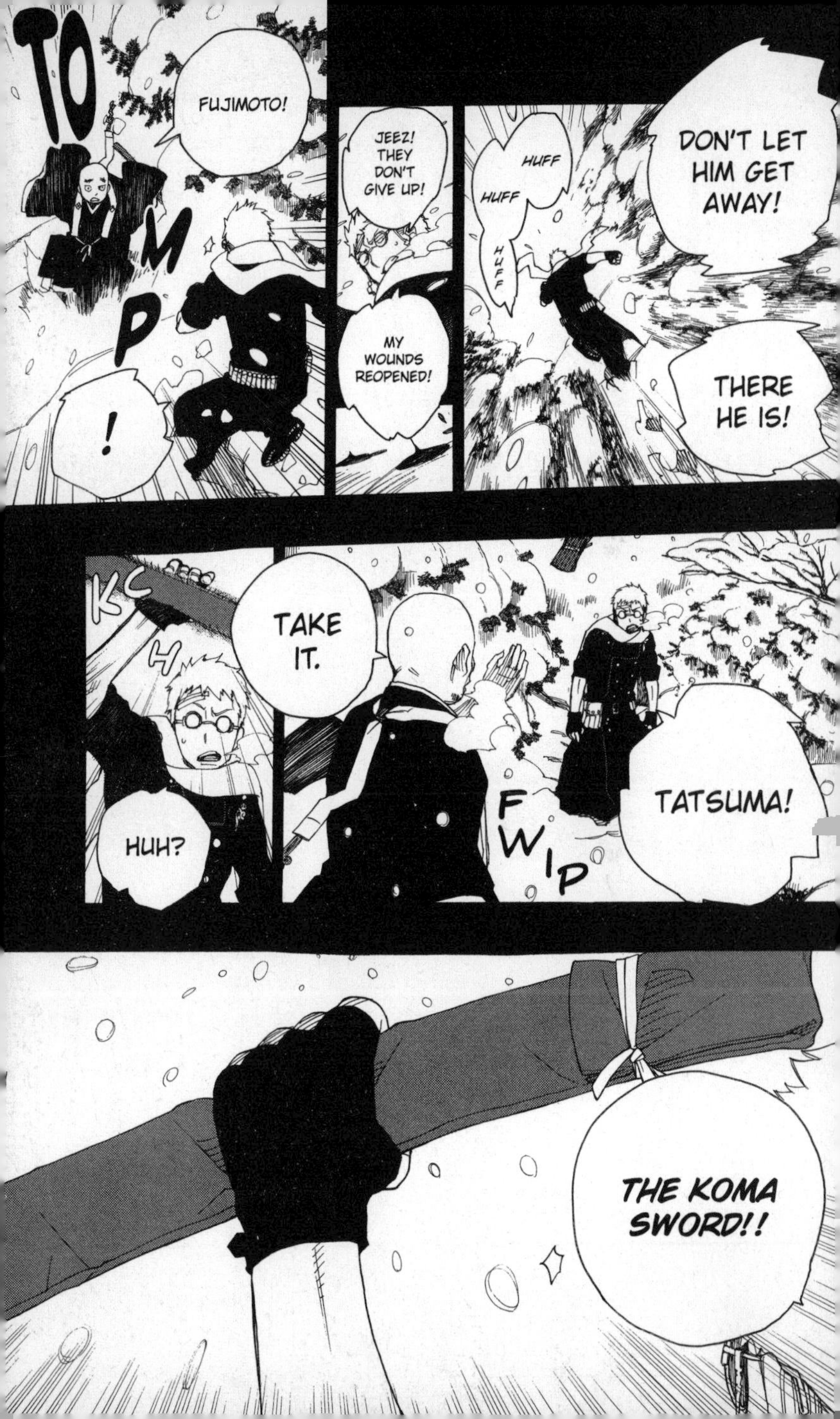
DON'T LET HIM GET AWAY!
HUFF
HUFF
HUFF
THERE HE IS!
JEEZ! THEY DON'T GIVE UP!
MY WOUNDS REOPENED!
FUJIMOTO!
TOMP
!
TATSUMA!
FWIP
TAKE IT.
KCH
HUH?
THE KOMA SWORD!!

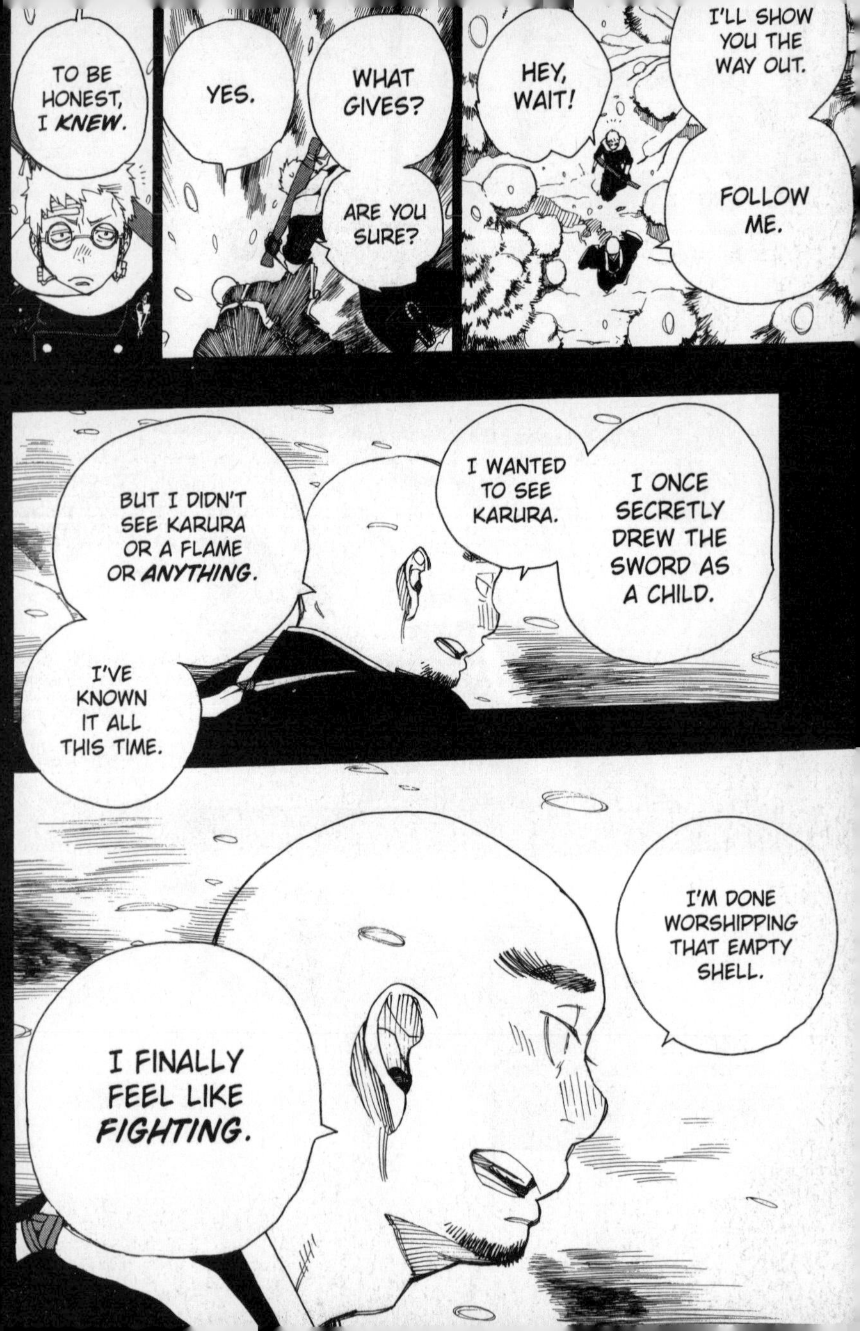
I'LL SHOW YOU THE WAY OUT.
FOLLOW ME.
HEY, WAIT!
WHAT GIVES?
ARE YOU SURE?
YES.
TO BE HONEST, I *KNEW*.
I ONCE SECRETLY DREW THE SWORD AS A CHILD.
I WANTED TO SEE KARURA.
BUT I DIDN'T SEE KARURA OR A FLAME OR *ANYTHING*.
I'VE KNOWN IT ALL THIS TIME.
I'M DONE WORSHIPPING THAT EMPTY SHELL.
I FINALLY FEEL LIKE *FIGHTING*.

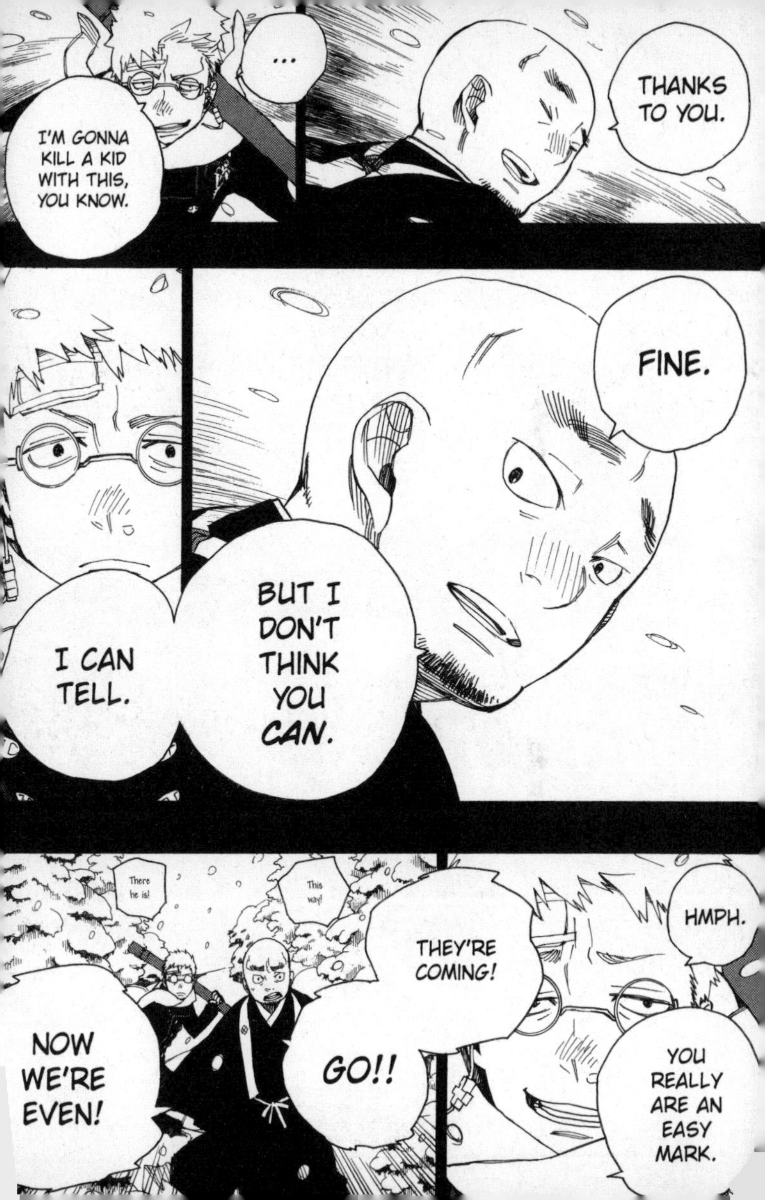
THANKS TO YOU.
...
I'M GONNA KILL A KID WITH THIS, YOU KNOW.
FINE.
BUT I DON'T THINK YOU CAN.
I CAN TELL.
HMPH.
YOU REALLY ARE AN EASY MARK.
THEY'RE COMING!
This way!
There he is!
GO!!
NOW WE'RE EVEN!

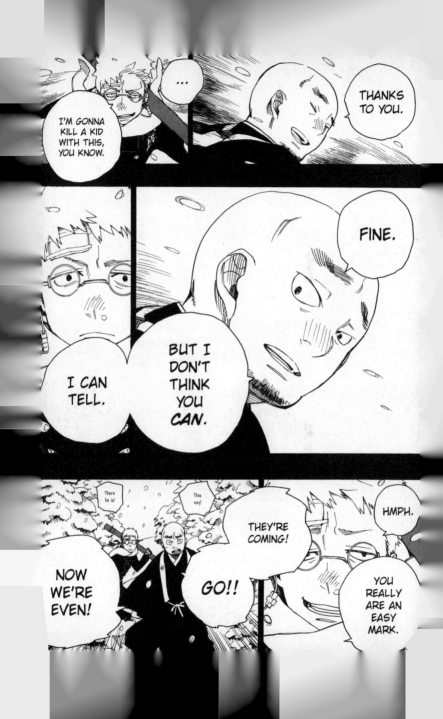

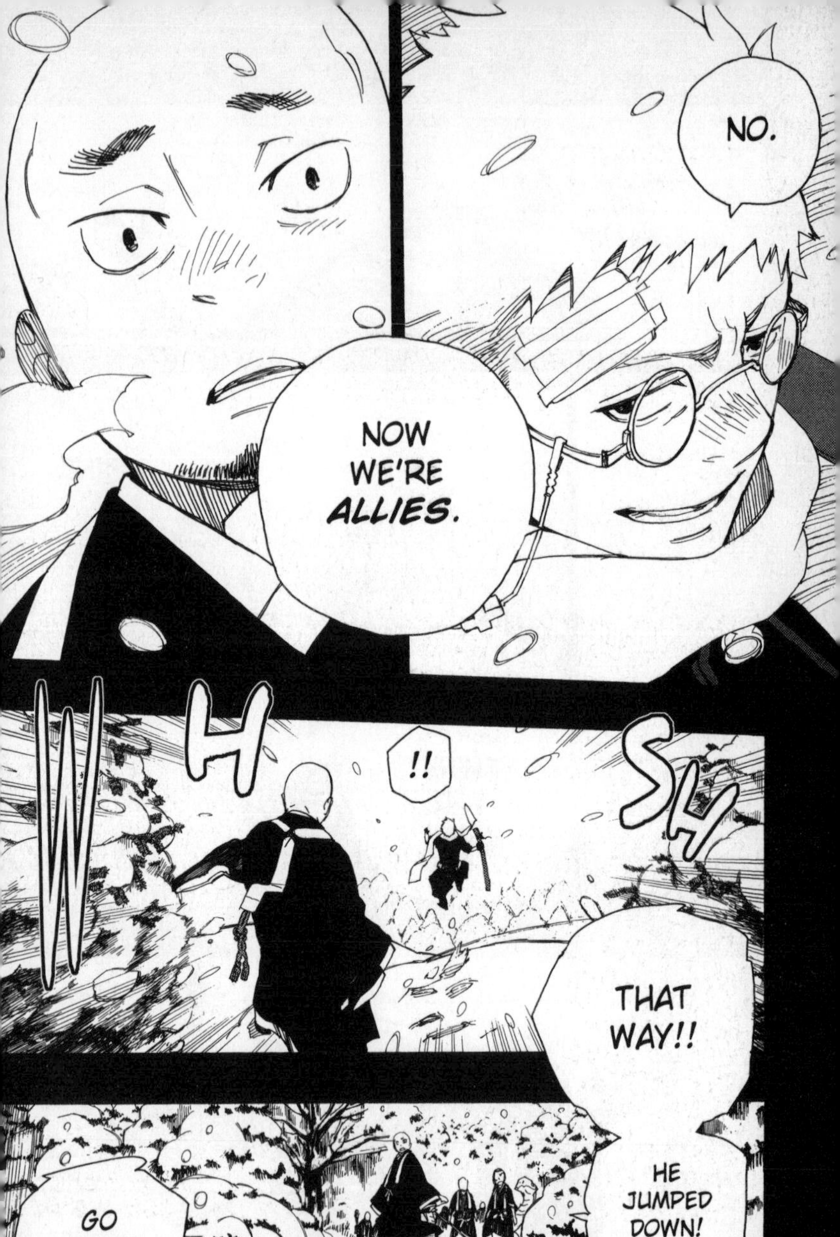
NO.
NOW WE'RE ALLIES.
WHSH
!!
THAT WAY!!
HE JUMPED DOWN!
GO AFTER HIM!

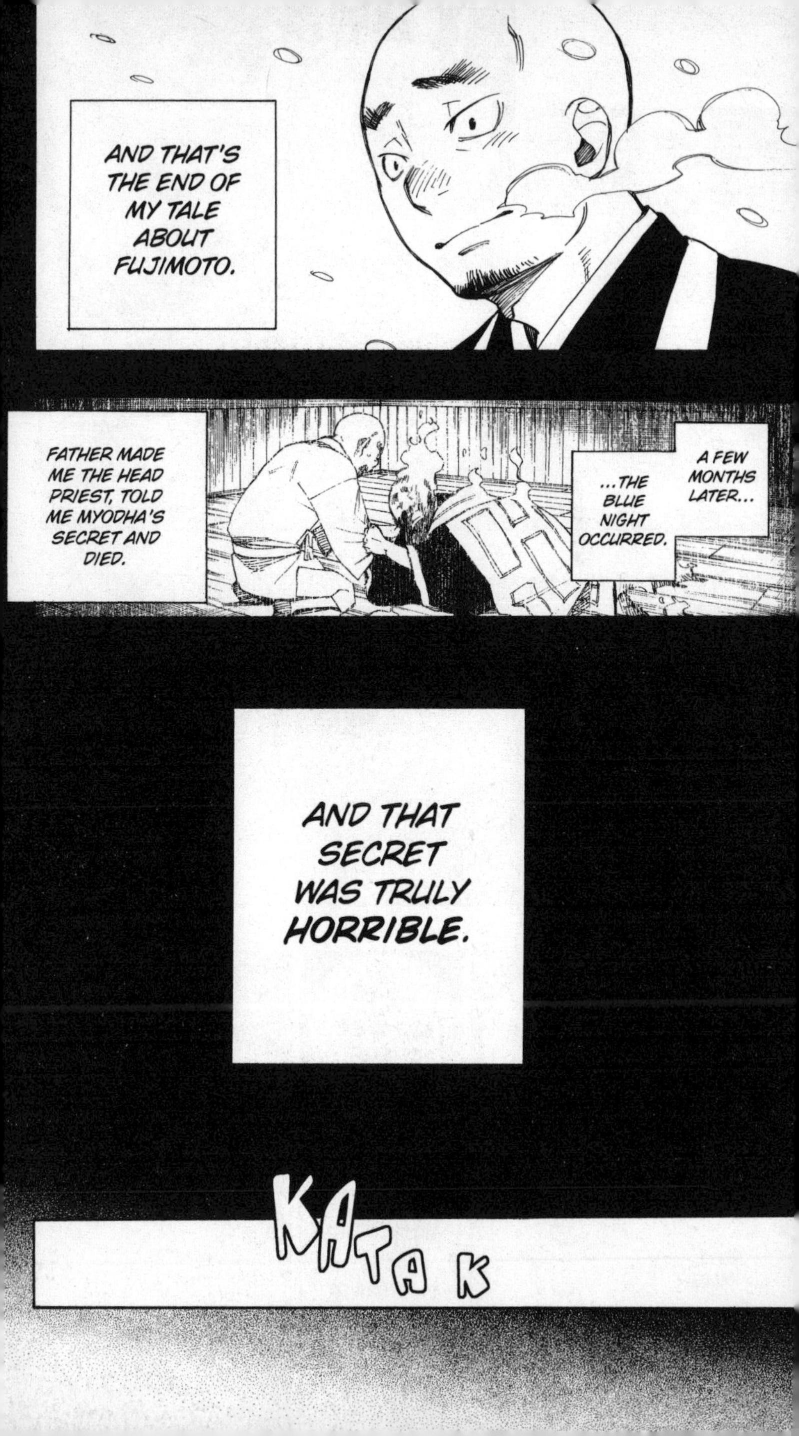
AND THAT'S THE END OF MY TALE ABOUT FUJIMOTO.
A FEW MONTHS LATER...
...THE BLUE NIGHT OCCURRED.
FATHER MADE ME THE HEAD PRIEST, TOLD ME MYODHA'S SECRET AND DIED.
AND THAT SECRET WAS TRULY HORRIBLE.
KATAK

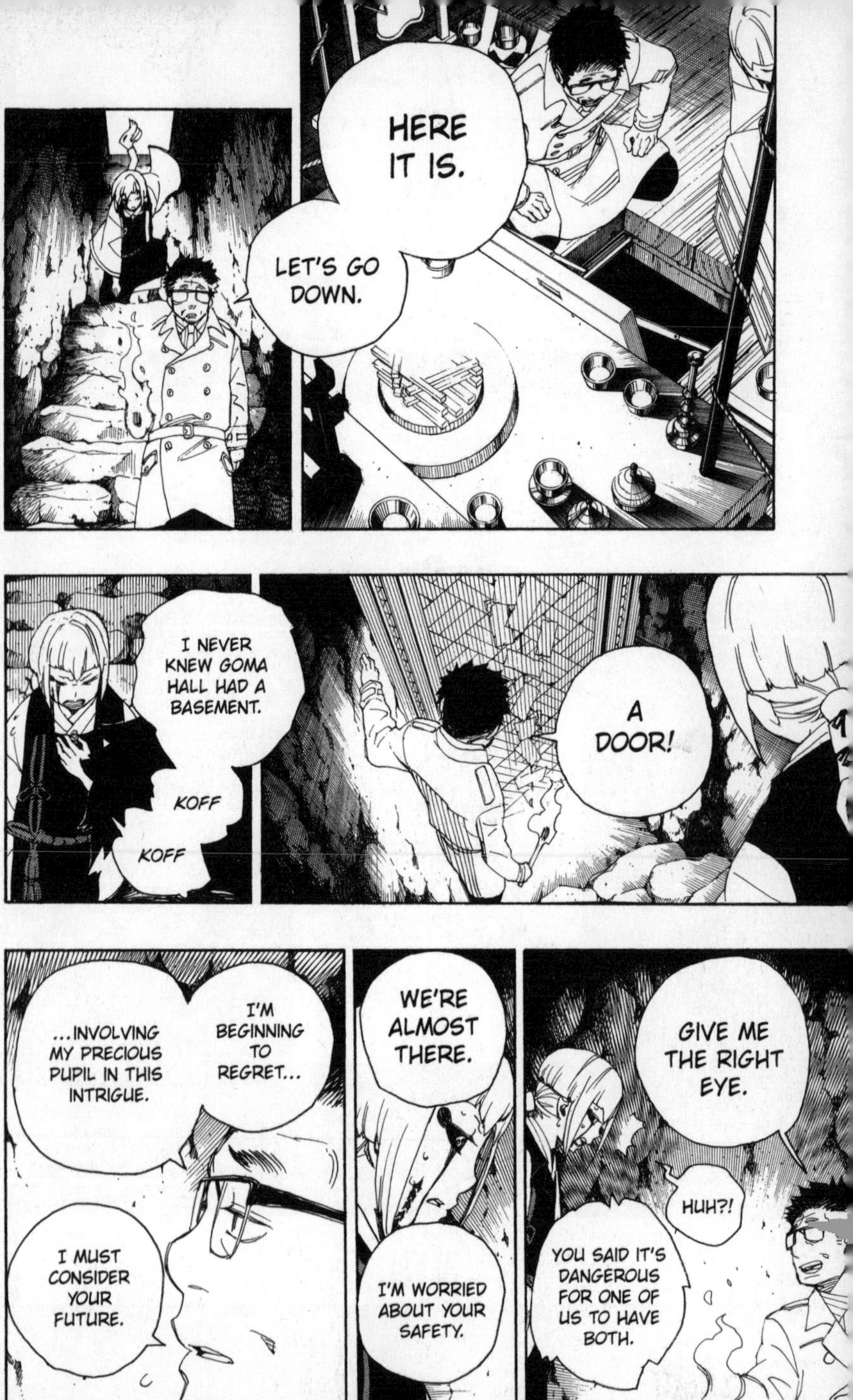
HERE IT IS.
LET'S GO DOWN.
A DOOR!
I NEVER KNEW GOMA HALL HAD A BASEMENT.
KOFF
KOFF
GIVE ME THE RIGHT EYE.
HUH?!
YOU SAID IT'S DANGEROUS FOR ONE OF US TO HAVE BOTH.
WE'RE ALMOST THERE.
I'M WORRIED ABOUT YOUR SAFETY.
I'M BEGINNING TO REGRET...
...INVOLVING MY PRECIOUS PUPIL IN THIS INTRIGUE.
I MUST CONSIDER YOUR FUTURE.

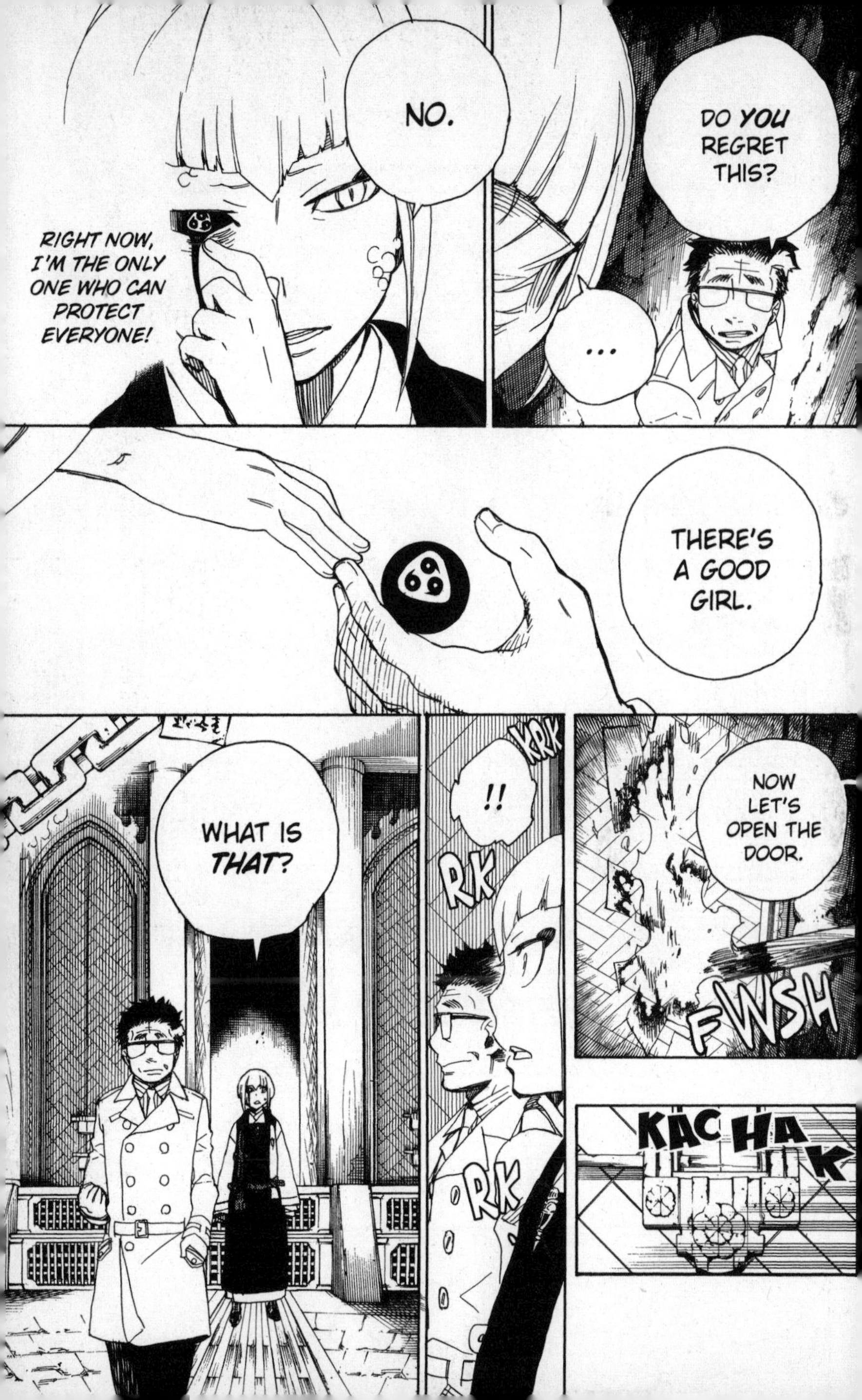
DO *YOU* REGRET THIS?
...
NO.
RIGHT NOW, I'M THE ONLY ONE WHO CAN PROTECT EVERYONE!
THERE'S A GOOD GIRL.
NOW LET'S OPEN THE DOOR.
FWSH
KACHAK
KRK
!!
RK
RK
WHAT IS *THAT*?

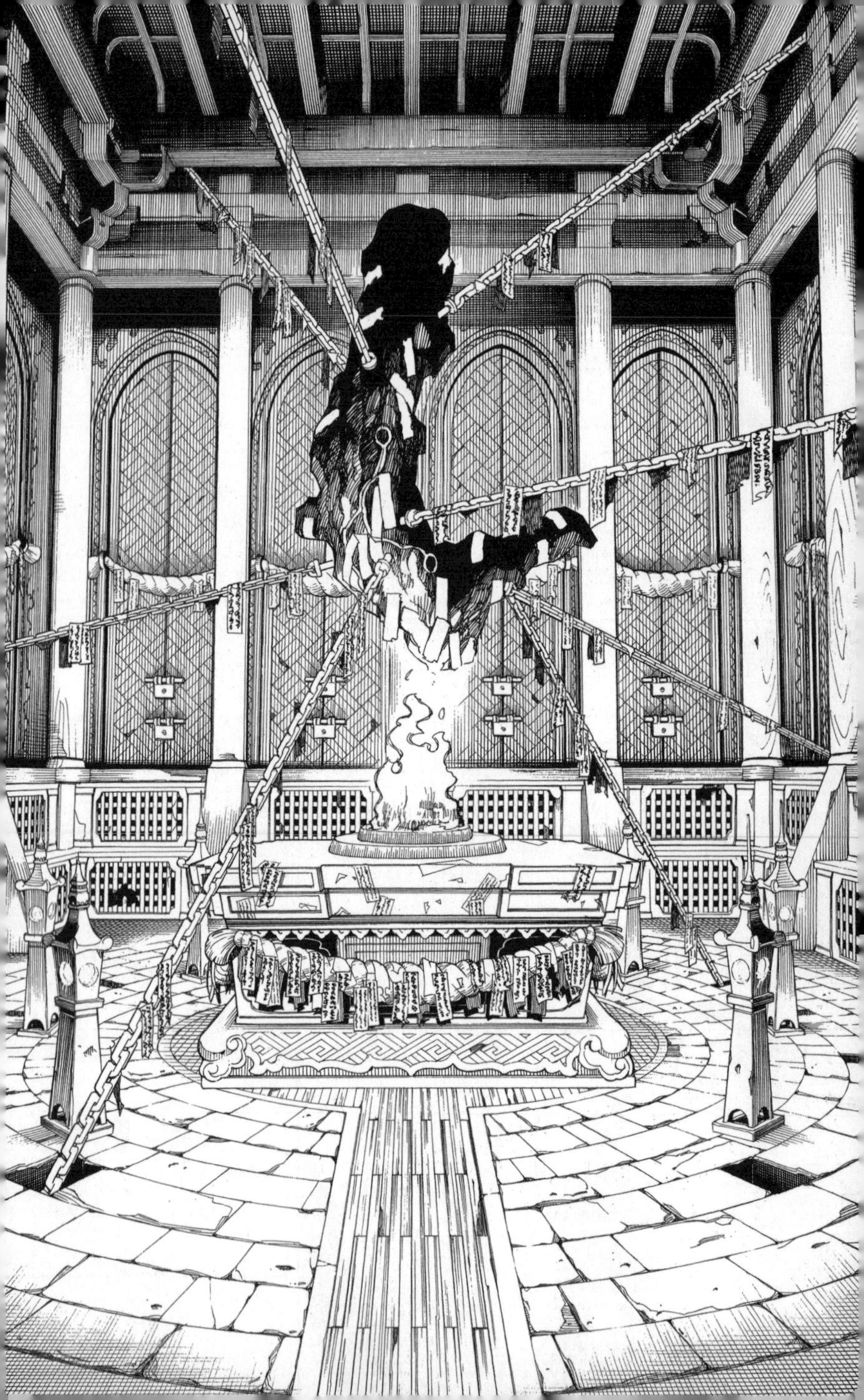

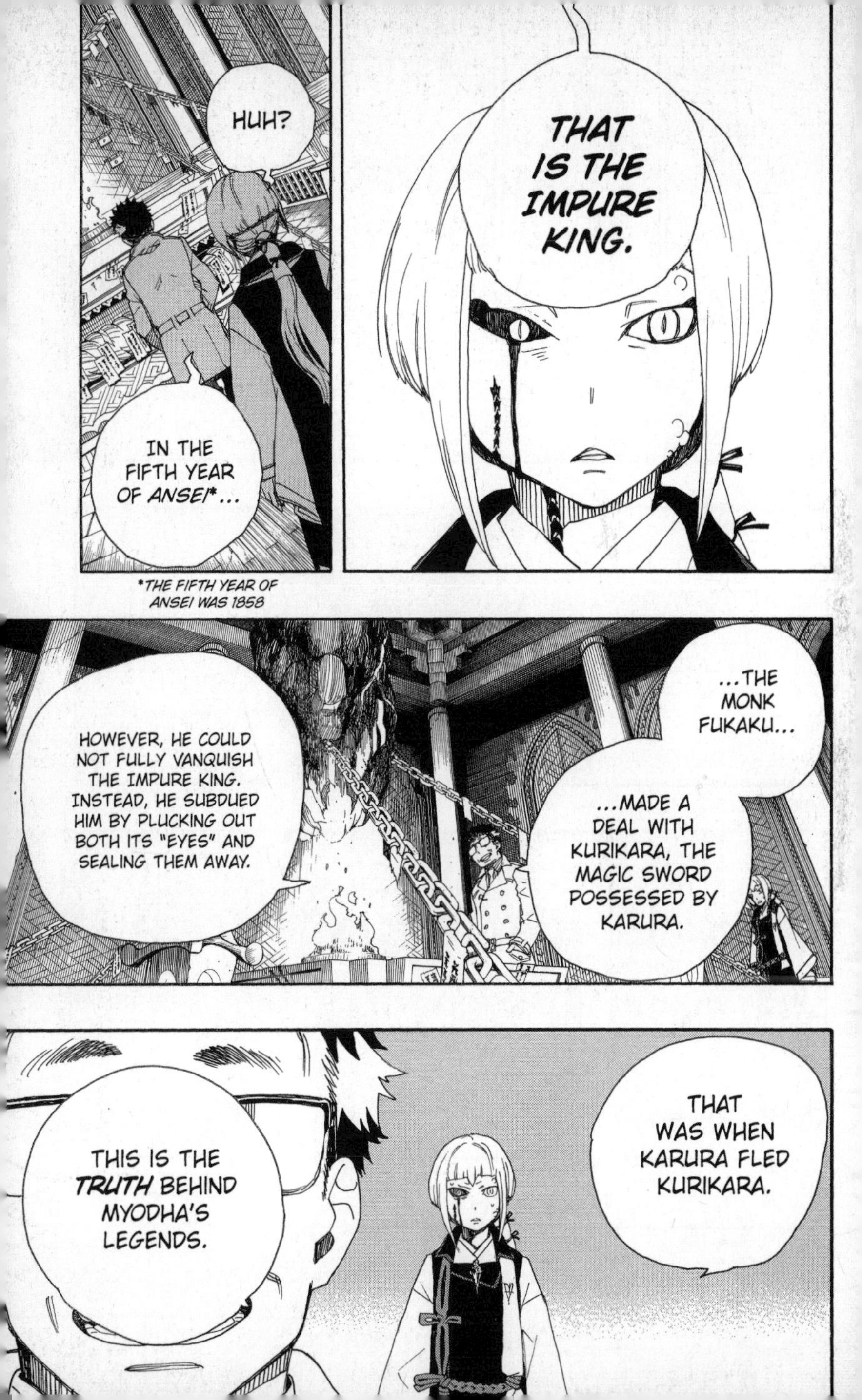
THAT IS THE IMPURE KING.
HUH?
IN THE FIFTH YEAR OF *ANSEI**...
...THE MONK FUKAKU...
...MADE A DEAL WITH KURIKARA, THE MAGIC SWORD POSSESSED BY KARURA.
HOWEVER, HE COULD NOT FULLY VANQUISH THE IMPURE KING. INSTEAD, HE SUBDUED HIM BY PLUCKING OUT BOTH ITS "EYES" AND SEALING THEM AWAY.
THAT WAS WHEN KARURA FLED KURIKARA.
THIS IS THE ***TRUTH*** BEHIND MYODHA'S LEGENDS.

**THE FIFTH YEAR OF ANSEI WAS 1858*

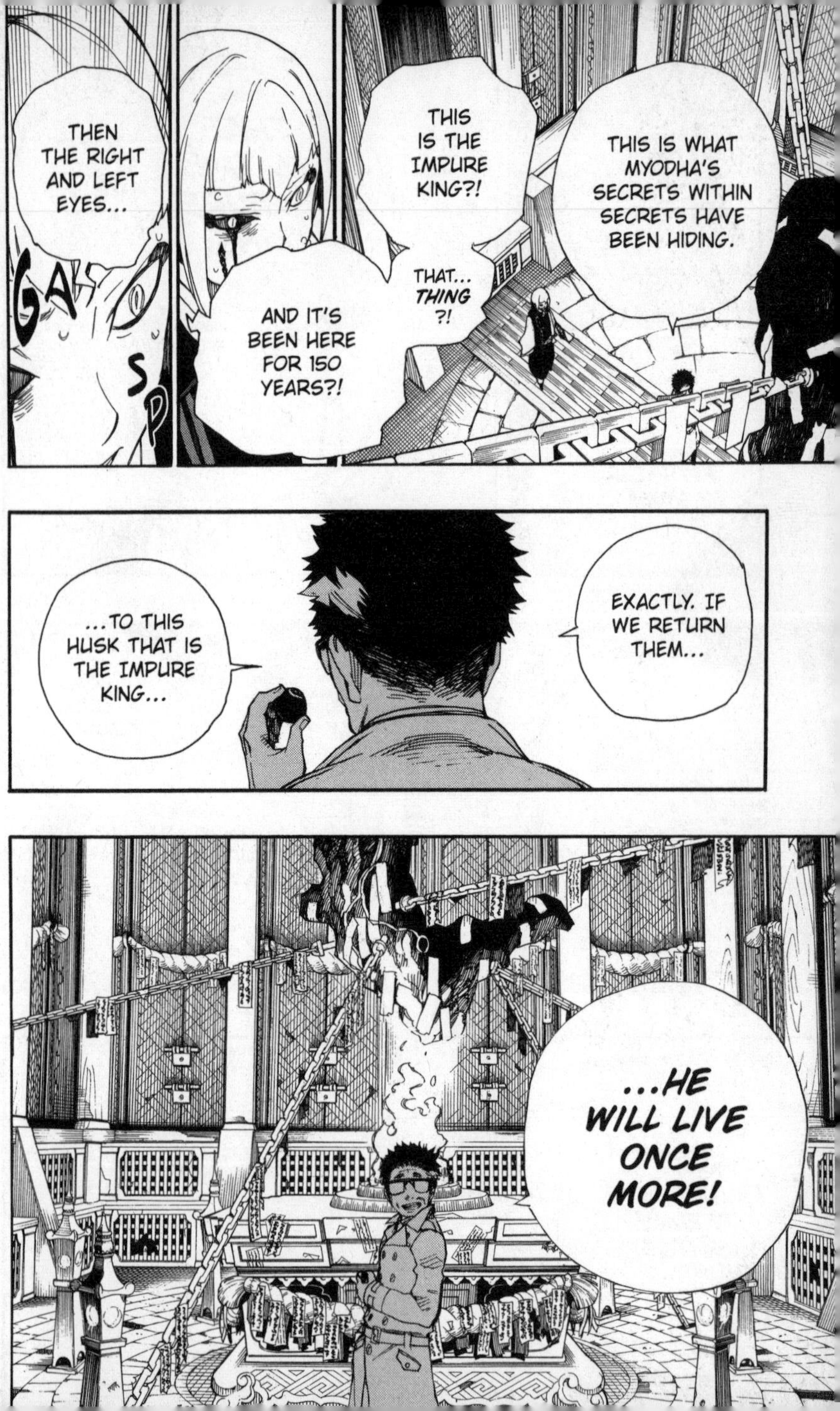
THIS IS WHAT MYODHA'S SECRETS WITHIN SECRETS HAVE BEEN HIDING.
THIS IS THE IMPURE KING?!
THAT... *THING*?!
AND IT'S BEEN HERE FOR 150 YEARS?!
THEN THE RIGHT AND LEFT EYES...
GASP
EXACTLY. IF WE RETURN THEM...
...TO THIS HUSK THAT IS THE IMPURE KING...
...HE WILL LIVE ONCE MORE!

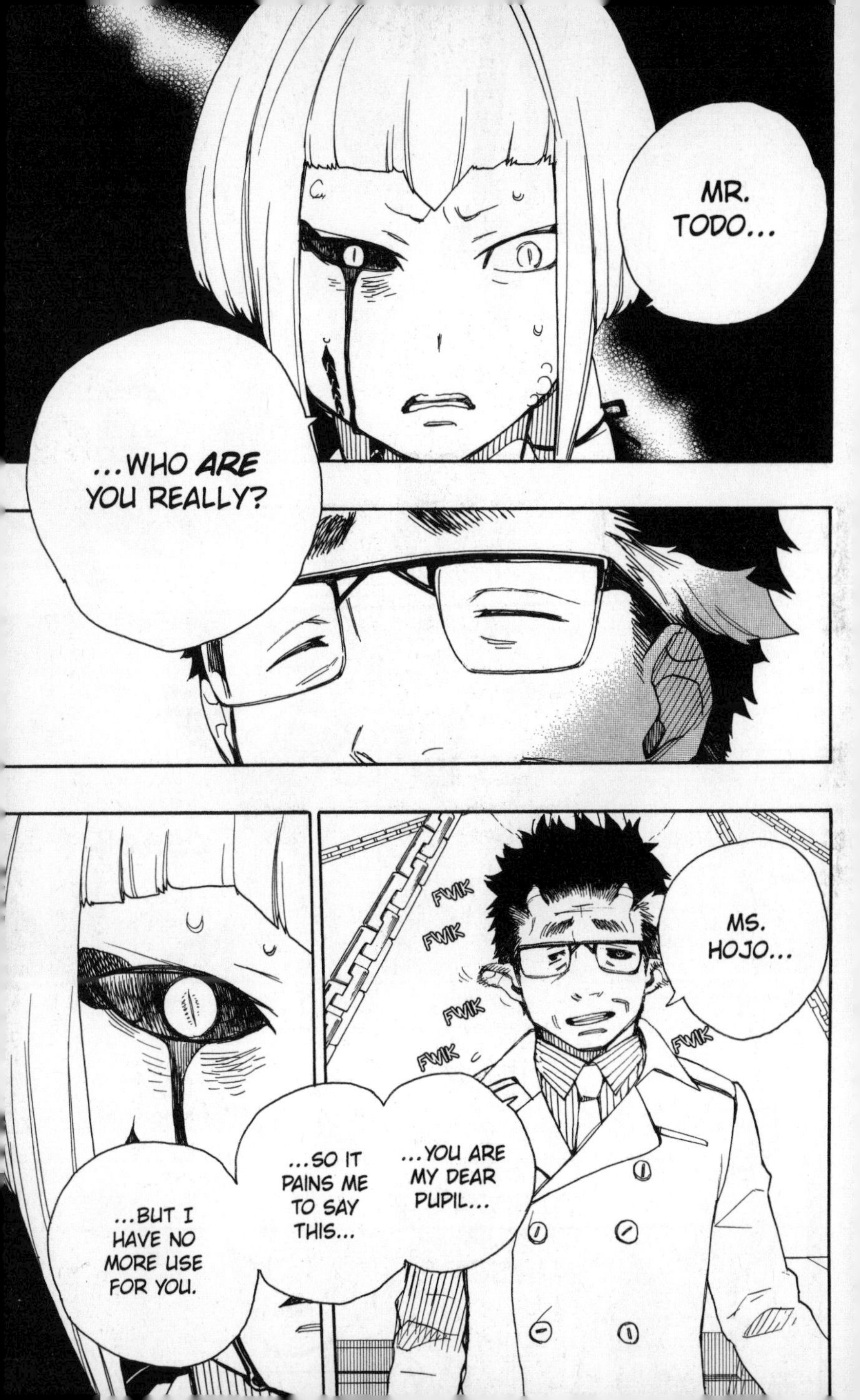
MR. TODO...
...WHO ARE YOU REALLY?
MS. HOJO...
FWIK
FWIK
FWIK
FWIK
FWIK
...YOU ARE MY DEAR PUPIL...
...SO IT PAINS ME TO SAY THIS...
...BUT I HAVE NO MORE USE FOR YOU.

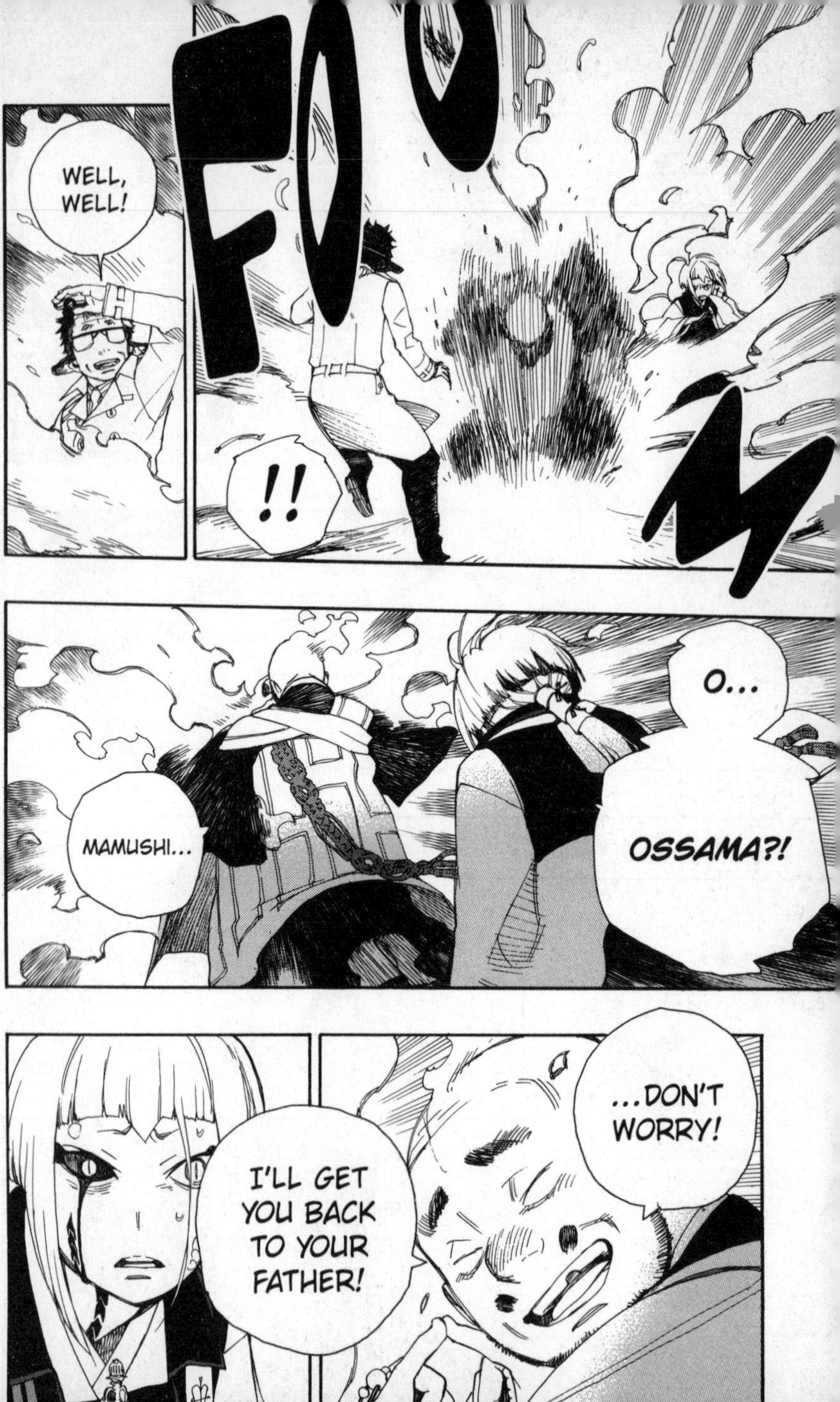
FOOM
!!
WELL, WELL!
O...
OSSAMA?!
MAMUSHI...
...DON'T WORRY!
I'LL GET YOU BACK TO YOUR FATHER!

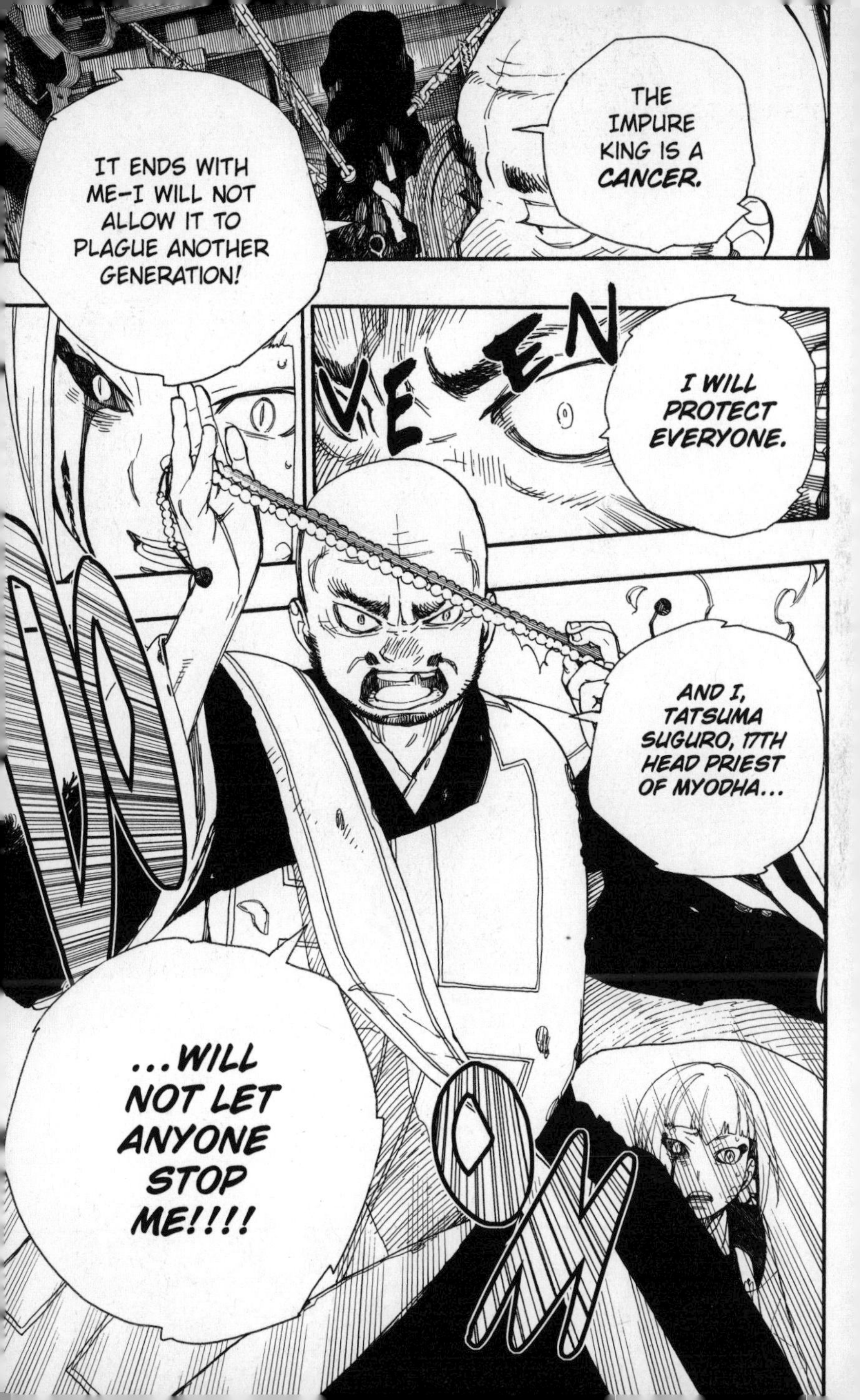
THE IMPURE KING IS A CANCER.
IT ENDS WITH ME—I WILL NOT ALLOW IT TO PLAGUE ANOTHER GENERATION!
VEEN
I WILL PROTECT EVERYONE.
AND I, TATSUMA SUGURO, 17TH HEAD PRIEST OF MYODHA...
...WILL NOT LET ANYONE STOP ME!!!!

Blue Exorcist Chapter 24 Empty Sword

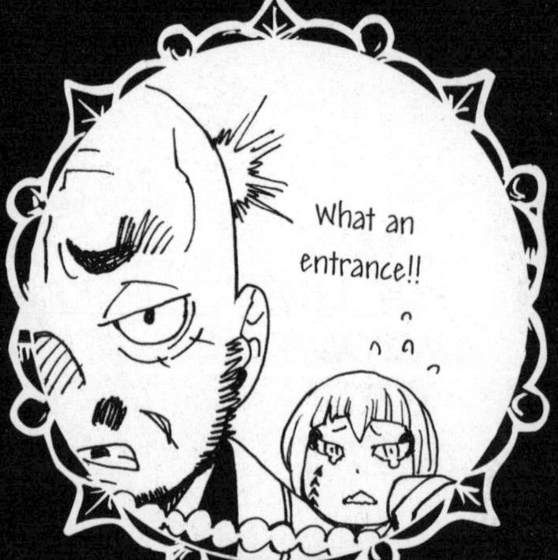
What an entrance!!

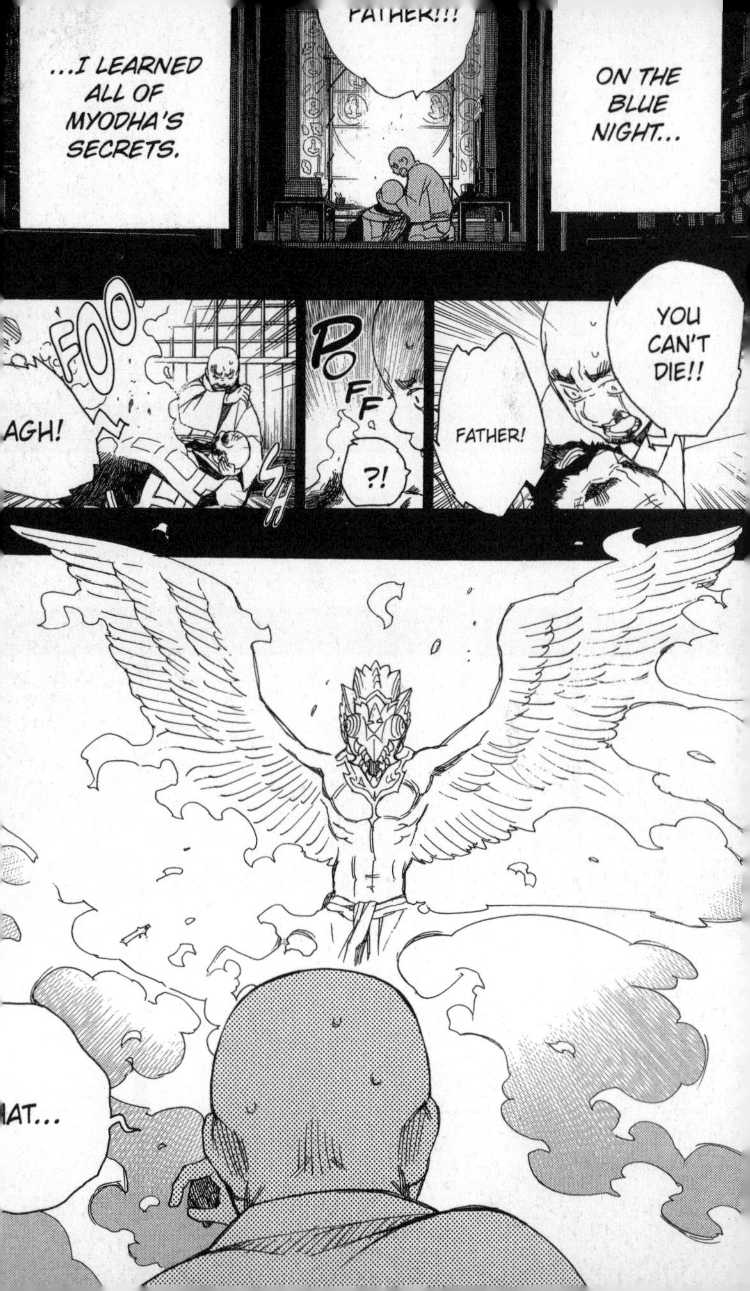
ON THE BLUE NIGHT...
FATHER!!!
...I LEARNED ALL OF MYODHA'S SECRETS.
YOU CAN'T DIE!!
FATHER!
POFF
?!
FOO
SH
AGH!
AT...

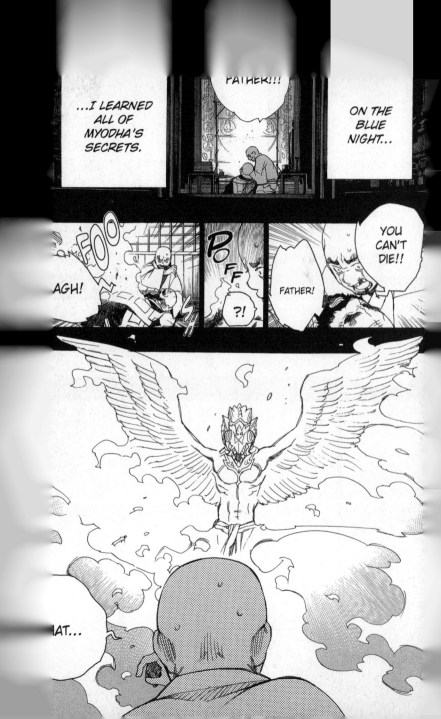

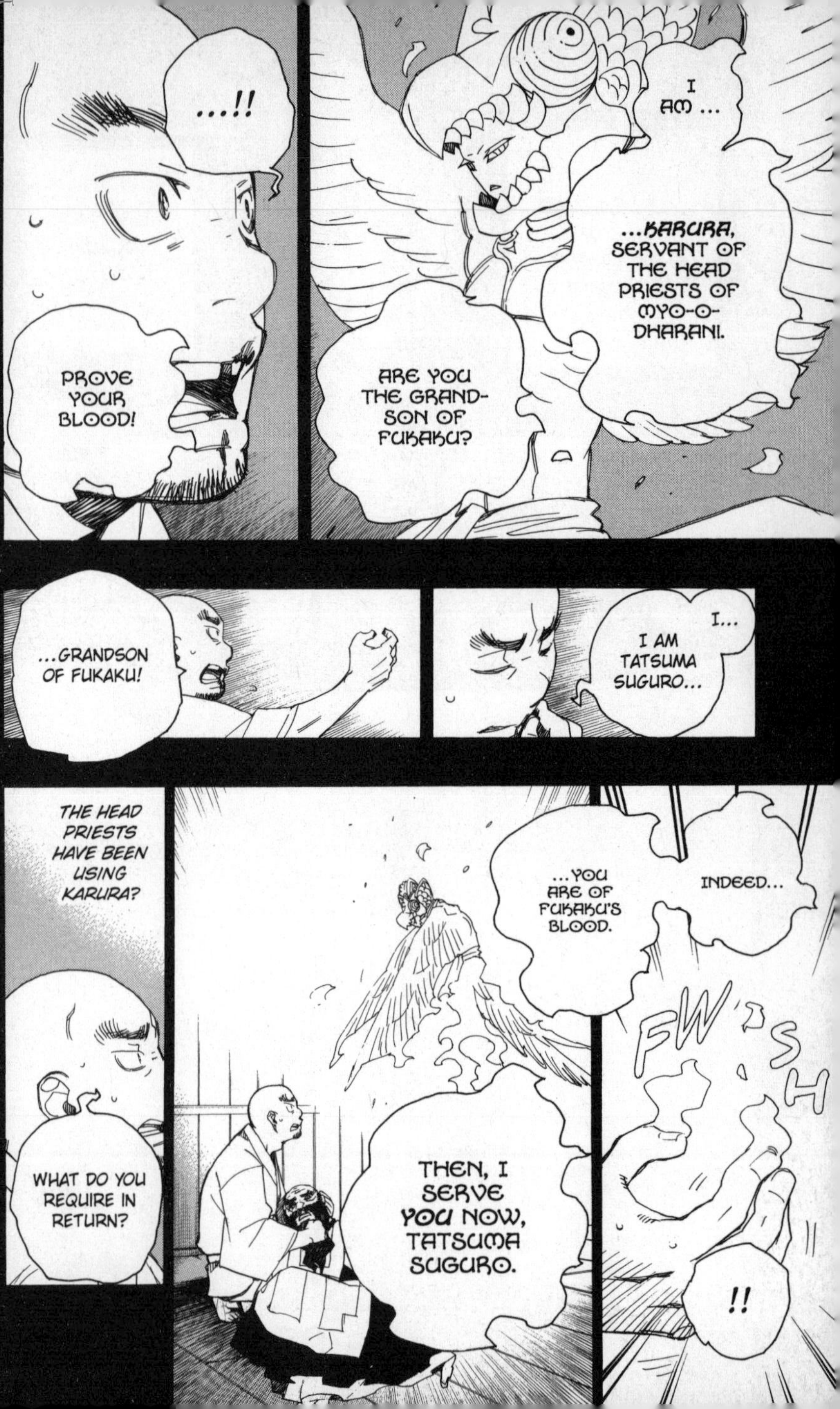
I AM ...
...KARURA, SERVANT OF THE HEAD PRIESTS OF MYO-O-DHARANI.
ARE YOU THE GRAND-SON OF FUKAKU?
...!!
PROVE YOUR BLOOD!
I...
I AM TATSUMA SUGURO...
...GRANDSON OF FUKAKU!
INDEED...
...YOU ARE OF FUKAKU'S BLOOD.
FWSSH
!!
THEN, I SERVE YOU NOW, TATSUMA SUGURO.
THE HEAD PRIESTS HAVE BEEN USING KARURA?
WHAT DO YOU REQUIRE IN RETURN?

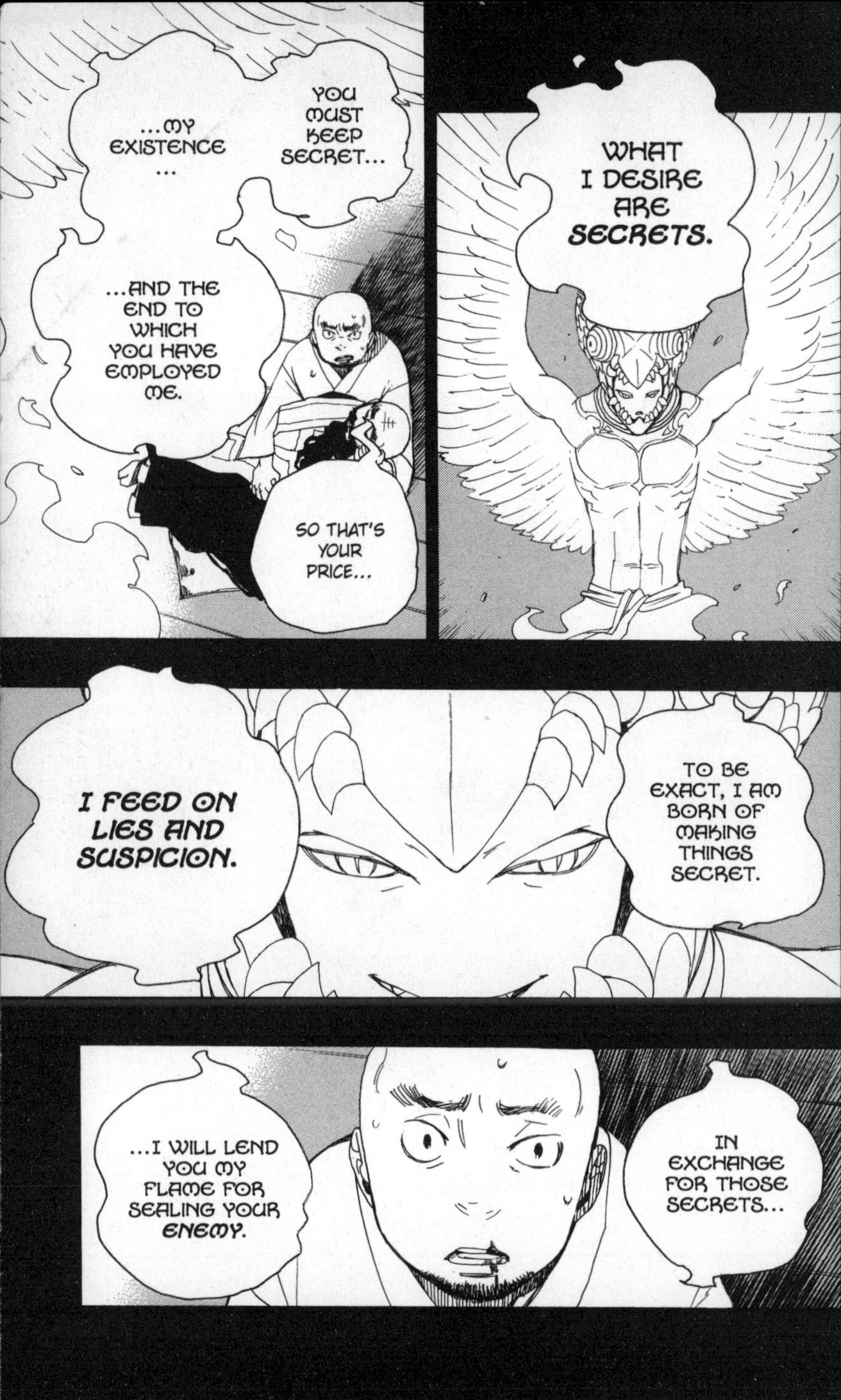
WHAT I DESIRE ARE SECRETS.
YOU MUST KEEP SECRET...
...MY EXISTENCE...
...AND THE END TO WHICH YOU HAVE EMPLOYED ME.
SO THAT'S YOUR PRICE...
TO BE EXACT, I AM BORN OF MAKING THINGS SECRET.
I FEED ON LIES AND SUSPICION.
IN EXCHANGE FOR THOSE SECRETS...
...I WILL LEND YOU MY FLAME FOR SEALING YOUR ENEMY.

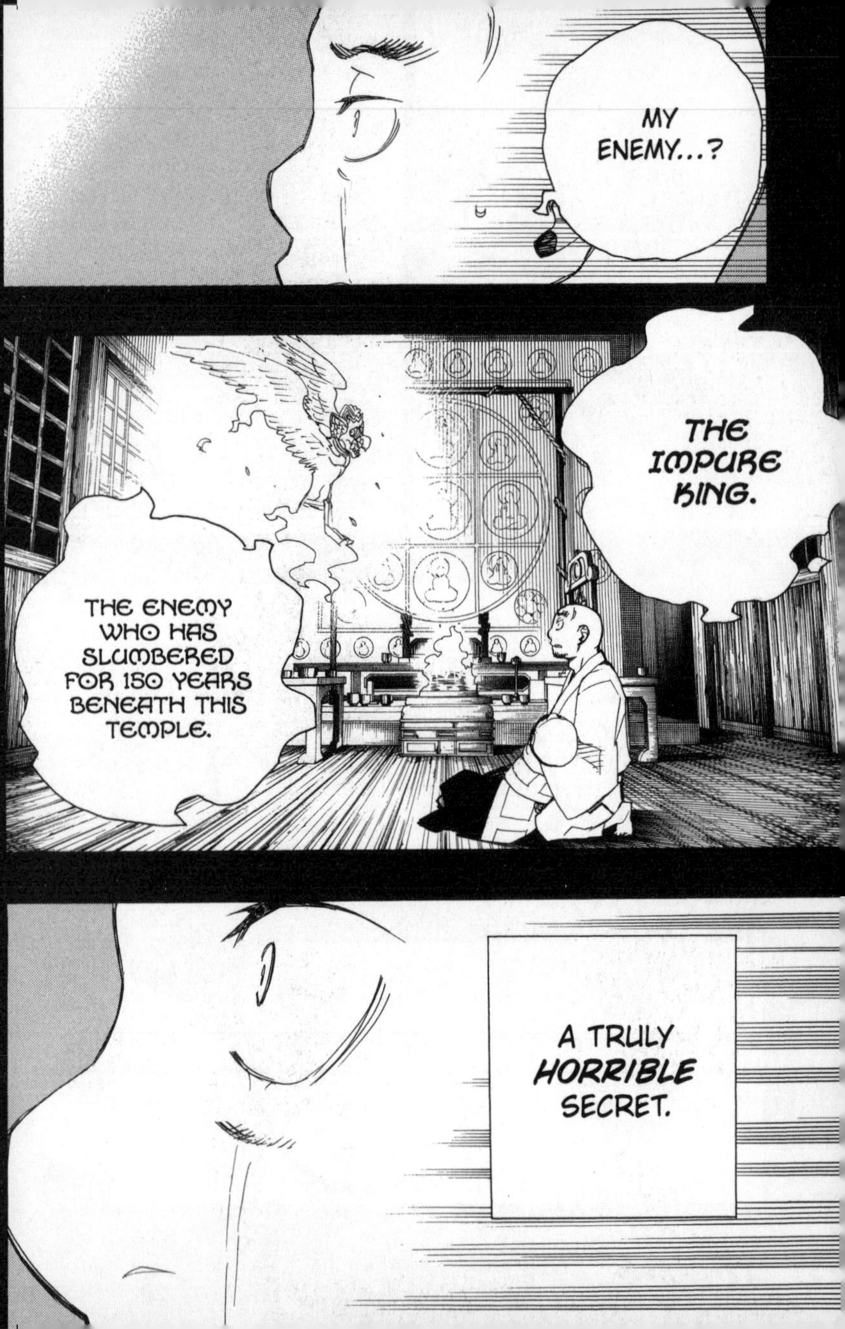
MY ENEMY...?
THE IMPURE KING.
THE ENEMY WHO HAS SLUMBERED FOR 150 YEARS BENEATH THIS TEMPLE.
A TRULY HORRIBLE SECRET.

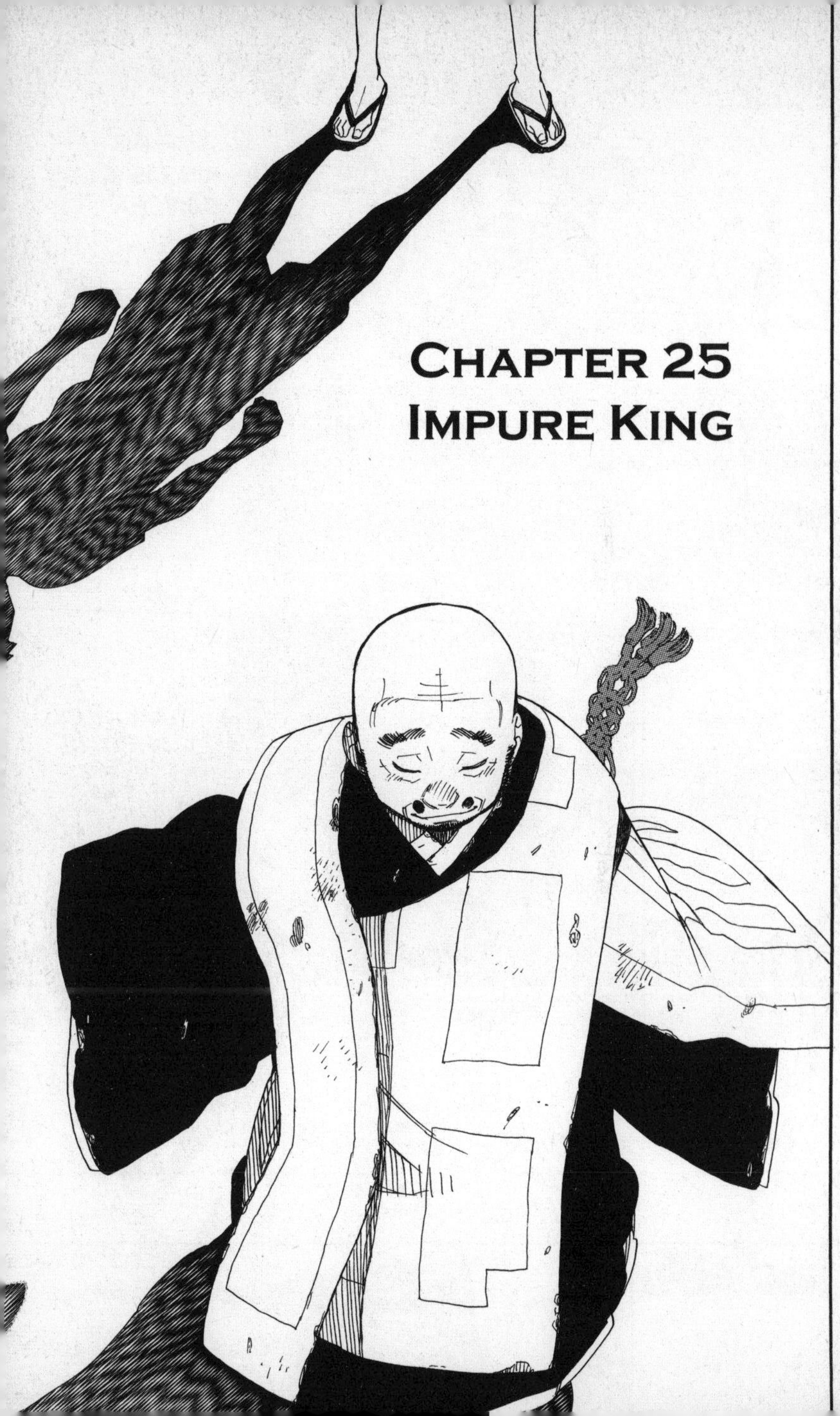
CHAPTER 25
IMPURE KING

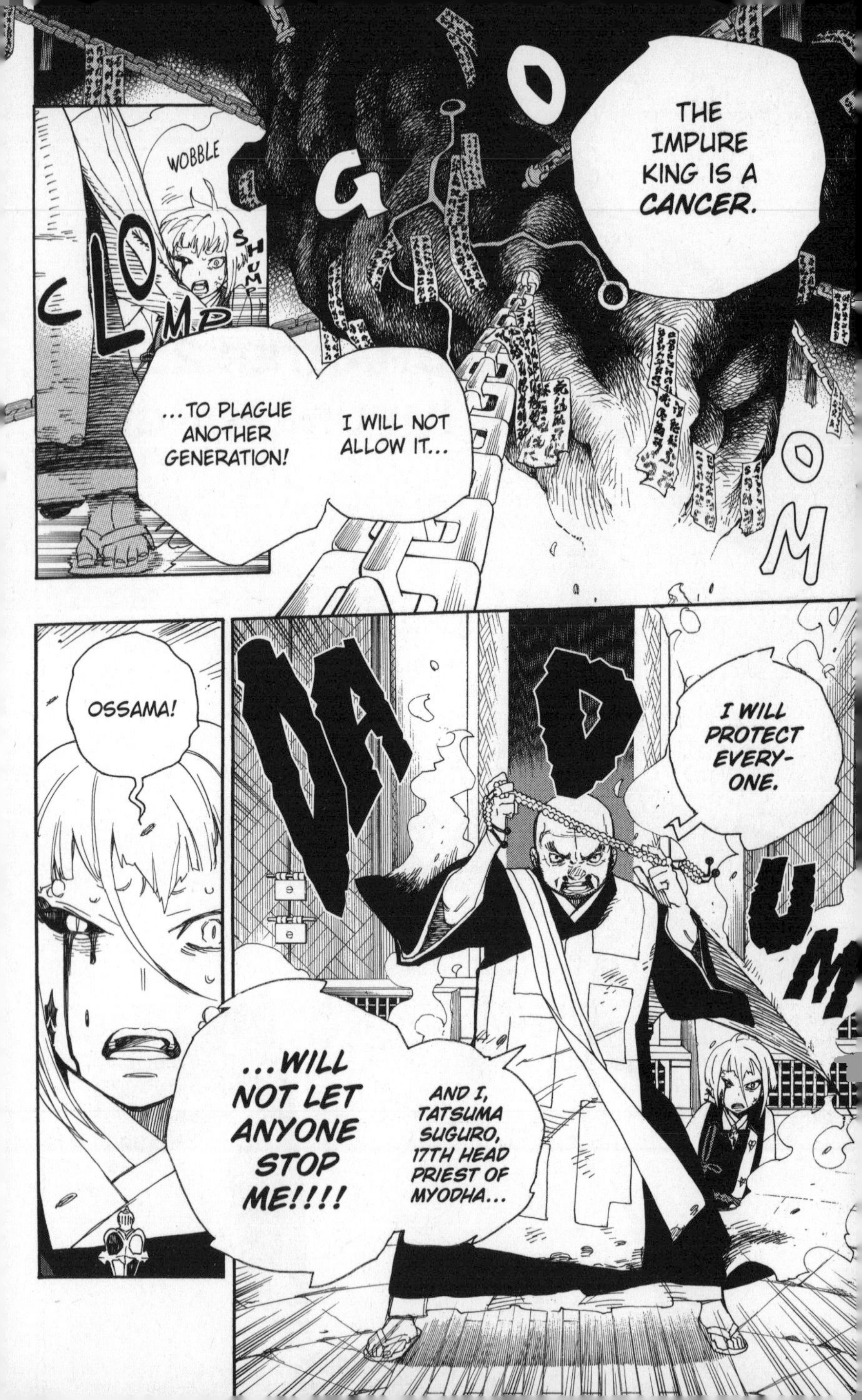
THE IMPURE KING IS A CANCER.
I WILL NOT ALLOW IT...
...TO PLAGUE ANOTHER GENERATION!
WOBBLE
SHUMP
CLOMP
I WILL PROTECT EVERY-ONE.
AND I, TATSUMA SUGURO, 17TH HEAD PRIEST OF MYODHA...
...WILL NOT LET ANYONE STOP ME!!!!
OSSAMA!

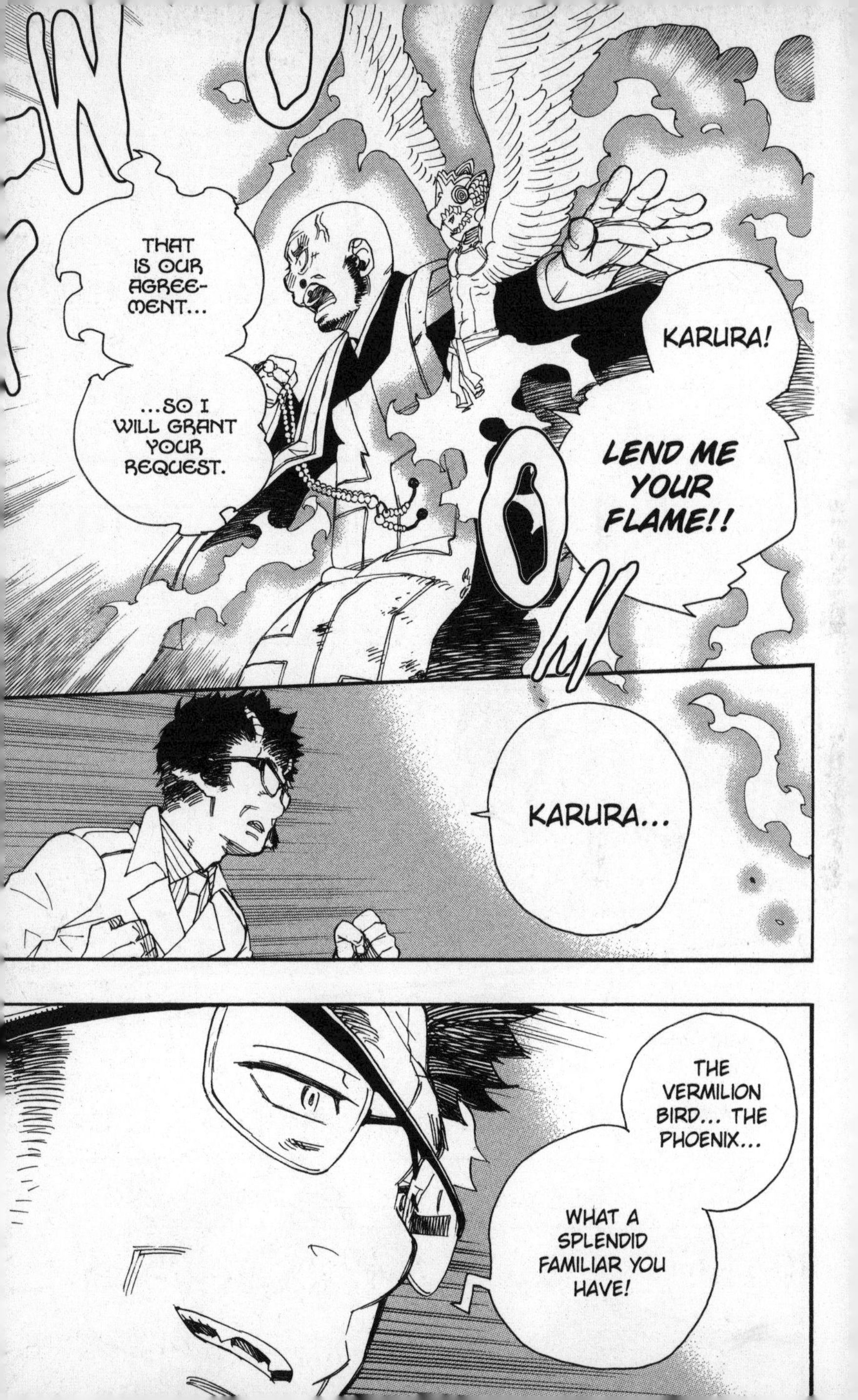
KARURA!
LEND ME YOUR FLAME!!
THAT IS OUR AGREEMENT...
...SO I WILL GRANT YOUR REQUEST.
KARURA...
THE VERMILION BIRD... THE PHOENIX...
WHAT A SPLENDID FAMILIAR YOU HAVE!

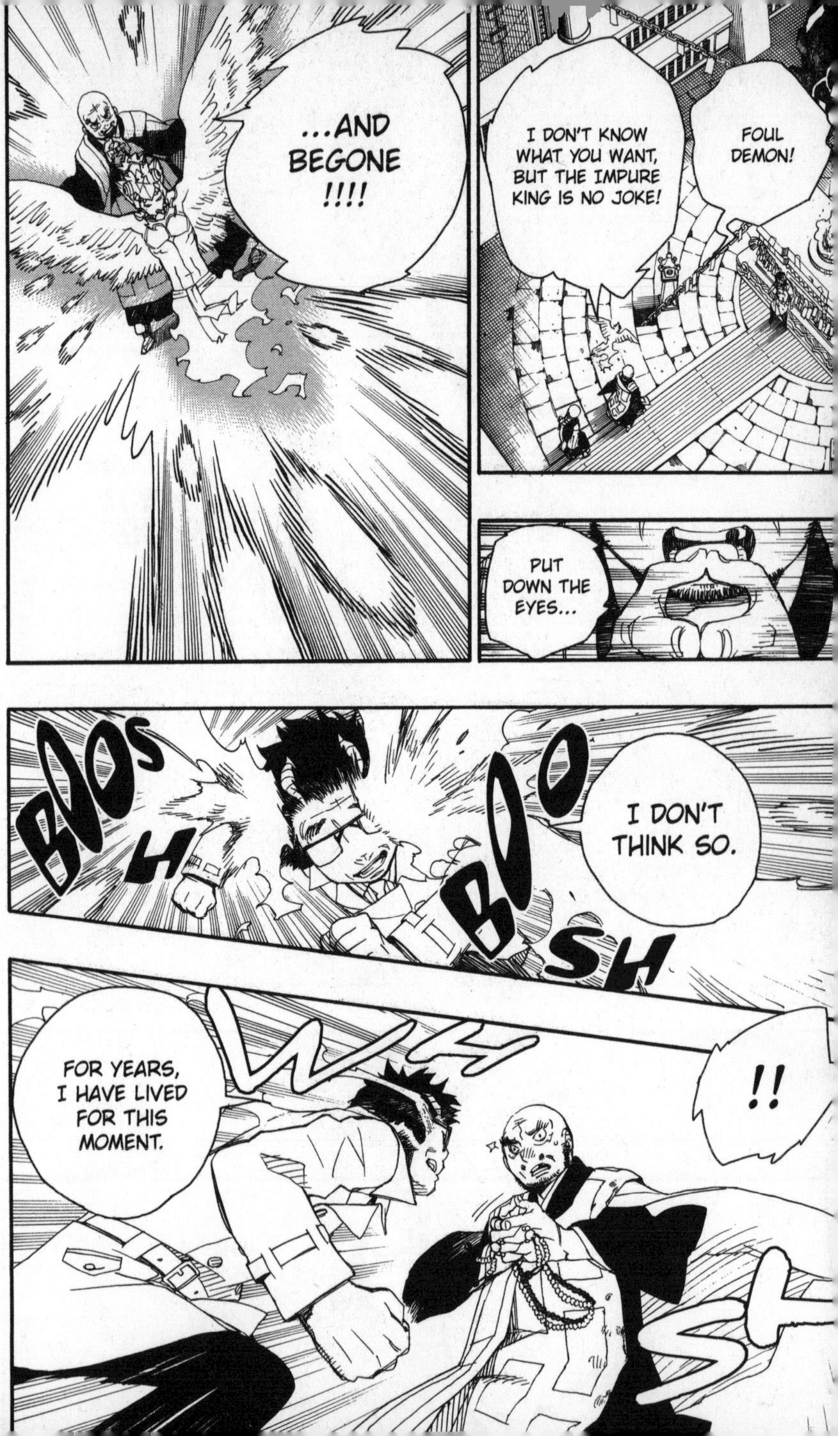
FOUL DEMON!
I DON'T KNOW WHAT YOU WANT, BUT THE IMPURE KING IS NO JOKE!
PUT DOWN THE EYES...
...AND BEGONE !!!!
I DON'T THINK SO.
BOOSH
BOOSH
!!
FOR YEARS, I HAVE LIVED FOR THIS MOMENT.

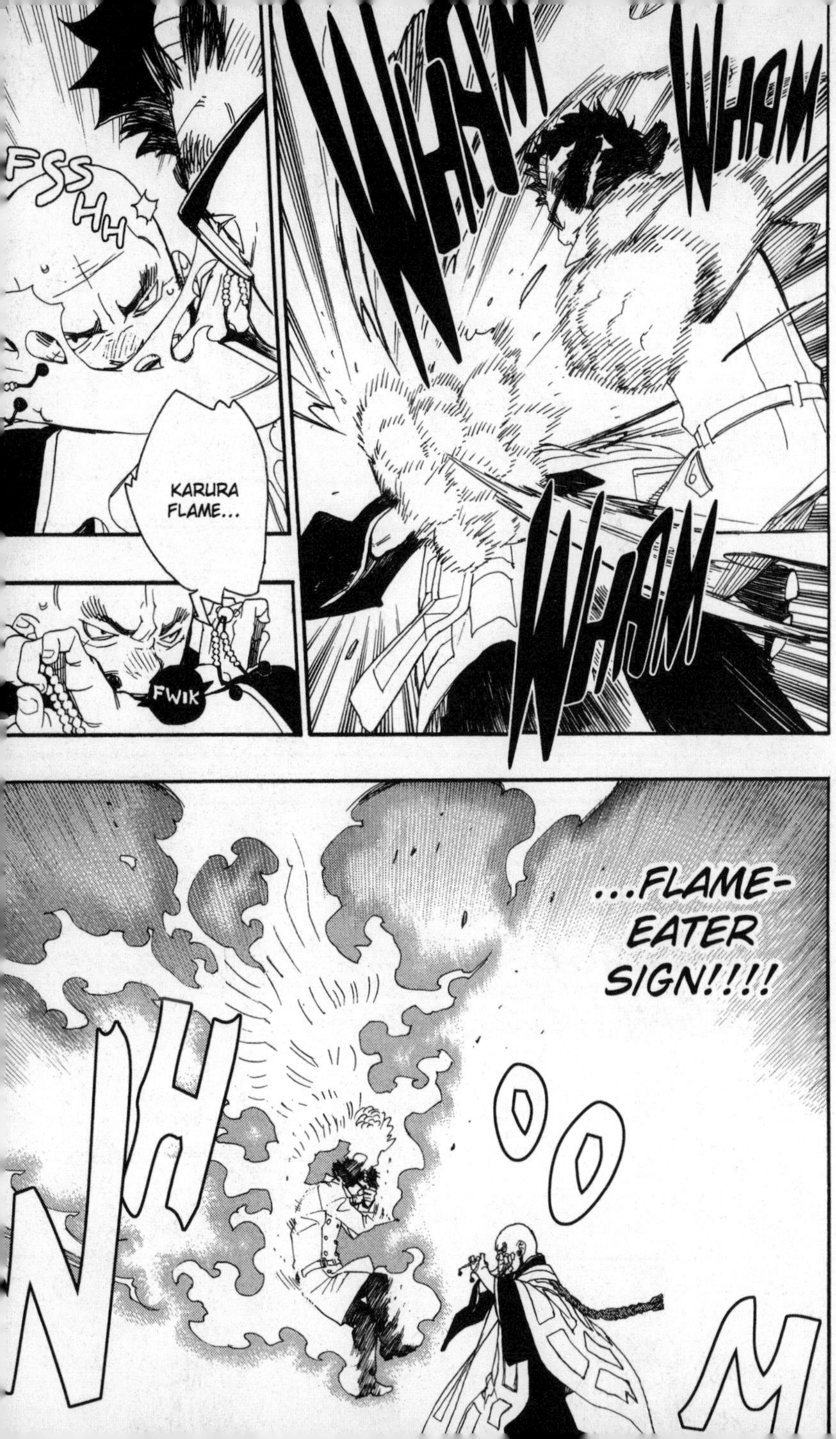
WHAM
WHAM
WHAM
FSSHH
KARURA FLAME...
FWIK
...FLAME-EATER SIGN!!!!
WHOOOM

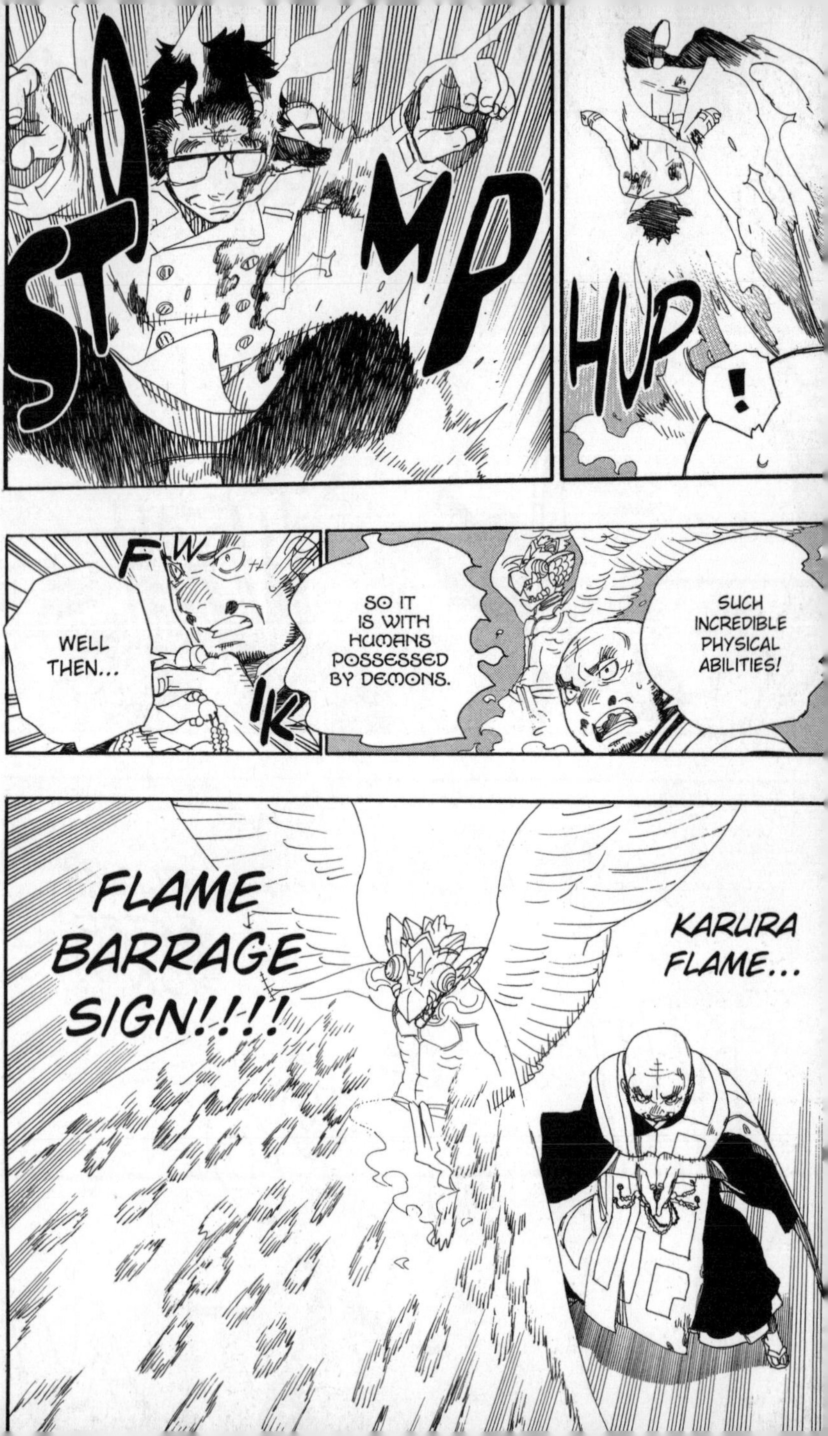
HUP
!
STOMP
SUCH INCREDIBLE PHYSICAL ABILITIES!
SO IT IS WITH HUMANS POSSESSED BY DEMONS.
FWIK
WELL THEN...
KARURA FLAME...
FLAME BARRAGE SIGN!!!!

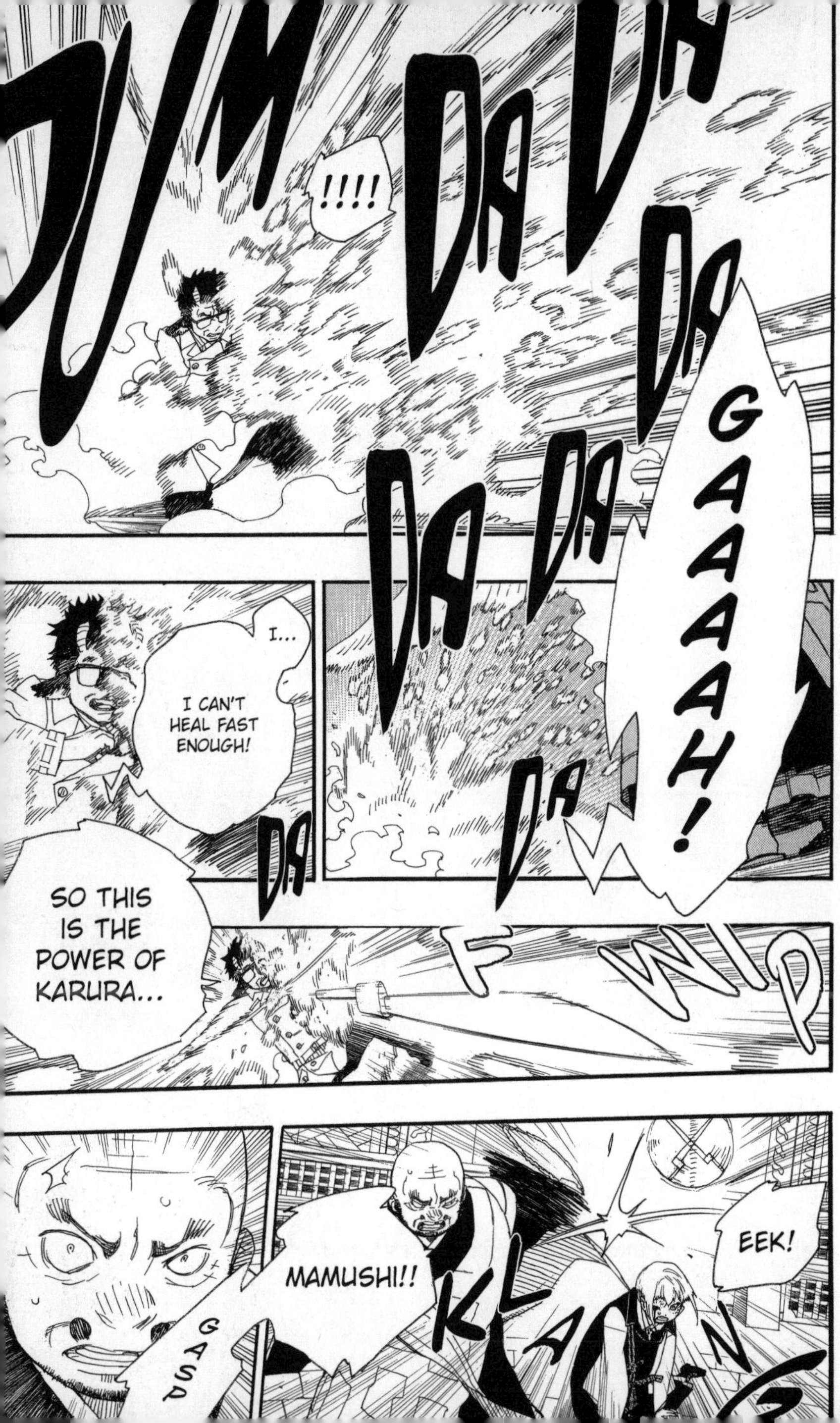
GAAAAAH!
DA DA DA DA DA DA DA
!!!!
I...
I CAN'T HEAL FAST ENOUGH!
FWIP
SO THIS IS THE POWER OF KARURA...
EEK!
KLANG
MAMUSHI!!
GASA

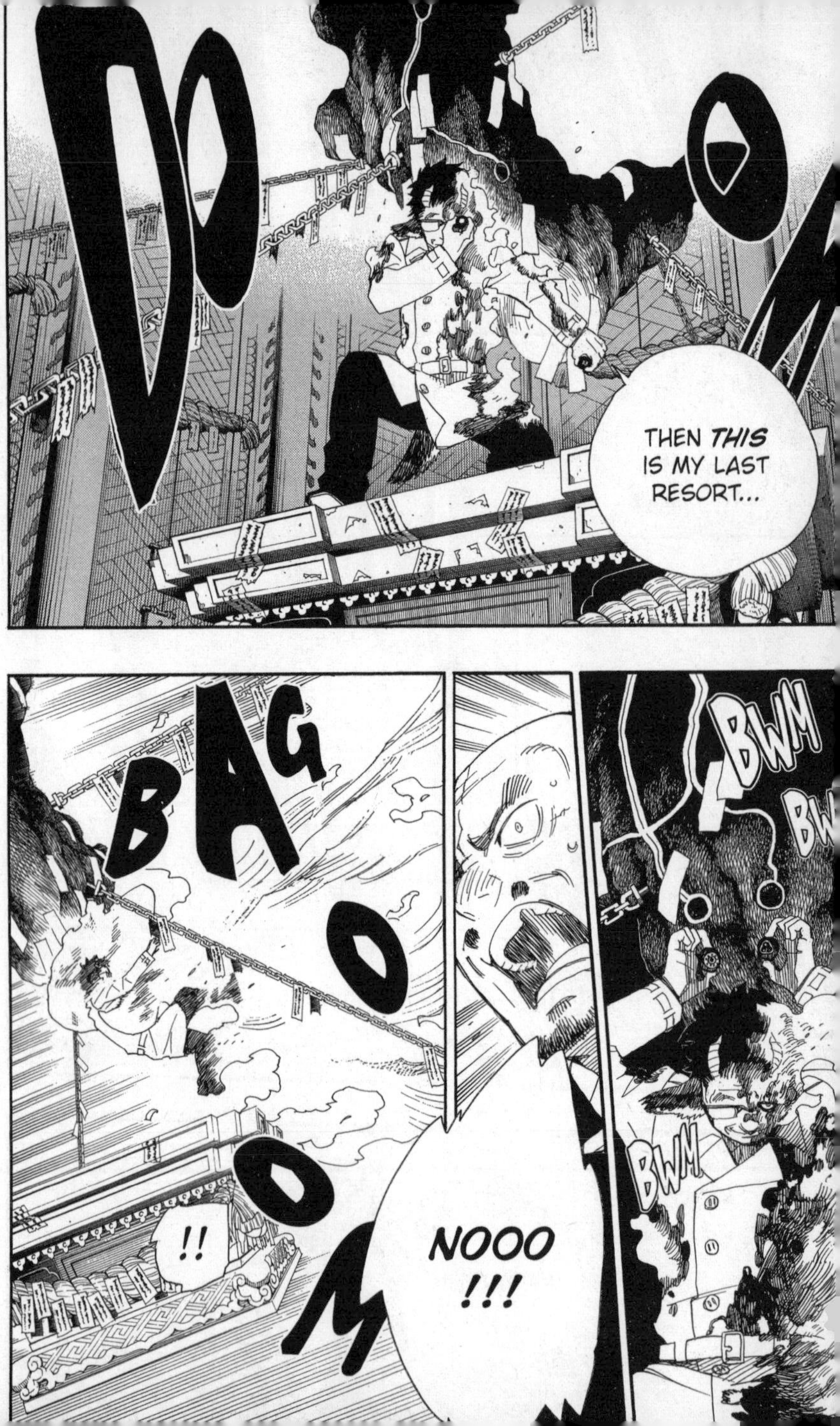
DOOM
THEN *THIS* IS MY LAST RESORT...
BWM
BW
BWM
NOOO !!!
BAGOOM
!!

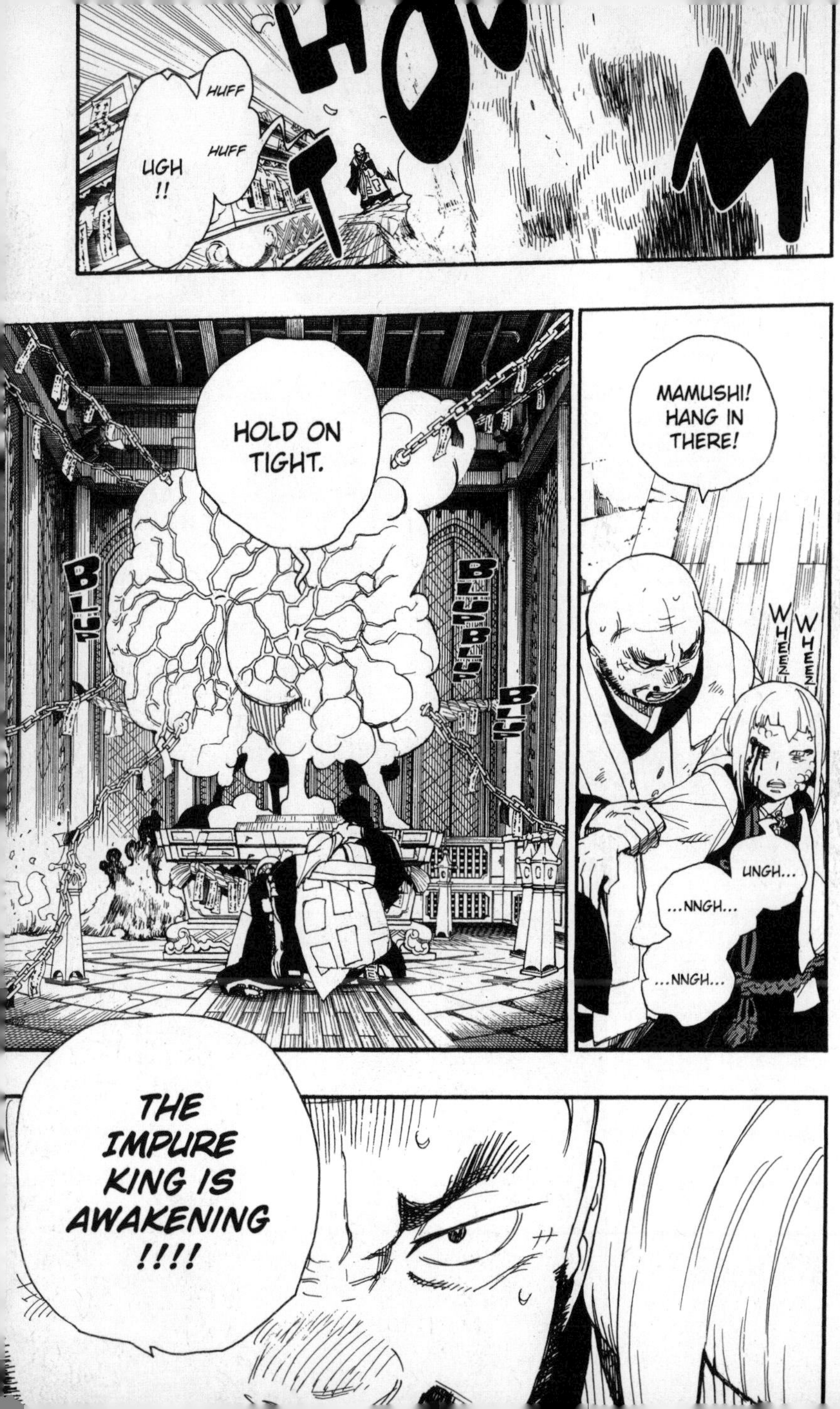
THOOM
HUFF
HUFF
UGH !!
MAMUSHI! HANG IN THERE!
WHEEZ
WHEEZ
UNGH...
...NNGH...
...NNGH...
HOLD ON TIGHT.
BLUP
BLUPBLUP
BLUP
THE IMPURE KING IS AWAKENING !!!!

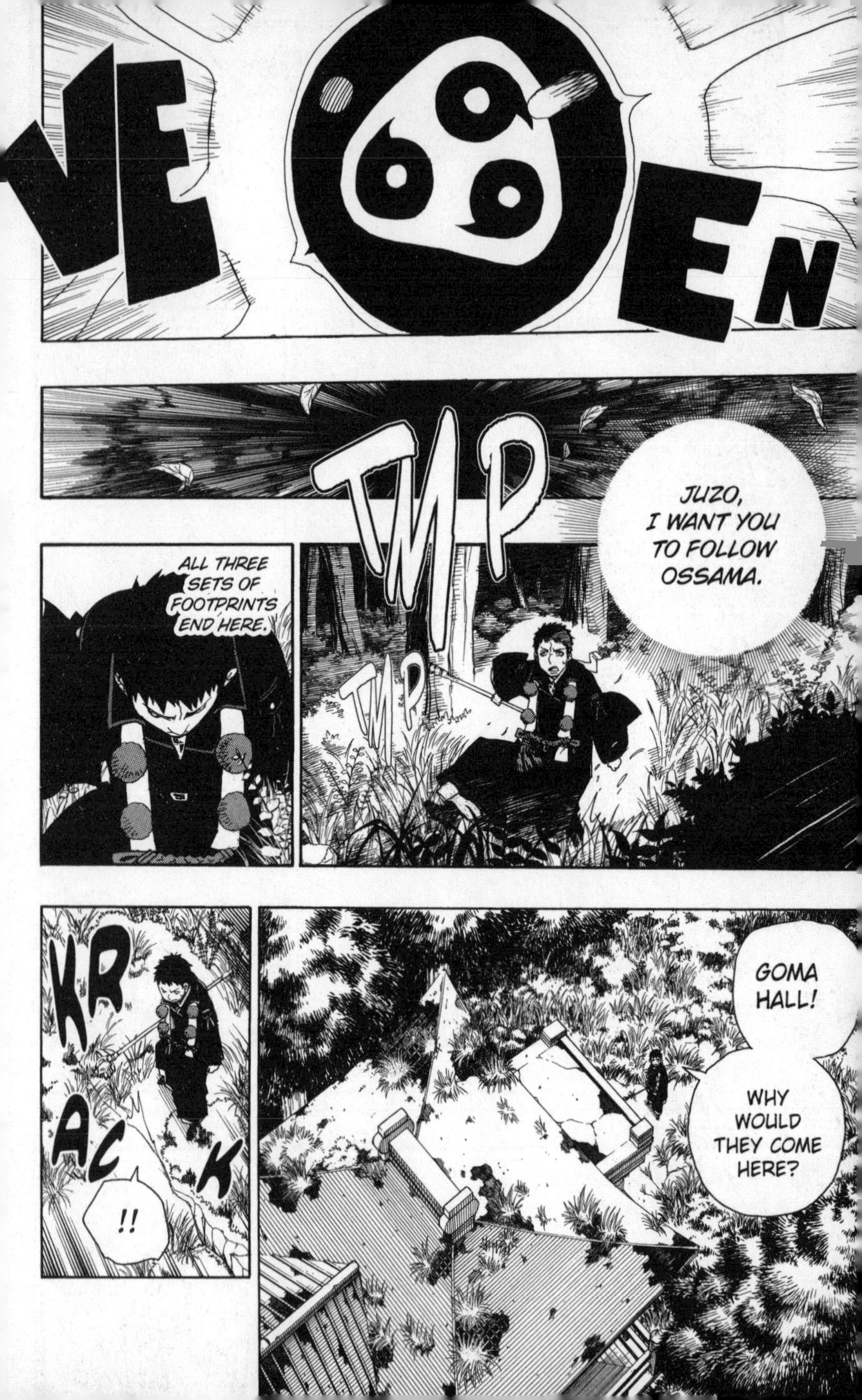
VE
EN
TMP
JUZO, I WANT YOU TO FOLLOW OSSAMA.
TMP
ALL THREE SETS OF FOOTPRINTS END HERE.
GOMA HALL!
WHY WOULD THEY COME HERE?
KRACK
!!

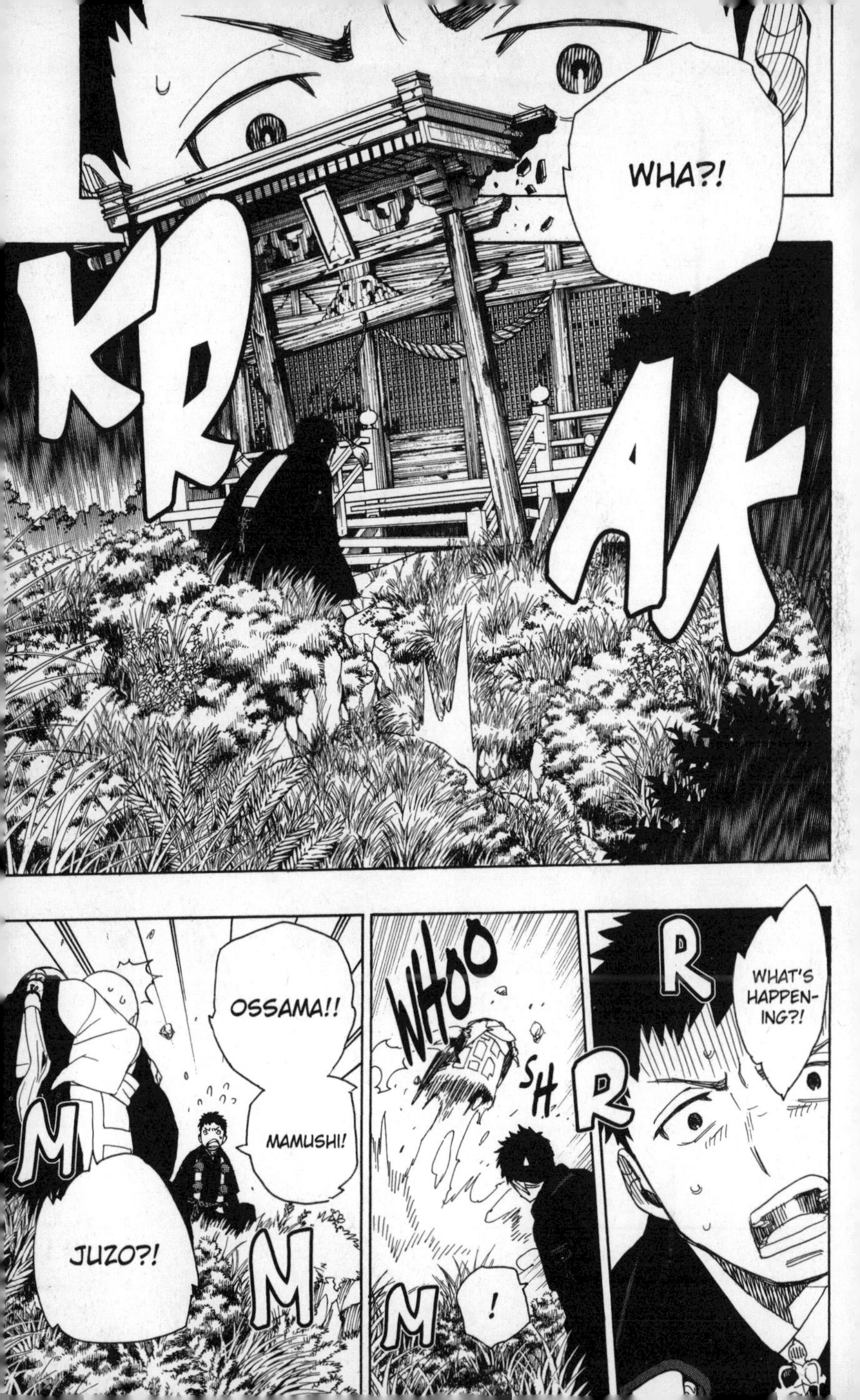
WHA?!
KR
AK
WHAT'S HAPPENING?!
R
R
WHOO
SH
!
M
OSSAMA!!
MAMUSHI!
JUZO?!
M
M

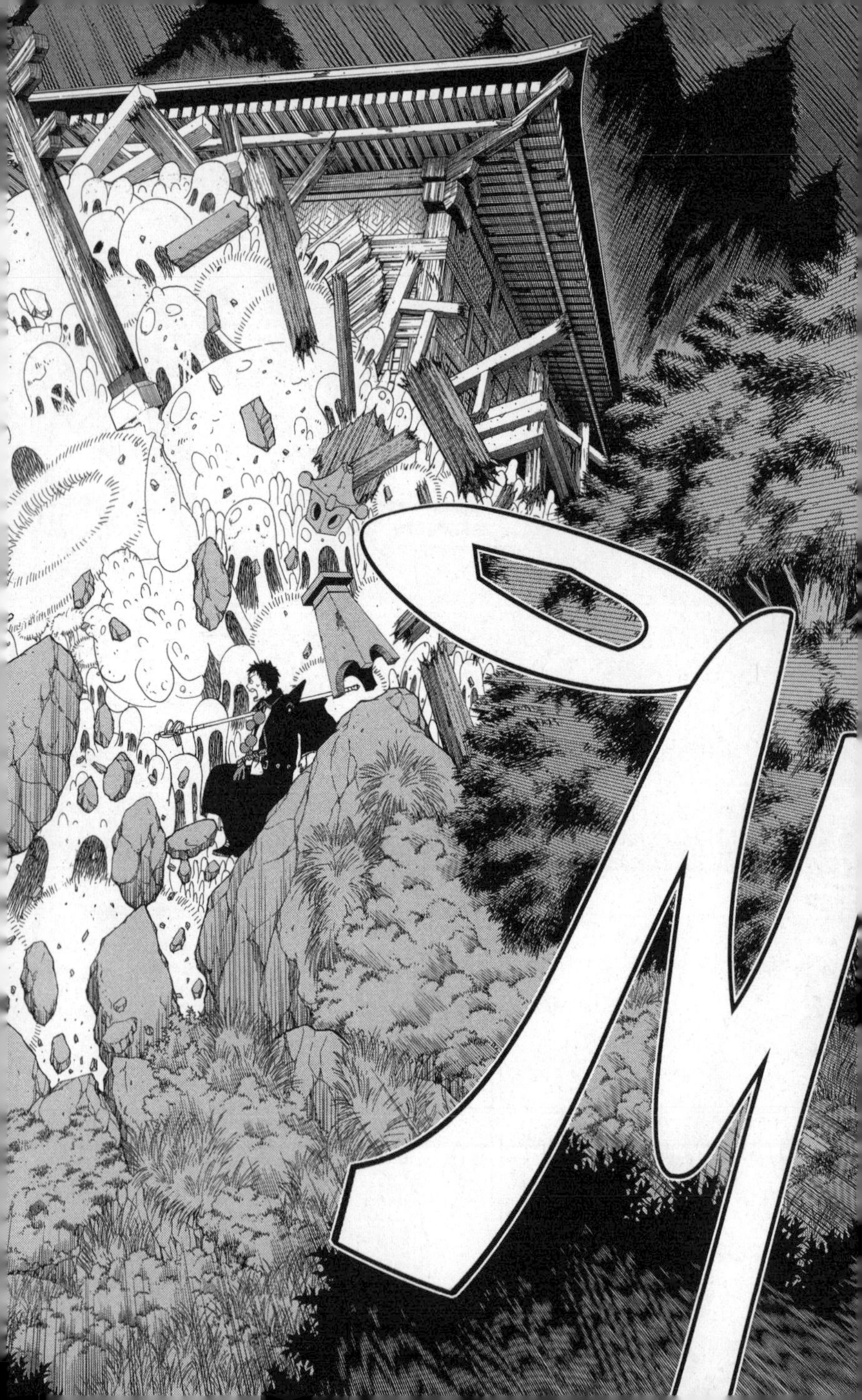

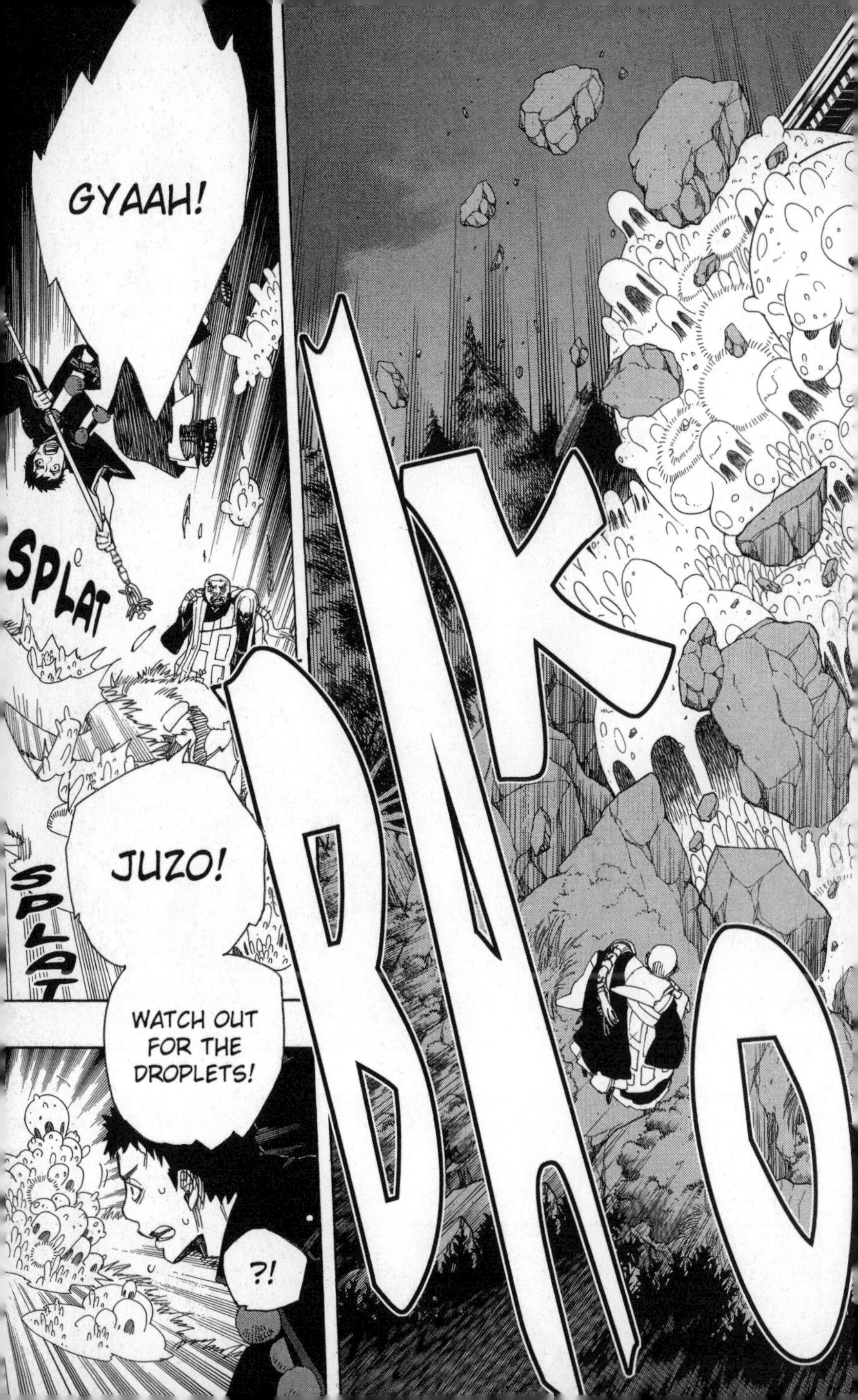
GYAAH!
SPLAT
JUZO!
SPLAT
WATCH OUT FOR THE DROPLETS!
?!

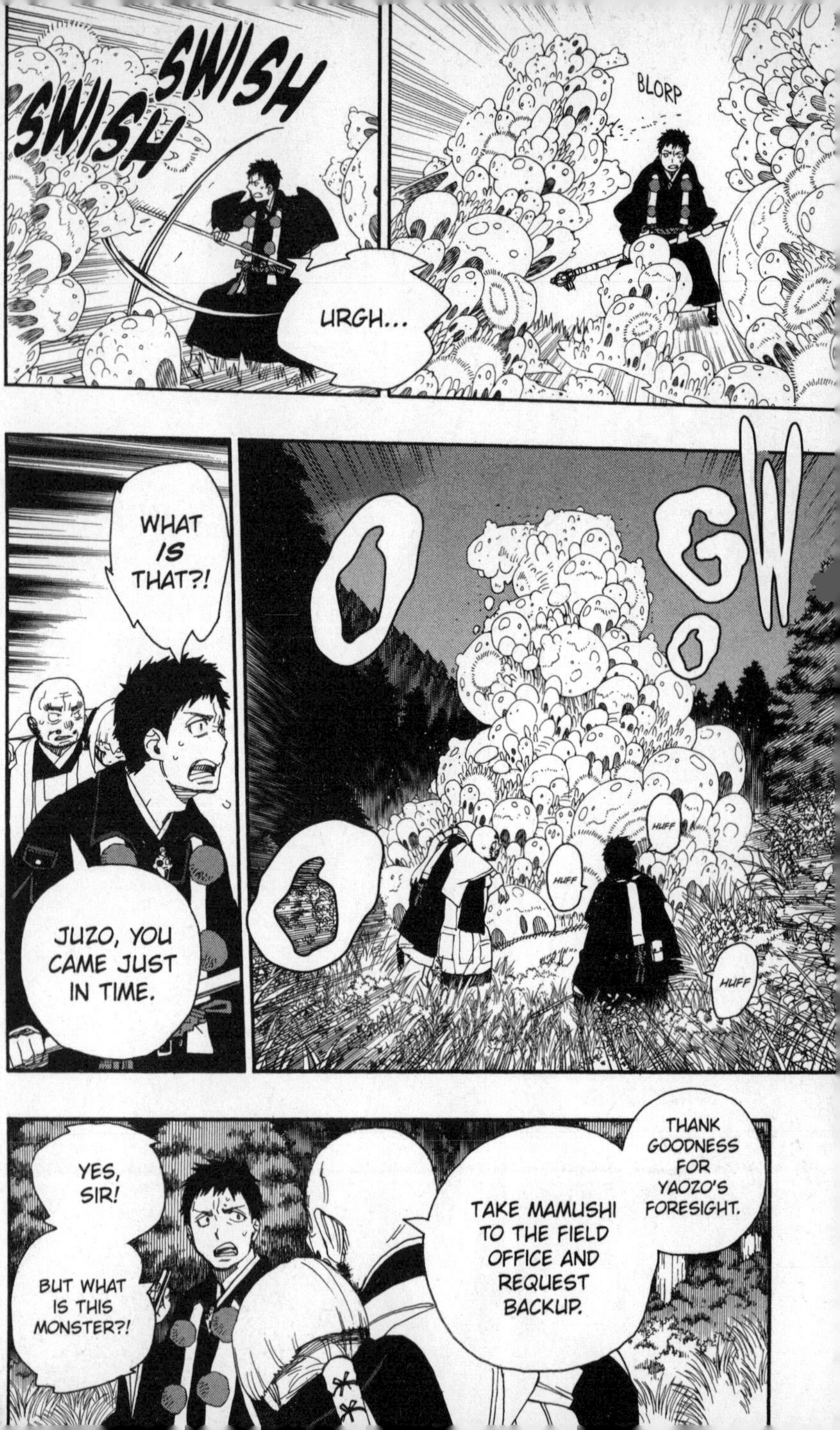
BLORP
SWISH SWISH
URGH...
HUFF
HUFF
HUFF
WHAT IS THAT?!
JUZO, YOU CAME JUST IN TIME.
THANK GOODNESS FOR YAOZO'S FORESIGHT.
TAKE MAMUSHI TO THE FIELD OFFICE AND REQUEST BACKUP.
YES, SIR!
BUT WHAT IS THIS MONSTER?!

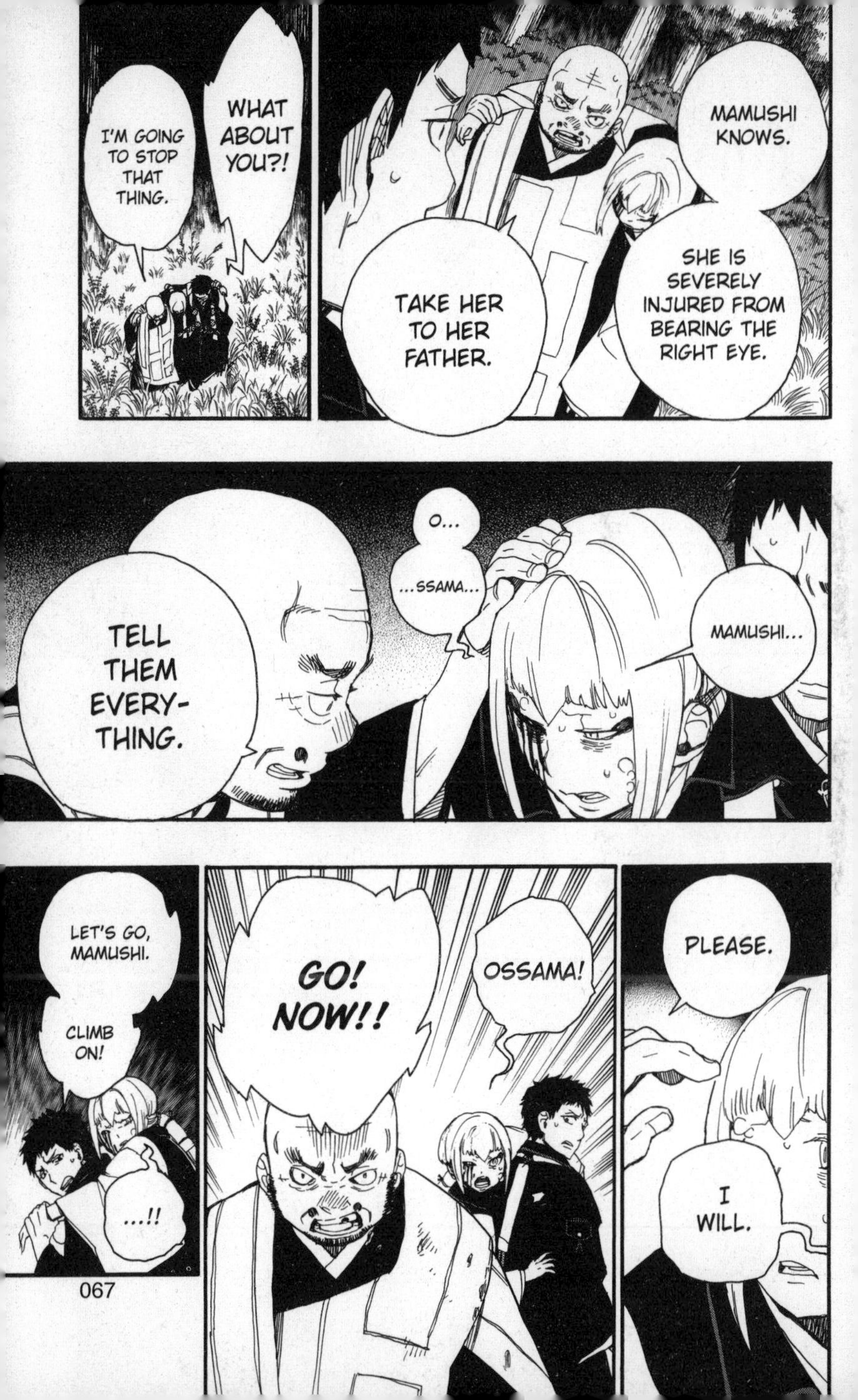

MAMUSHI KNOWS.
SHE IS SEVERELY INJURED FROM BEARING THE RIGHT EYE.
TAKE HER TO HER FATHER.
WHAT ABOUT YOU?!
I'M GOING TO STOP THAT THING.
MAMUSHI...
O...
...SSAMA...
TELL THEM EVERY-THING.
PLEASE.
I WILL.
OSSAMA!
GO! NOW!!
LET'S GO, MAMUSHI.
CLIMB ON!
...!!

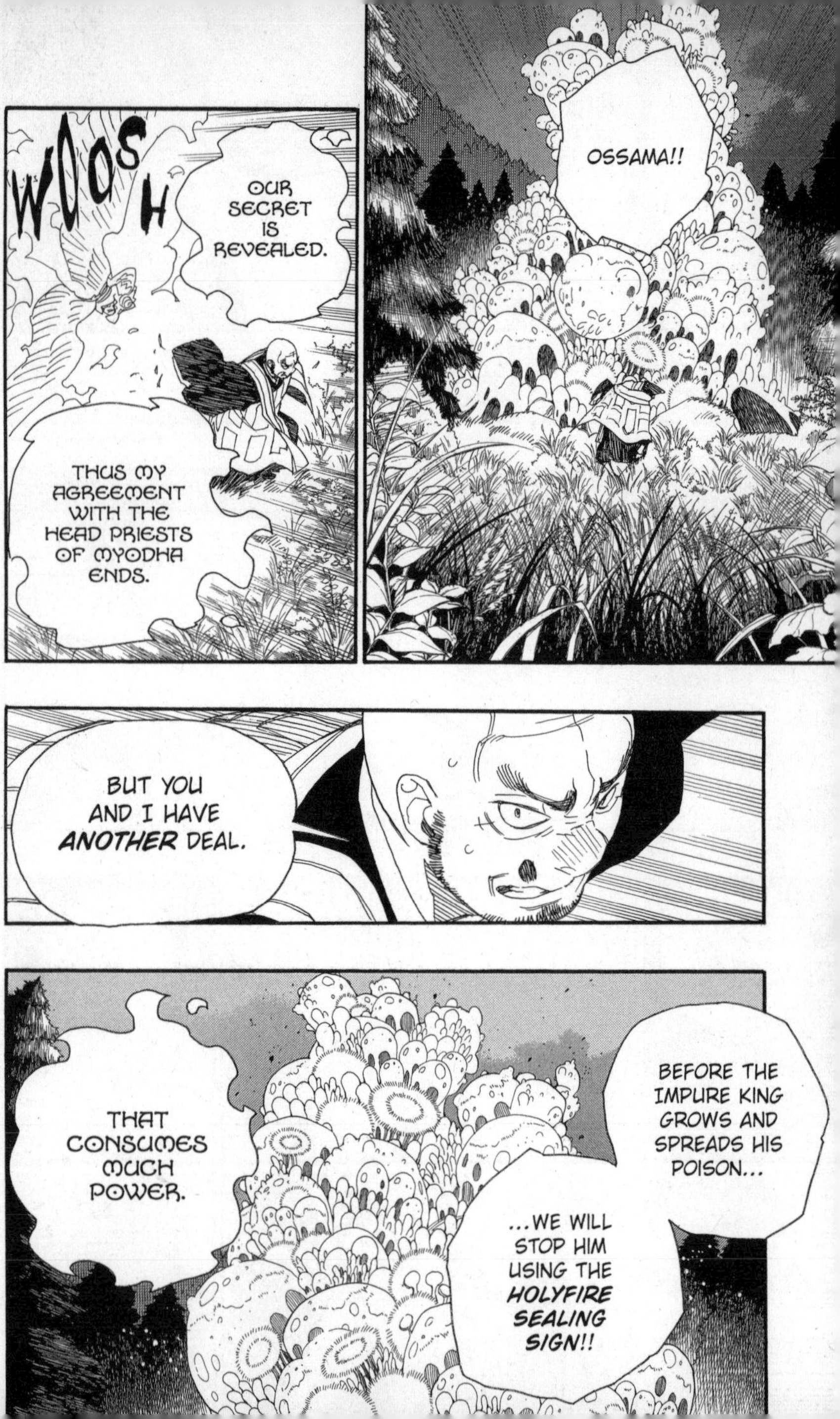
OSSAMA!!
WOOSH
OUR SECRET IS REVEALED.
THUS MY AGREEMENT WITH THE HEAD PRIESTS OF MYODHA ENDS.
BUT YOU AND I HAVE *ANOTHER* DEAL.
BEFORE THE IMPURE KING GROWS AND SPREADS HIS POISON...
...WE WILL STOP HIM USING THE *HOLYFIRE SEALING SIGN*!!
THAT CONSUMES MUCH POWER.

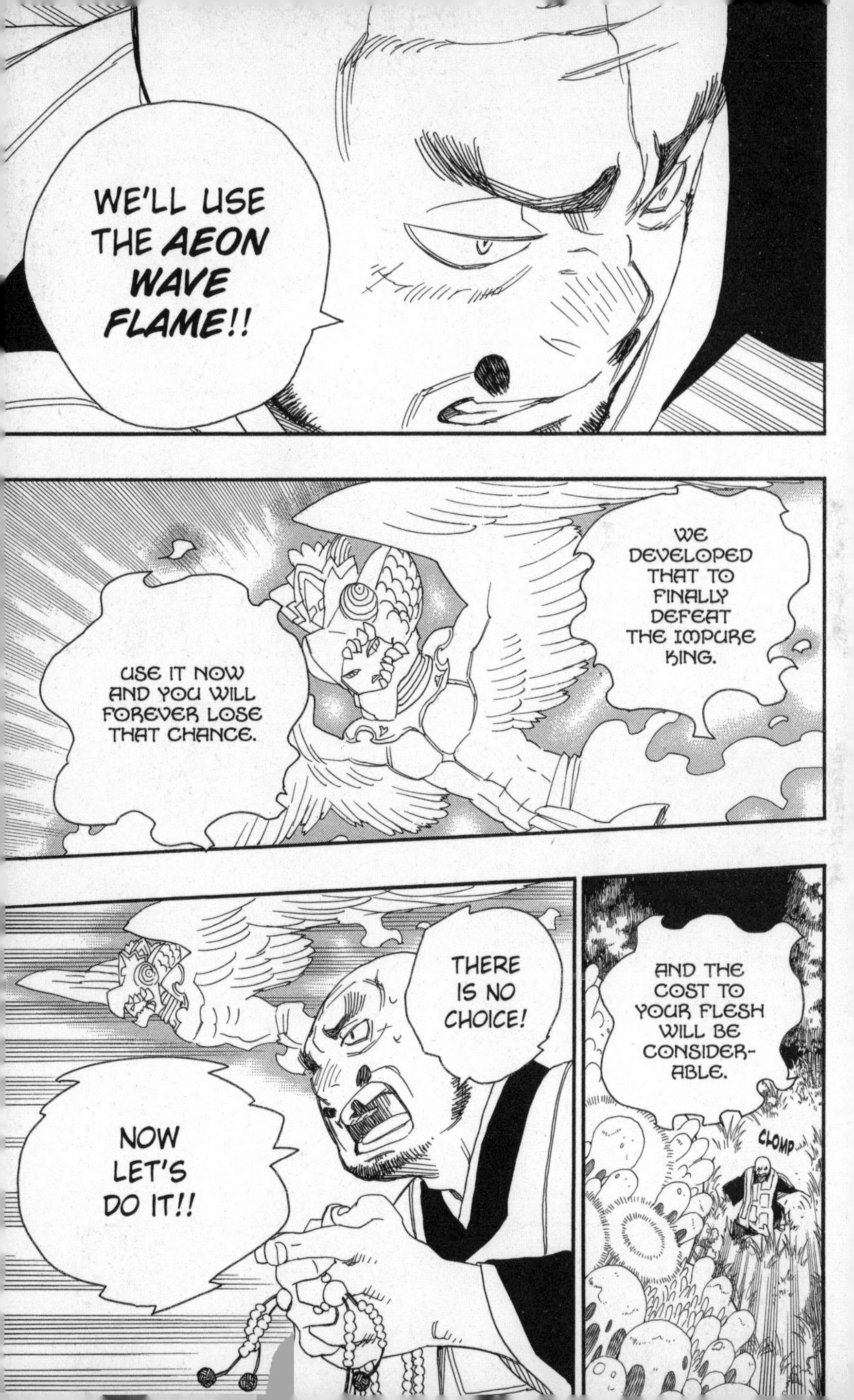
WE'LL USE THE AEON WAVE FLAME!!
WE DEVELOPED THAT TO FINALLY DEFEAT THE IMPURE KING.
USE IT NOW AND YOU WILL FOREVER LOSE THAT CHANCE.
AND THE COST TO YOUR FLESH WILL BE CONSIDER-ABLE.
CLOMP
THERE IS NO CHOICE!
NOW LET'S DO IT!!

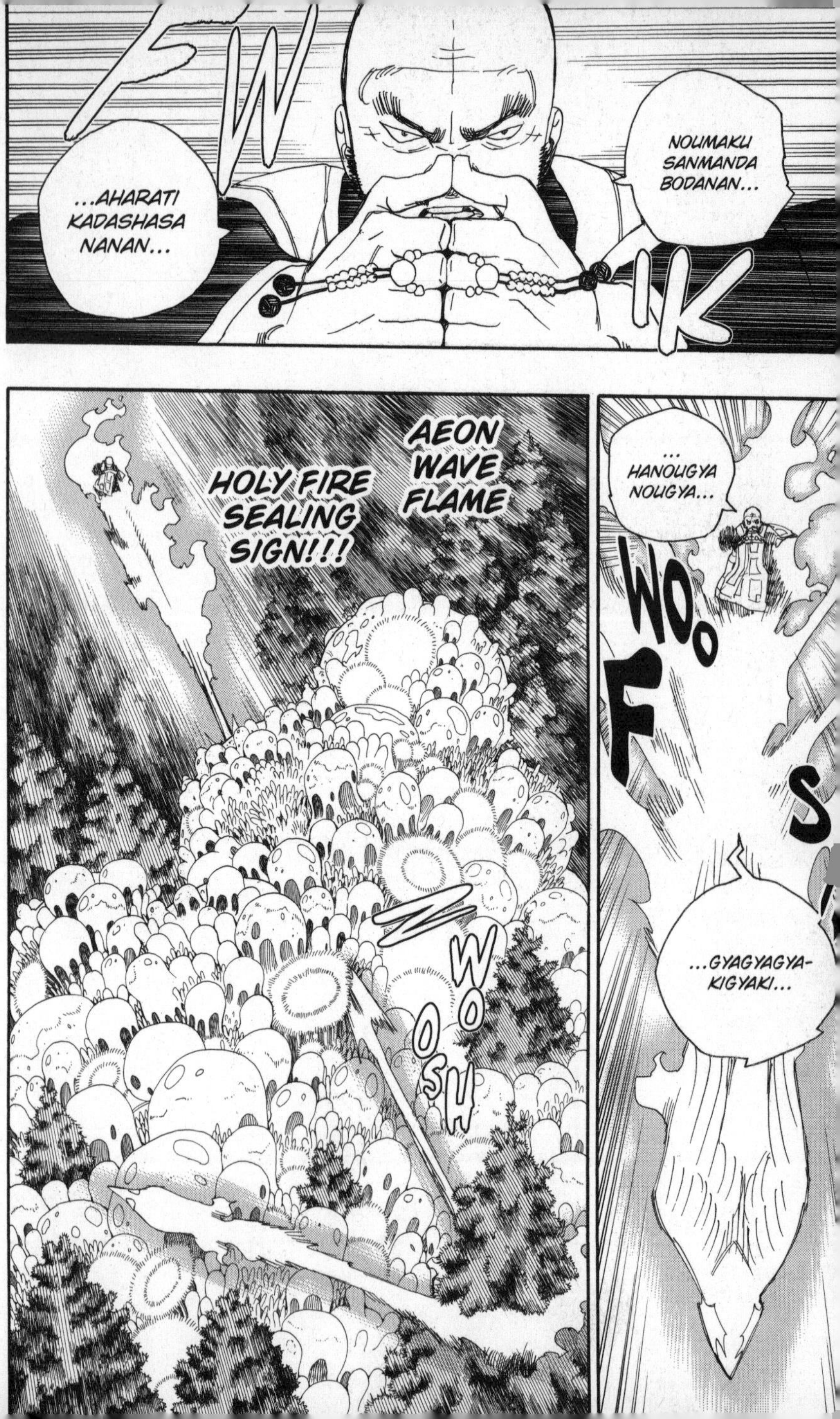

NOUMAKU SANMANDA BODANAN...
...AHARATI KADASHASA NANAN...
FW
IK
... HANOUGYA NOUGYA...
WOOF
...GYAGYAGYA-KIGYAKI...
AEON WAVE FLAME
HOLY FIRE SEALING SIGN!!!
WOOSH

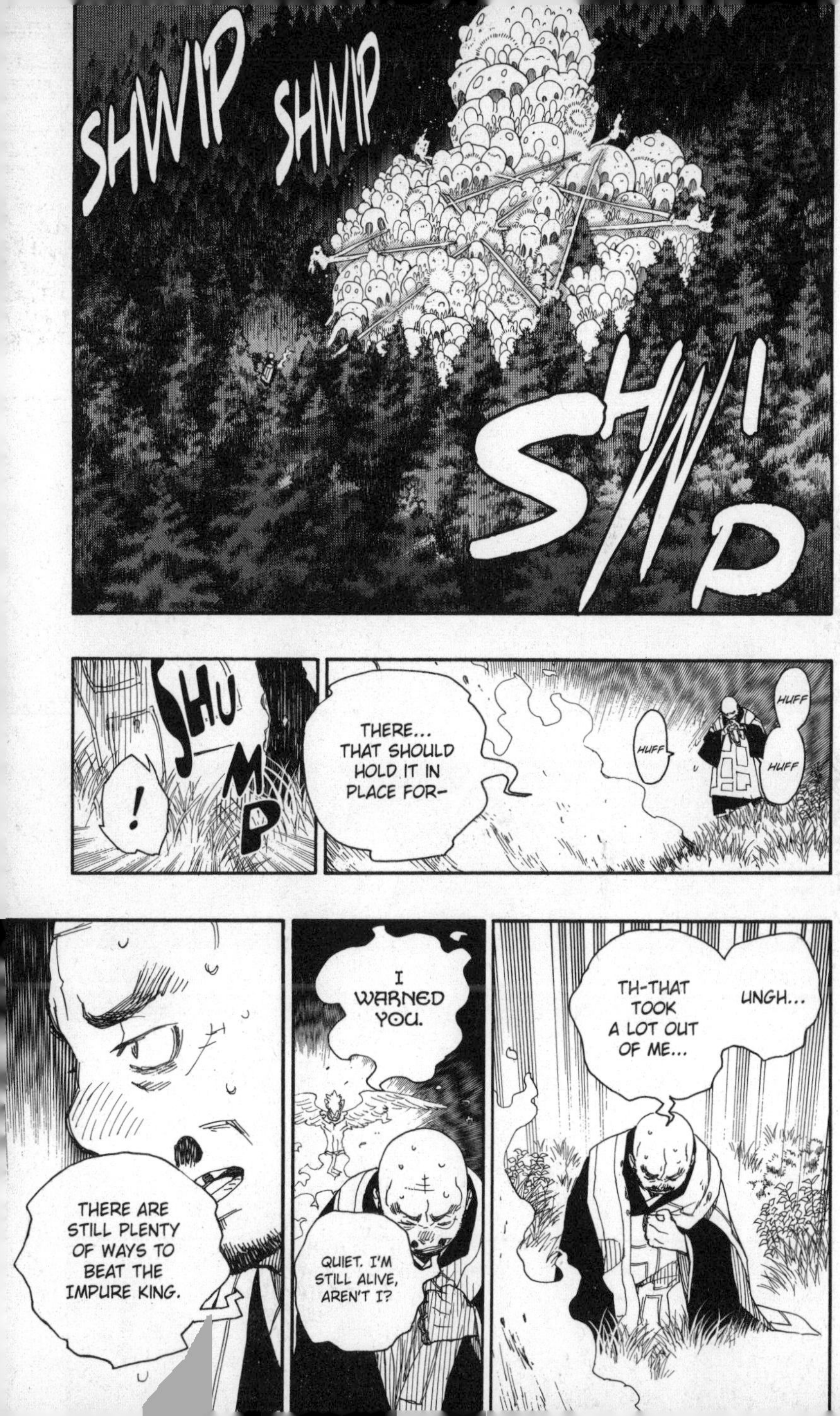
SHWIP SHWIP
SHWIP
HUFF
HUFF
HUFF
THERE... THAT SHOULD HOLD IT IN PLACE FOR-
SHUMP
!
UNGH...
TH-THAT TOOK A LOT OUT OF ME...
I WARNED YOU.
QUIET. I'M STILL ALIVE, AREN'T I?
THERE ARE STILL PLENTY OF WAYS TO BEAT THE IMPURE KING.

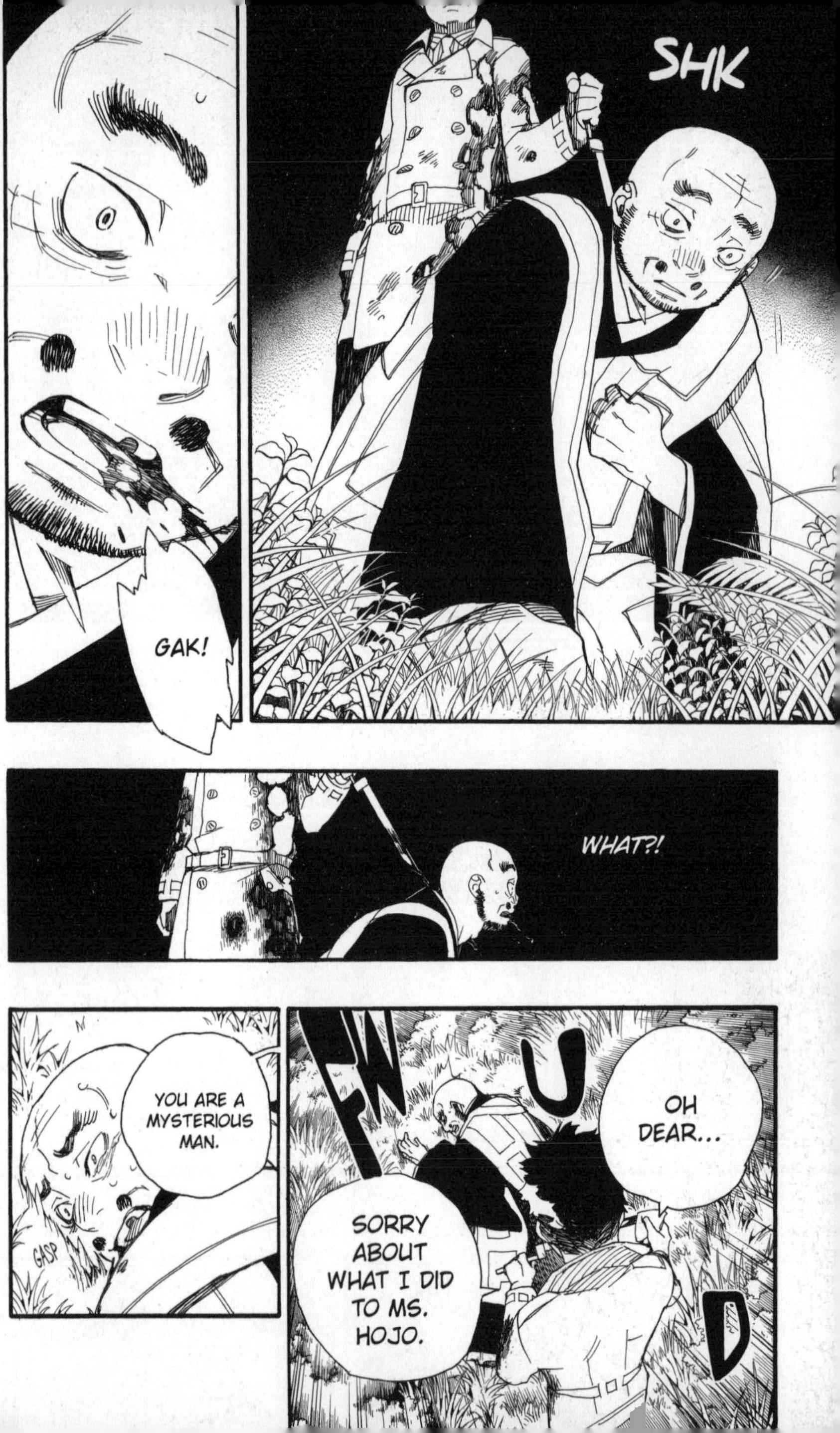
SHK
GAK!
WHAT?!
FWUD
OH DEAR...
SORRY ABOUT WHAT I DID TO MS. HOJO.
YOU ARE A MYSTERIOUS MAN.
GASP

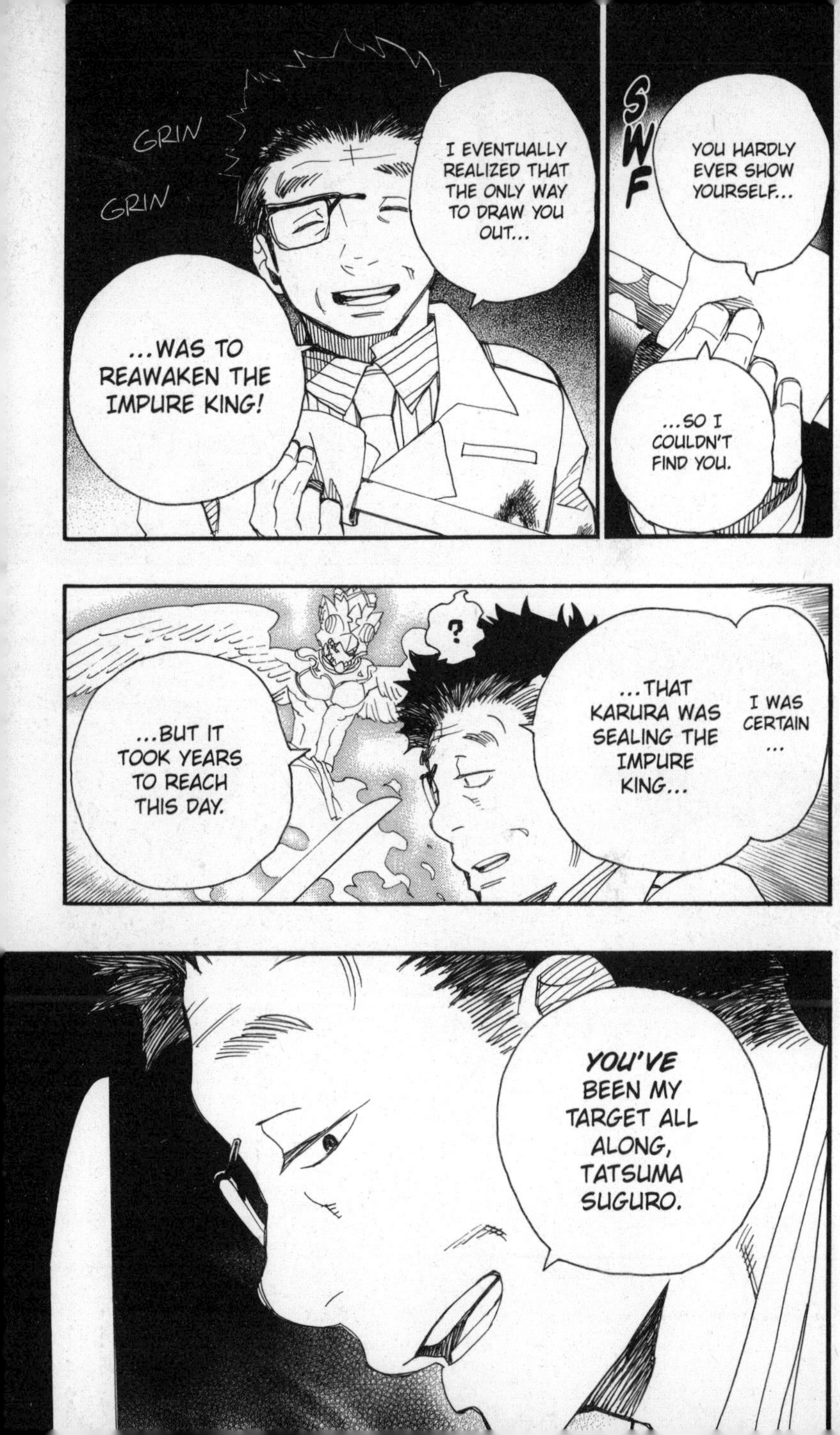
SWF
YOU HARDLY EVER SHOW YOURSELF...
...SO I COULDN'T FIND YOU.
I EVENTUALLY REALIZED THAT THE ONLY WAY TO DRAW YOU OUT...
GRIN
GRIN
...WAS TO REAWAKEN THE IMPURE KING!
I WAS CERTAIN...
...THAT KARURA WAS SEALING THE IMPURE KING...
?
...BUT IT TOOK YEARS TO REACH THIS DAY.
YOU'VE BEEN MY TARGET ALL ALONG, TATSUMA SUGURO.

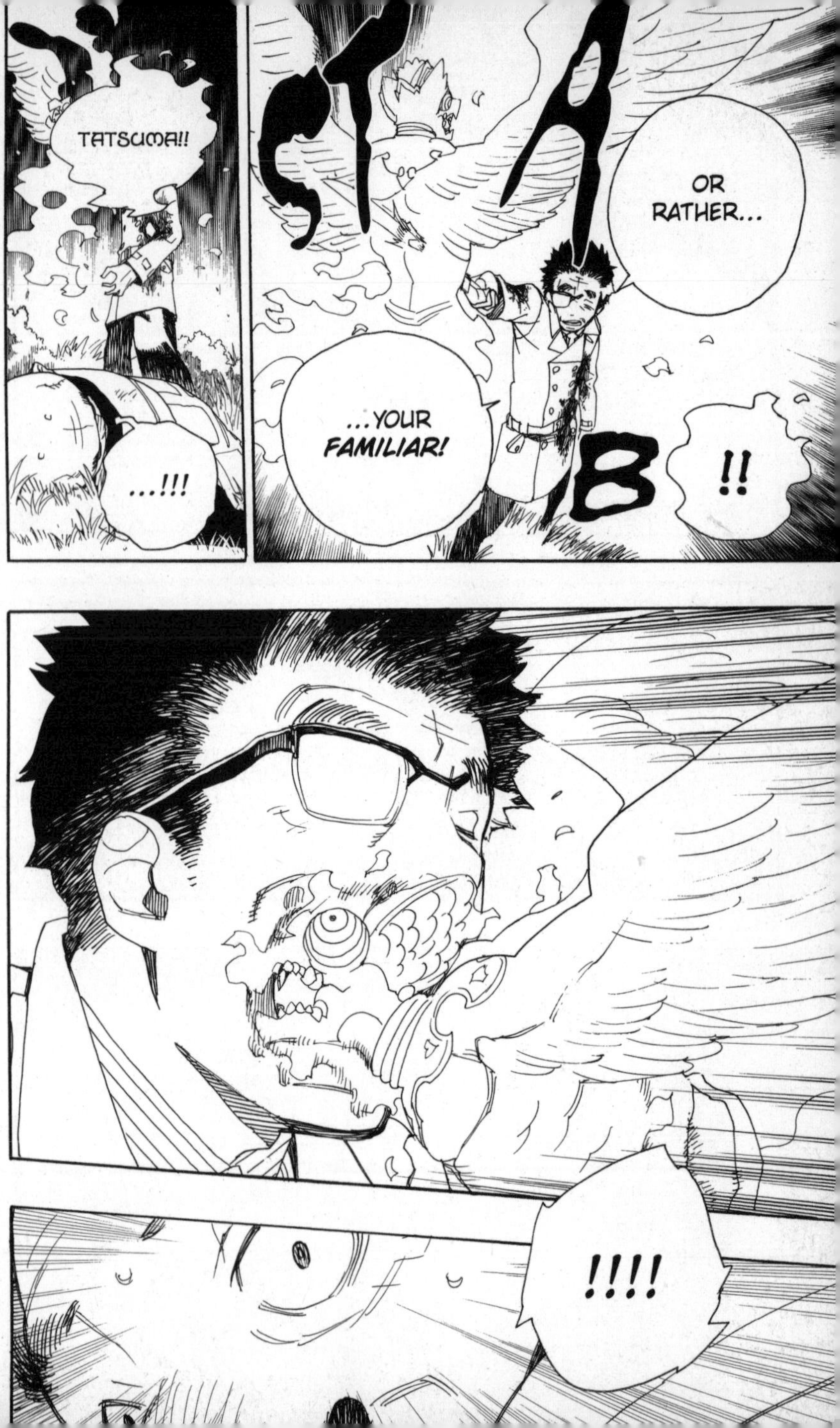
OR RATHER...
...YOUR FAMILIAR!
!!
TATSUMA!!
...!!!
!!!!

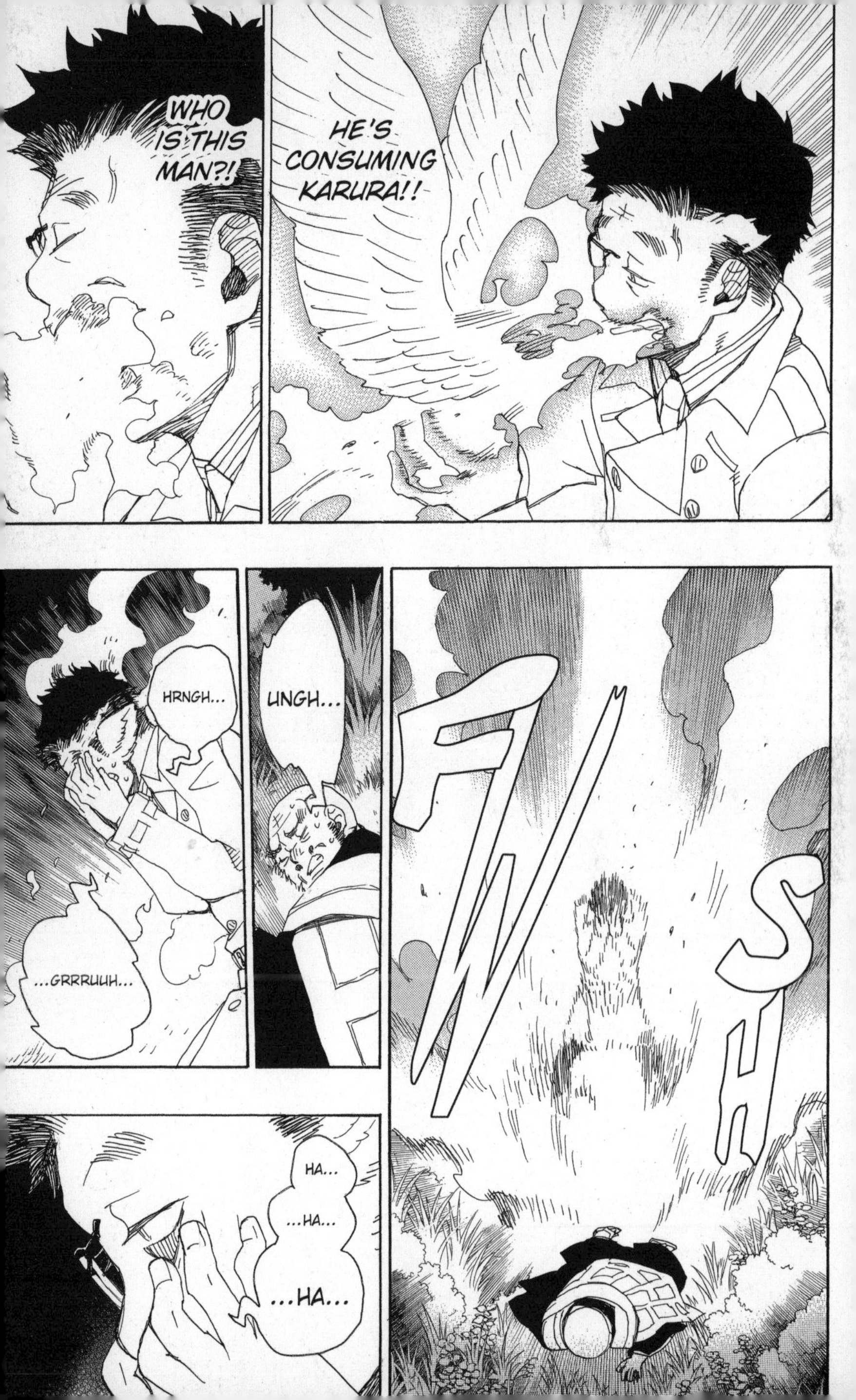
HE'S CONSUMING KARURA!!
WHO IS THIS MAN?!
FWSH
UNGH...
HRNGH...
...GRRRUUH...
HA...
...HA...
...HA...

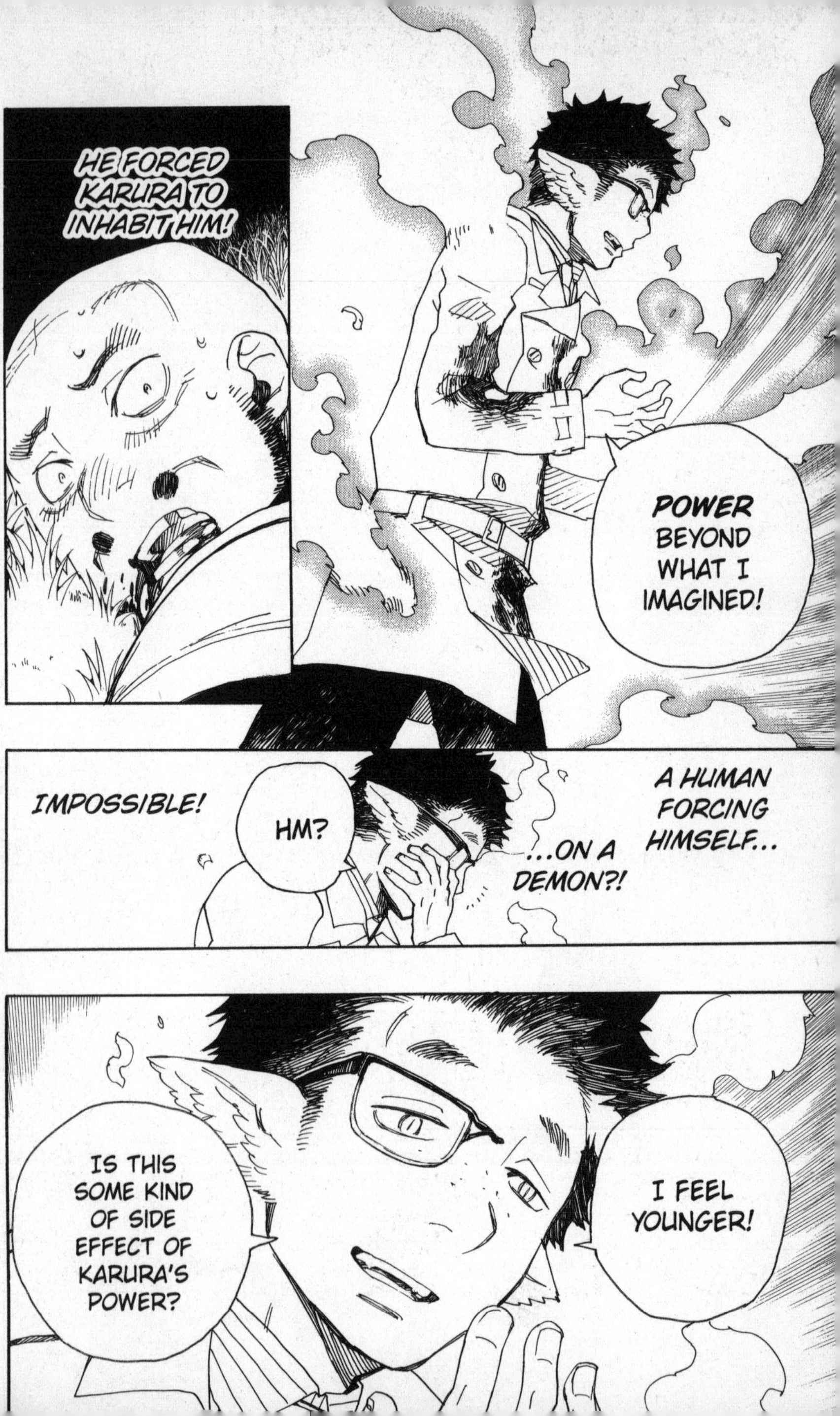
POWER BEYOND WHAT I IMAGINED!
HE FORCED KARURA TO INHABIT HIM!
A HUMAN FORCING HIMSELF...
...ON A DEMON?!
HM?
IMPOSSIBLE!
I FEEL YOUNGER!
IS THIS SOME KIND OF SIDE EFFECT OF KARURA'S POWER?

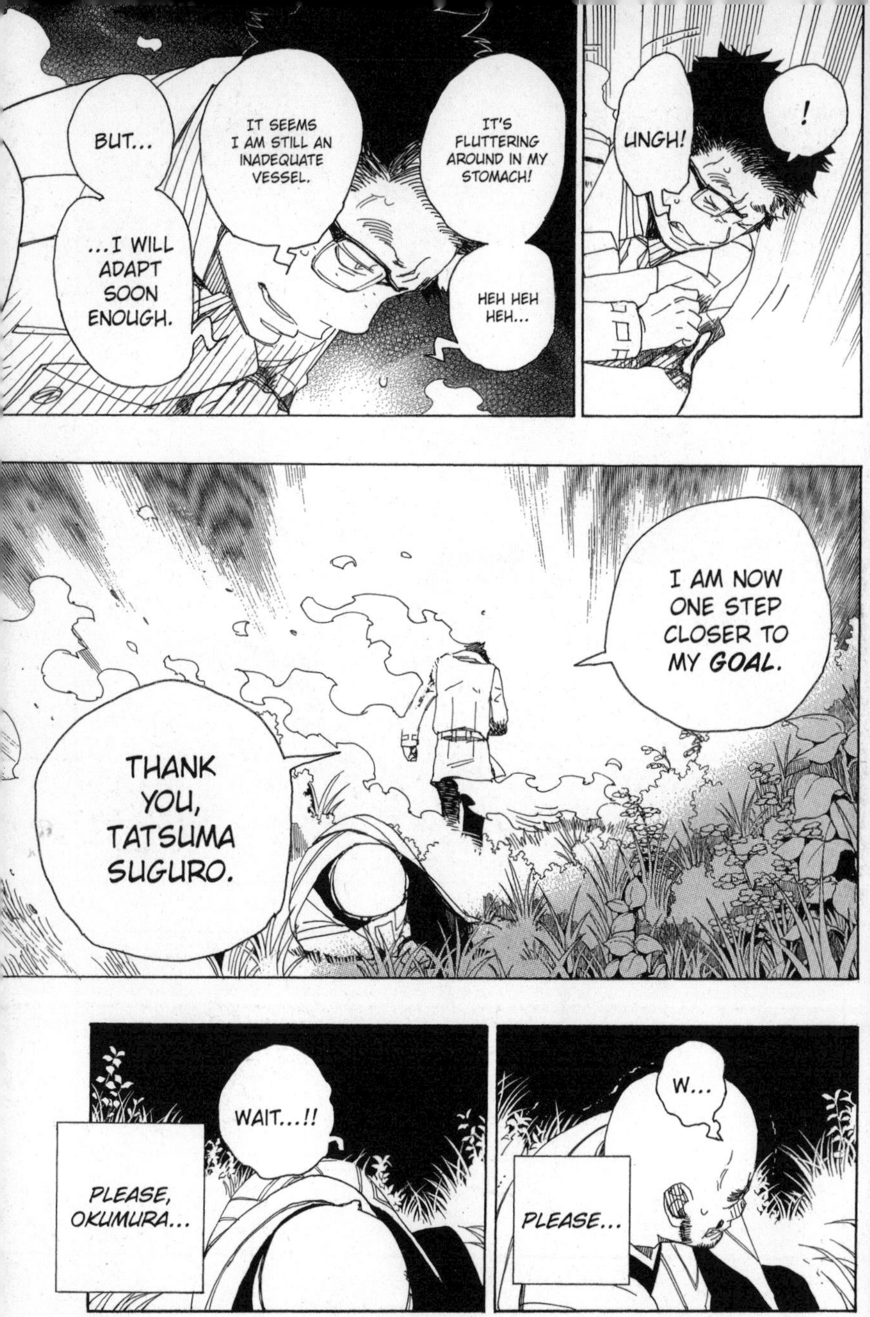
!
UNGH!
IT'S FLUTTERING AROUND IN MY STOMACH!
HEH HEH HEH...
IT SEEMS I AM STILL AN INADEQUATE VESSEL.
BUT...
...I WILL ADAPT SOON ENOUGH.
I AM NOW ONE STEP CLOSER TO MY **GOAL**.
THANK YOU, TATSUMA SUGURO.
W...
PLEASE...
WAIT...!!
PLEASE, OKUMURA...

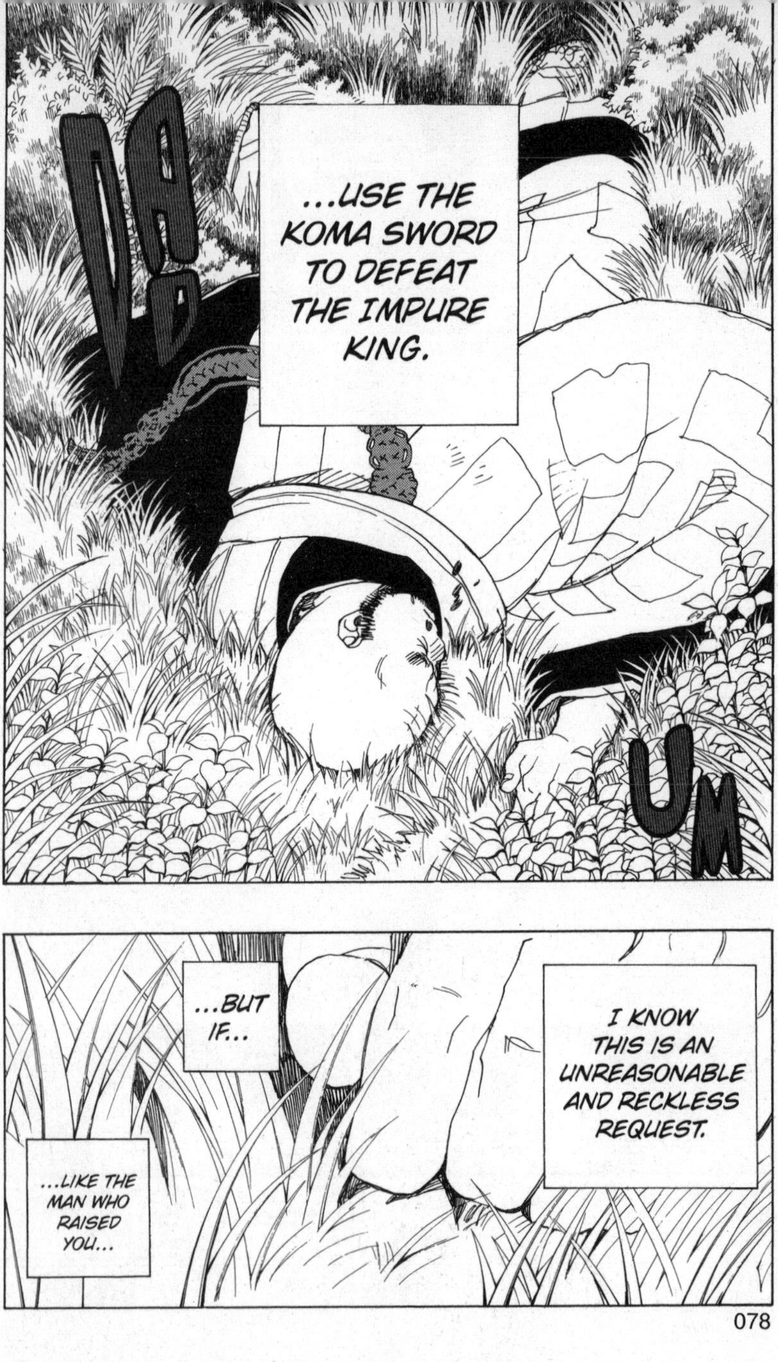
...USE THE KOMA SWORD TO DEFEAT THE IMPURE KING.
DAD
UM
I KNOW THIS IS AN UNREASONABLE AND RECKLESS REQUEST.
...BUT IF...
...LIKE THE MAN WHO RAISED YOU...

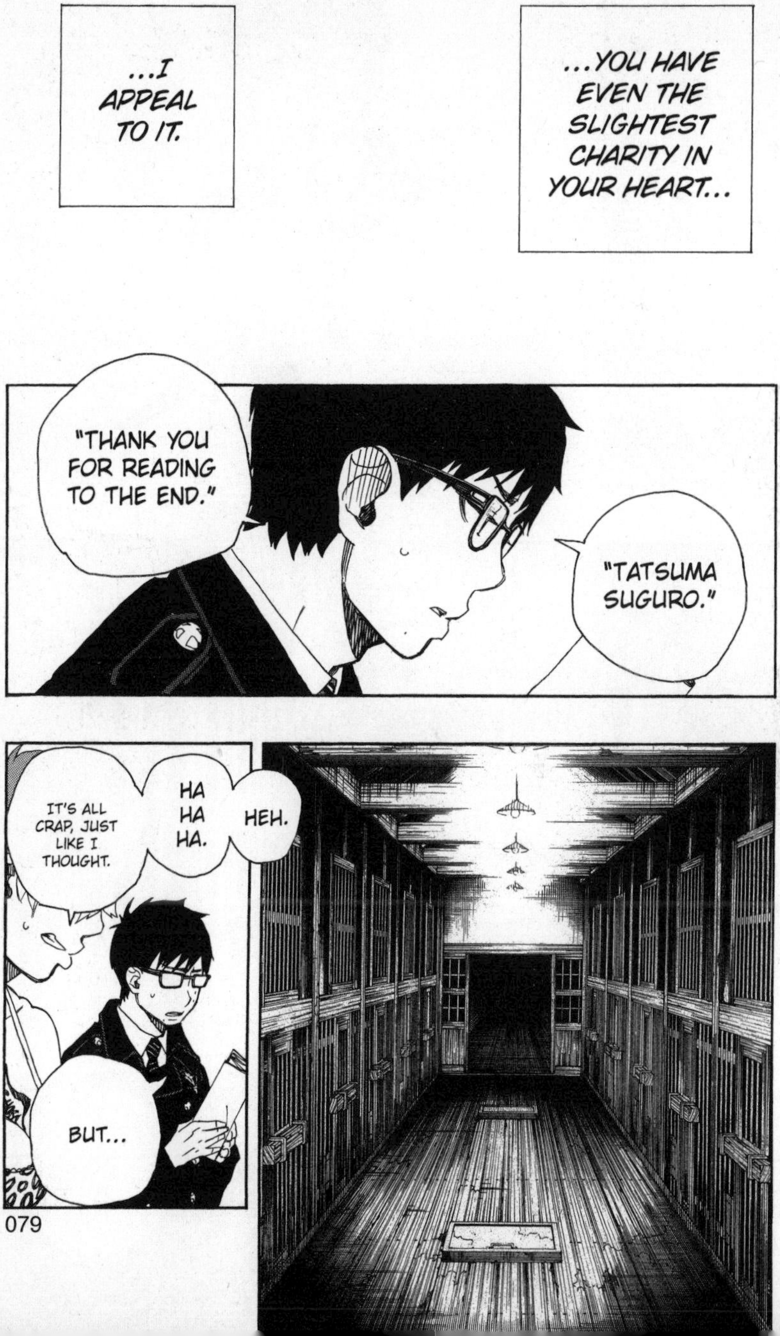
...YOU HAVE EVEN THE SLIGHTEST CHARITY IN YOUR HEART...
...I APPEAL TO IT.
"TATSUMA SUGURO."
"THANK YOU FOR READING TO THE END."
HEH.
HA HA HA.
IT'S ALL CRAP, JUST LIKE I THOUGHT.
BUT...

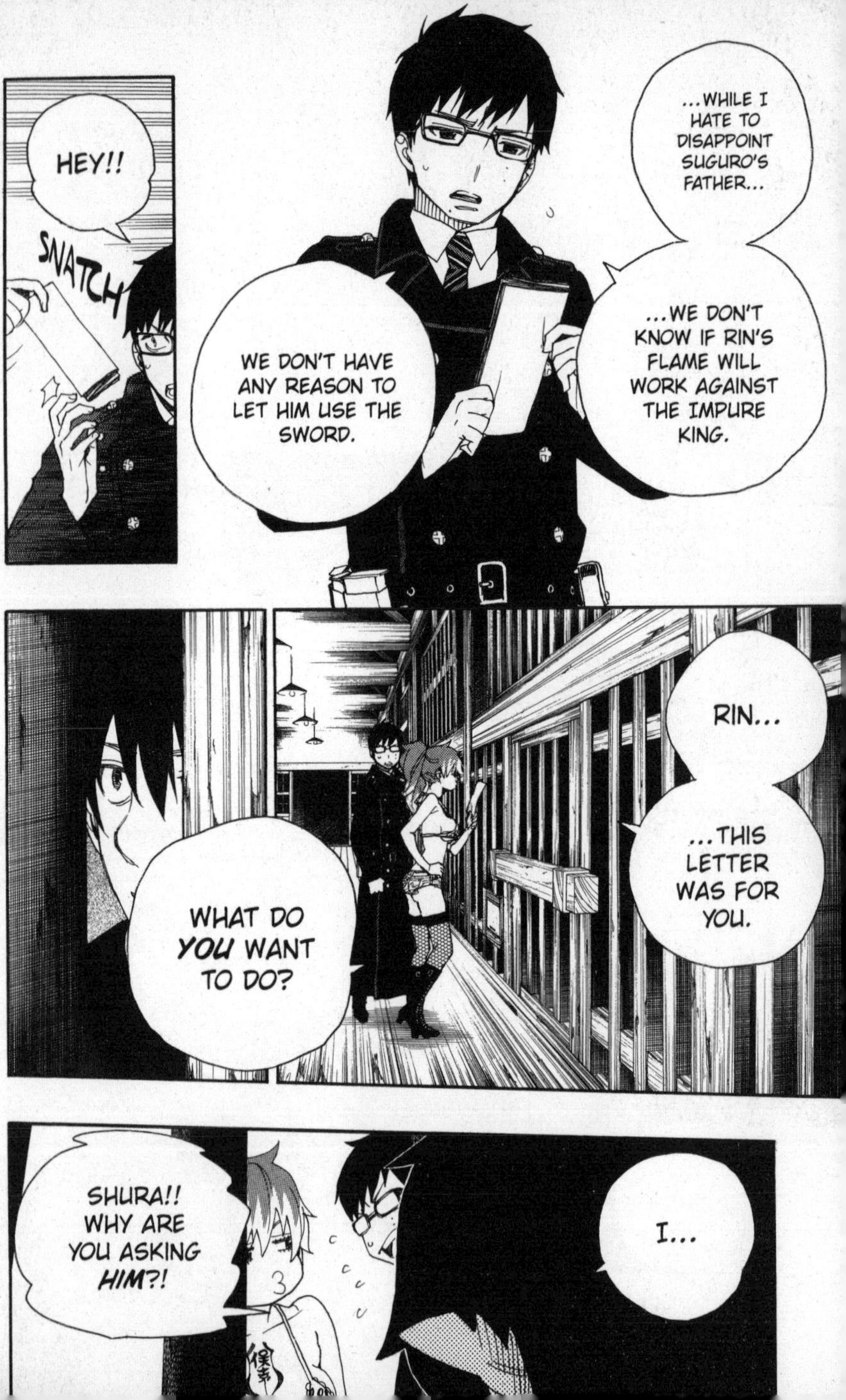
...WHILE I HATE TO DISAPPOINT SUGURO'S FATHER...
...WE DON'T KNOW IF RIN'S FLAME WILL WORK AGAINST THE IMPURE KING.
WE DON'T HAVE ANY REASON TO LET HIM USE THE SWORD.
HEY!!
SNATCH
RIN...
...THIS LETTER WAS FOR YOU.
WHAT DO *YOU* WANT TO DO?
I...
SHURA!! WHY ARE YOU ASKING *HIM*?!

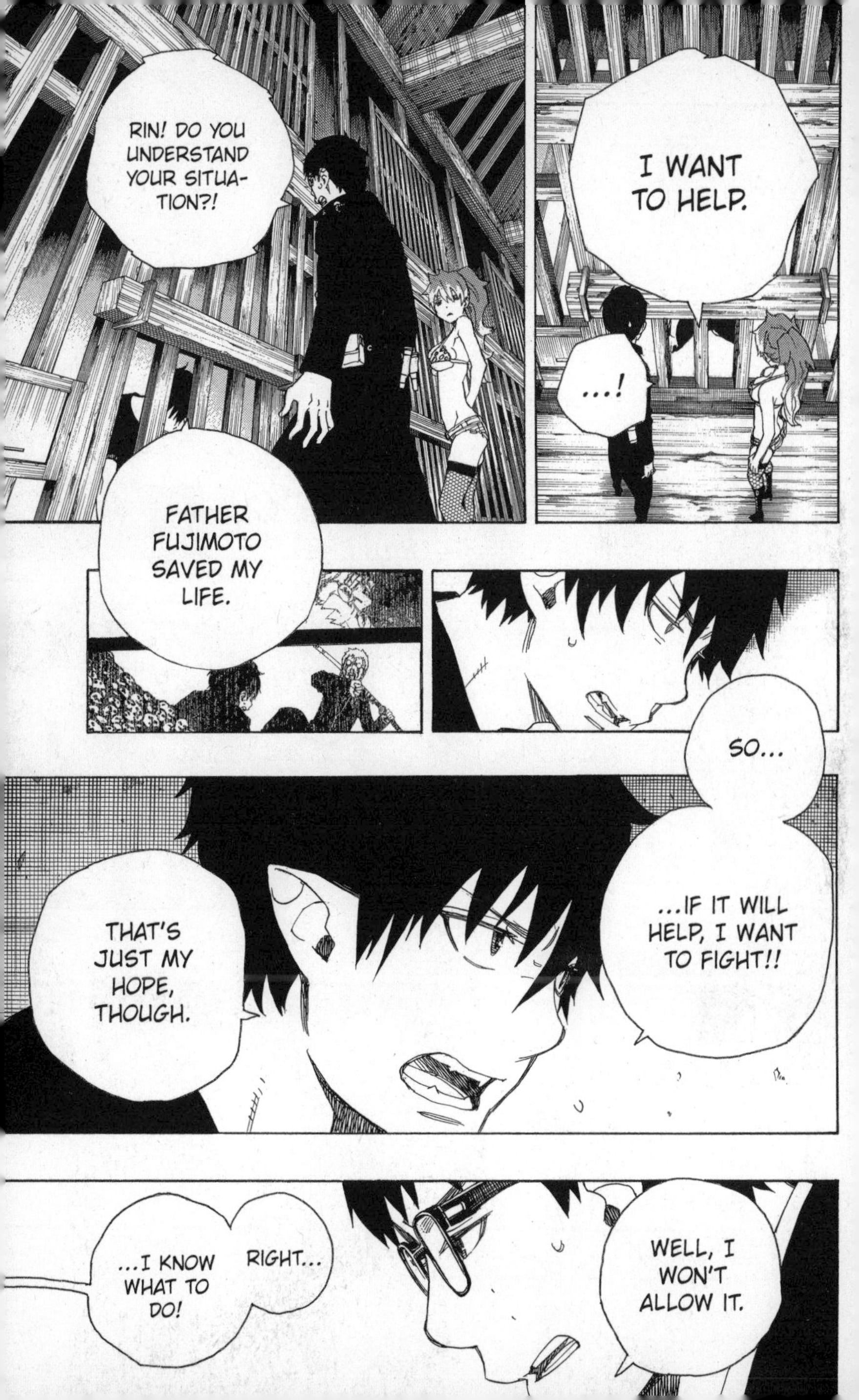
I WANT TO HELP.
...!
RIN! DO YOU UNDERSTAND YOUR SITUATION?!
FATHER FUJIMOTO SAVED MY LIFE.
SO...
...IF IT WILL HELP, I WANT TO FIGHT!!
THAT'S JUST MY HOPE, THOUGH.
WELL, I WON'T ALLOW IT.
RIGHT...
...I KNOW WHAT TO DO!

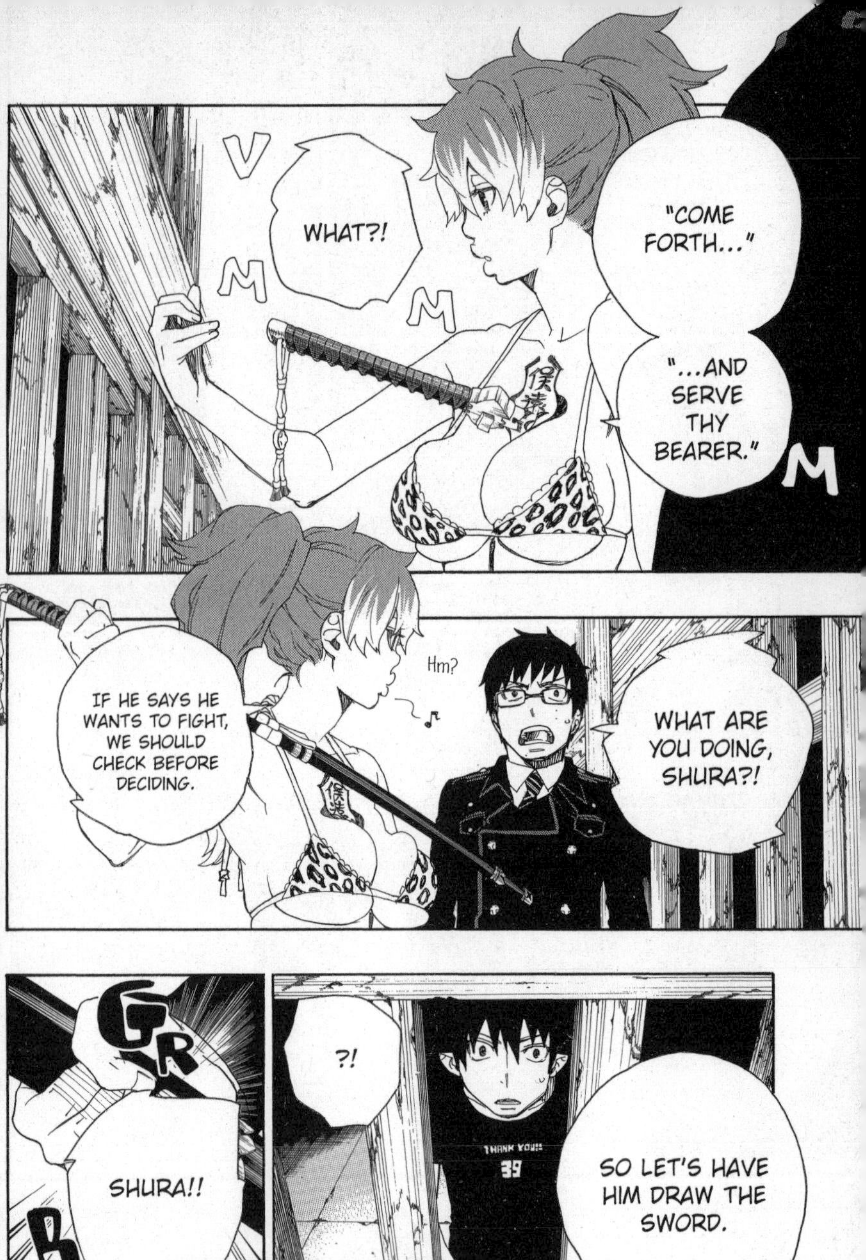
"COME FORTH..."
"...AND SERVE THY BEARER."
WHAT?!
VMMM
WHAT ARE YOU DOING, SHURA?!
Hm?
IF HE SAYS HE WANTS TO FIGHT, WE SHOULD CHECK BEFORE DECIDING.
SO LET'S HAVE HIM DRAW THE SWORD.
?!
THANK YOU!!
39
GR
SHURA!!
B

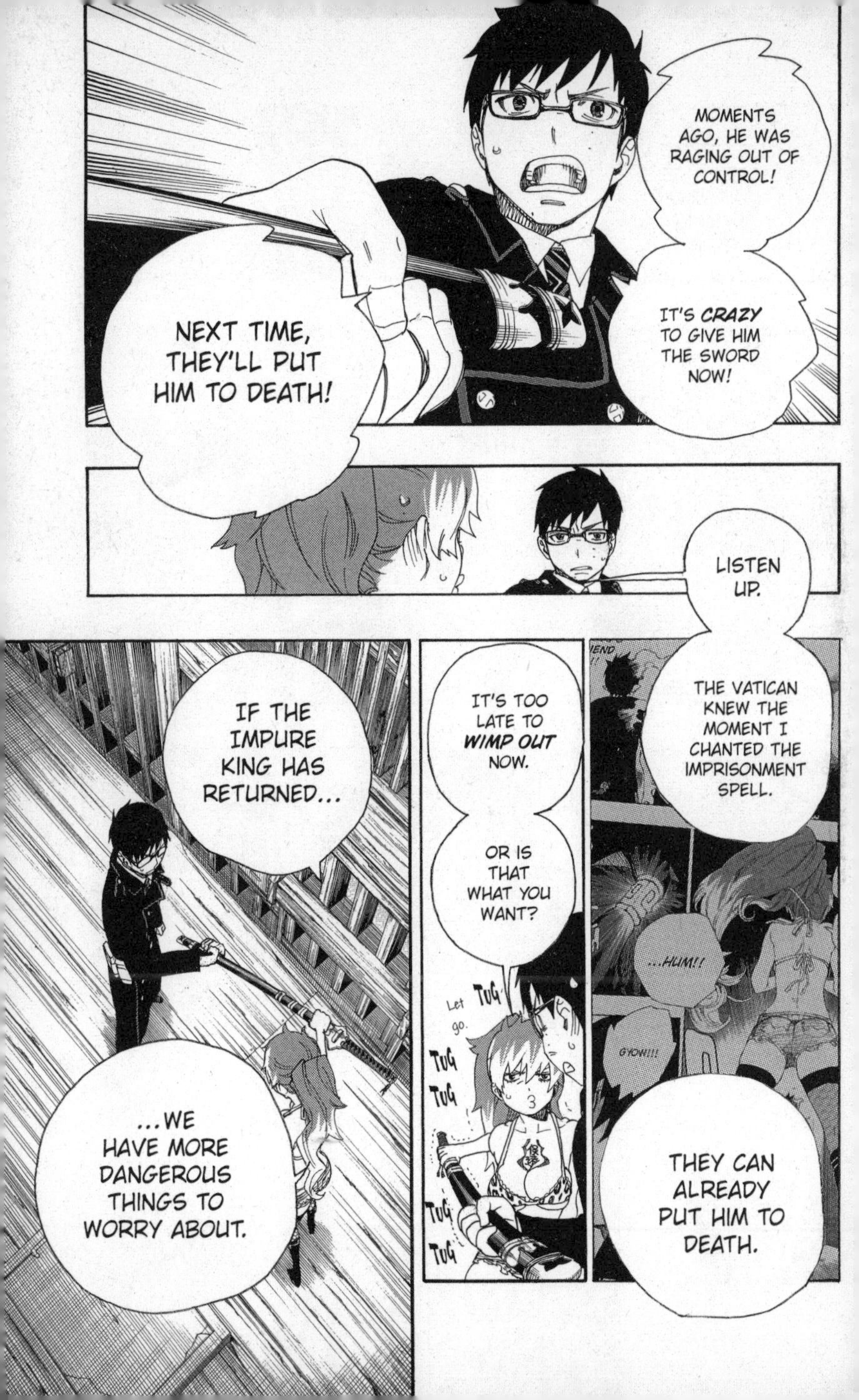
MOMENTS AGO, HE WAS RAGING OUT OF CONTROL!
IT'S *CRAZY* TO GIVE HIM THE SWORD NOW!
NEXT TIME, THEY'LL PUT HIM TO DEATH!
LISTEN UP.
THE VATICAN KNEW THE MOMENT I CHANTED THE IMPRISONMENT SPELL.
...HUM!!
GYOW!!!
THEY CAN ALREADY PUT HIM TO DEATH.
IT'S TOO LATE TO *WIMP OUT* NOW.
OR IS THAT WHAT YOU WANT?
TUG
Let go.
TUG
TUG
TUG
TUG
IF THE IMPURE KING HAS RETURNED...
...WE HAVE MORE DANGEROUS THINGS TO WORRY ABOUT.

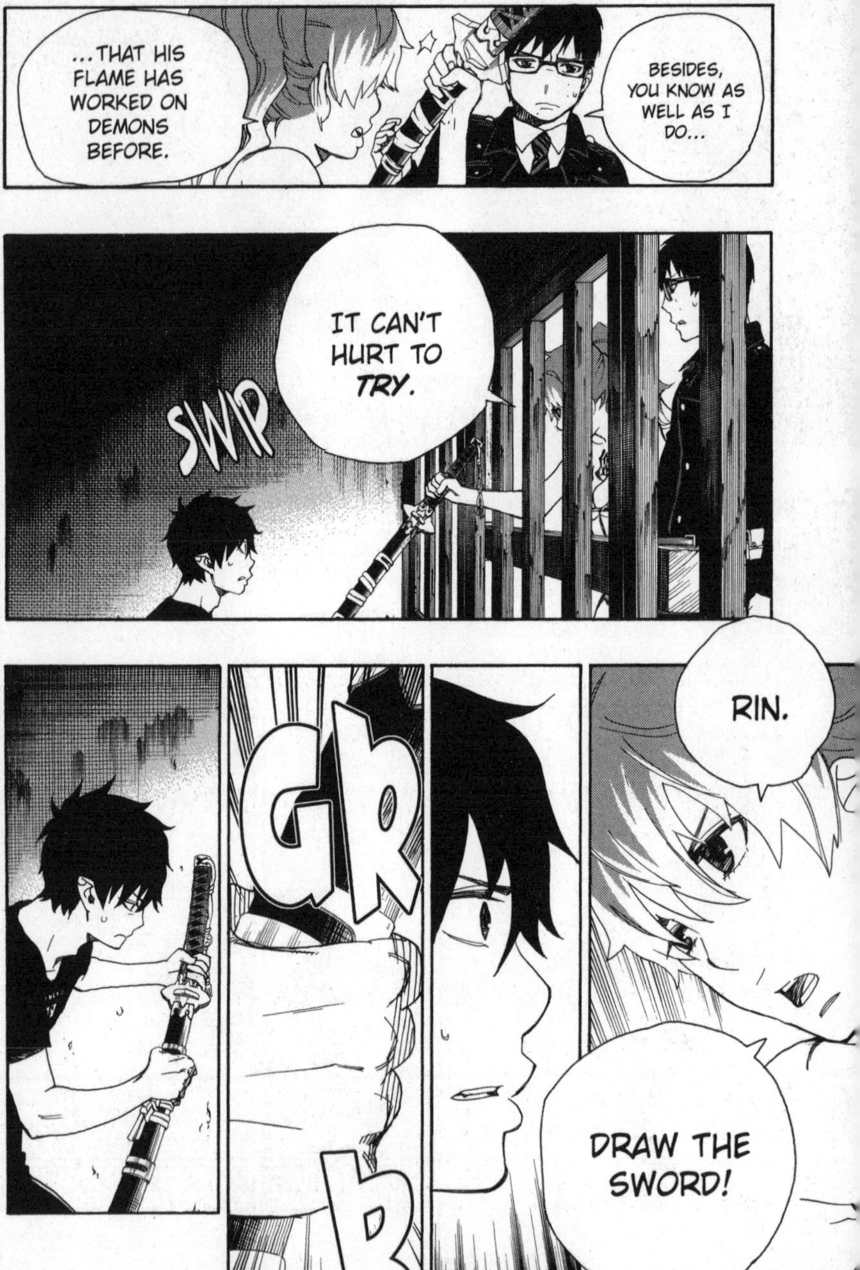
BESIDES, YOU KNOW AS WELL AS I DO...
...THAT HIS FLAME HAS WORKED ON DEMONS BEFORE.
IT CAN'T HURT TO *TRY*.
SWIP
RIN.
DRAW THE SWORD!
GRb

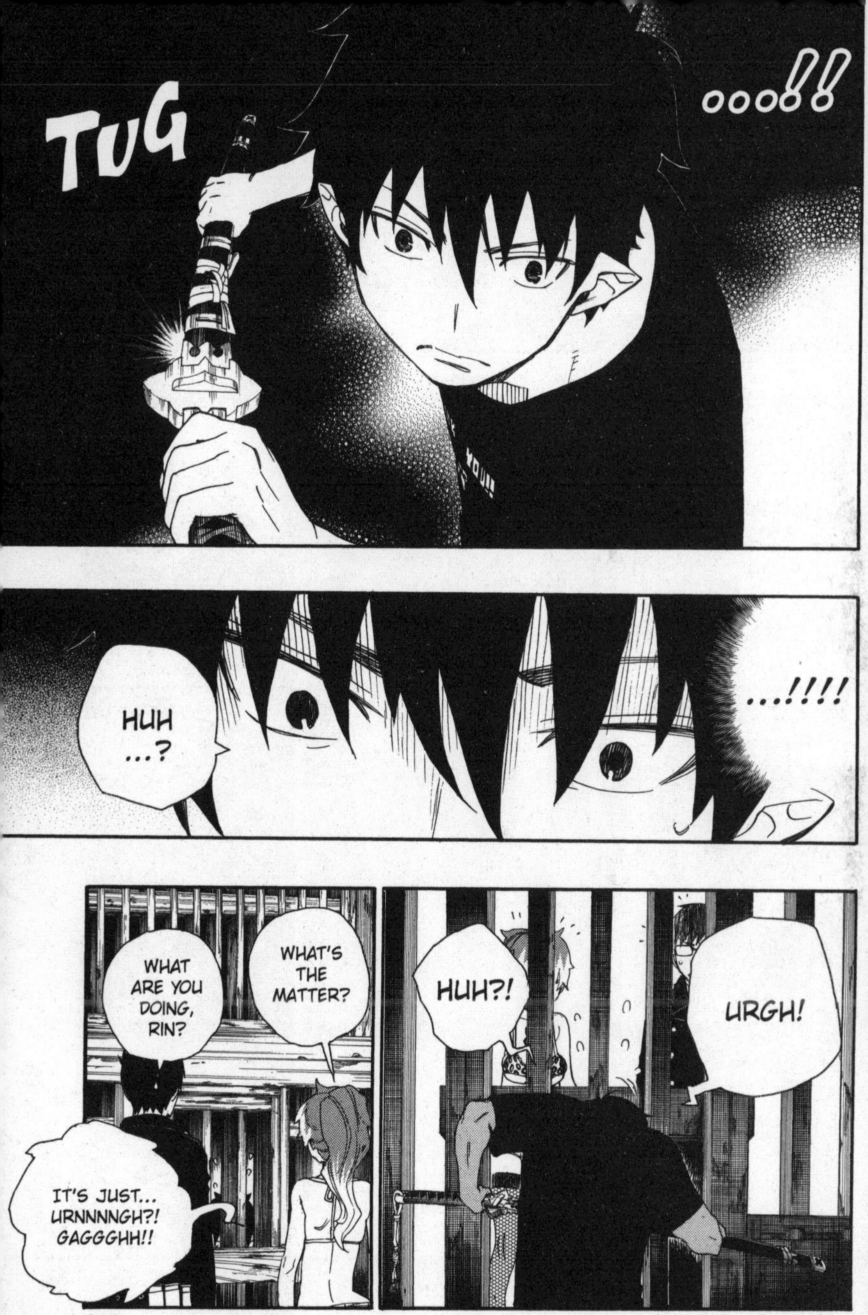
ooo!!
TUG
...!!!!
HUH ...?
URGH!
HUH?!
WHAT'S THE MATTER?
WHAT ARE YOU DOING, RIN?
IT'S JUST... URNNNNGH?! GAGGGHH!!

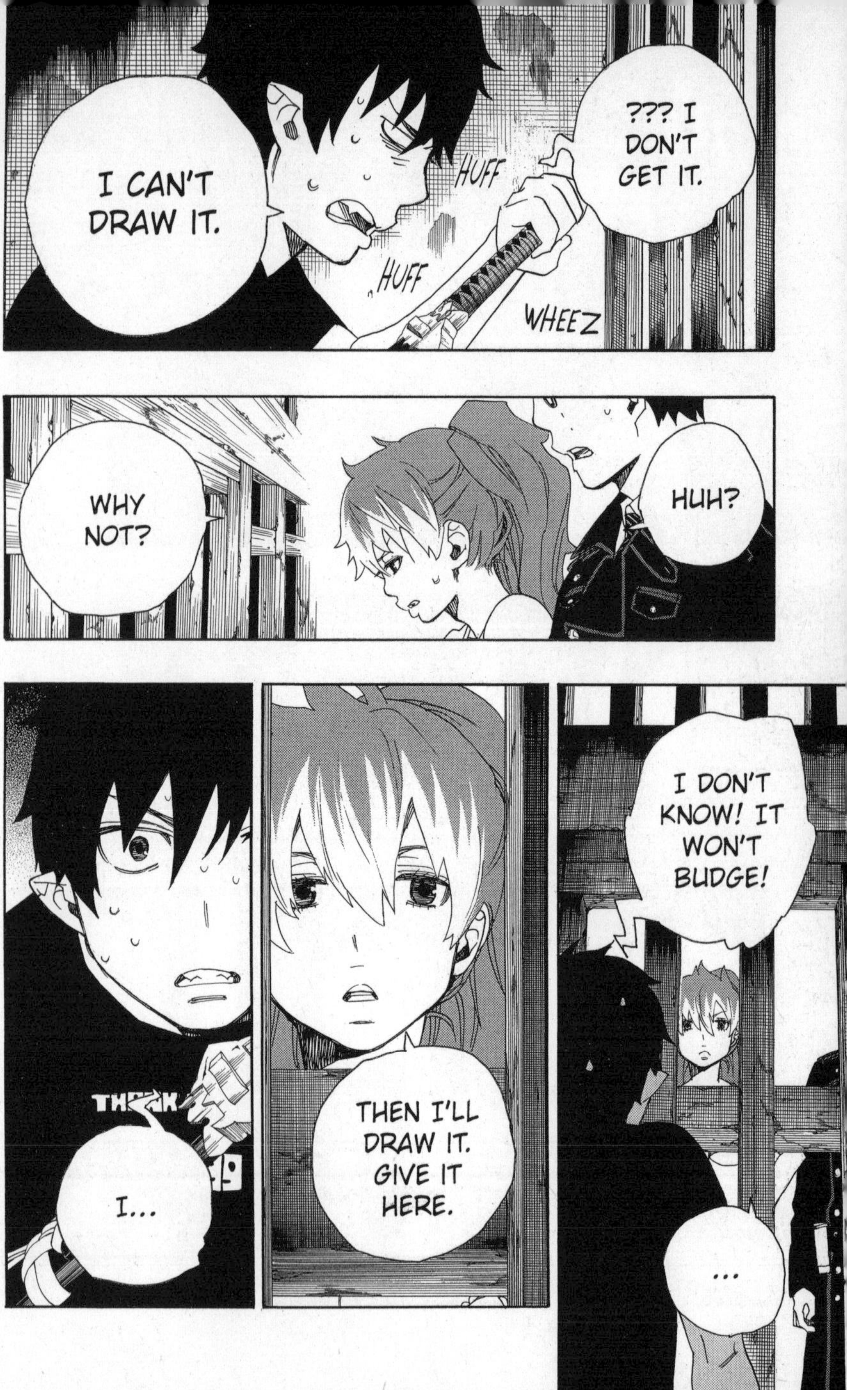
??? I DON'T GET IT.
HUFF
HUFF
WHEEZ
I CAN'T DRAW IT.
HUH?
WHY NOT?
I DON'T KNOW! IT WON'T BUDGE!
...
THEN I'LL DRAW IT. GIVE IT HERE.
I...

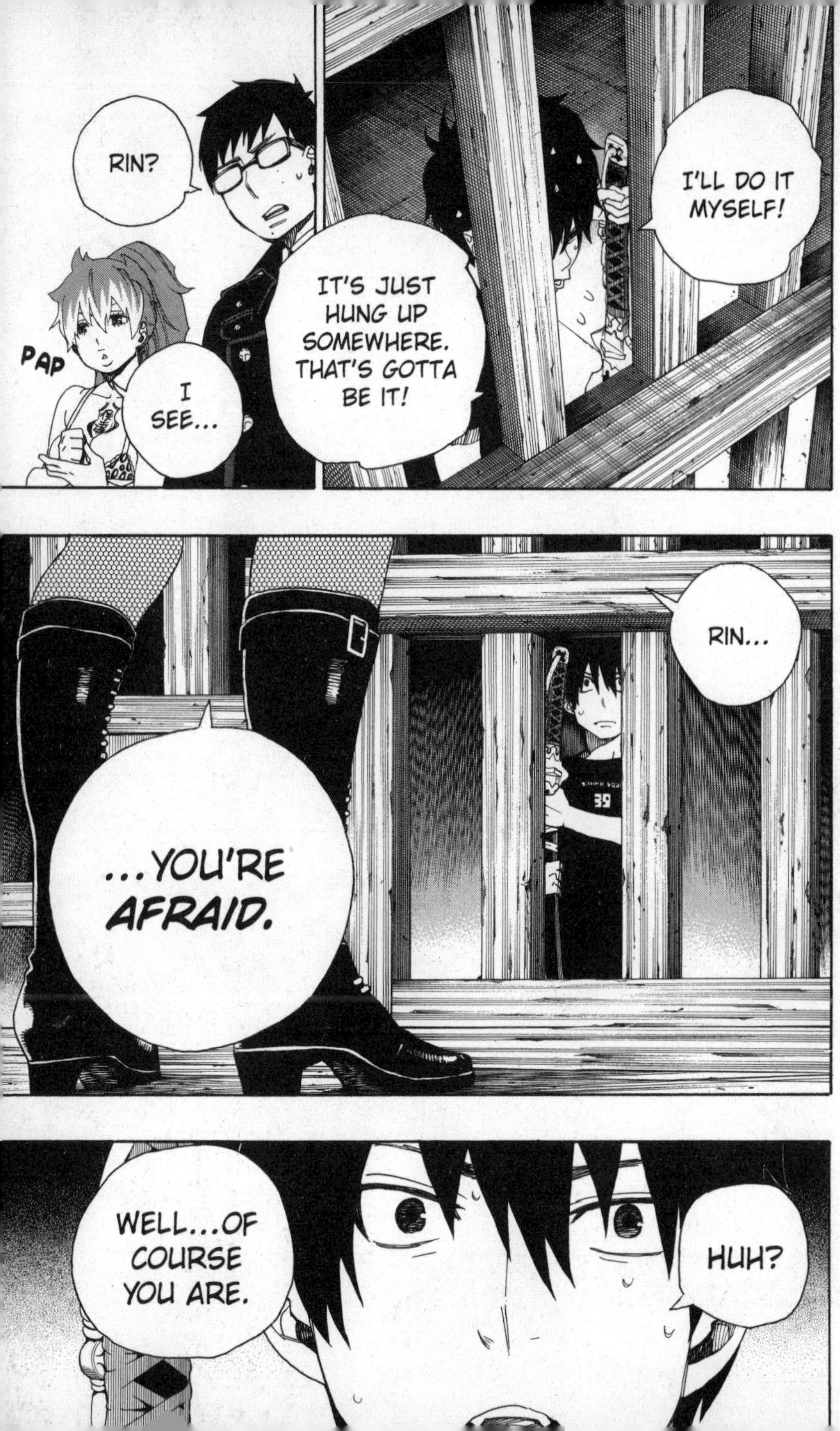
I'LL DO IT MYSELF!
IT'S JUST HUNG UP SOMEWHERE. THAT'S GOTTA BE IT!
RIN?
PAP
I SEE...
RIN...
...YOU'RE AFRAID.
HUH?
WELL...OF COURSE YOU ARE.

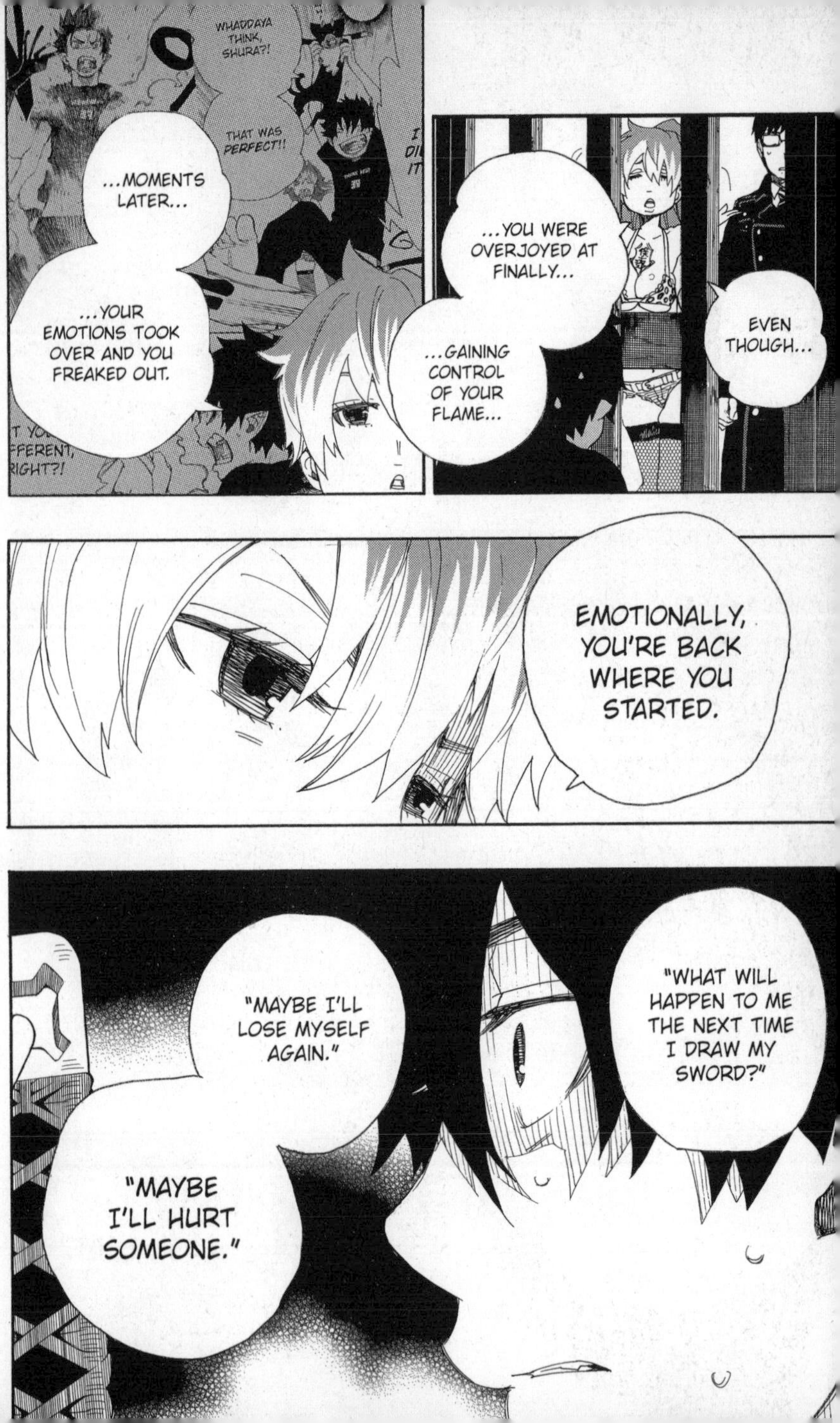
EVEN THOUGH...
...YOU WERE OVERJOYED AT FINALLY...
...GAINING CONTROL OF YOUR FLAME...
WHADDAYA THINK, SHURA?!
THAT WAS PERFECT!!
...MOMENTS LATER...
...YOUR EMOTIONS TOOK OVER AND YOU FREAKED OUT.
EMOTIONALLY, YOU'RE BACK WHERE YOU STARTED.
"WHAT WILL HAPPEN TO ME THE NEXT TIME I DRAW MY SWORD?"
"MAYBE I'LL LOSE MYSELF AGAIN."
"MAYBE I'LL HURT SOMEONE."

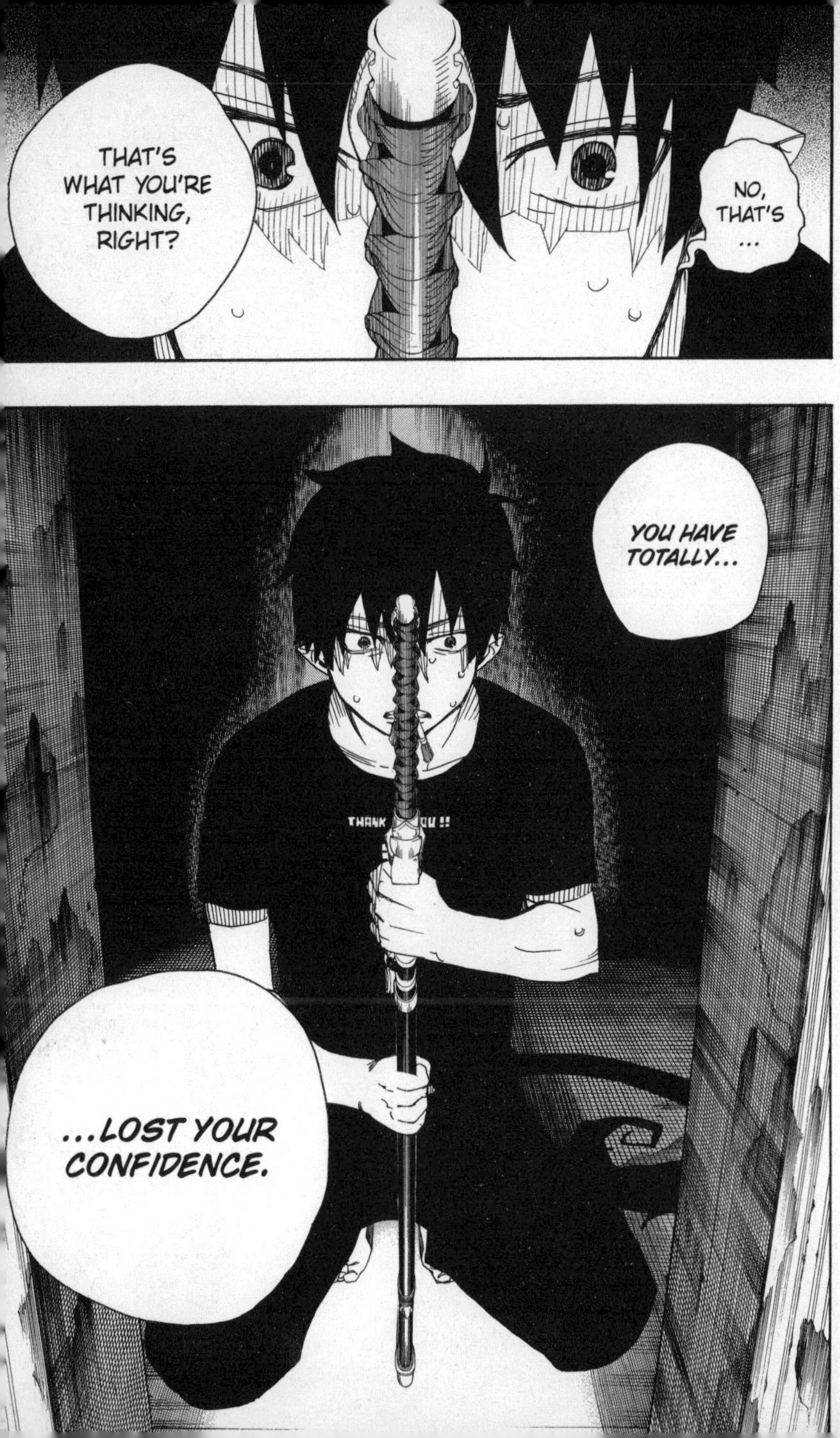
NO, THAT'S ...
THAT'S WHAT YOU'RE THINKING, RIGHT?
YOU HAVE TOTALLY...
...LOST YOUR CONFIDENCE.

Blue Exorcist Chapter 25 Impure King

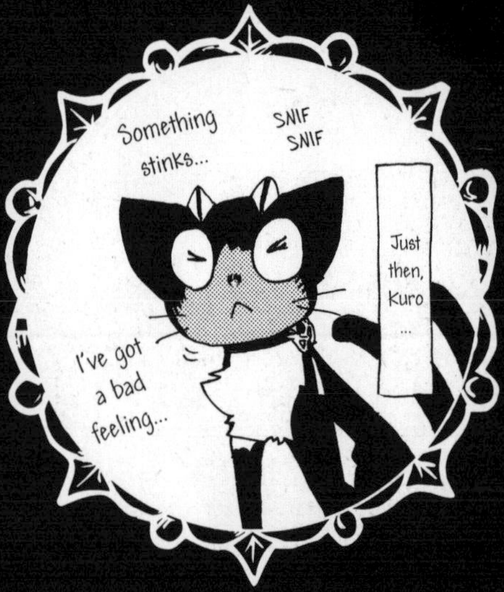
Just then, Kuro ...
SNIF SNIF
Something stinks...
I've got a bad feeling...

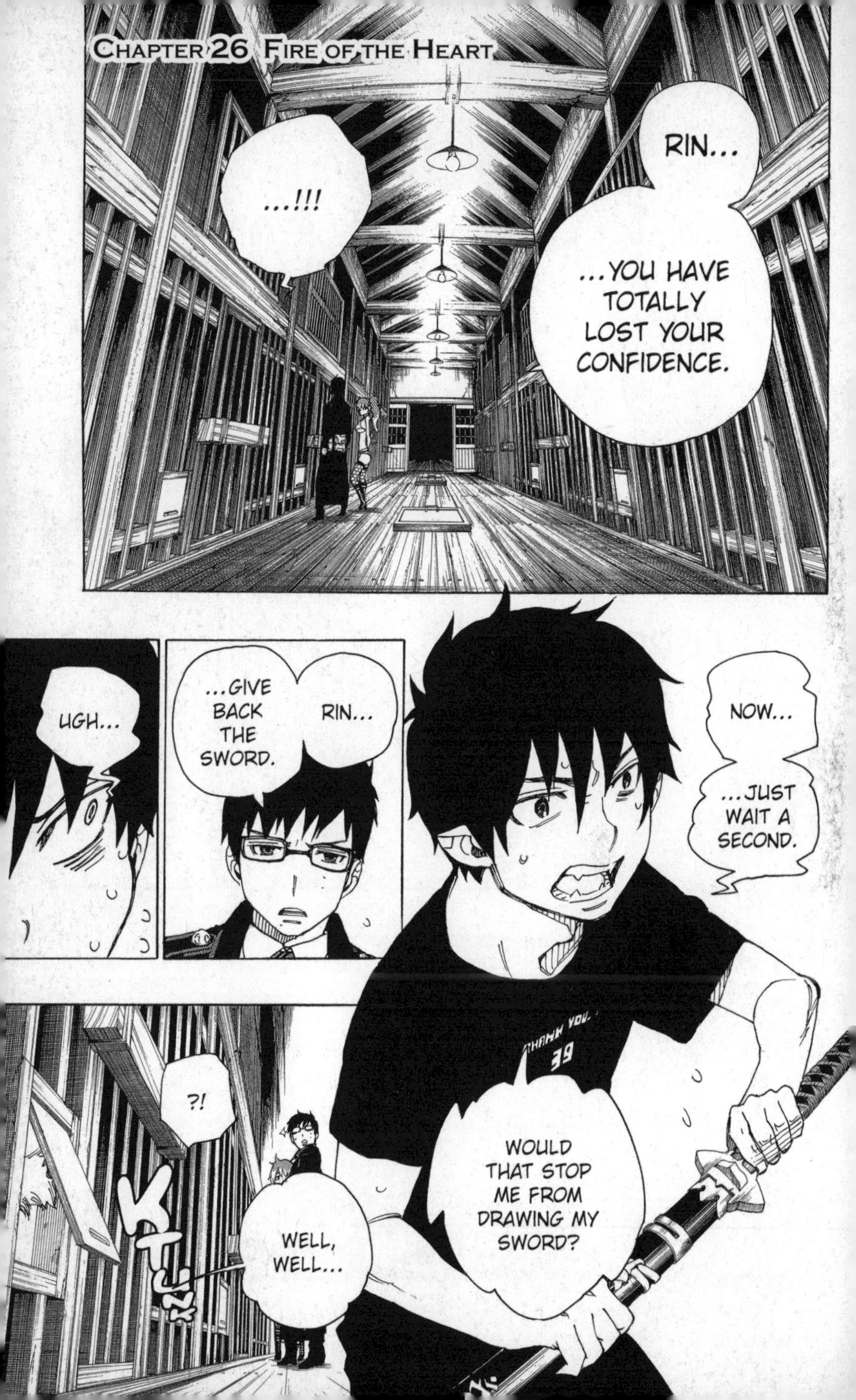
Chapter 26 Fire of the Heart
RIN...
...YOU HAVE TOTALLY LOST YOUR CONFIDENCE.
...!!!
NOW...
...JUST WAIT A SECOND.
WOULD THAT STOP ME FROM DRAWING MY SWORD?
RIN...
...GIVE BACK THE SWORD.
UGH...
?!
WELL, WELL...
KTUNK

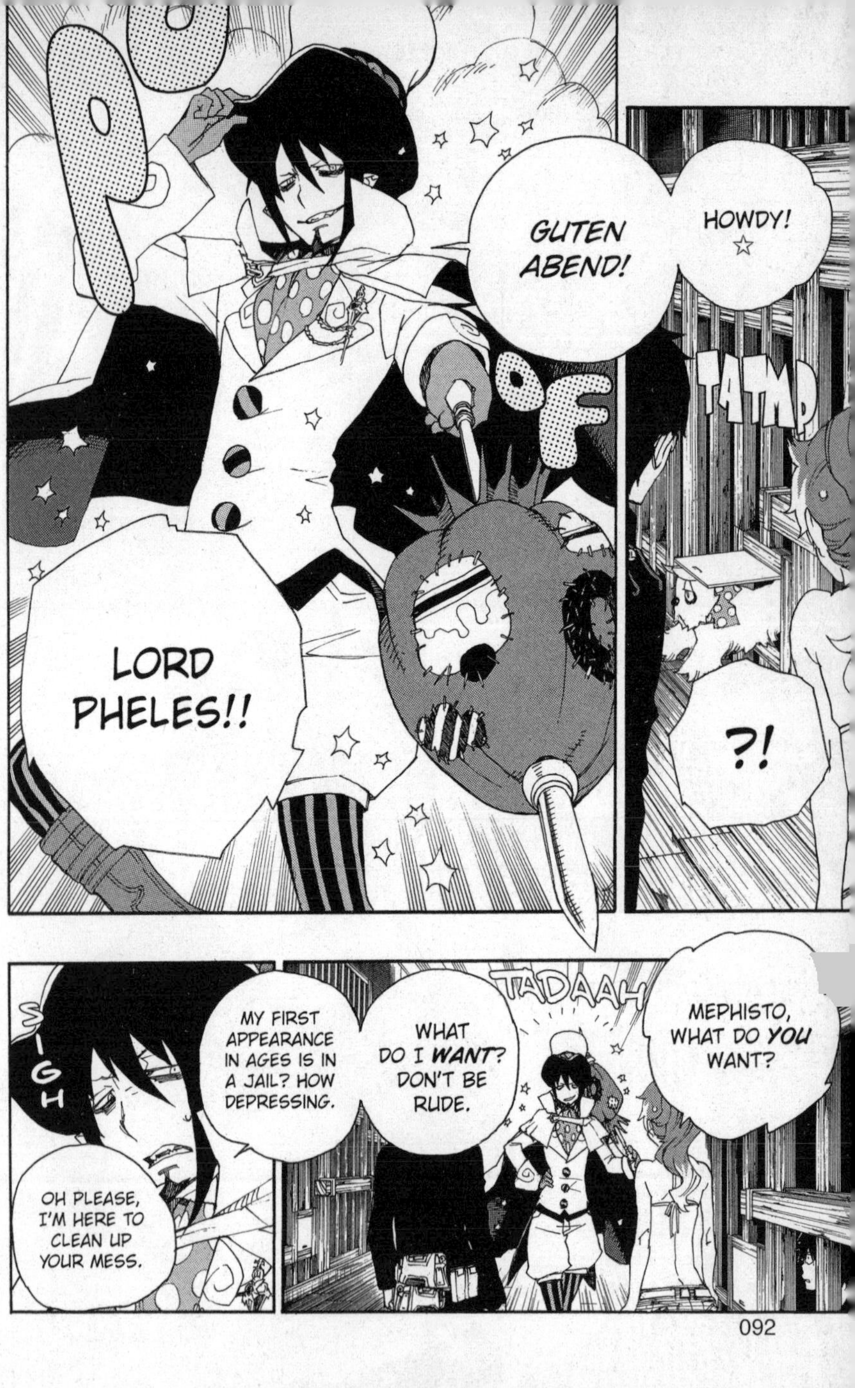
HOWDY! ☆
TATMP
?!
GUTEN ABEND!
POOF
LORD PHELES!!
MEPHISTO, WHAT DO *YOU* WANT?
TADAAH
WHAT DO I *WANT*? DON'T BE RUDE.
MY FIRST APPEARANCE IN AGES IS IN A JAIL? HOW DEPRESSING.
SIGH
OH PLEASE, I'M HERE TO CLEAN UP YOUR MESS.

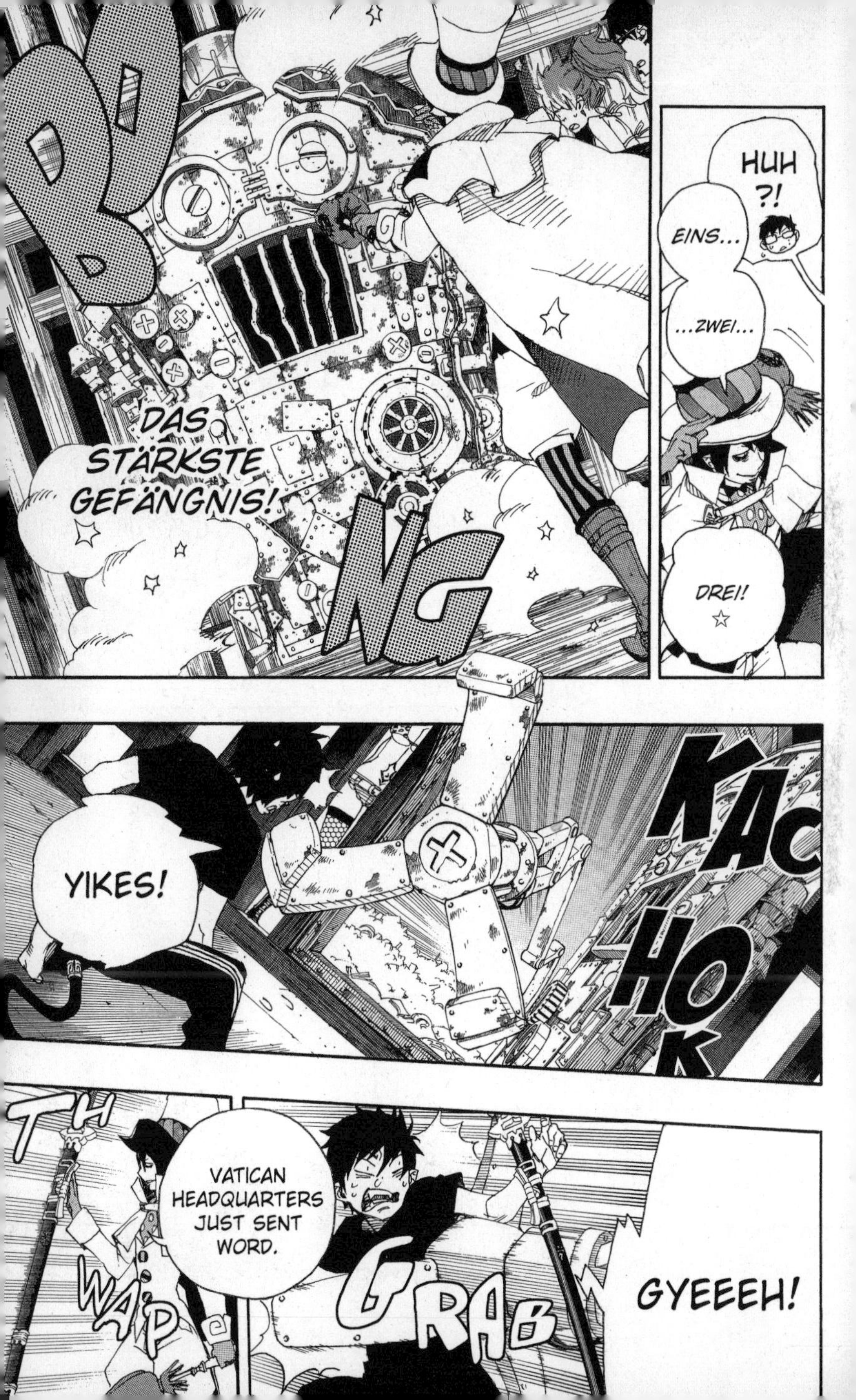
HUH ?!
EINS...
...ZWEI...
DREI! ☆
DAS STÄRKSTE GEFÄNGNIS!
NG
YIKES!
GYEEEH!
GRAB
VATICAN HEADQUARTERS JUST SENT WORD.
TH
WAP

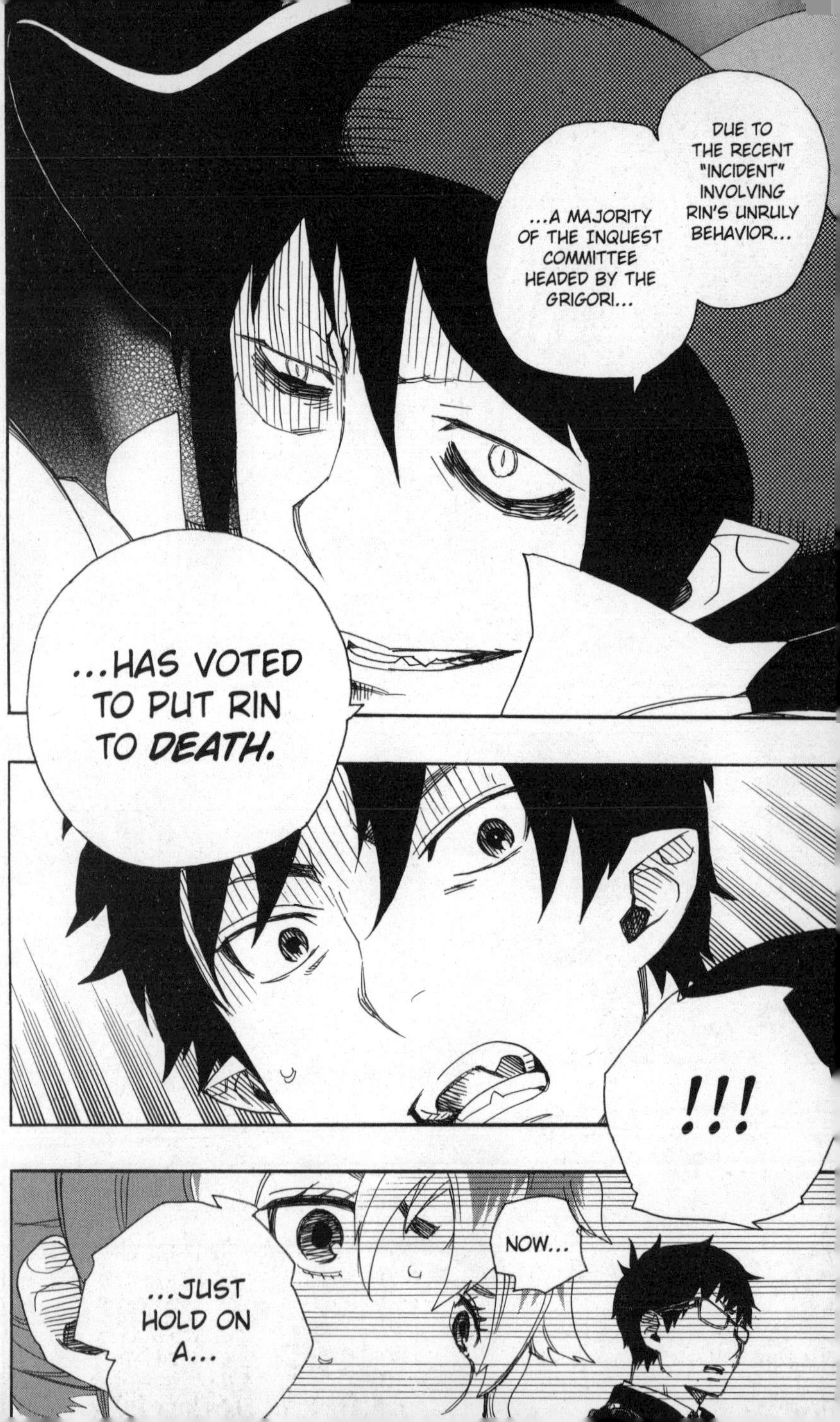
DUE TO THE RECENT "INCIDENT" INVOLVING RIN'S UNRULY BEHAVIOR...
...A MAJORITY OF THE INQUEST COMMITTEE HEADED BY THE GRIGORI...
...HAS VOTED TO PUT RIN TO *DEATH.*
!!!
NOW...
...JUST HOLD ON A...

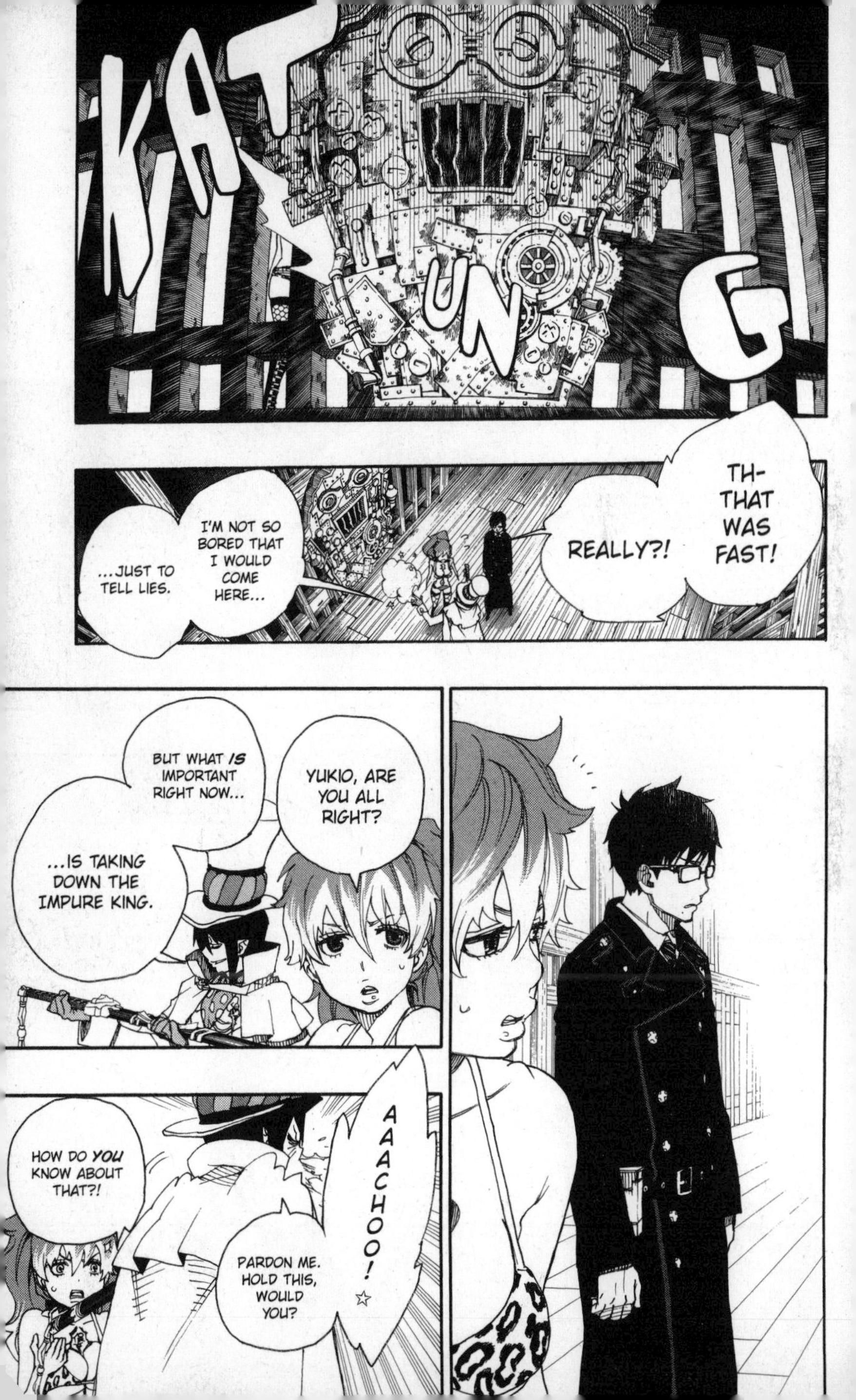
KATUNG
TH-THAT WAS FAST!
REALLY?!
I'M NOT SO BORED THAT I WOULD COME HERE...
...JUST TO TELL LIES.
YUKIO, ARE YOU ALL RIGHT?
BUT WHAT *IS* IMPORTANT RIGHT NOW...
...IS TAKING DOWN THE IMPURE KING.
AAACHOO! ☆
PARDON ME. HOLD THIS, WOULD YOU?
HOW DO *YOU* KNOW ABOUT THAT?!

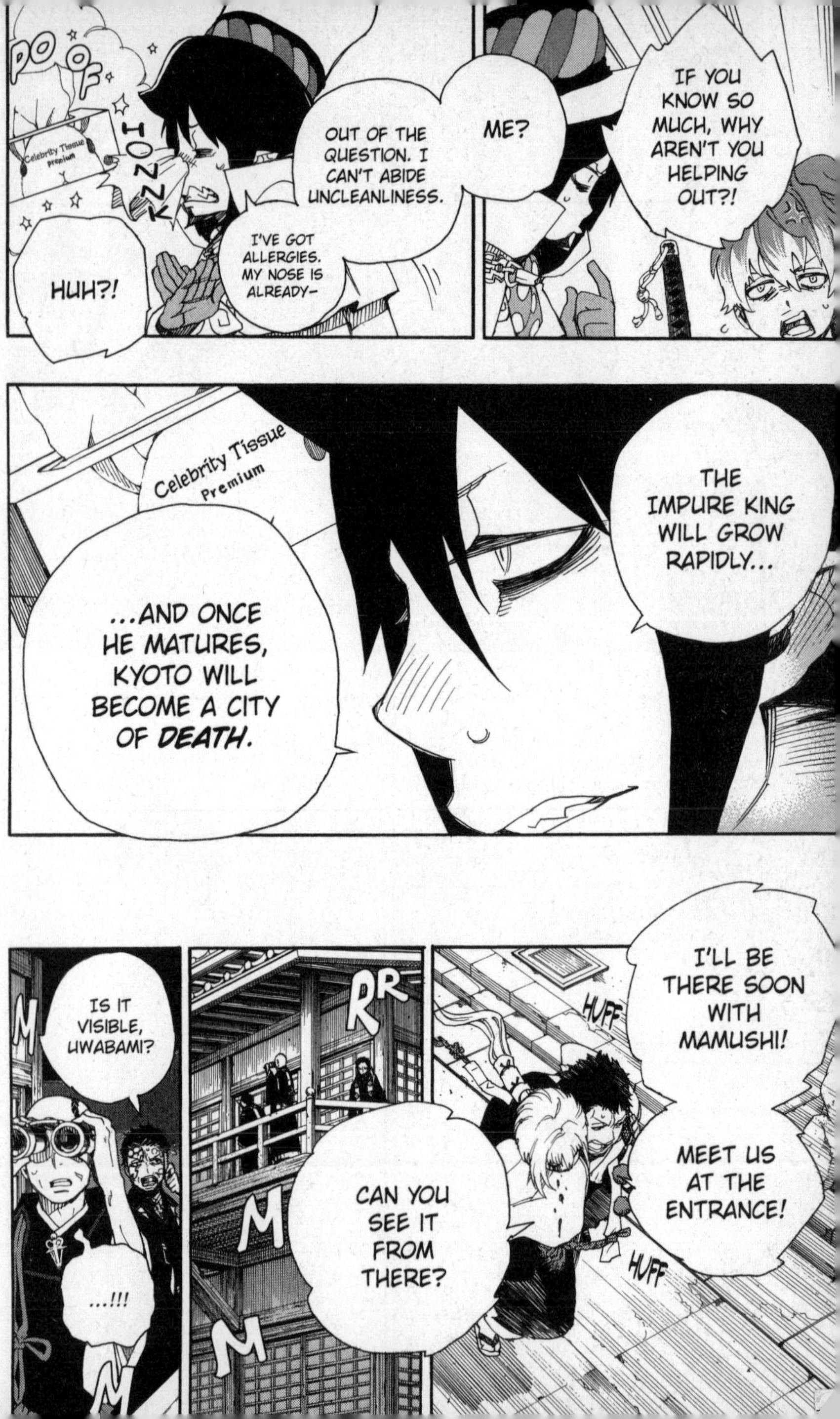
IF YOU KNOW SO MUCH, WHY AREN'T YOU HELPING OUT?!
ME?
OUT OF THE QUESTION. I CAN'T ABIDE UNCLEANLINESS.
I'VE GOT ALLERGIES. MY NOSE IS ALREADY–
HONNK
POOF
Celebrity Tissue premium
HUH?!
THE IMPURE KING WILL GROW RAPIDLY...
Celebrity Tissue Premium
...AND ONCE HE MATURES, KYOTO WILL BECOME A CITY OF DEATH.
I'LL BE THERE SOON WITH MAMUSHI!
HUFF
MEET US AT THE ENTRANCE!
HUFF
RR
CAN YOU SEE IT FROM THERE?
MMM
IS IT VISIBLE, UWABAMI?
M
...!!!

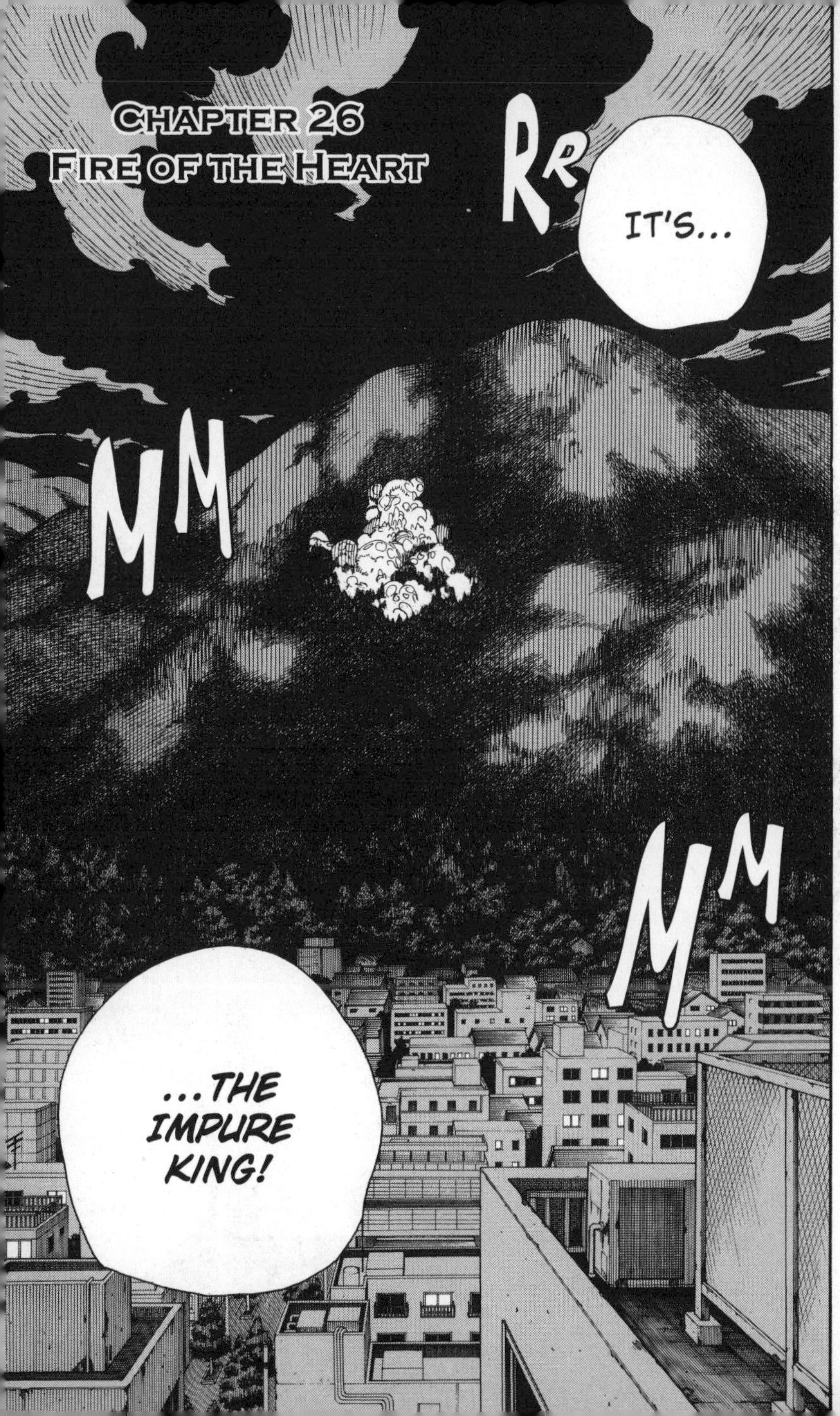
CHAPTER 26
FIRE OF THE HEART
RR
IT'S...
MM
MM
...THE IMPURE KING!

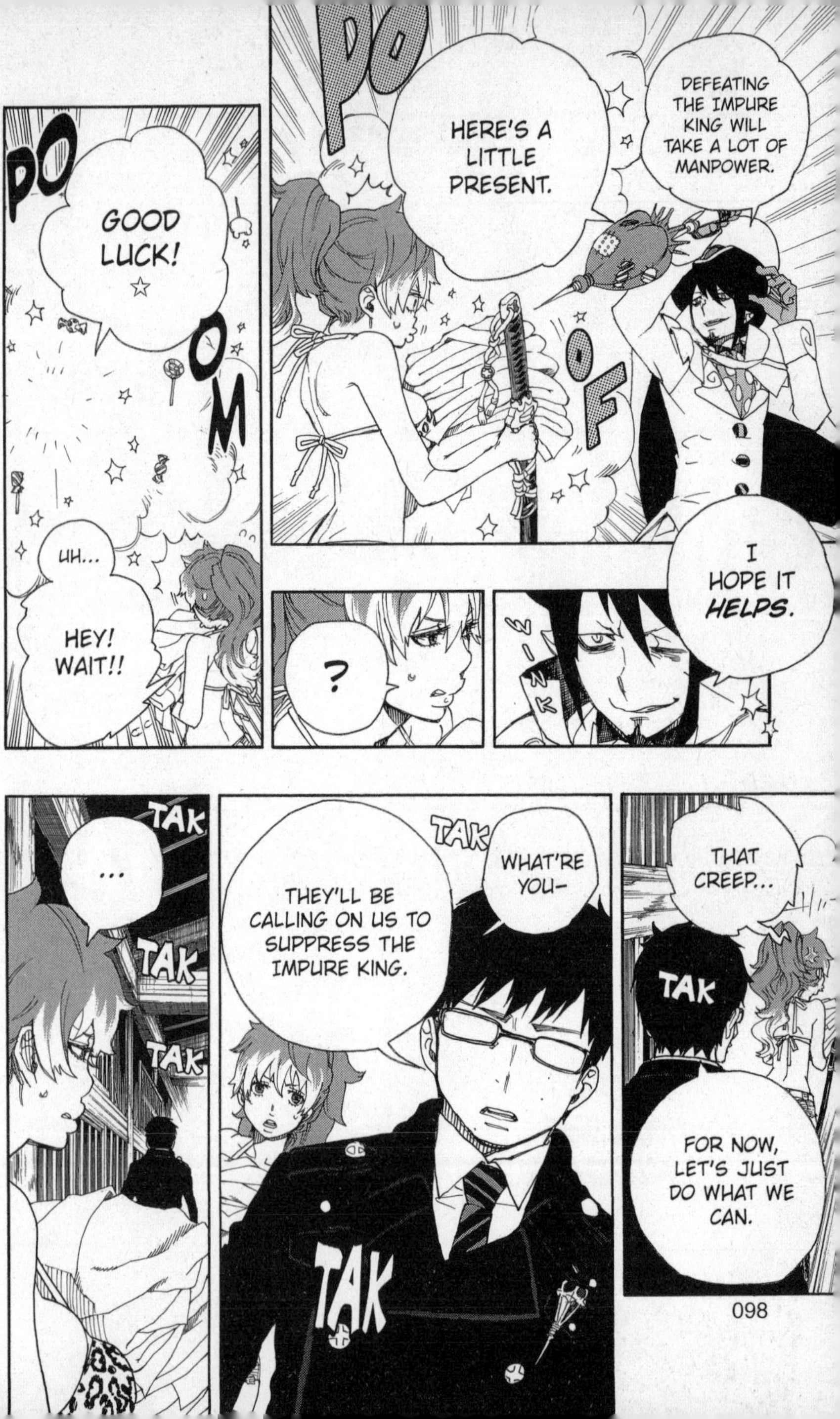
DEFEATING THE IMPURE KING WILL TAKE A LOT OF MANPOWER.
HERE'S A LITTLE PRESENT.
PO
POOF
I HOPE IT HELPS.
WINK
?
PO
GOOD LUCK!
POOM
UH...
HEY! WAIT!!
THAT CREEP...
TAK
FOR NOW, LET'S JUST DO WHAT WE CAN.
TAK
WHAT'RE YOU-
THEY'LL BE CALLING ON US TO SUPPRESS THE IMPURE KING.
TAK
TAK
...
TAK
TAK

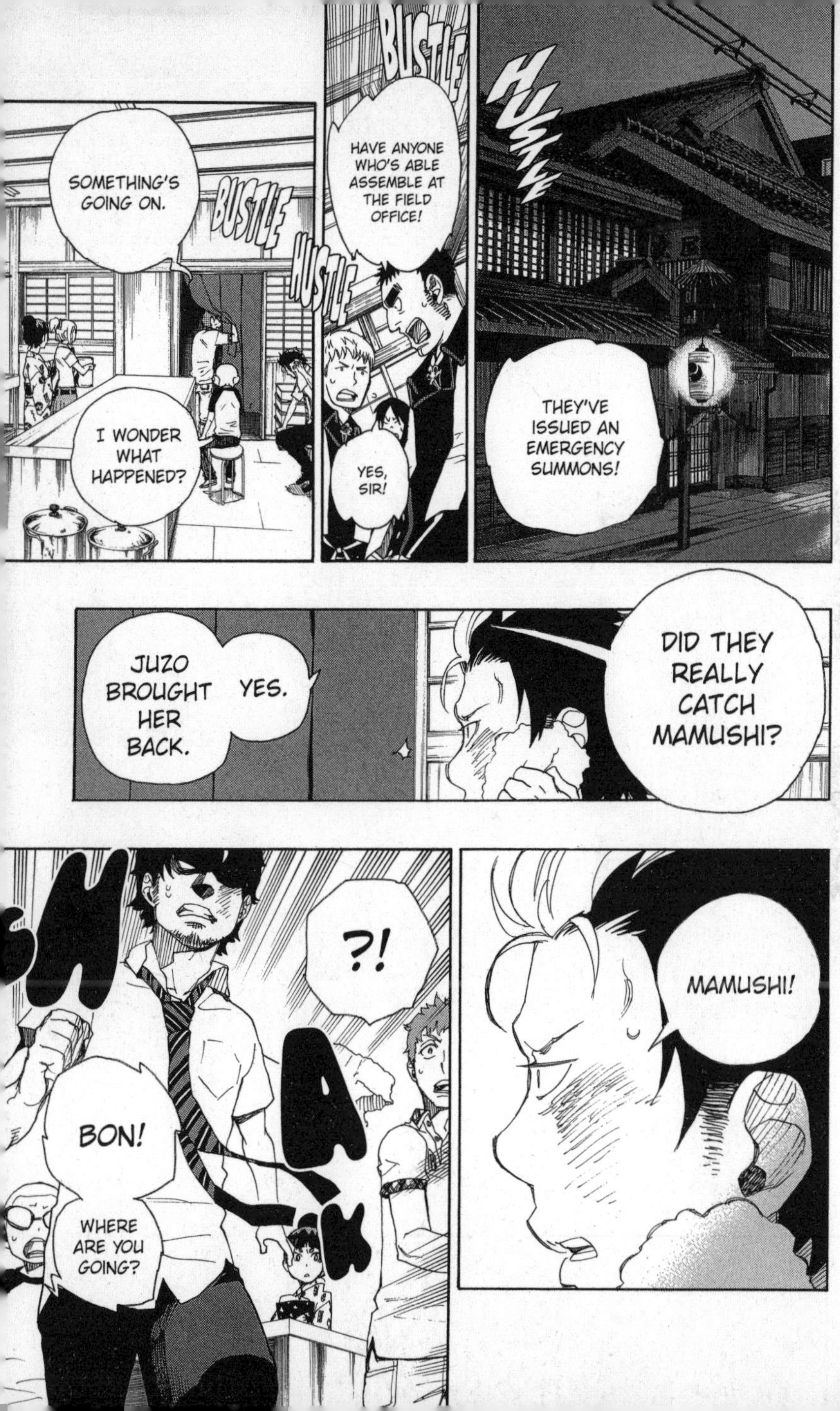
HUSTLE
THEY'VE ISSUED AN EMERGENCY SUMMONS!
BUSTLE
HAVE ANYONE WHO'S ABLE ASSEMBLE AT THE FIELD OFFICE!
YES, SIR!
SOMETHING'S GOING ON.
BUSTLE
HUSTLE
I WONDER WHAT HAPPENED?
DID THEY REALLY CATCH MAMUSHI?
YES.
JUZO BROUGHT HER BACK.
MAMUSHI!
?!
BON!
WHERE ARE YOU GOING?

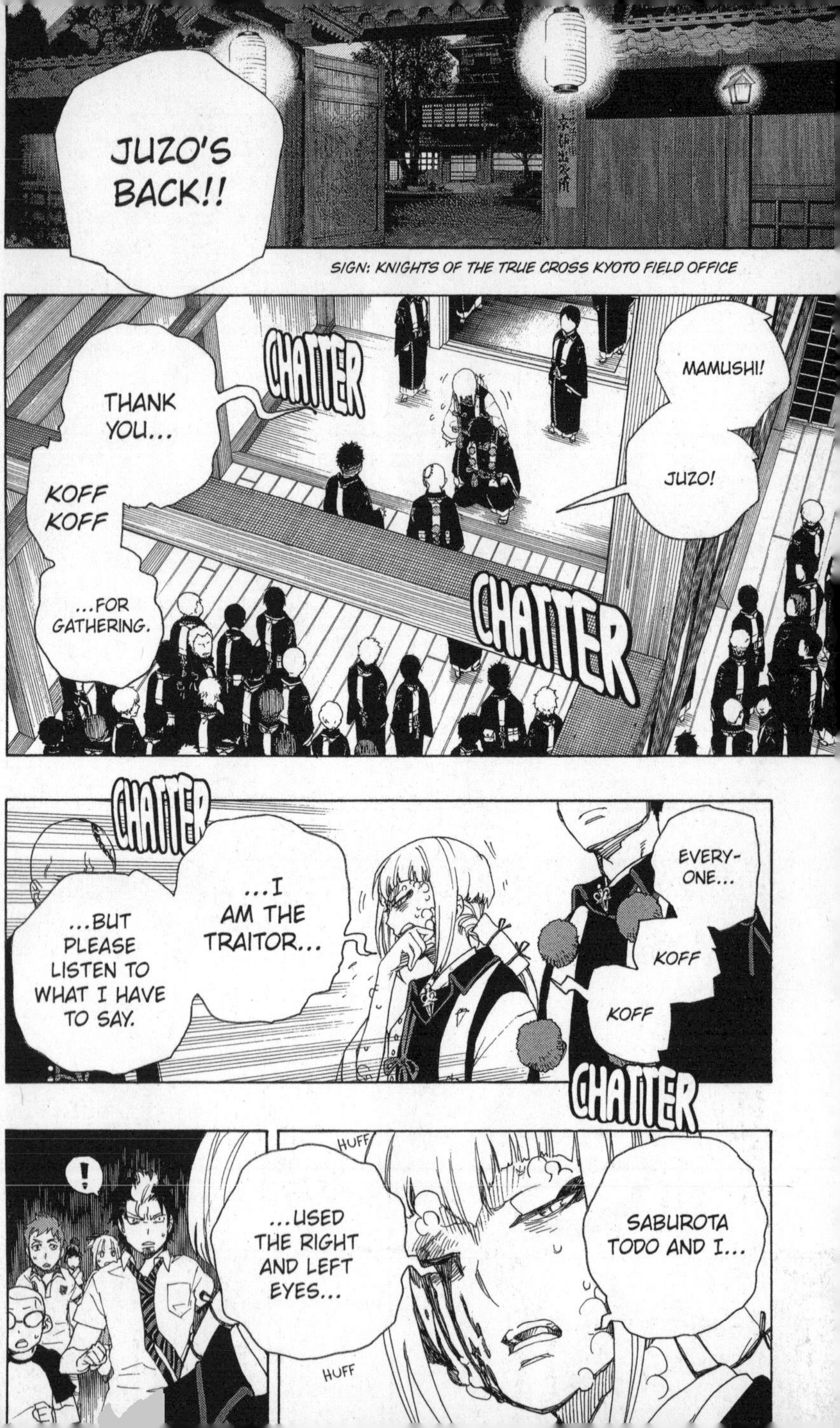
JUZO'S BACK!!
SIGN: KNIGHTS OF THE TRUE CROSS KYOTO FIELD OFFICE
MAMUSHI!
JUZO!
CHATTER
CHATTER
THANK YOU...
KOFF KOFF
...FOR GATHERING.
EVERY-ONE...
KOFF
KOFF
CHATTER
...I AM THE TRAITOR...
...BUT PLEASE LISTEN TO WHAT I HAVE TO SAY.
CHATTER
HUFF
SABUROTA TODO AND I...
...USED THE RIGHT AND LEFT EYES...
HUFF
!

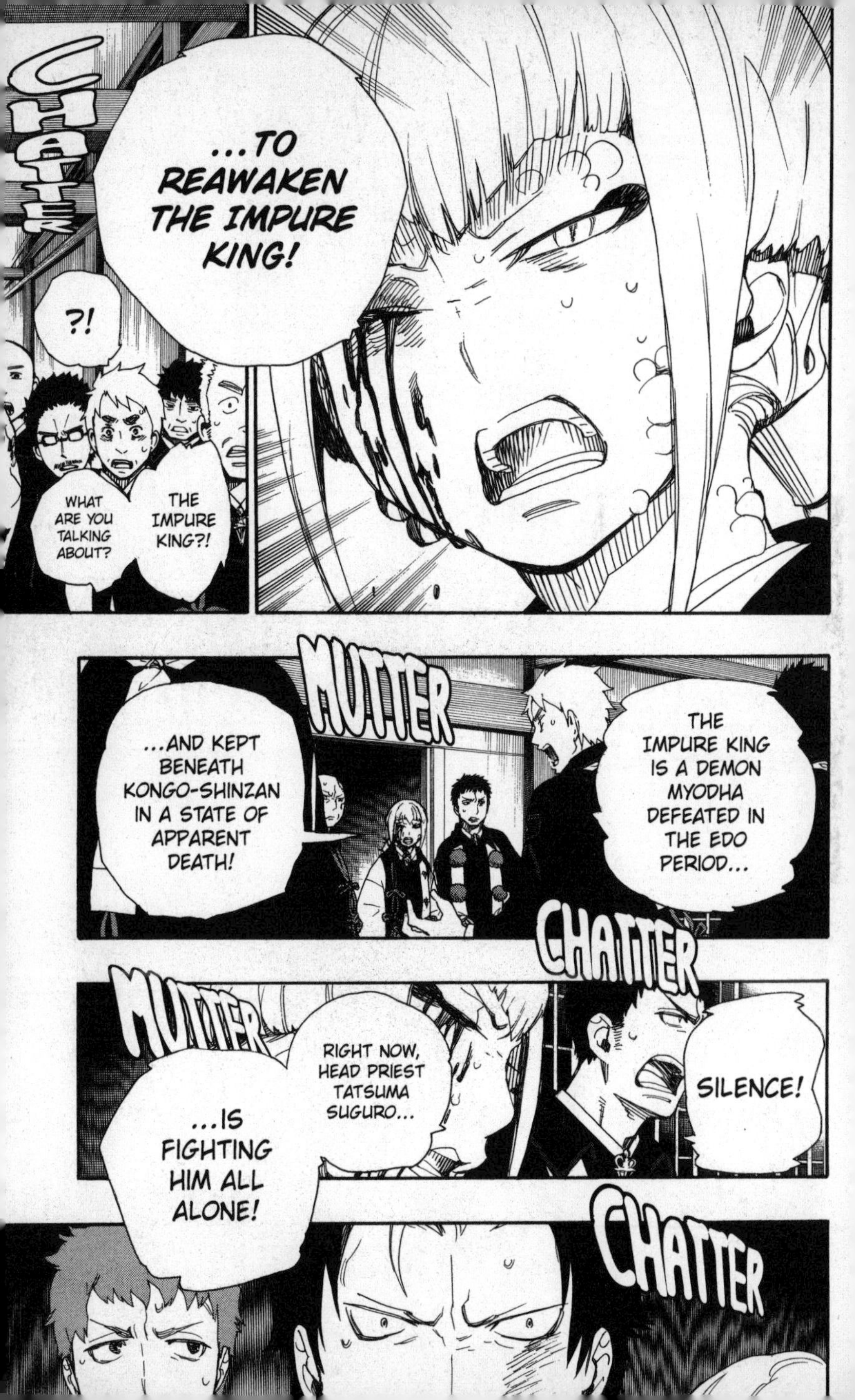
...TO REAWAKEN THE IMPURE KING!
CHATTER
?!
THE IMPURE KING?!
WHAT ARE YOU TALKING ABOUT?
MUTTER
THE IMPURE KING IS A DEMON MYODHA DEFEATED IN THE EDO PERIOD...
...AND KEPT BENEATH KONGO-SHINZAN IN A STATE OF APPARENT DEATH!
CHATTER
SILENCE!
RIGHT NOW, HEAD PRIEST TATSUMA SUGURO...
MUTTER
...IS FIGHTING HIM ALL ALONE!
CHATTER

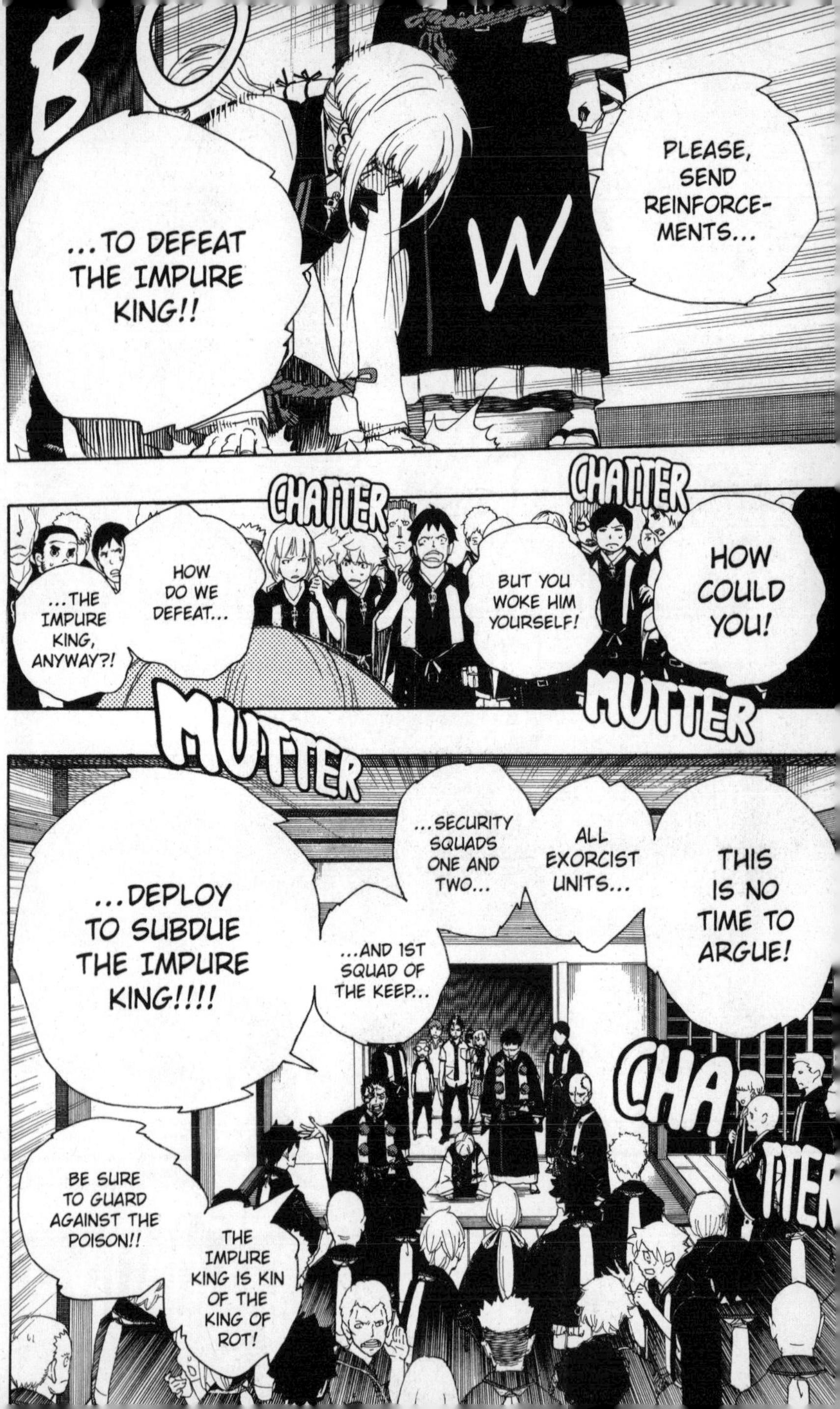
BOW
PLEASE, SEND REINFORCEMENTS...
...TO DEFEAT THE IMPURE KING!!
CHATTER
HOW COULD YOU!
BUT YOU WOKE HIM YOURSELF!
CHATTER
HOW DO WE DEFEAT...
...THE IMPURE KING, ANYWAY?!
MUTTER
MUTTER
THIS IS NO TIME TO ARGUE!
ALL EXORCIST UNITS...
...SECURITY SQUADS ONE AND TWO...
...AND 1ST SQUAD OF THE KEEP...
...DEPLOY TO SUBDUE THE IMPURE KING!!!!
CHATTER
THE IMPURE KING IS KIN OF THE KING OF ROT!
BE SURE TO GUARD AGAINST THE POISON!!

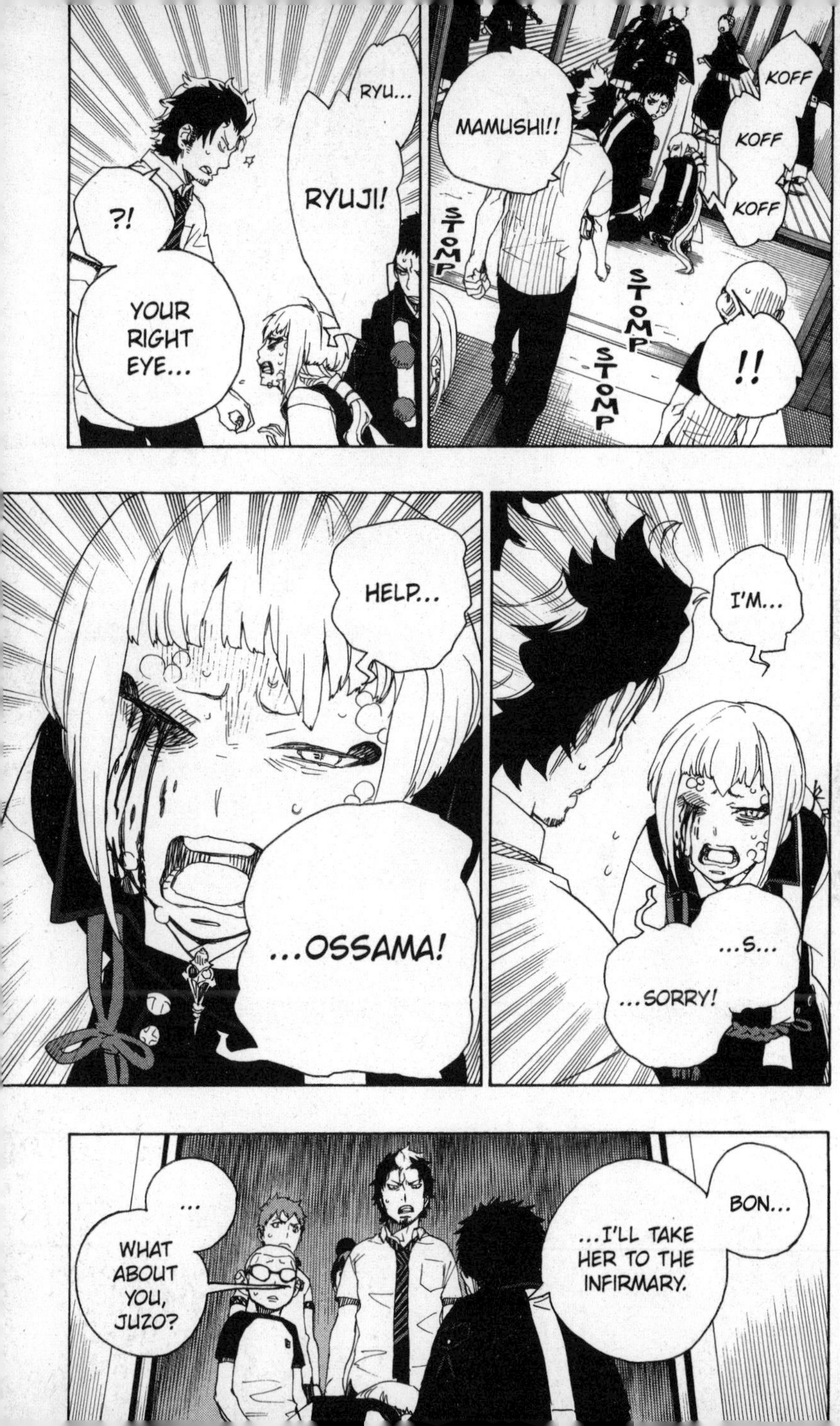
KOFF
KOFF
KOFF
MAMUSHI!!
STOMP
STOMP
STOMP
!!
RYU...
RYUJI!
?!
YOUR RIGHT EYE...
I'M...
...S...
...SORRY!
HELP...
...OSSAMA!
BON...
...I'LL TAKE HER TO THE INFIRMARY.
...
WHAT ABOUT YOU, JUZO?

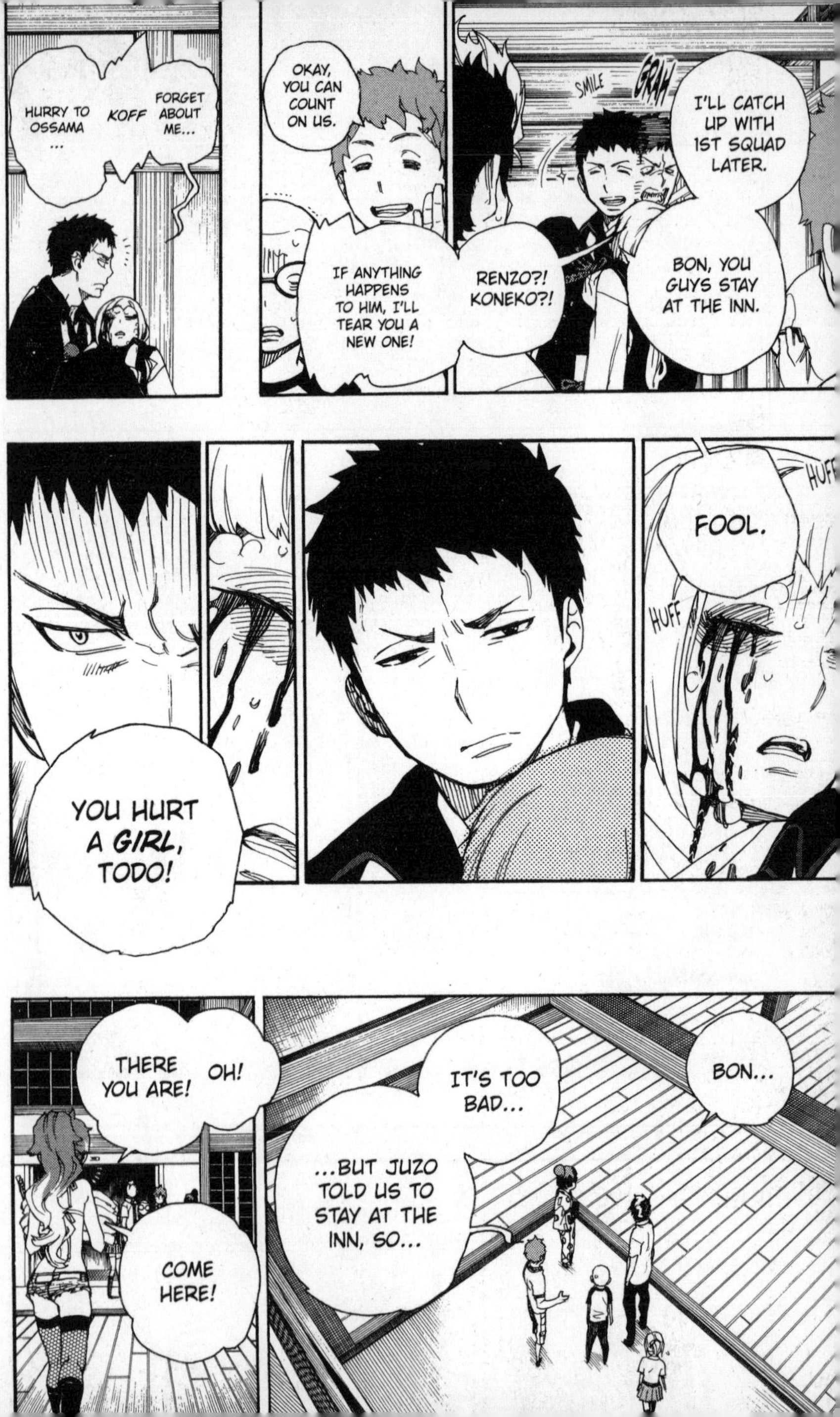
SMILE
GRAH
I'LL CATCH UP WITH 1ST SQUAD LATER.
BON, YOU GUYS STAY AT THE INN.
RENZO?! KONEKO?!
OKAY, YOU CAN COUNT ON US.
IF ANYTHING HAPPENS TO HIM, I'LL TEAR YOU A NEW ONE!
FORGET ABOUT ME...
KOFF
HURRY TO OSSAMA ...
HUFF
FOOL.
HUFF
YOU HURT A *GIRL*, TODO!
BON...
IT'S TOO BAD...
...BUT JUZO TOLD US TO STAY AT THE INN, SO...
OH!
THERE YOU ARE!
COME HERE!

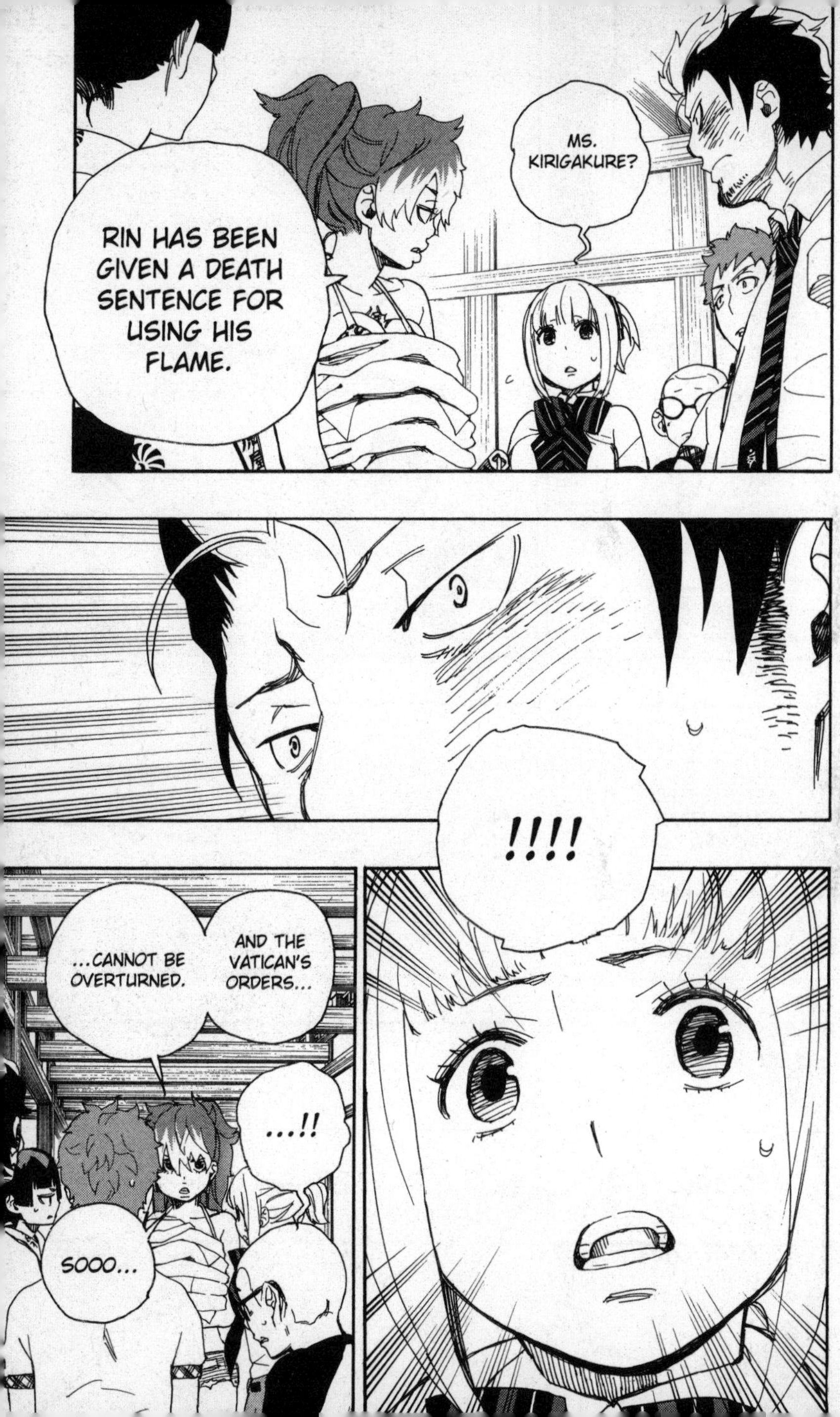
MS. KIRIGAKURE?
RIN HAS BEEN GIVEN A DEATH SENTENCE FOR USING HIS FLAME.
!!!!
AND THE VATICAN'S ORDERS...
...CANNOT BE OVERTURNED.
...!!
SOOO...

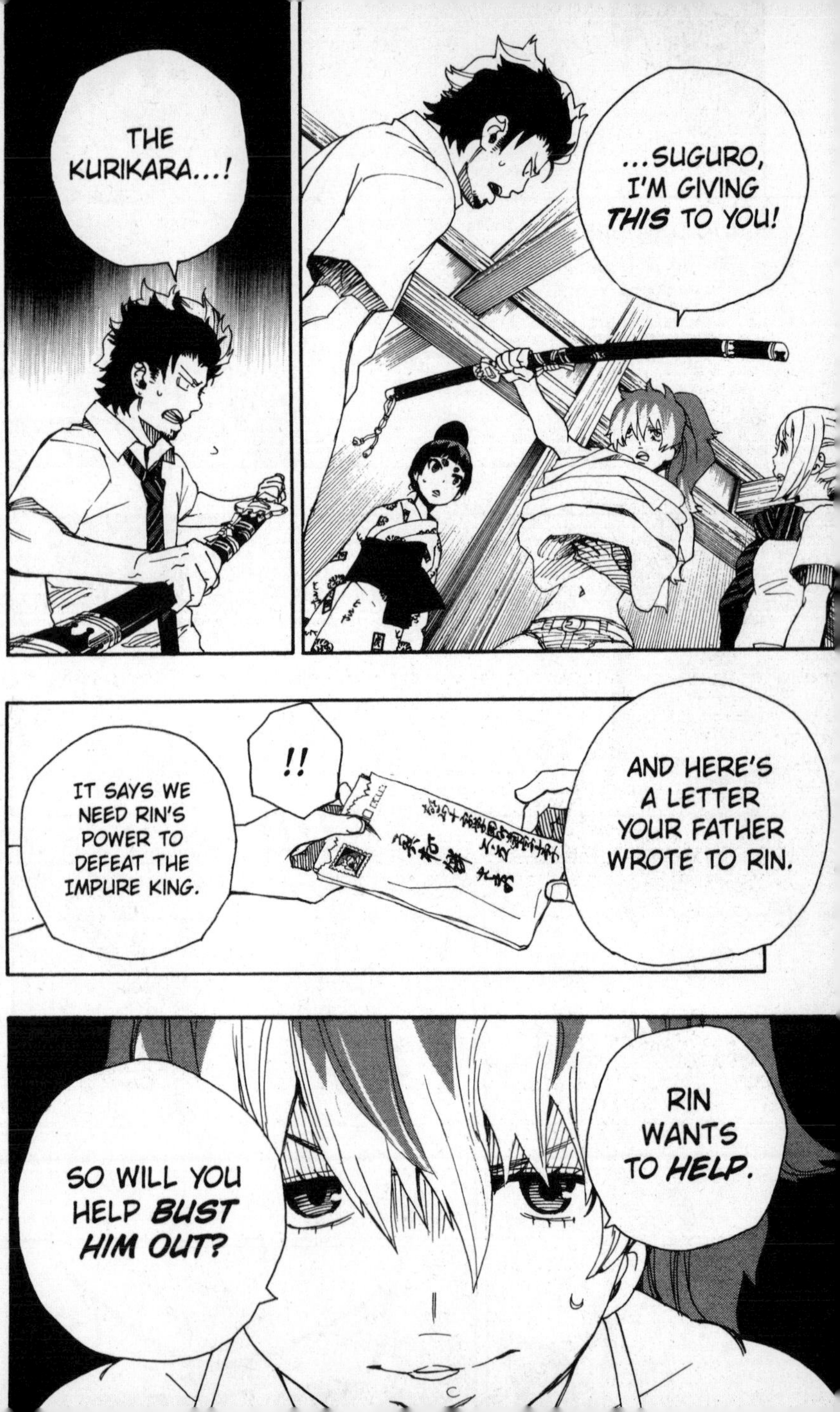
...SUGURO, I'M GIVING *THIS* TO YOU!
THE KURIKARA...!
AND HERE'S A LETTER YOUR FATHER WROTE TO RIN.
!!
IT SAYS WE NEED RIN'S POWER TO DEFEAT THE IMPURE KING.
RIN WANTS TO *HELP*.
SO WILL YOU HELP *BUST HIM OUT?*

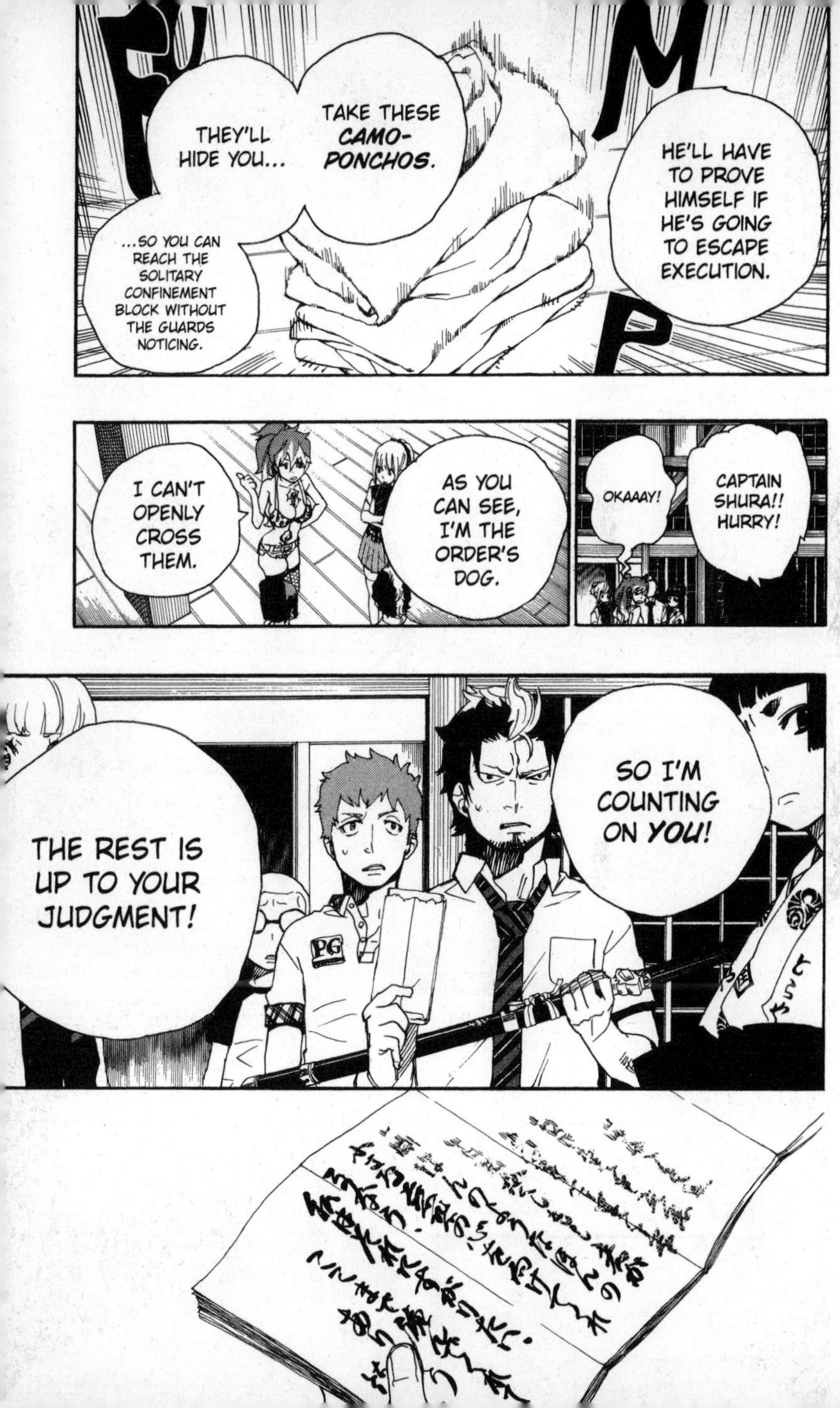
FUMP
TAKE THESE CAMO-PONCHOS.
THEY'LL HIDE YOU...
...SO YOU CAN REACH THE SOLITARY CONFINEMENT BLOCK WITHOUT THE GUARDS NOTICING.
HE'LL HAVE TO PROVE HIMSELF IF HE'S GOING TO ESCAPE EXECUTION.
CAPTAIN SHURA!! HURRY!
OKAAAY!
AS YOU CAN SEE, I'M THE ORDER'S DOG.
I CAN'T OPENLY CROSS THEM.
SO I'M COUNTING ON YOU!
THE REST IS UP TO YOUR JUDGMENT!
PG

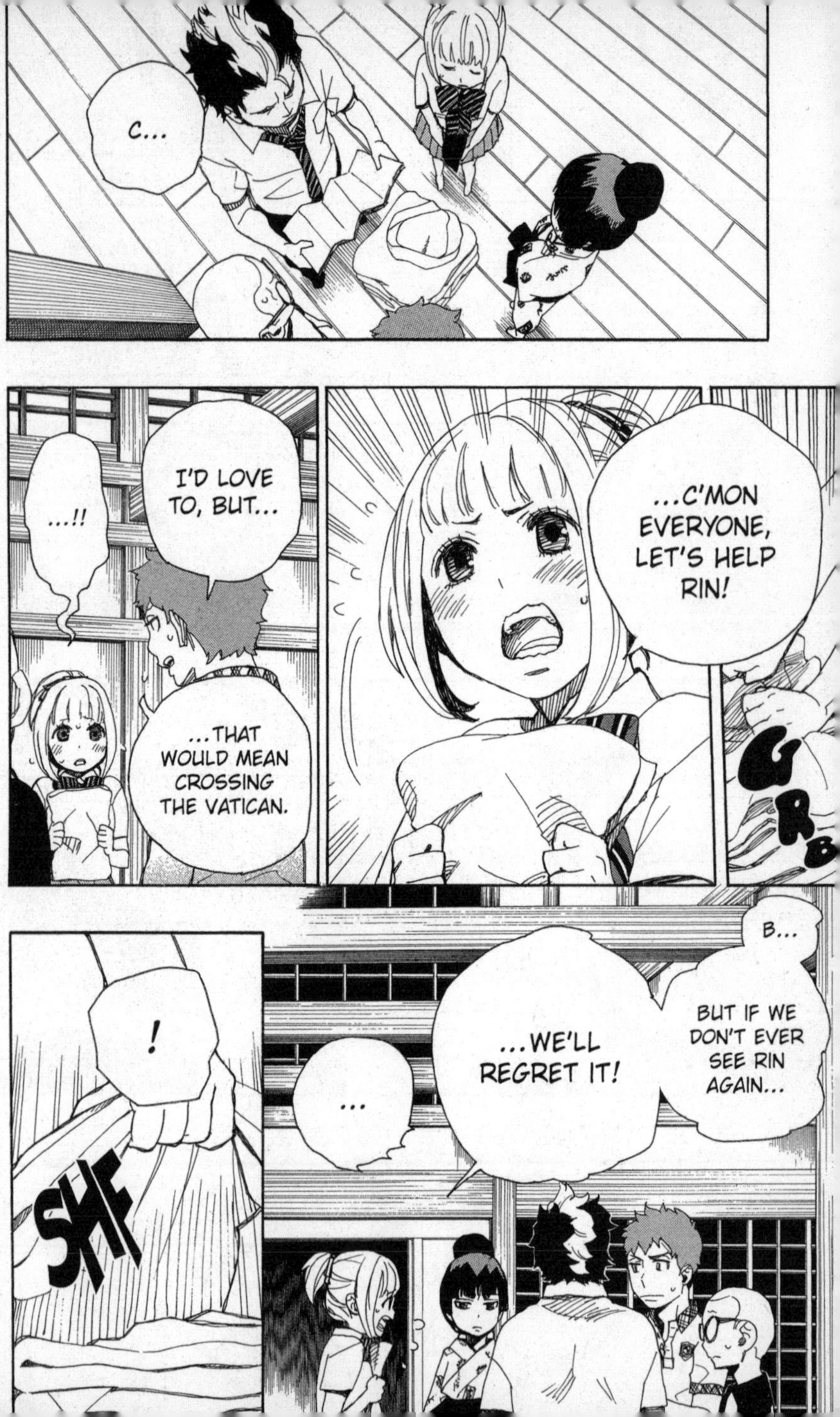
C...
GRB
...C'MON EVERYONE, LET'S HELP RIN!
I'D LOVE TO, BUT...
...!!
...THAT WOULD MEAN CROSSING THE VATICAN.
B...
BUT IF WE DON'T EVER SEE RIN AGAIN...
...WE'LL REGRET IT!
...
!
SHF

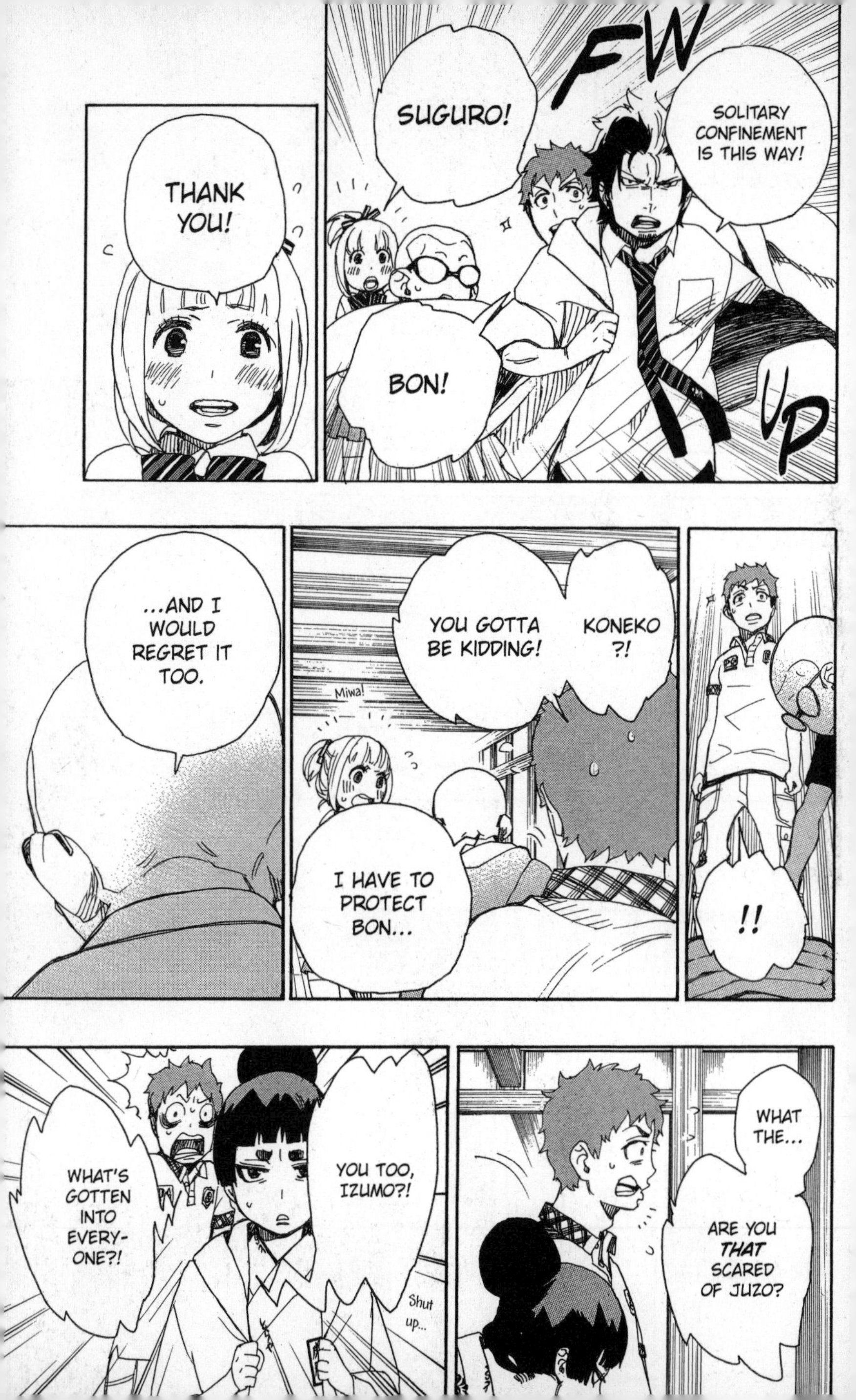
FW
SOLITARY CONFINEMENT IS THIS WAY!
SUGURO!
BON!
UP
THANK YOU!
!!
KONEKO?!
YOU GOTTA BE KIDDING!
Miwa!
I HAVE TO PROTECT BON...
...AND I WOULD REGRET IT TOO.
WHAT THE...
ARE YOU *THAT* SCARED OF JUZO?
YOU TOO, IZUMO?!
Shut up...
WHAT'S GOTTEN INTO EVERYONE?!

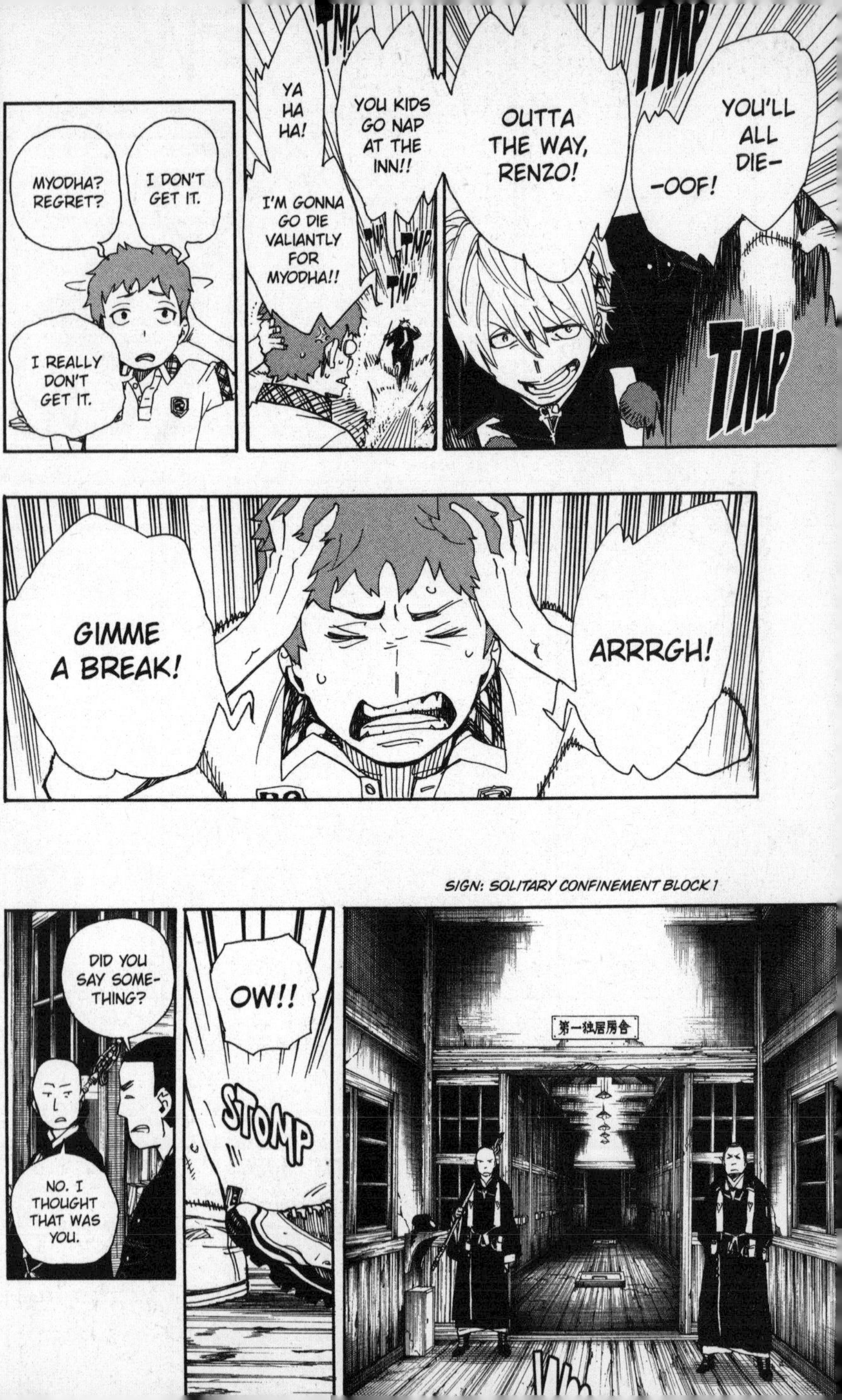
TMP
YOU'LL ALL DIE-
-OOF!
OUTTA THE WAY, RENZO!
TMP
YOU KIDS GO NAP AT THE INN!!
YA HA HA!
I'M GONNA GO DIE VALIANTLY FOR MYODHA!!
TMP TMP TMP
I DON'T GET IT.
MYODHA? REGRET?
I REALLY DON'T GET IT.
ARRRGH!
GIMME A BREAK!
SIGN: SOLITARY CONFINEMENT BLOCK 1
第一独居房舎
OW!!
STOMP
DID YOU SAY SOME-THING?
NO. I THOUGHT THAT WAS YOU.

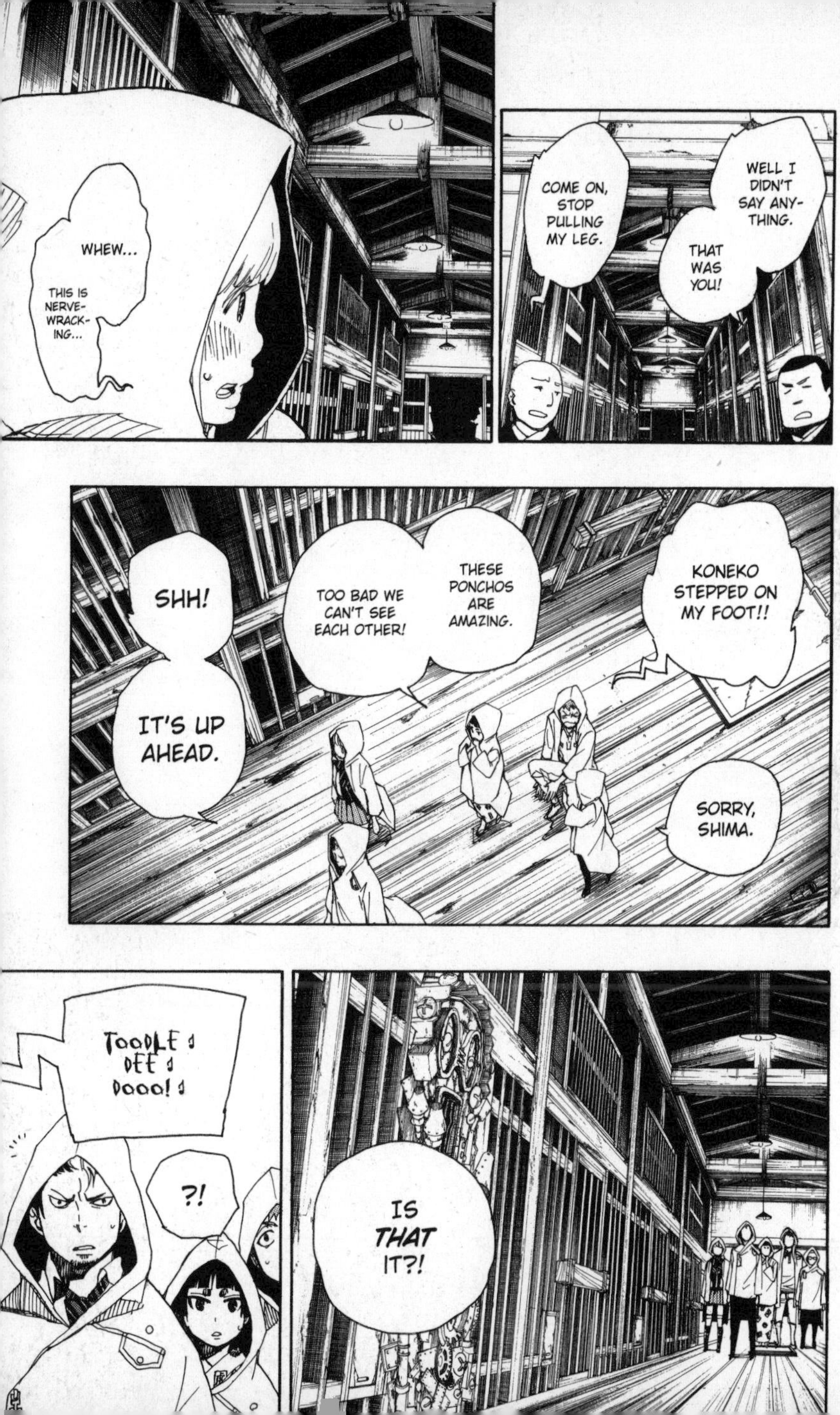
WELL I DIDN'T SAY ANYTHING.
THAT WAS YOU!
COME ON, STOP PULLING MY LEG.
WHEW...
THIS IS NERVE-WRACKING...
KONEKO STEPPED ON MY FOOT!!
SORRY, SHIMA.
THESE PONCHOS ARE AMAZING.
TOO BAD WE CAN'T SEE EACH OTHER!
SHH!
IT'S UP AHEAD.
IS THAT IT?!
TOODLE ♪ DEE ♪ DOOO! ♪
?!

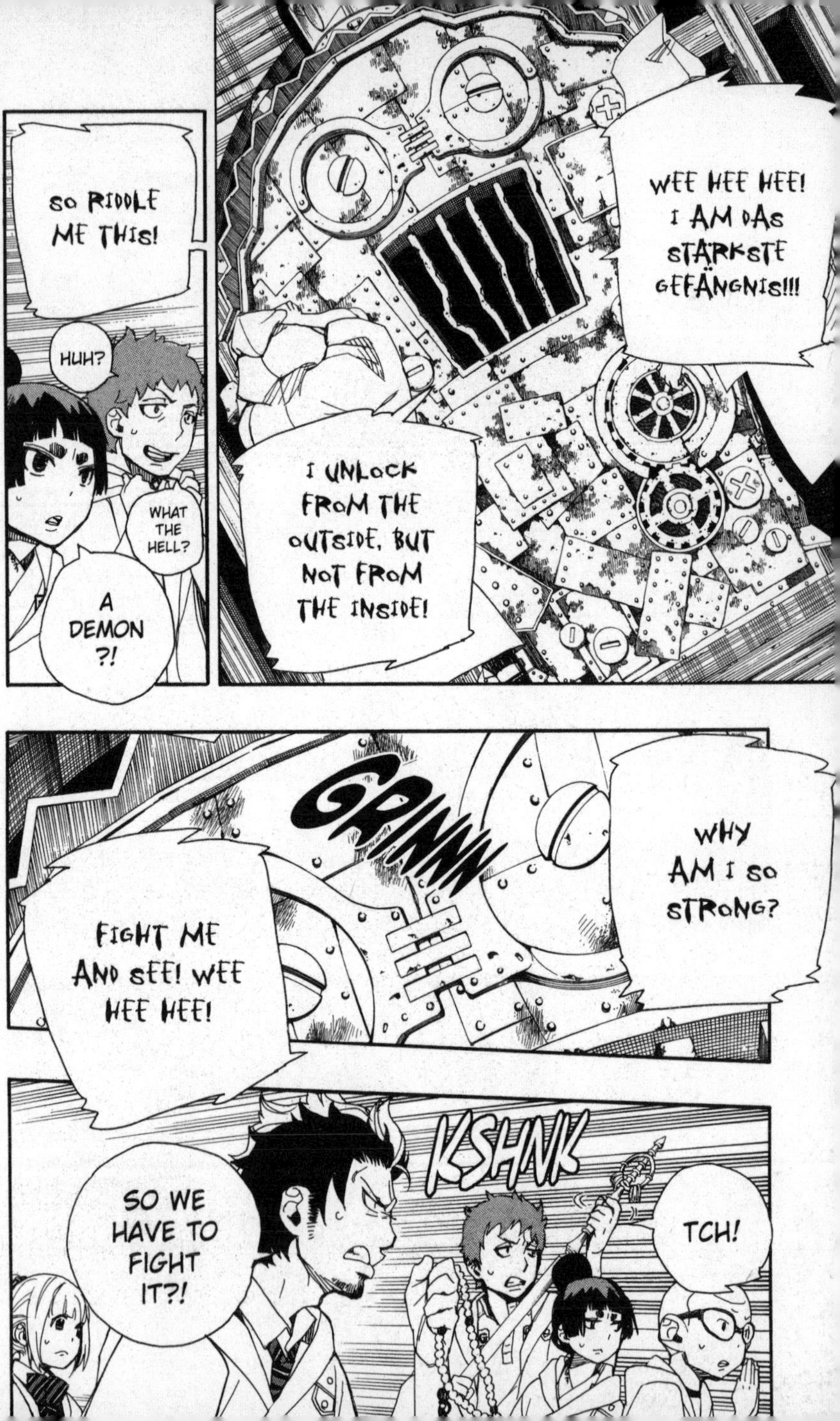
WEE HEE HEE! I AM DAS STÄRKSTE GEFÄNGNIS!!!
I UNLOCK FROM THE OUTSIDE, BUT NOT FROM THE INSIDE!
SO RIDDLE ME THIS!
HUH?
WHAT THE HELL?
A DEMON?!
WHY AM I SO STRONG?
GRINNN
FIGHT ME AND SEE! WEE HEE HEE!
KSHNK
TCH!
SO WE HAVE TO FIGHT IT?!

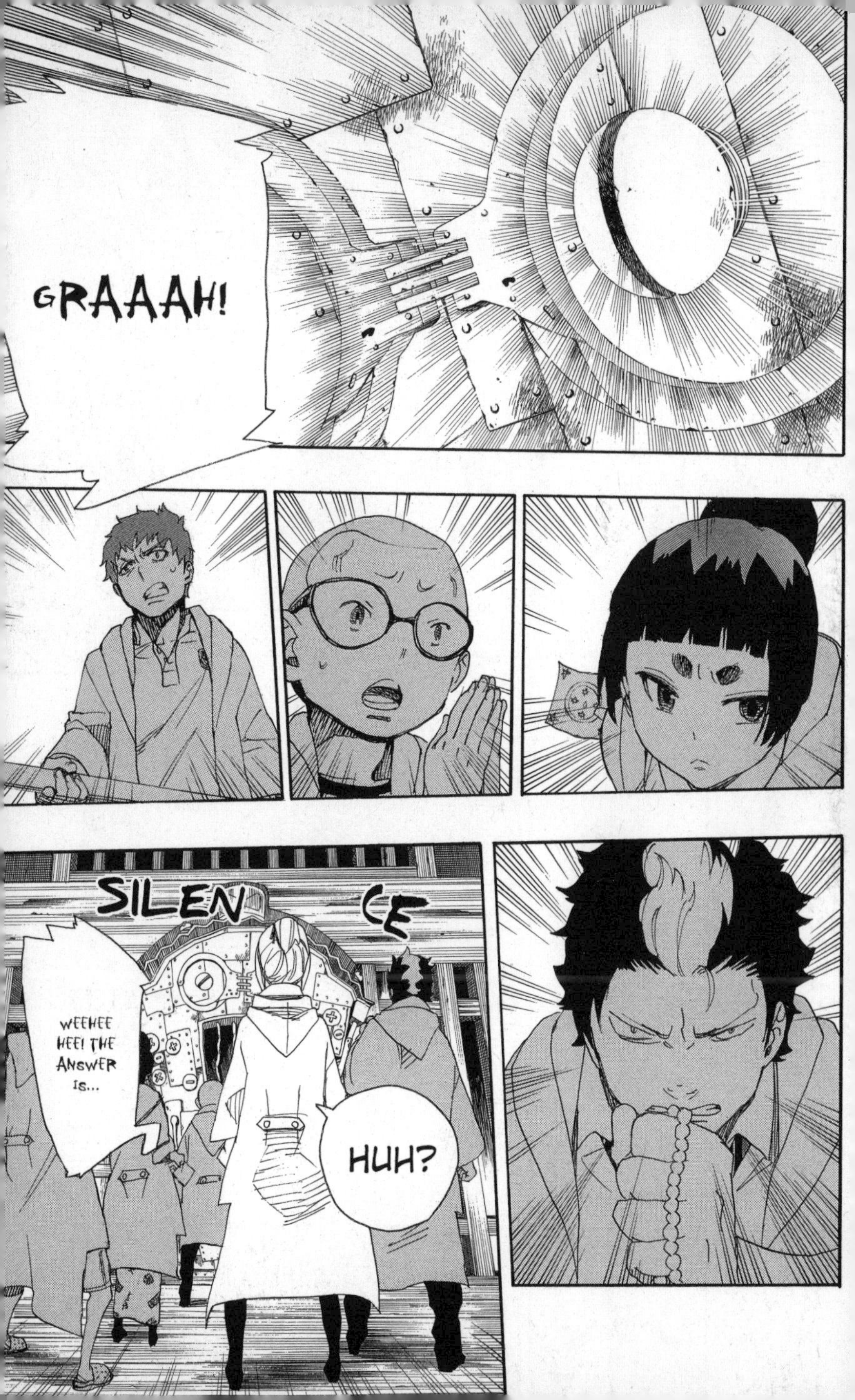
GRAAAH!
SILEN CE
HUH?
WEEHEE HEE! THE ANSWER IS...

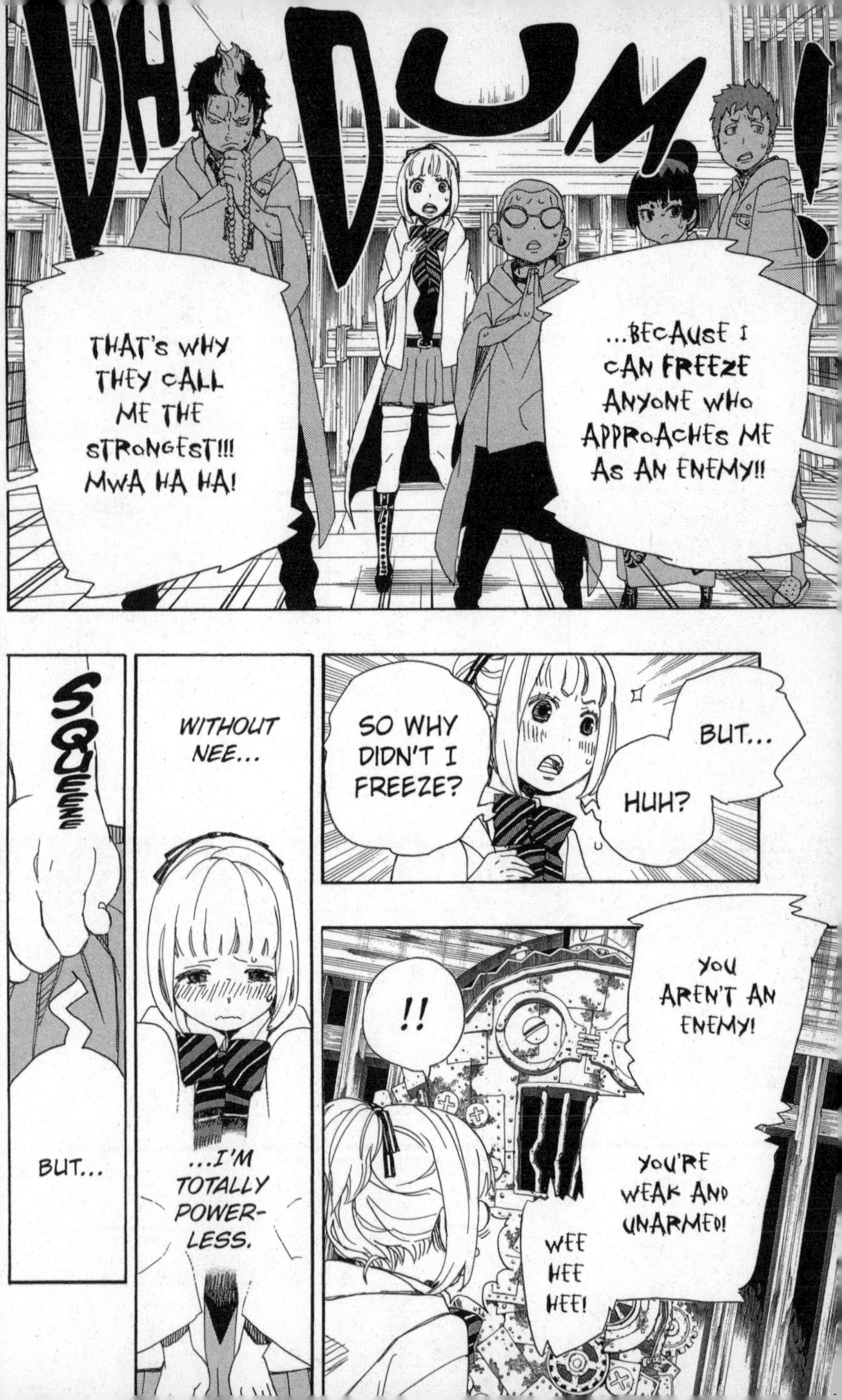
VH DUM!!
...BECAUSE I CAN FREEZE ANYONE WHO APPROACHES ME AS AN ENEMY!!
THAT'S WHY THEY CALL ME THE STRONGEST!!! MWA HA HA!
BUT...
HUH?
SO WHY DIDN'T I FREEZE?
YOU AREN'T AN ENEMY!
!!
YOU'RE WEAK AND UNARMED!
WEE HEE HEE!
WITHOUT NEE...
...I'M TOTALLY POWERLESS.
SQUEEZE
BUT...

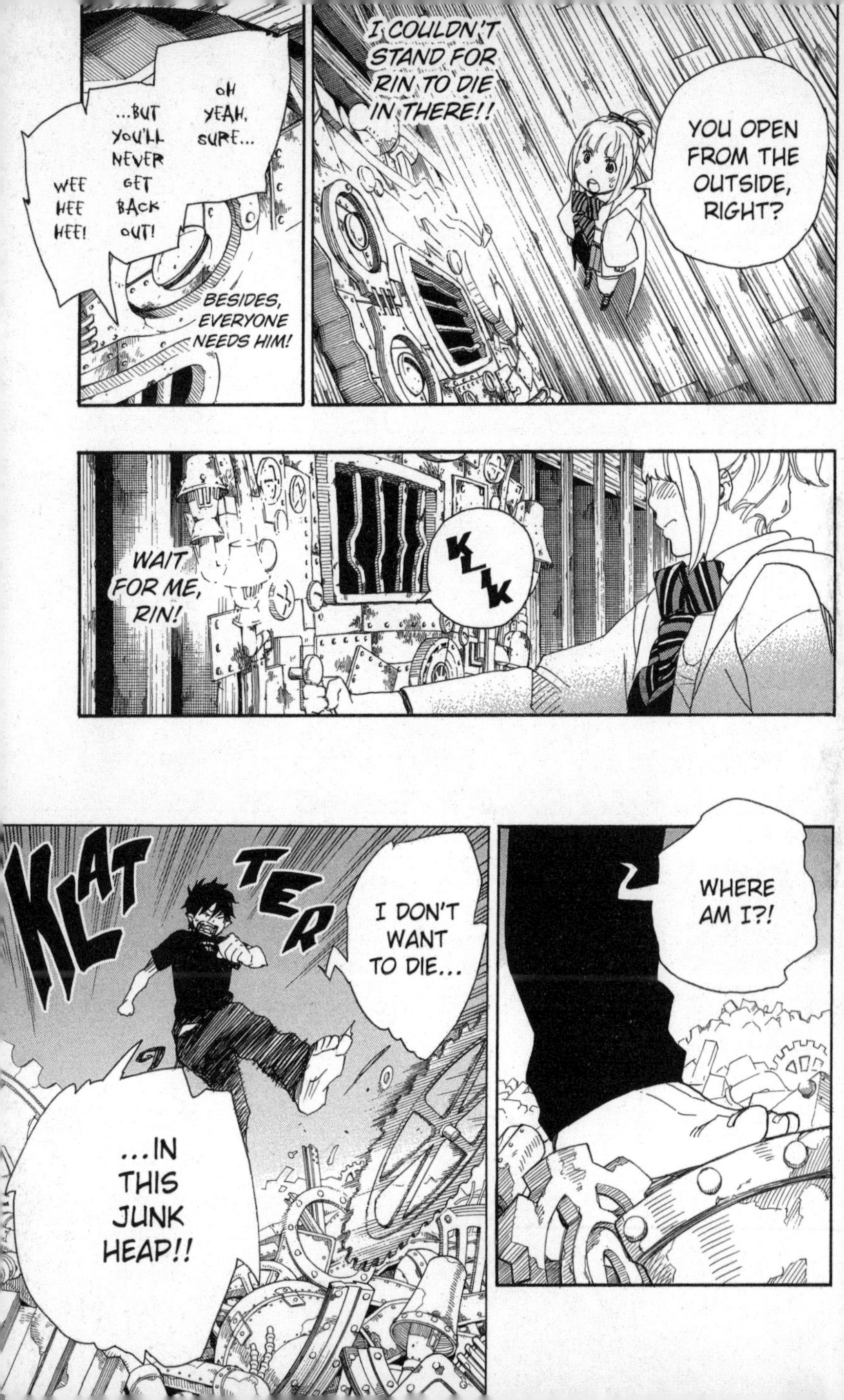
YOU OPEN FROM THE OUTSIDE, RIGHT?
I COULDN'T STAND FOR RIN TO DIE IN THERE!!
OH YEAH, SURE... ...BUT YOU'LL NEVER GET BACK OUT! WEE HEE HEE!
BESIDES, EVERYONE NEEDS HIM!
KLIK
WAIT FOR ME, RIN!
WHERE AM I?!
KLATTER
I DON'T WANT TO DIE...
...IN THIS JUNK HEAP!!

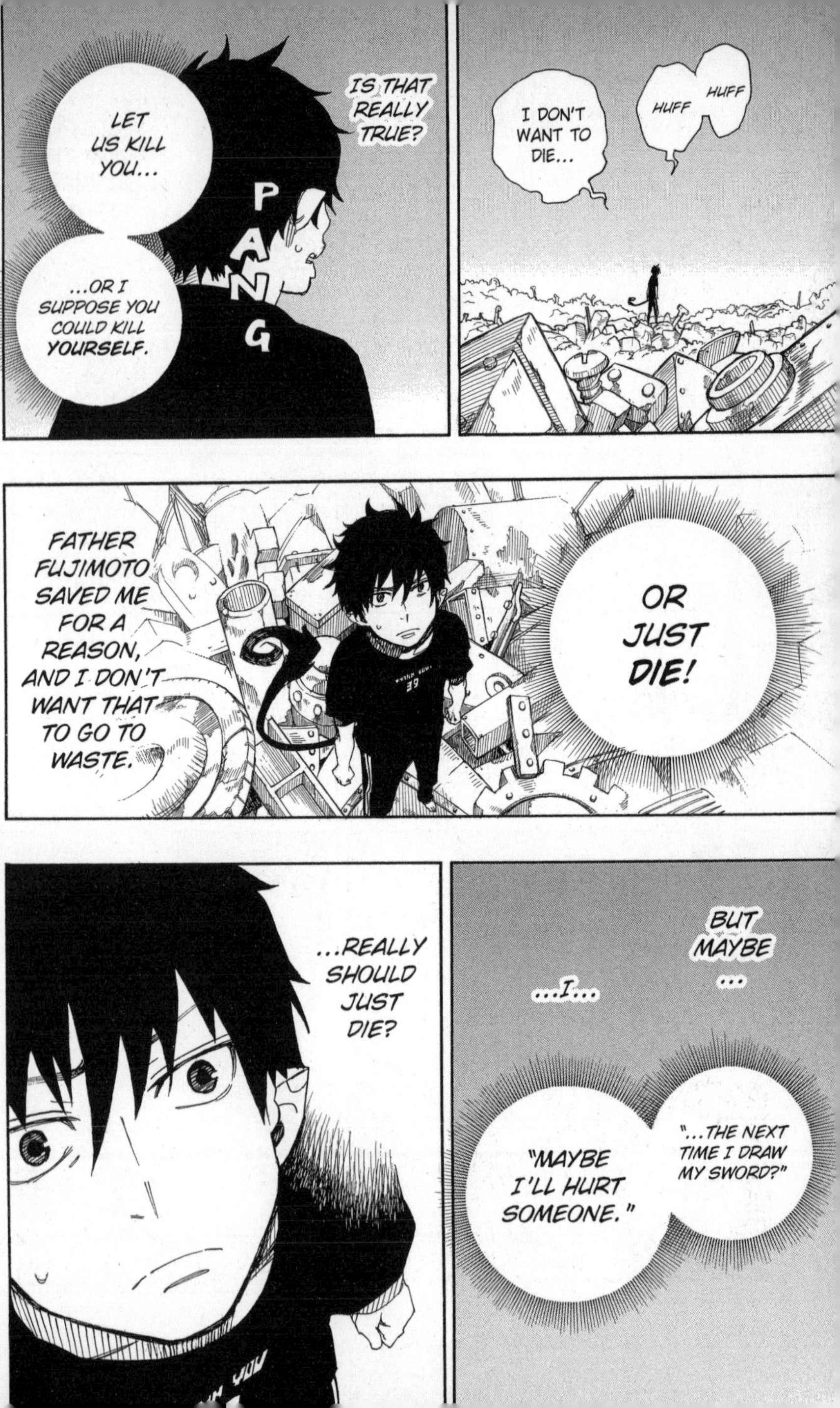
HUFF HUFF
I DON'T WANT TO DIE...
IS THAT REALLY TRUE?
LET US KILL YOU...
PANG
...OR I SUPPOSE YOU COULD KILL YOURSELF.
OR JUST DIE!
FATHER FUJIMOTO SAVED ME FOR A REASON, AND I DON'T WANT THAT TO GO TO WASTE.
BUT MAYBE ...
...I...
"...THE NEXT TIME I DRAW MY SWORD?"
"MAYBE I'LL HURT SOMEONE."
...REALLY SHOULD JUST DIE?

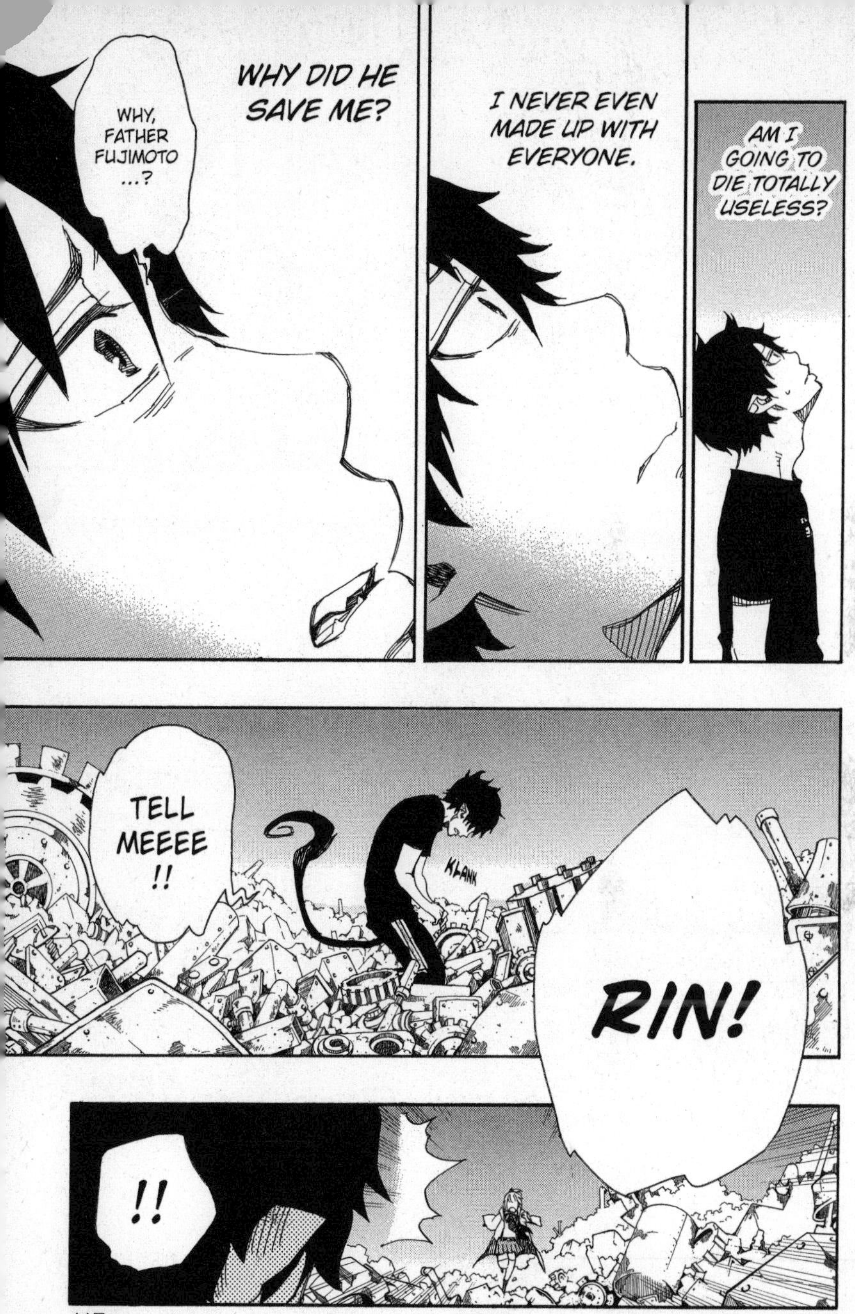
AM I GOING TO DIE TOTALLY USELESS?
I NEVER EVEN MADE UP WITH EVERYONE.
WHY DID HE SAVE ME?
WHY, FATHER FUJIMOTO ...?
TELL MEEEE !!
KLANK
RIN!
!!

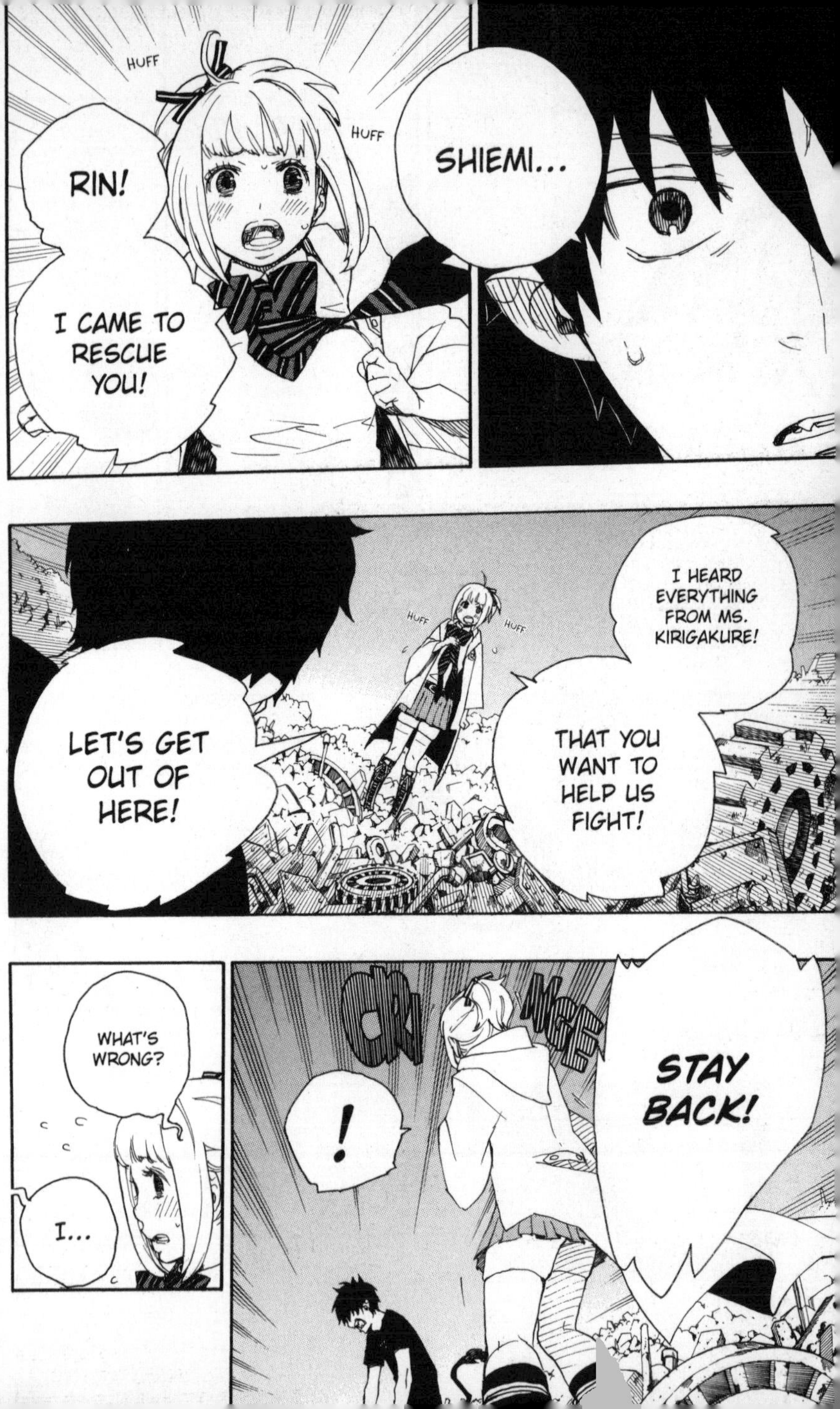
SHIEMI...
HUFF
HUFF
RIN!
I CAME TO RESCUE YOU!
I HEARD EVERYTHING FROM MS. KIRIGAKURE!
THAT YOU WANT TO HELP US FIGHT!
HUFF
HUFF
LET'S GET OUT OF HERE!
STAY BACK!
CRINGE
!
WHAT'S WRONG?
I...

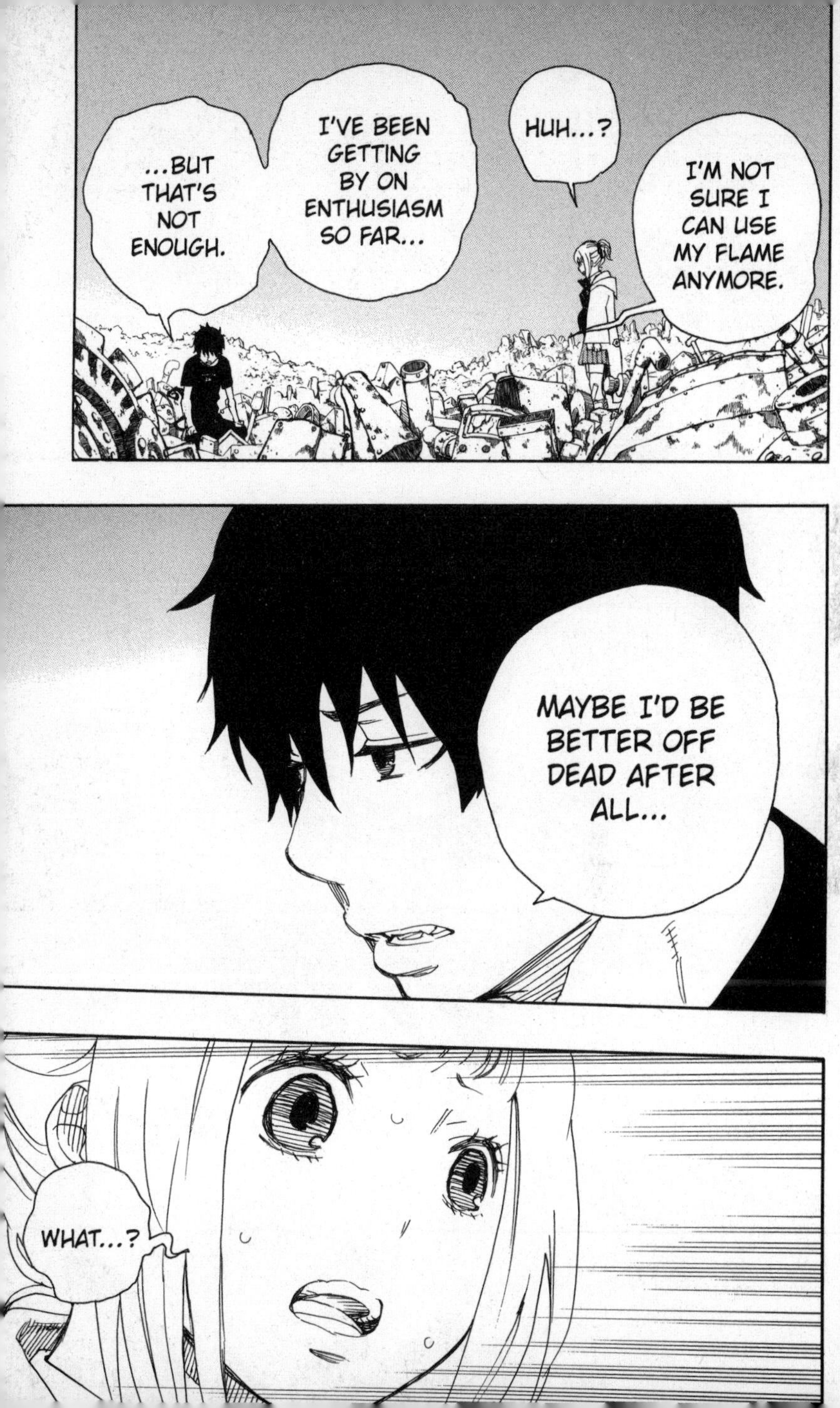
I'M NOT SURE I CAN USE MY FLAME ANYMORE.
HUH...?
I'VE BEEN GETTING BY ON ENTHUSIASM SO FAR...
...BUT THAT'S NOT ENOUGH.
MAYBE I'D BE BETTER OFF DEAD AFTER ALL...
WHAT...?

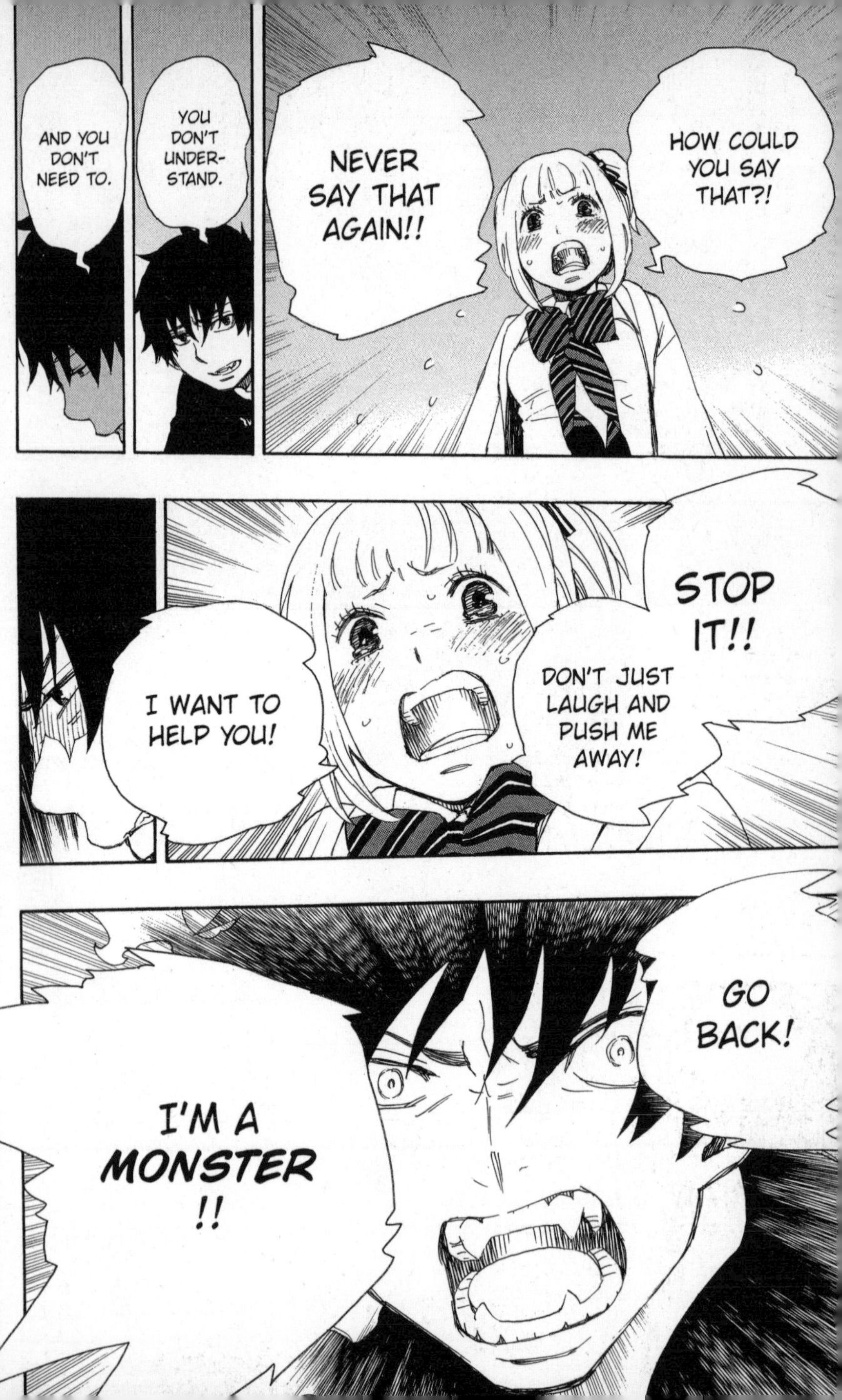
HOW COULD YOU SAY THAT?!
NEVER SAY THAT AGAIN!!
YOU DON'T UNDER-STAND.
AND YOU DON'T NEED TO.
STOP IT!!
DON'T JUST LAUGH AND PUSH ME AWAY!
I WANT TO HELP YOU!
GO BACK!
I'M A MONSTER!!

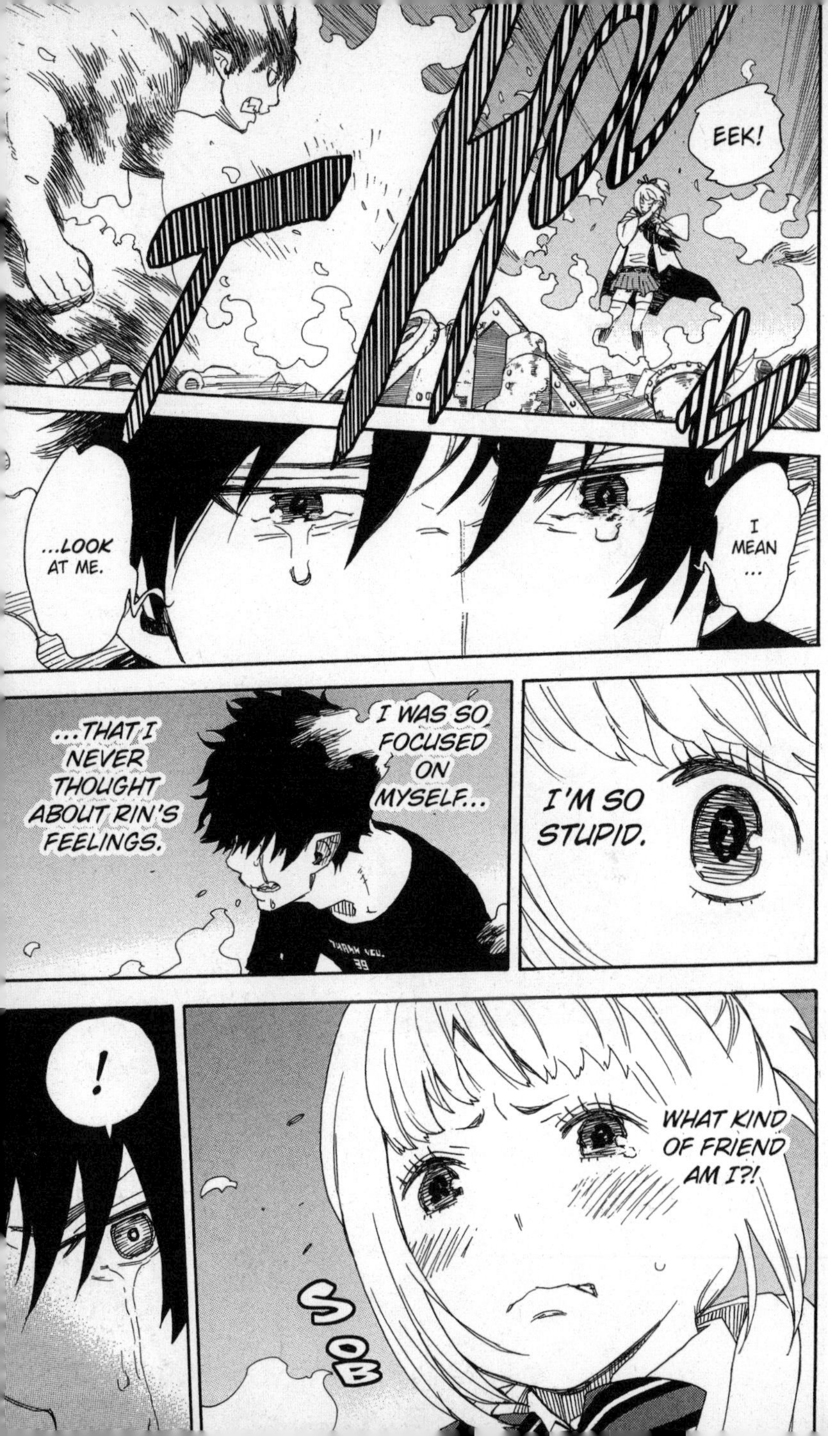
EEK!
I MEAN...
...LOOK AT ME.
I'M SO STUPID.
I WAS SO FOCUSED ON MYSELF...
...THAT I NEVER THOUGHT ABOUT RIN'S FEELINGS.
WHAT KIND OF FRIEND AM I?!
SOB
!

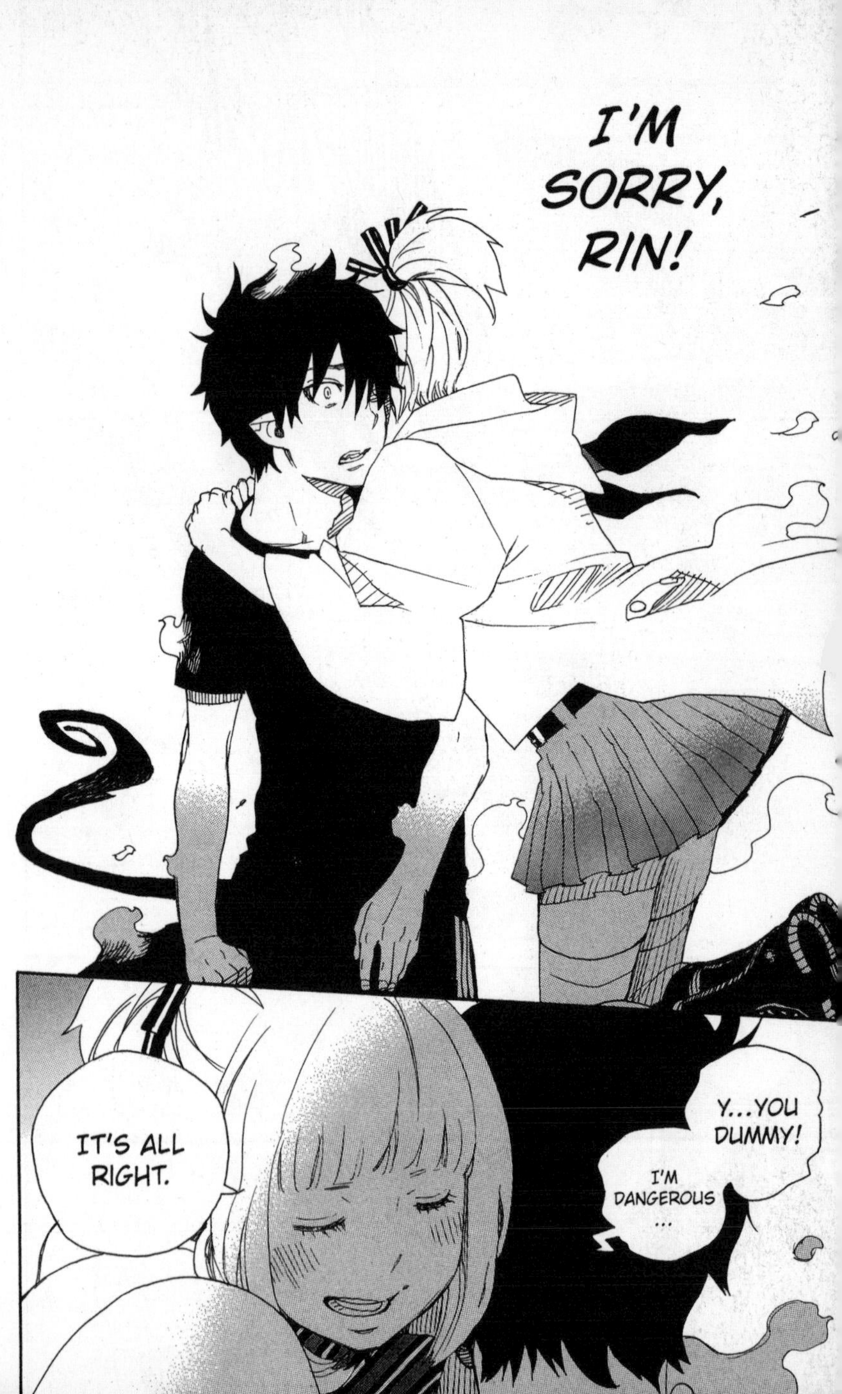
I'M SORRY, RIN!
Y...YOU DUMMY!
I'M DANGEROUS ...
IT'S ALL RIGHT.

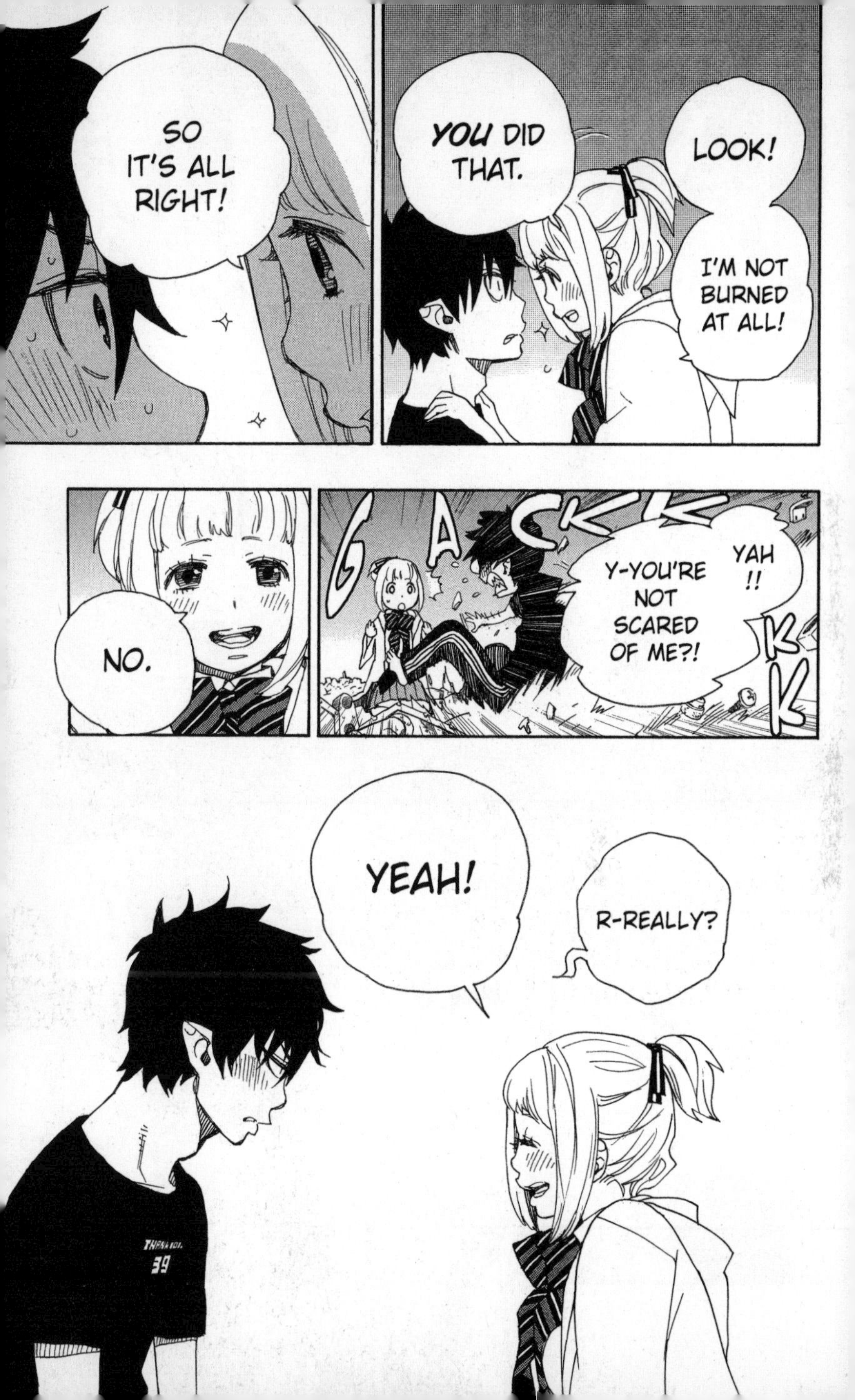
LOOK!
I'M NOT BURNED AT ALL!
YOU DID THAT.
SO IT'S ALL RIGHT!
YAH!!
Y-YOU'RE NOT SCARED OF ME?!
GACKKKK
NO.
R-REALLY?
YEAH!

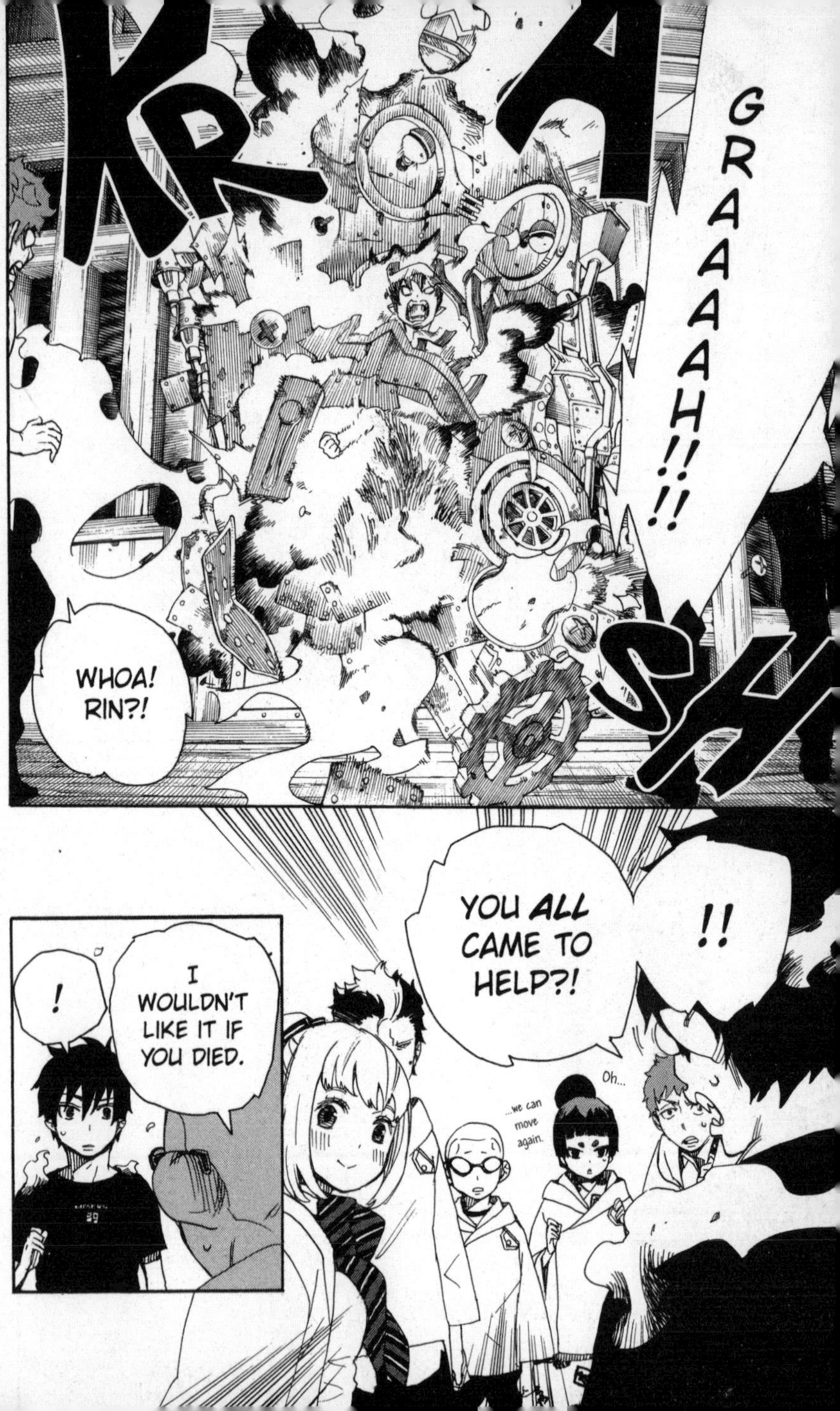
KRA
GRAAAAH!!!
SH
WHOA! RIN?!
!!
YOU *ALL* CAME TO HELP?!
Oh...
...we can move again.
I WOULDN'T LIKE IT IF YOU DIED.
!

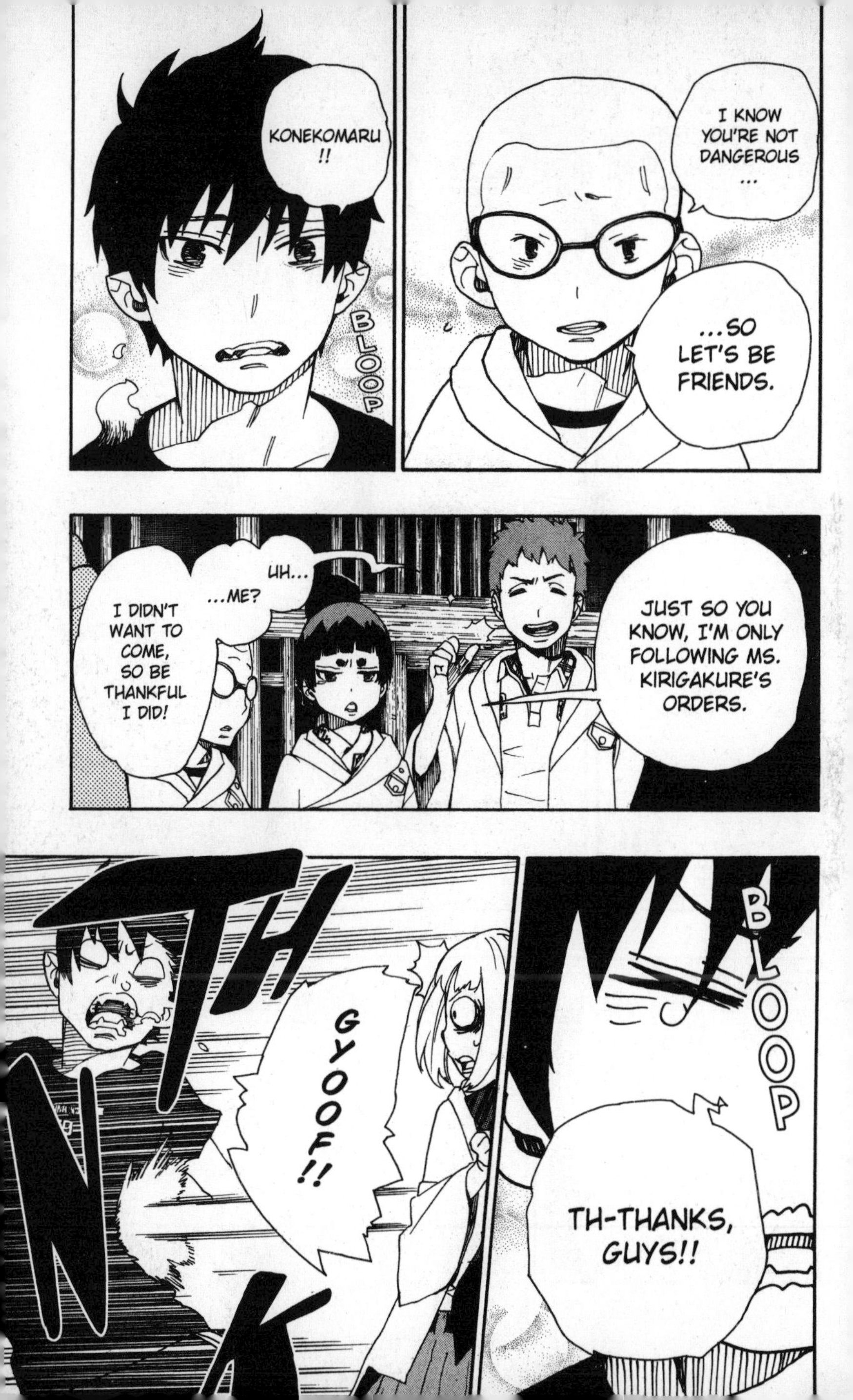
I KNOW YOU'RE NOT DANGEROUS ...
...SO LET'S BE FRIENDS.
KONEKOMARU !!
BLOOP
JUST SO YOU KNOW, I'M ONLY FOLLOWING MS. KIRIGAKURE'S ORDERS.
UH...
...ME?
I DIDN'T WANT TO COME, SO BE THANKFUL I DID!
BLOOP
TH-THANKS, GUYS!!
GYOOOF!!

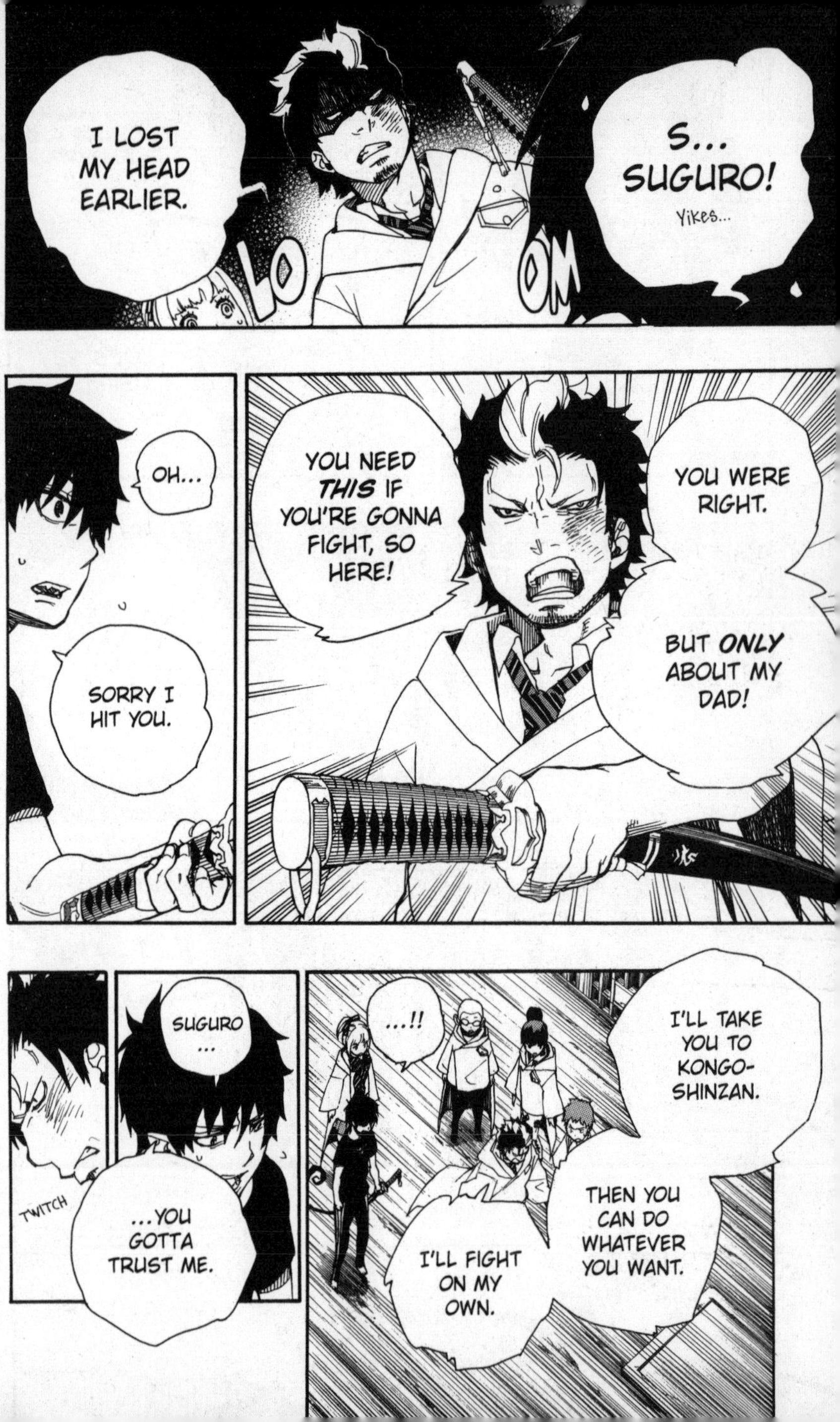
S... SUGURO!
Yikes...
I LOST MY HEAD EARLIER.
LO OM
YOU WERE RIGHT.
BUT ONLY ABOUT MY DAD!
YOU NEED THIS IF YOU'RE GONNA FIGHT, SO HERE!
OH...
SORRY I HIT YOU.
I'LL TAKE YOU TO KONGO-SHINZAN.
THEN YOU CAN DO WHATEVER YOU WANT.
I'LL FIGHT ON MY OWN.
...!!
SUGURO ...
...YOU GOTTA TRUST ME.
TWITCH

SO PLEASE TRUST ME!!

I CAN'T HELP IT THAT I'M SATAN'S CHILD...

...BUT I'LL USE MY FLAME FOR US!

?!

WHO CARES ABOUT THAT!!

...IS HOW YOU TAKE EVERYTHING ON YOUR-SELF.

WHAT I CAN'T FORGIVE...

WHY SHOULD I TRUST A GUY LIKE THAT?

YOU'RE THE ONE WHO PUSHED US AWAY!

!

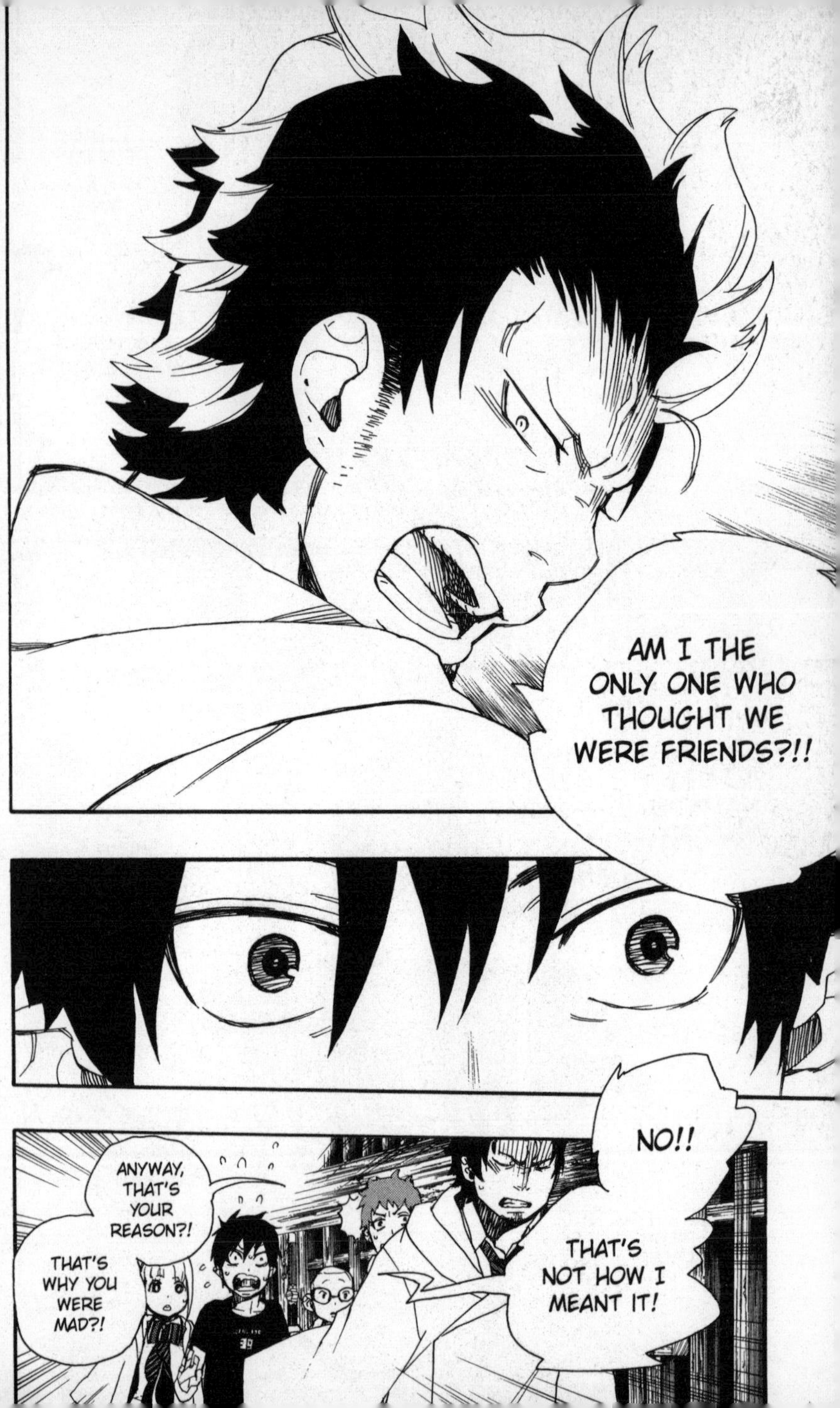
AM I THE ONLY ONE WHO THOUGHT WE WERE FRIENDS?!!
NO!!
THAT'S NOT HOW I MEANT IT!
ANYWAY, THAT'S YOUR REASON?!
THAT'S WHY YOU WERE MAD?!

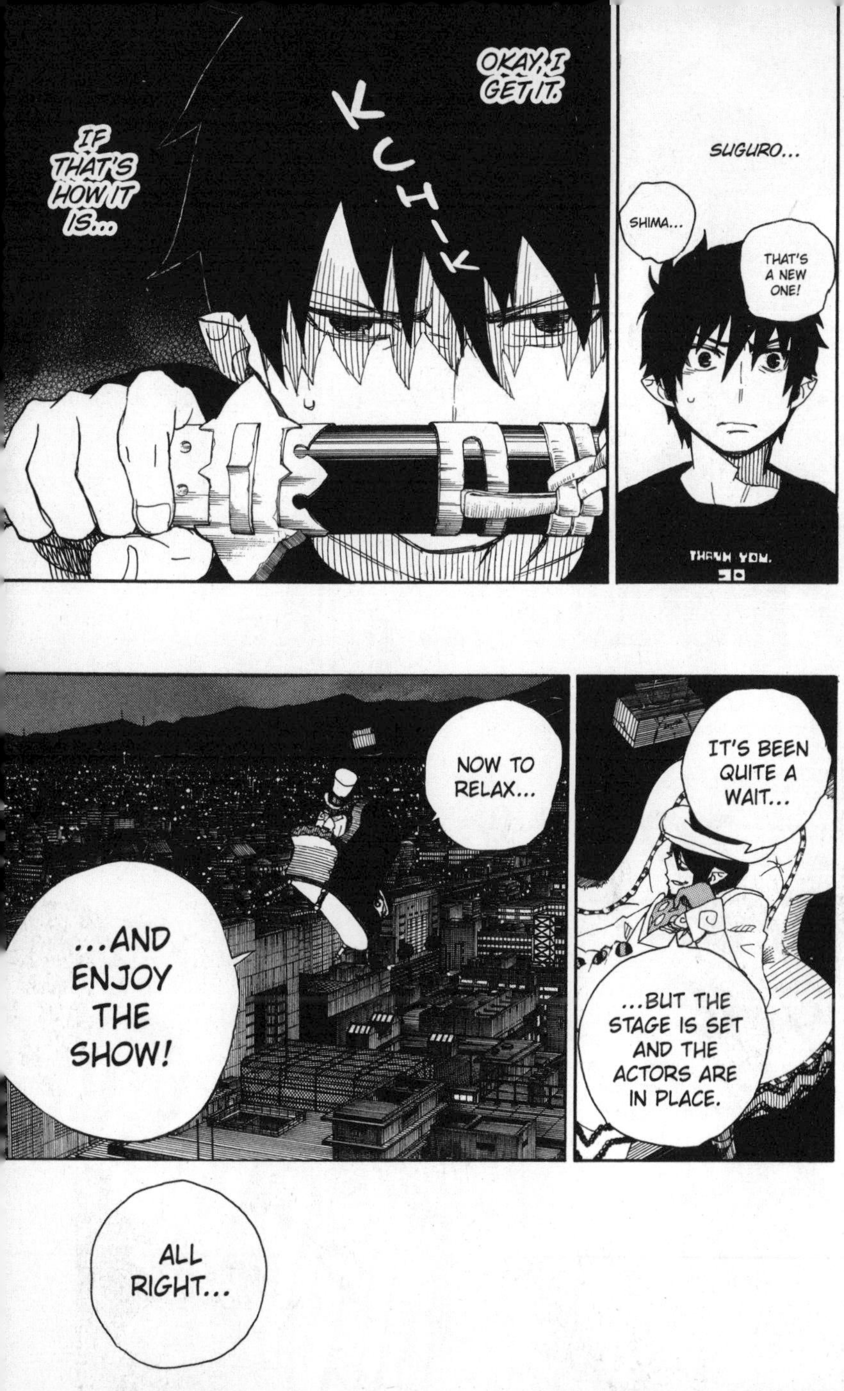
SUGURO...
SHIMA...
THAT'S A NEW ONE!
OKAY, I GET IT.
KUCHIK
IF THAT'S HOW IT IS...
IT'S BEEN QUITE A WAIT...
...BUT THE STAGE IS SET AND THE ACTORS ARE IN PLACE.
NOW TO RELAX...
...AND ENJOY THE SHOW!
ALL RIGHT...

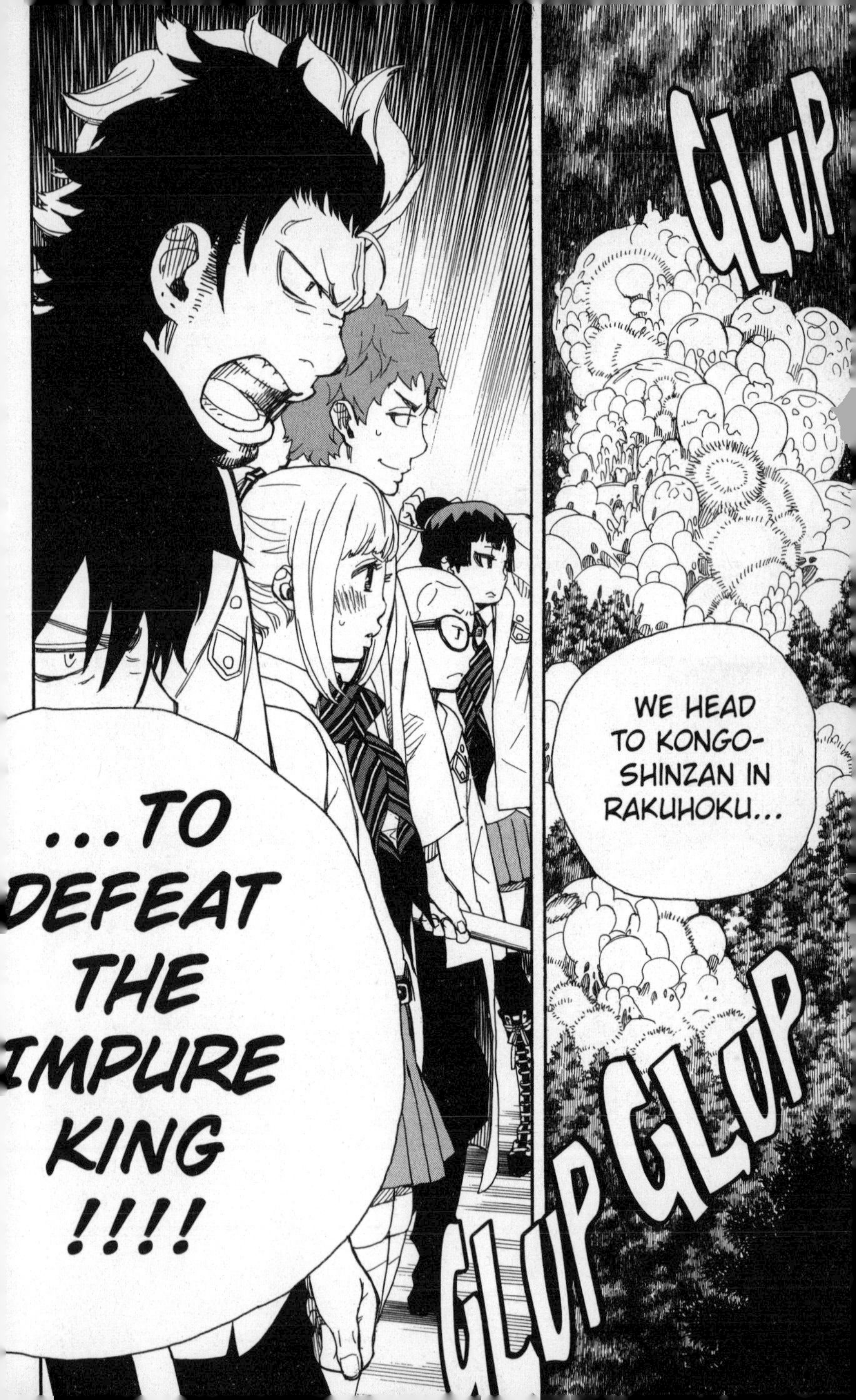
GLUP
WE HEAD TO KONGO-SHINZAN IN RAKUHOKU...
GLUP GLUP
...TO DEFEAT THE IMPURE KING!!!!

...I HAVE TO DO SOMETHING TO PROVE MYSELF!!!!

Blue Exorcist Chapter 26 Fire of the Heart

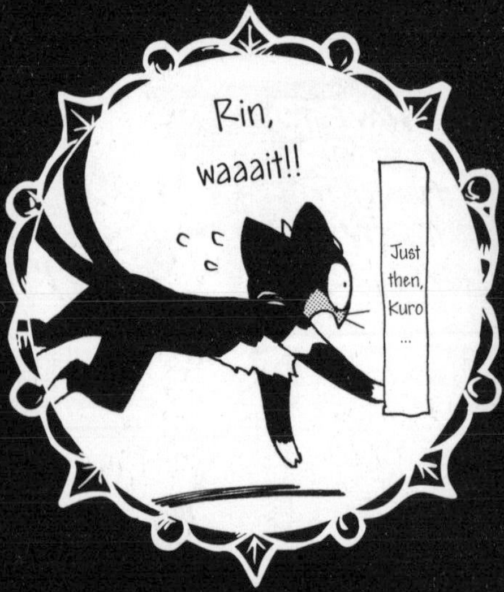

Just then, Kuro ...
Rin, waaait!!

Chapter 27
Battle at Kongo-Shinzan!

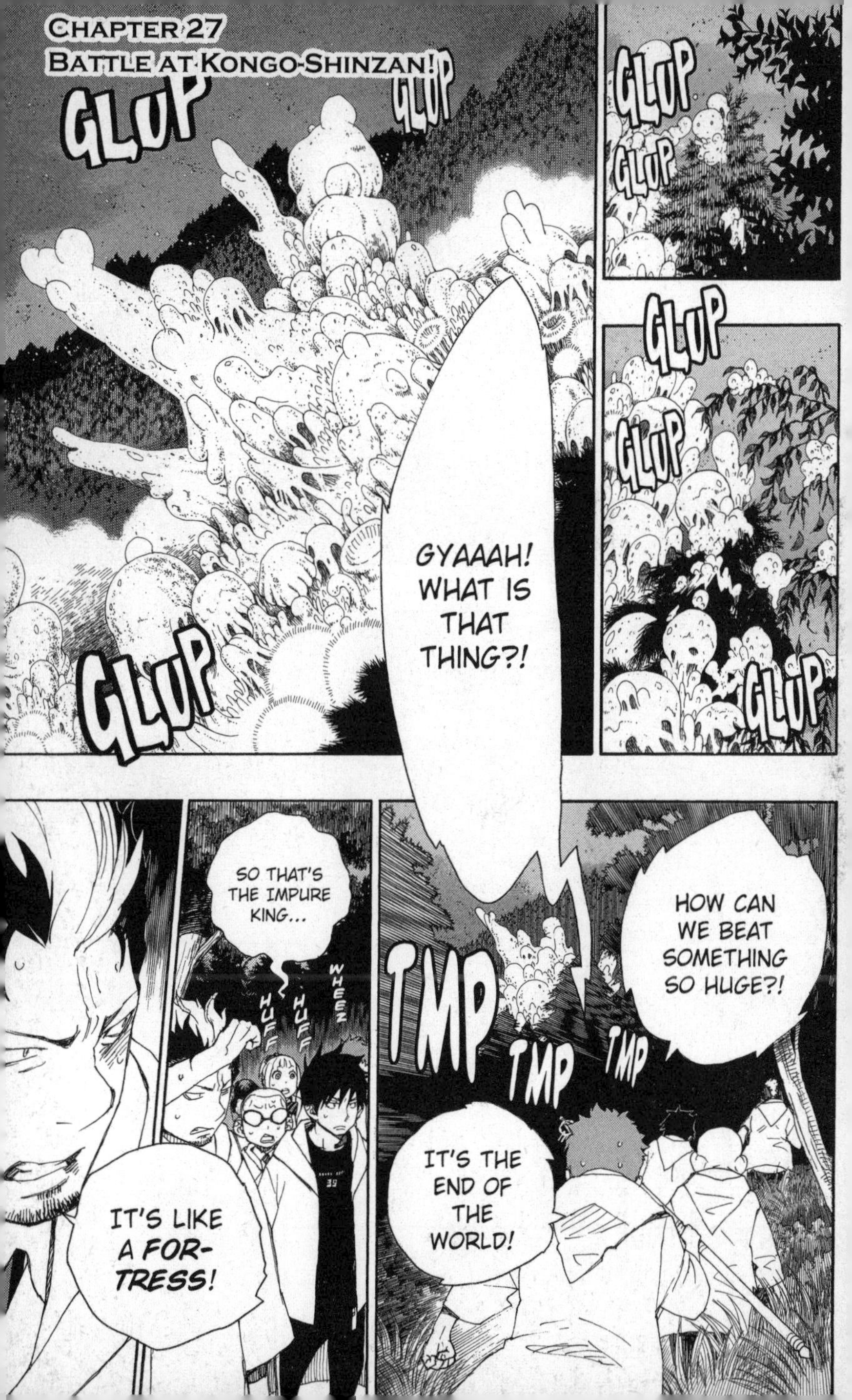
GLUP
GLUP
GLUP
GLUP
GLUP
GLUP
GLUP
GLUP
GYAAAH! WHAT IS THAT THING?!
HOW CAN WE BEAT SOMETHING SO HUGE?!
TMP
TMP
TMP
IT'S THE END OF THE WORLD!
SO THAT'S THE IMPURE KING...
WHEEZ
HUFF
HUFF
IT'S LIKE A FOR-TRESS!

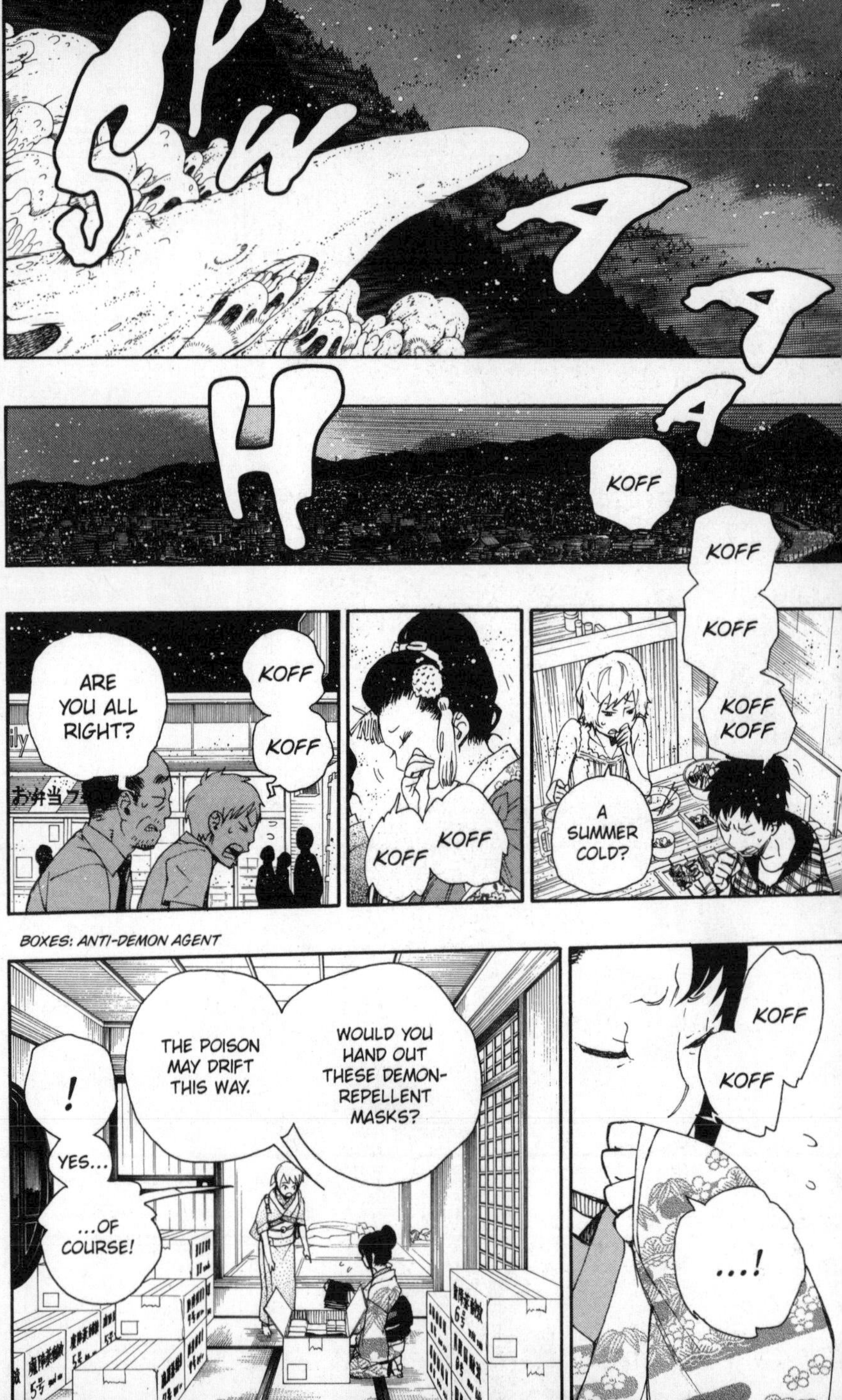
SPWAAAAH
KOFF
KOFF
KOFF
KOFF KOFF
A SUMMER COLD?
KOFF
KOFF
KOFF
KOFF
ARE YOU ALL RIGHT?
BOXES: ANTI-DEMON AGENT
KOFF
KOFF
...!
WOULD YOU HAND OUT THESE DEMON-REPELLENT MASKS?
THE POISON MAY DRIFT THIS WAY.
!
YES...
...OF COURSE!

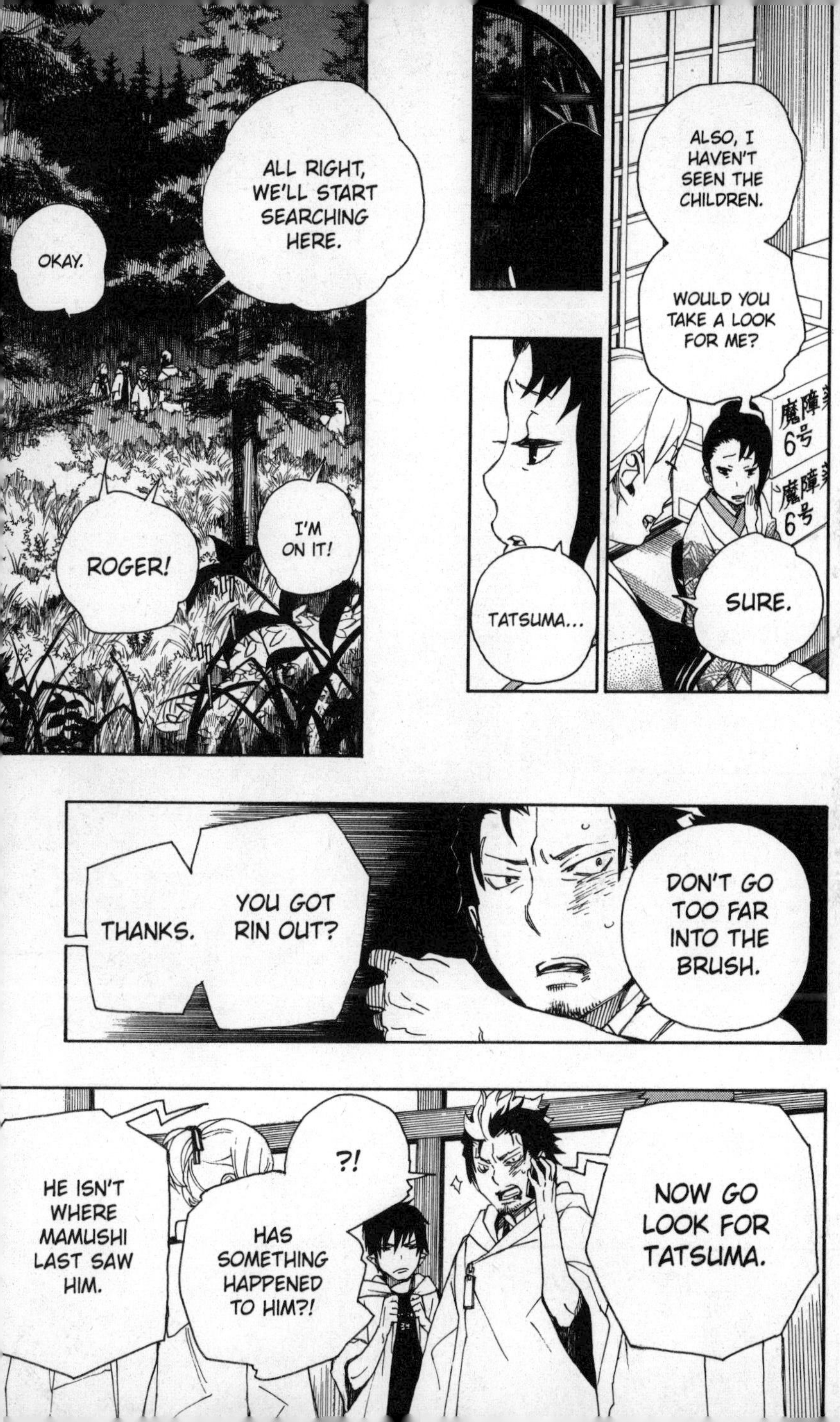
ALSO, I HAVEN'T SEEN THE CHILDREN.
WOULD YOU TAKE A LOOK FOR ME?
SURE.
TATSUMA...
ALL RIGHT, WE'LL START SEARCHING HERE.
OKAY.
I'M ON IT!
ROGER!
DON'T GO TOO FAR INTO THE BRUSH.
YOU GOT RIN OUT?
THANKS.
NOW GO LOOK FOR TATSUMA.
?!
HAS SOMETHING HAPPENED TO HIM?!
HE ISN'T WHERE MAMUSHI LAST SAW HIM.

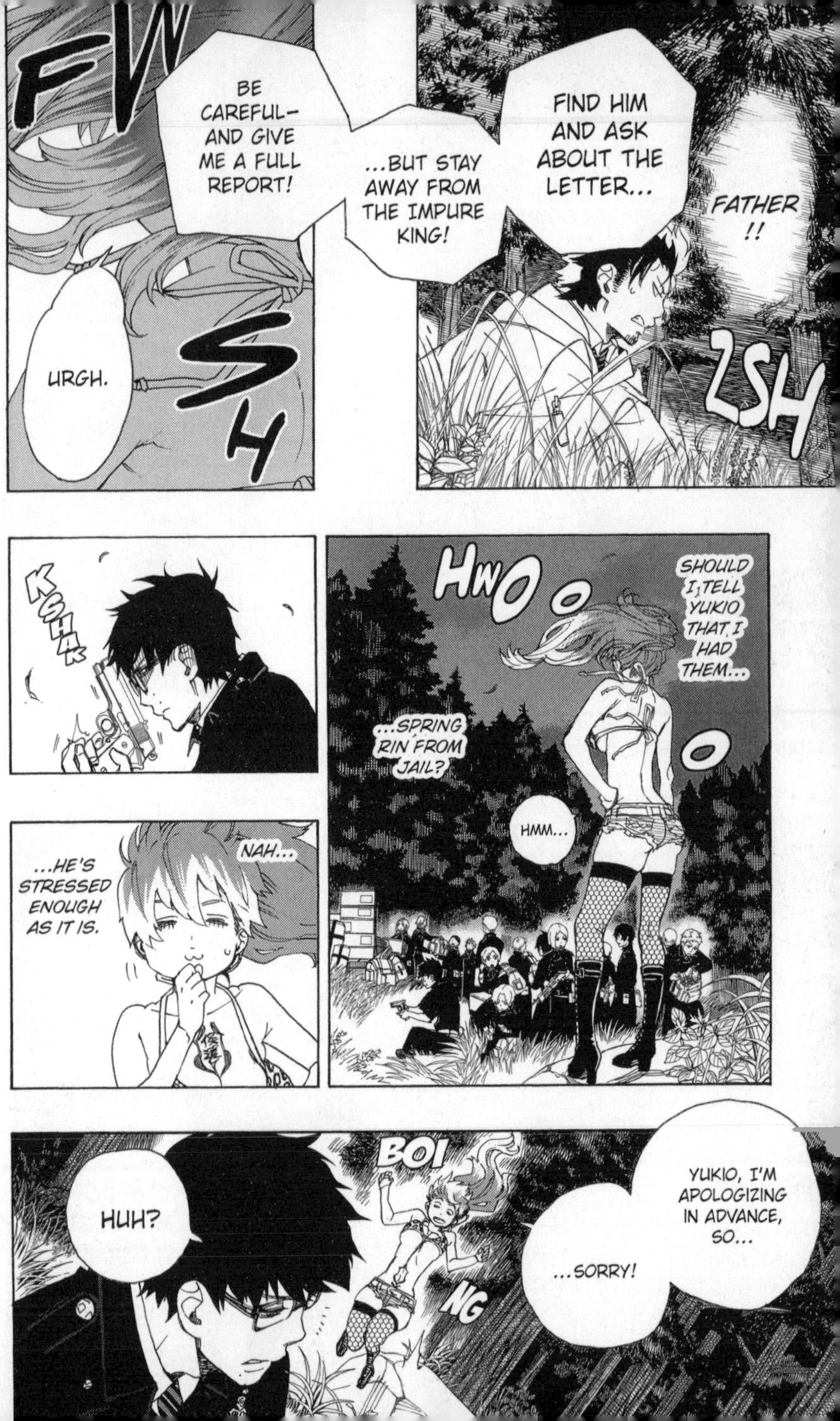
FATHER!!
FIND HIM AND ASK ABOUT THE LETTER...
...BUT STAY AWAY FROM THE IMPURE KING!
ZSH
BE CAREFUL- AND GIVE ME A FULL REPORT!
FW
SH
URGH.
HWOOOO
SHOULD I TELL YUKIO THAT I HAD THEM...
...SPRING RIN FROM JAIL?
HMM...
KSHAK
NAH...
...HE'S STRESSED ENOUGH AS IT IS.
YUKIO, I'M APOLOGIZING IN ADVANCE, SO...
...SORRY!
BOI
NG
HUH?

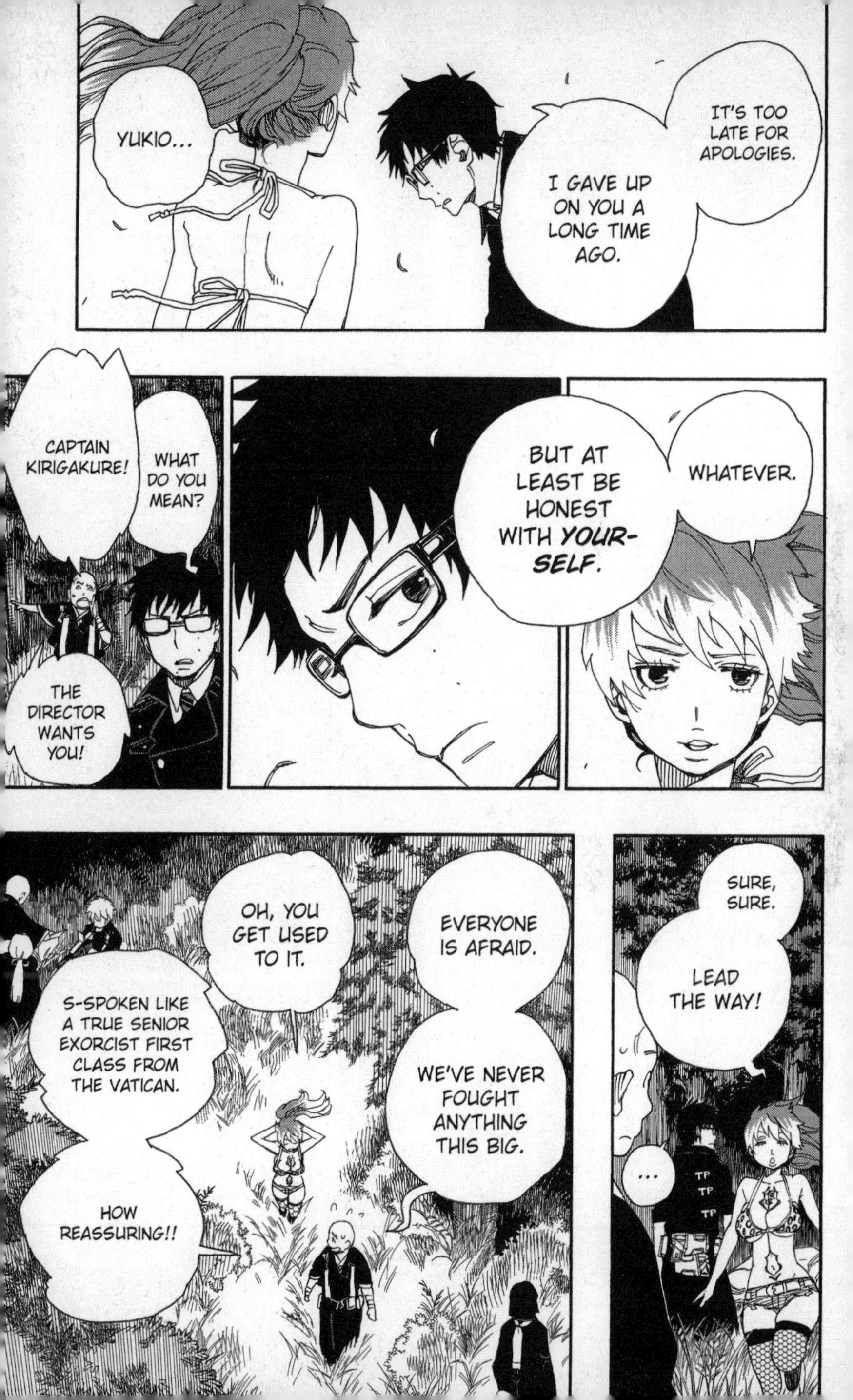
IT'S TOO LATE FOR APOLOGIES.
I GAVE UP ON YOU A LONG TIME AGO.
YUKIO...
WHATEVER.
BUT AT LEAST BE HONEST WITH *YOURSELF*.
WHAT DO YOU MEAN?
CAPTAIN KIRIGAKURE!
THE DIRECTOR WANTS YOU!
SURE, SURE.
LEAD THE WAY!
...
EVERYONE IS AFRAID.
WE'VE NEVER FOUGHT ANYTHING THIS BIG.
OH, YOU GET USED TO IT.
S-SPOKEN LIKE A TRUE SENIOR EXORCIST FIRST CLASS FROM THE VATICAN.
HOW REASSURING!!

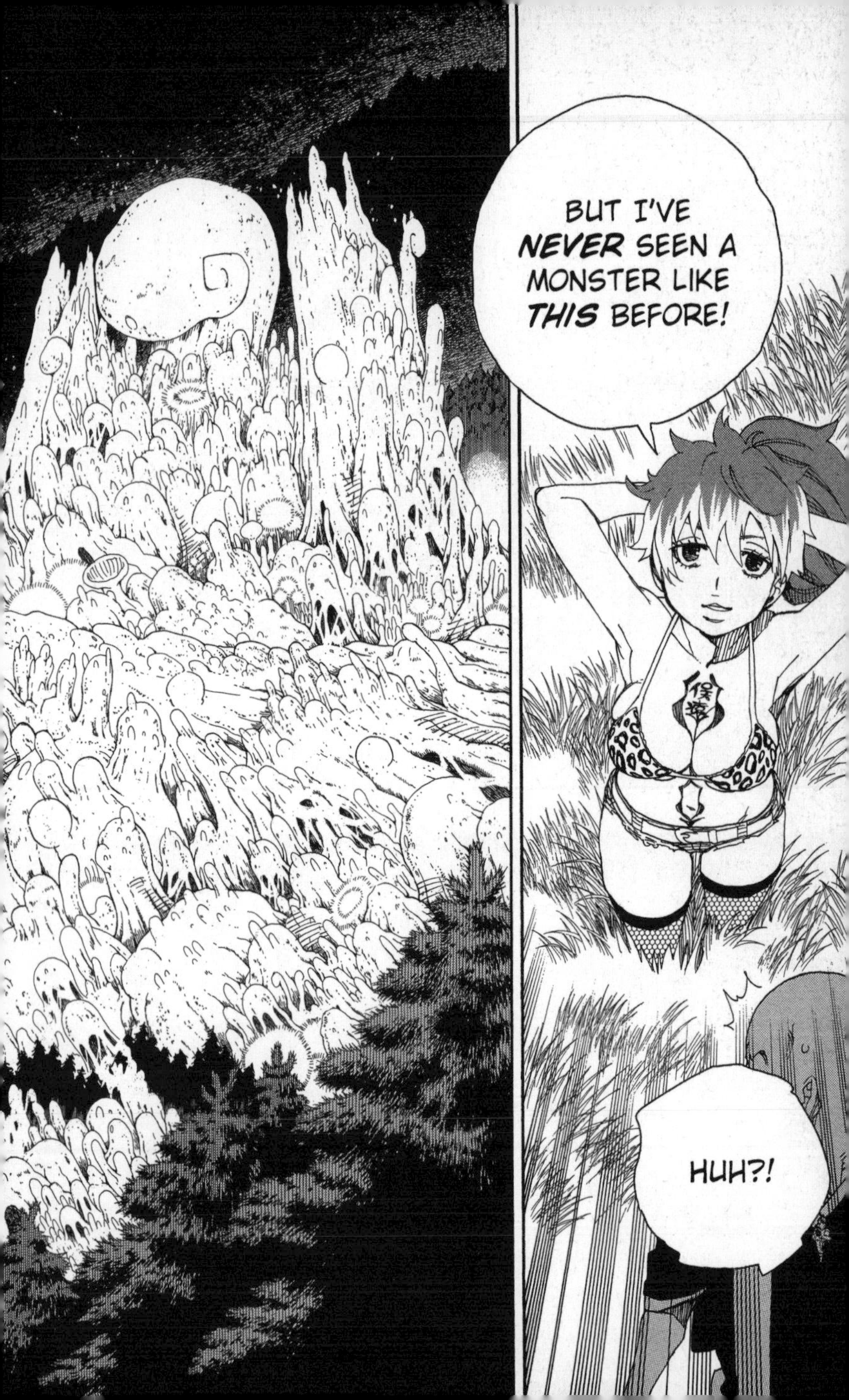
BUT I'VE **NEVER** SEEN A MONSTER LIKE **THIS** BEFORE!
HUH?!

CHAPTER 27
BATTLE AT KONGO-SHINZAN!

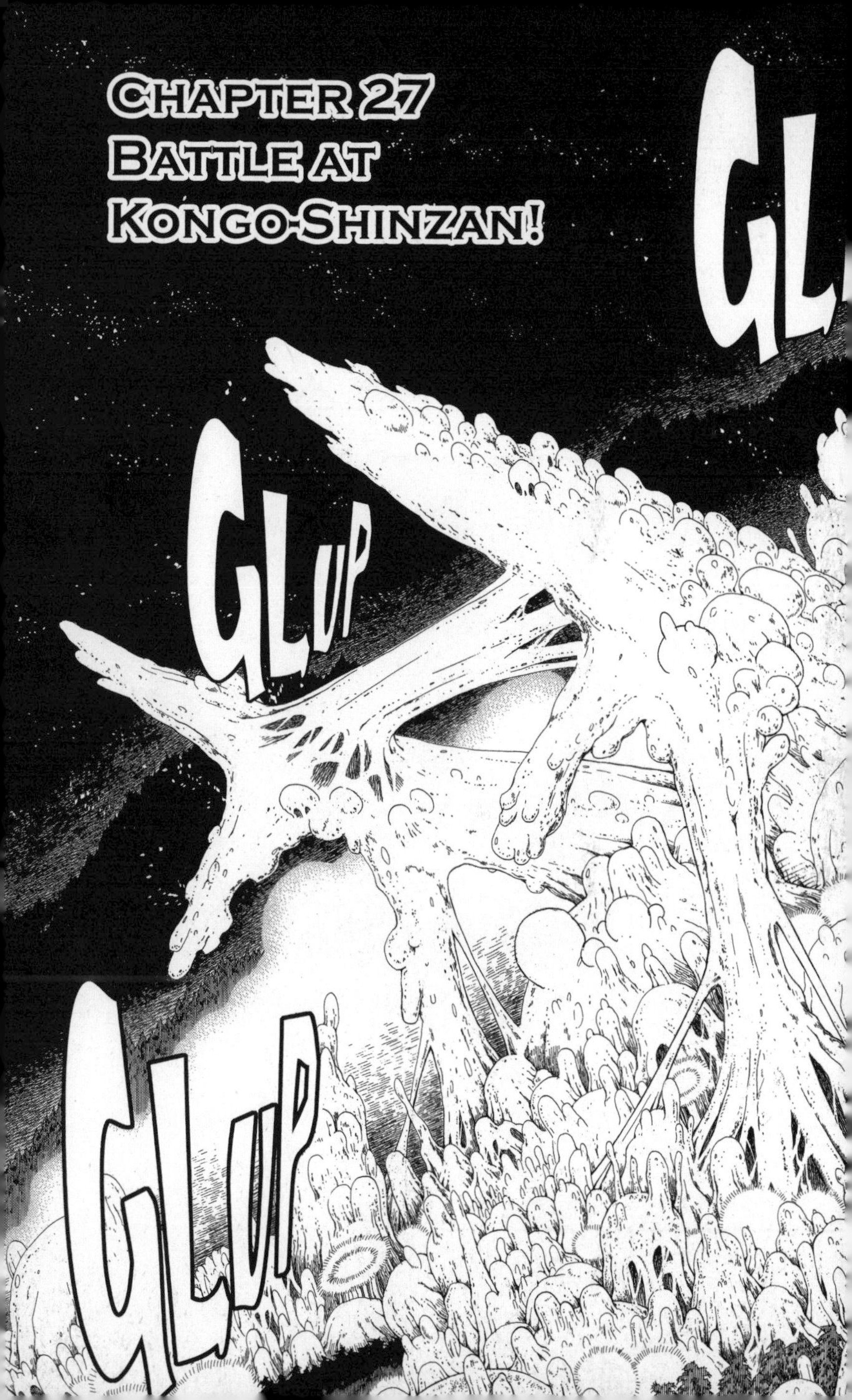
GL
GLUP
GLUP

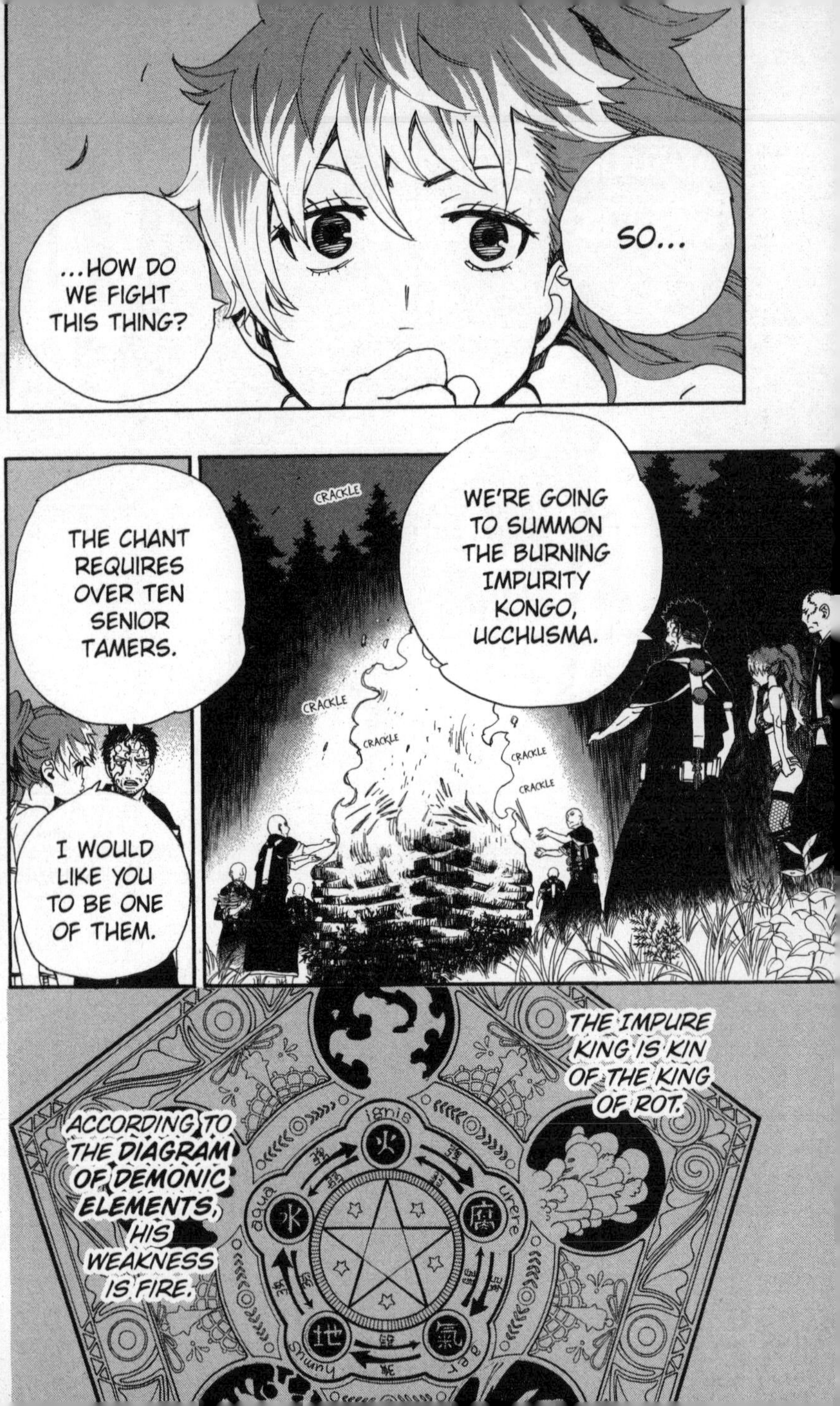
SO...
...HOW DO WE FIGHT THIS THING?
CRACKLE
WE'RE GOING TO SUMMON THE BURNING IMPURITY KONGO, UCCHUSMA.
CRACKLE
CRACKLE
CRACKLE
CRACKLE
THE CHANT REQUIRES OVER TEN SENIOR TAMERS.
I WOULD LIKE YOU TO BE ONE OF THEM.
THE IMPURE KING IS KIN OF THE KING OF ROT.
ACCORDING TO THE DIAGRAM OF DEMONIC ELEMENTS, HIS WEAKNESS IS FIRE.
ignis
aqua
urere

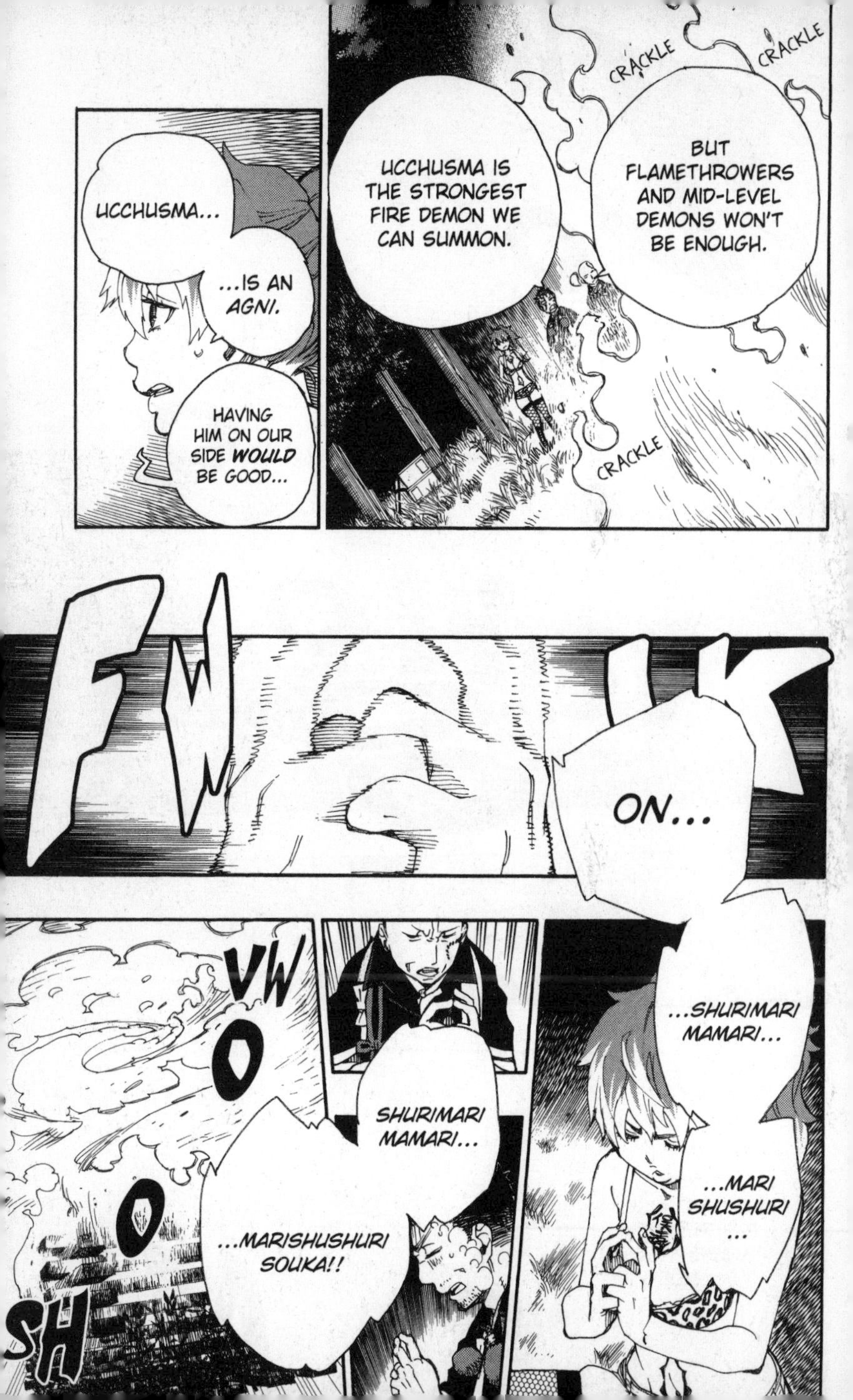
CRACKLE
CRACKLE
BUT FLAMETHROWERS AND MID-LEVEL DEMONS WON'T BE ENOUGH.
UCCHUSMA IS THE STRONGEST FIRE DEMON WE CAN SUMMON.
CRACKLE
UCCHUSMA...
...IS AN AGNI.
HAVING HIM ON OUR SIDE WOULD BE GOOD...
ON...
...SHURIMARI MAMARI...
...MARI SHUSHURI ...
SHURIMARI MAMARI...
...MARISHUSHURI SOUKA!!
VWOOSH

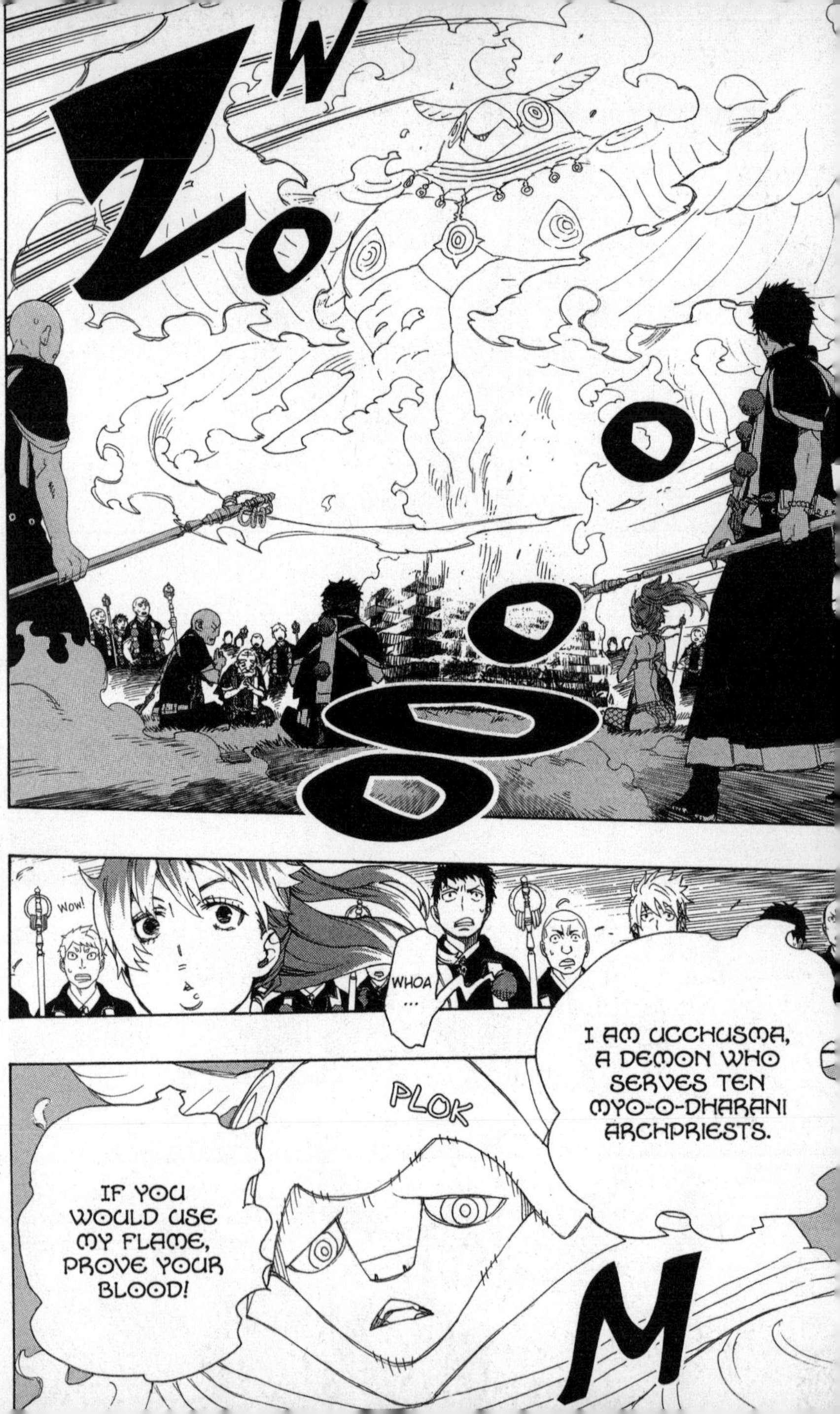
ZWOOOOM
WOW!
WHOA...
I AM UCCHUSMA, A DEMON WHO SERVES TEN MYO-O-DHARANI ARCHPRIESTS.
PLOK
IF YOU WOULD USE MY FLAME, PROVE YOUR BLOOD!
M

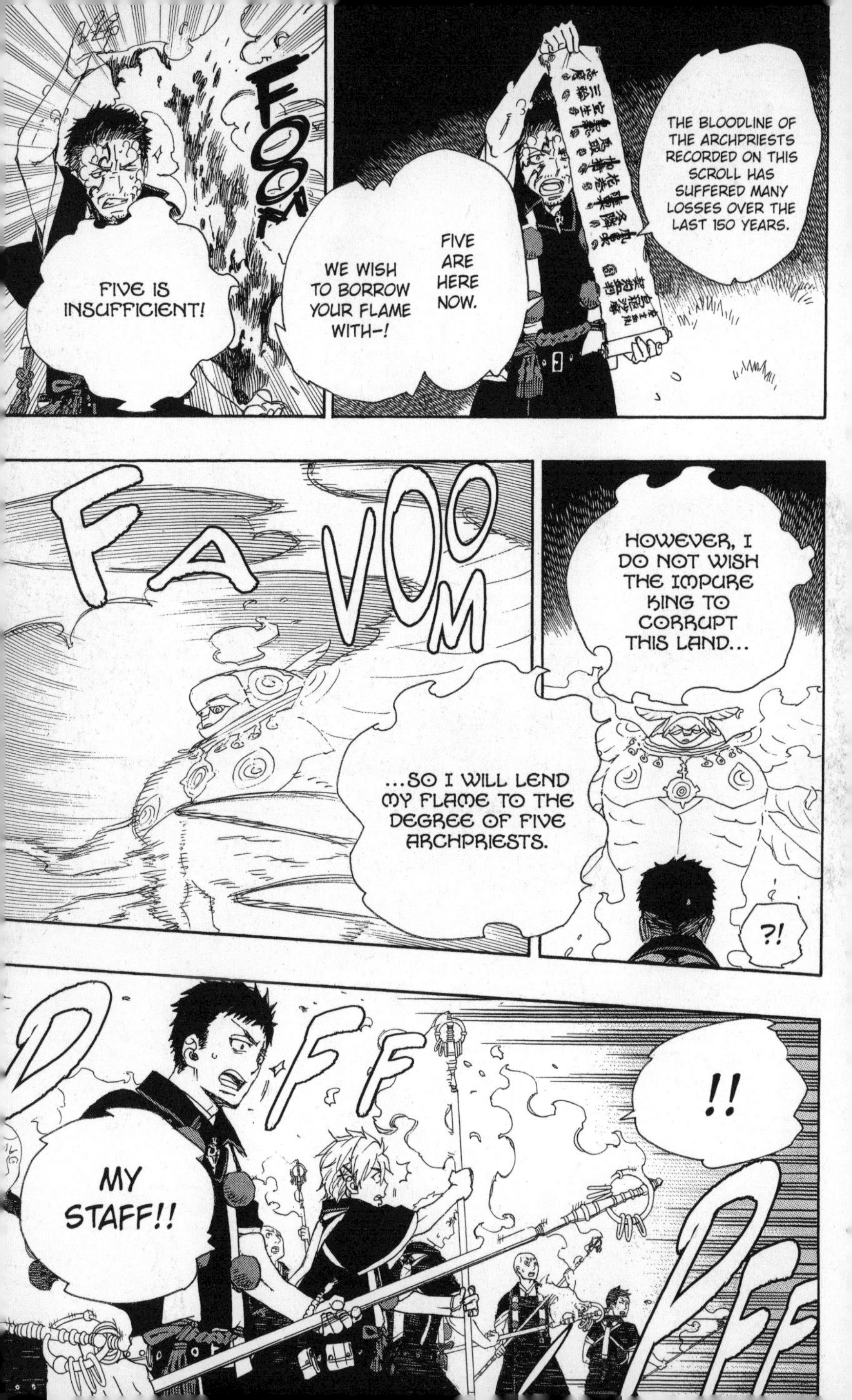
THE BLOODLINE OF THE ARCHPRIESTS RECORDED ON THIS SCROLL HAS SUFFERED MANY LOSSES OVER THE LAST 150 YEARS.
FIVE ARE HERE NOW.
WE WISH TO BORROW YOUR FLAME WITH-!
FOOOM
FIVE IS INSUFFICIENT!
HOWEVER, I DO NOT WISH THE IMPURE KING TO CORRUPT THIS LAND...
?!
FAVOOM
...SO I WILL LEND MY FLAME TO THE DEGREE OF FIVE ARCHPRIESTS.
DFF
!!
DFF
MY STAFF!!

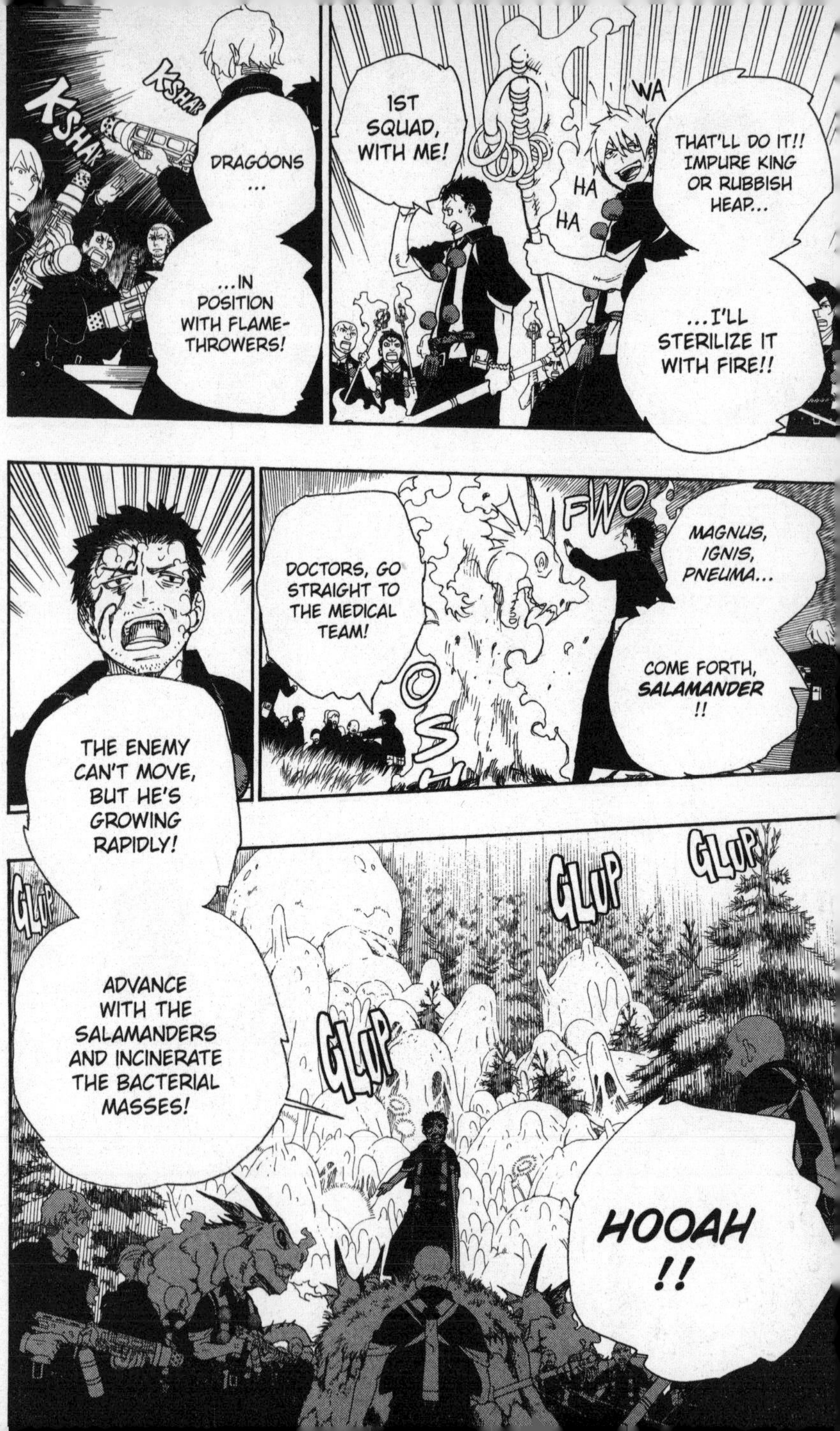
WA
HA
HA
THAT'LL DO IT!! IMPURE KING OR RUBBISH HEAP...
...I'LL STERILIZE IT WITH FIRE!!
1ST SQUAD, WITH ME!
KSHAK
KSHAK
DRAGOONS...
...IN POSITION WITH FLAME-THROWERS!
FWO
MAGNUS, IGNIS, PNEUMA...
COME FORTH, SALAMANDER!!
DOCTORS, GO STRAIGHT TO THE MEDICAL TEAM!
OOSH
THE ENEMY CAN'T MOVE, BUT HE'S GROWING RAPIDLY!
ADVANCE WITH THE SALAMANDERS AND INCINERATE THE BACTERIAL MASSES!
GLUP
GLUP
GLUP
GLUP
HOOAH!!

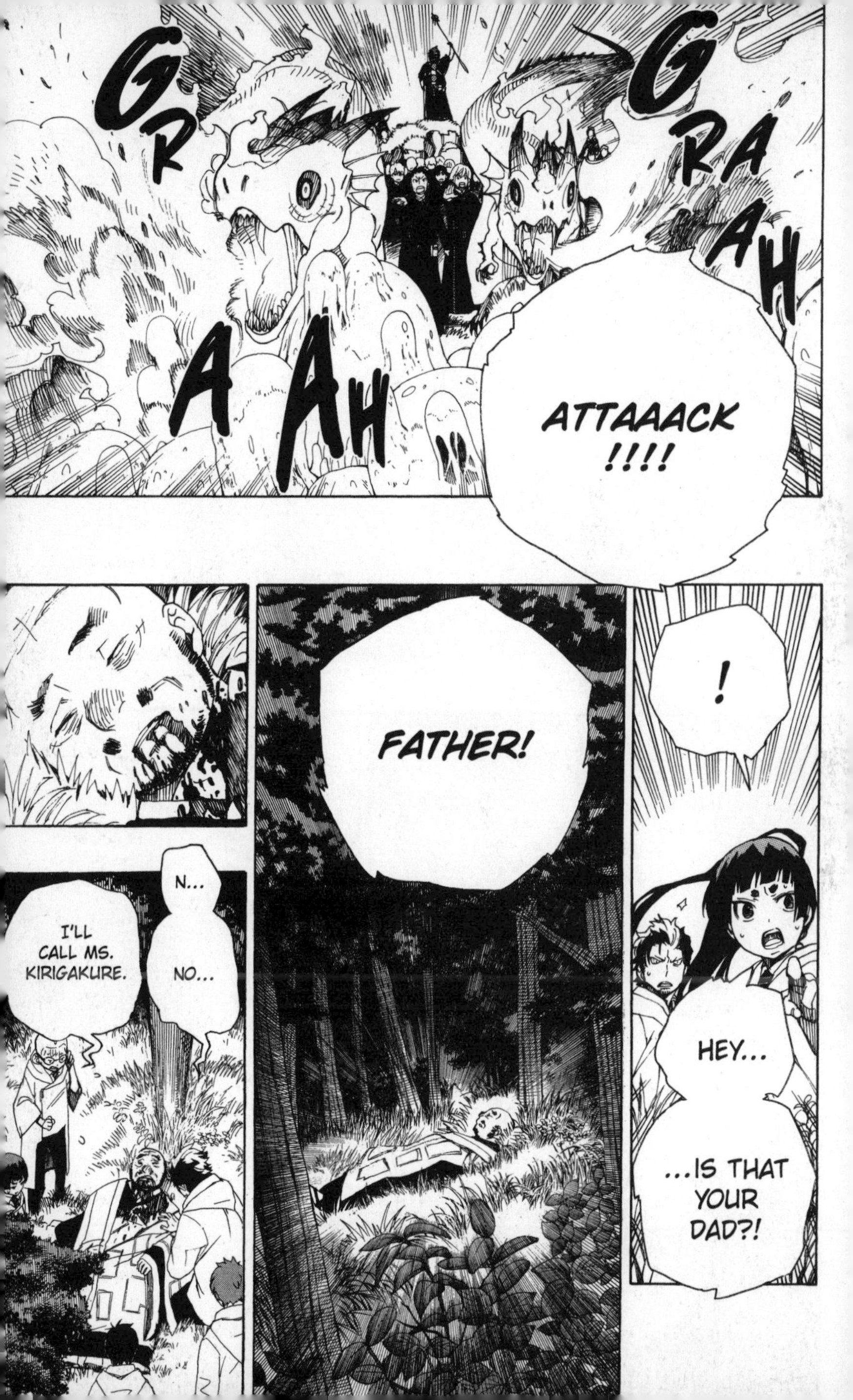
GRAAH
ATTAAACK!!!!
GRAAAH
!
HEY...
...IS THAT YOUR DAD?!
FATHER!
N...
NO...
I'LL CALL MS. KIRIGAKURE.

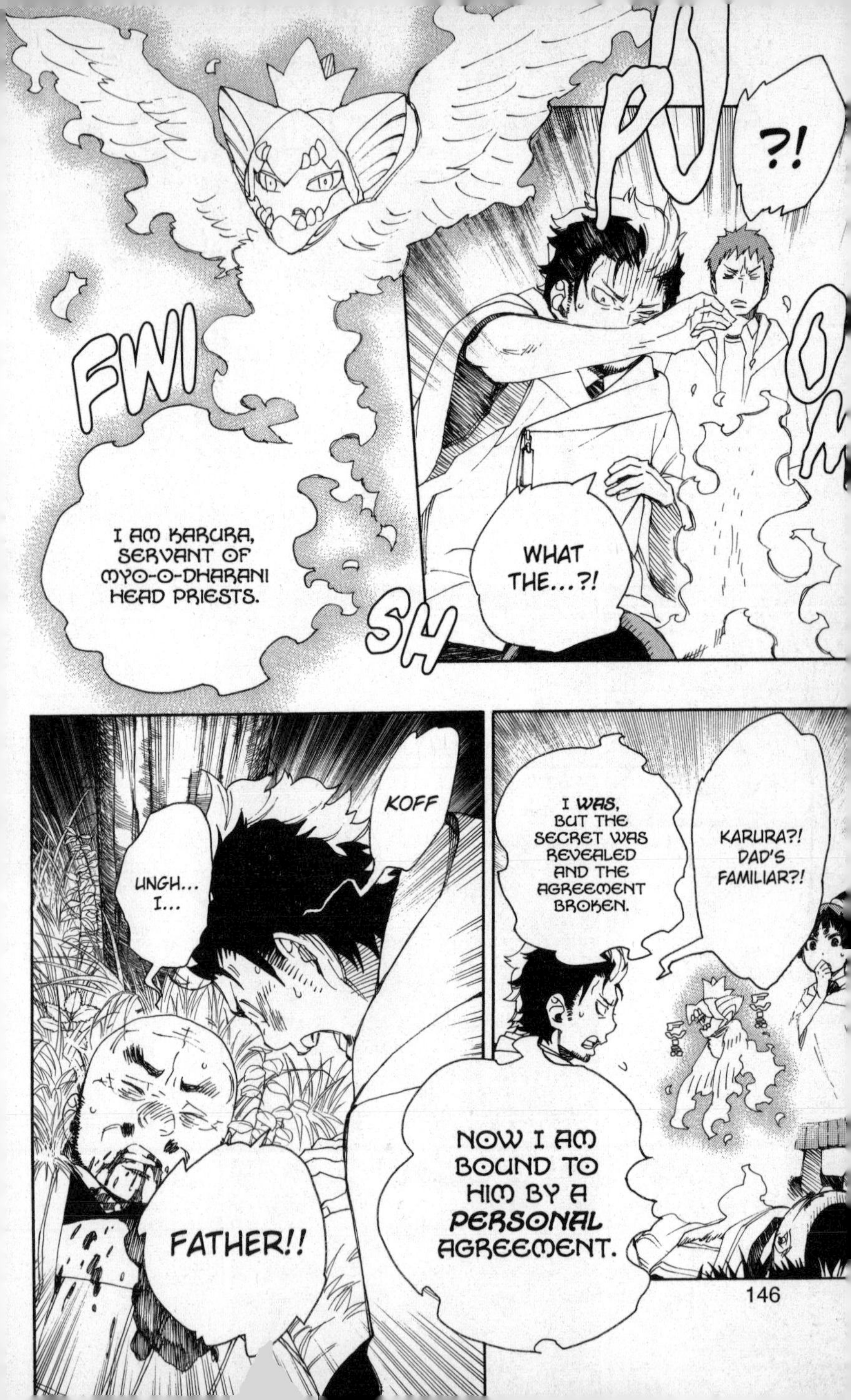
PU
?!
WHAT THE...?!
FWI
SH
I AM KARURA, SERVANT OF MYO-O-DHARANI HEAD PRIESTS.
KARURA?! DAD'S FAMILIAR?!
I WAS, BUT THE SECRET WAS REVEALED AND THE AGREEMENT BROKEN.
NOW I AM BOUND TO HIM BY A PERSONAL AGREEMENT.
KOFF
UNGH... I...
FATHER!!

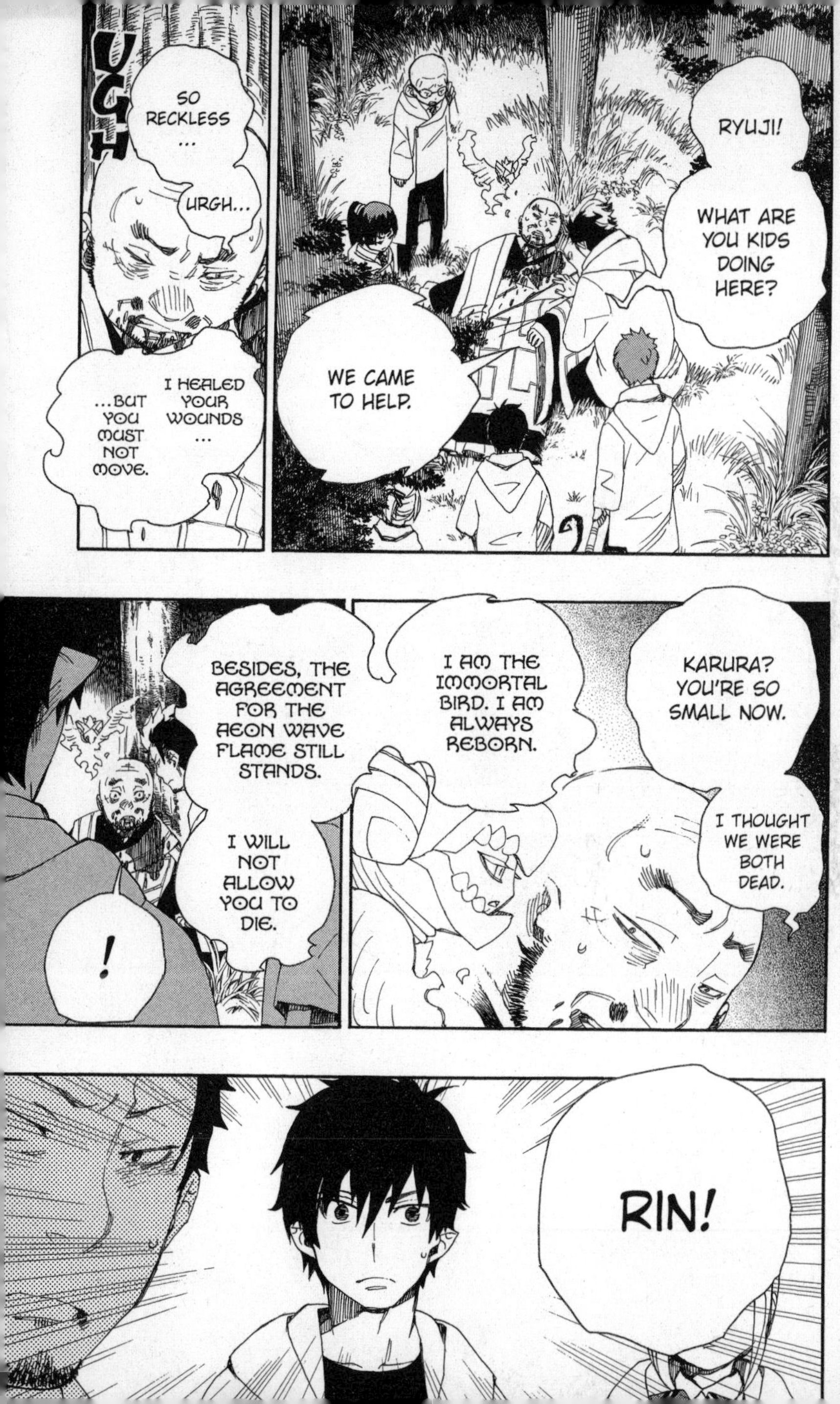
RYUJI!
WHAT ARE YOU KIDS DOING HERE?
WE CAME TO HELP.
UGH
SO RECKLESS ...
URGH...
I HEALED YOUR WOUNDS ...
...BUT YOU MUST NOT MOVE.
KARURA? YOU'RE SO SMALL NOW.
I THOUGHT WE WERE BOTH DEAD.
I AM THE IMMORTAL BIRD. I AM ALWAYS REBORN.
BESIDES, THE AGREEMENT FOR THE AEON WAVE FLAME STILL STANDS.
I WILL NOT ALLOW YOU TO DIE.
!
RIN!

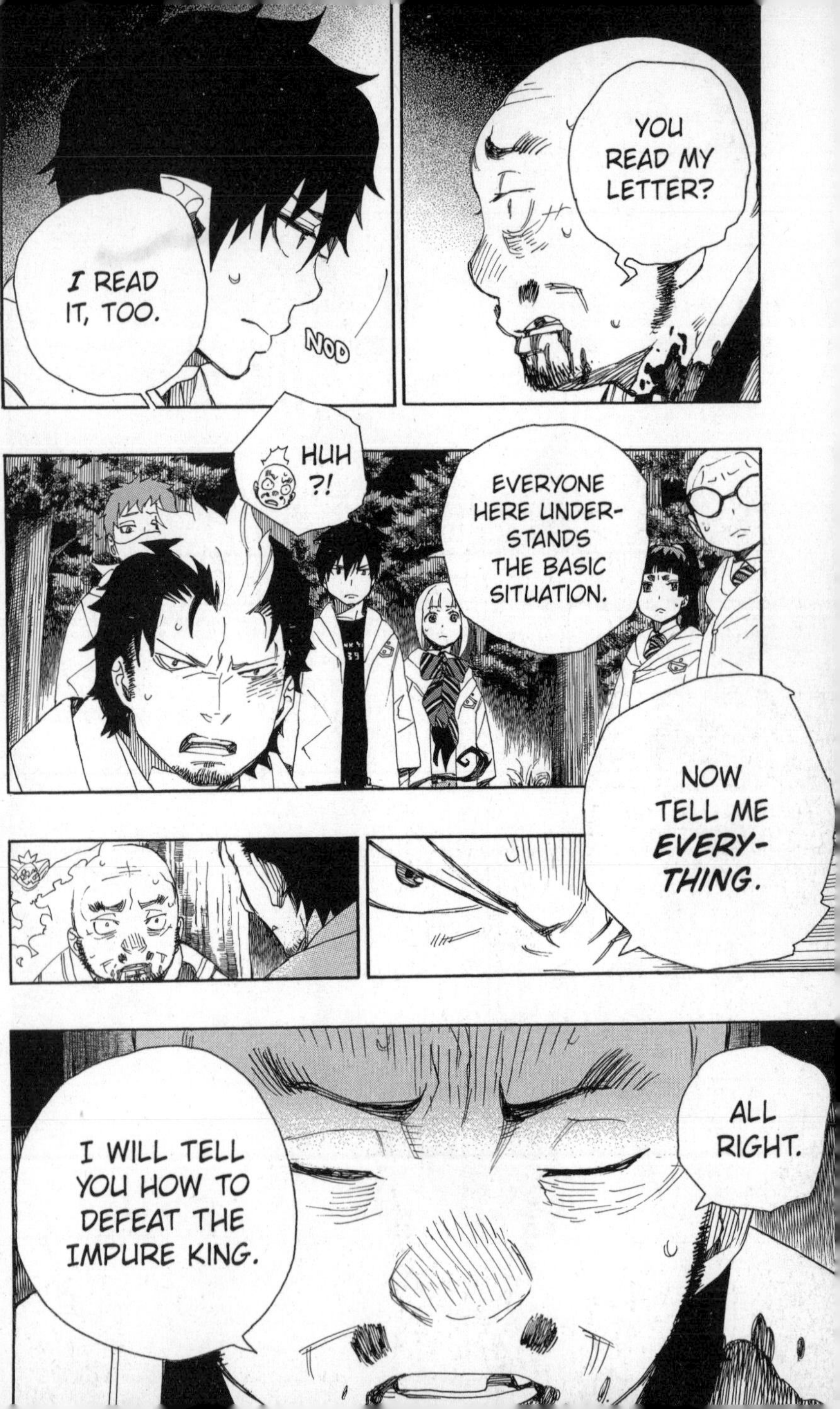
YOU READ MY LETTER?
I READ IT, TOO.
NOD
EVERYONE HERE UNDER-STANDS THE BASIC SITUATION.
HUH ?!
NOW TELL ME *EVERY-THING*.
ALL RIGHT.
I WILL TELL YOU HOW TO DEFEAT THE IMPURE KING.

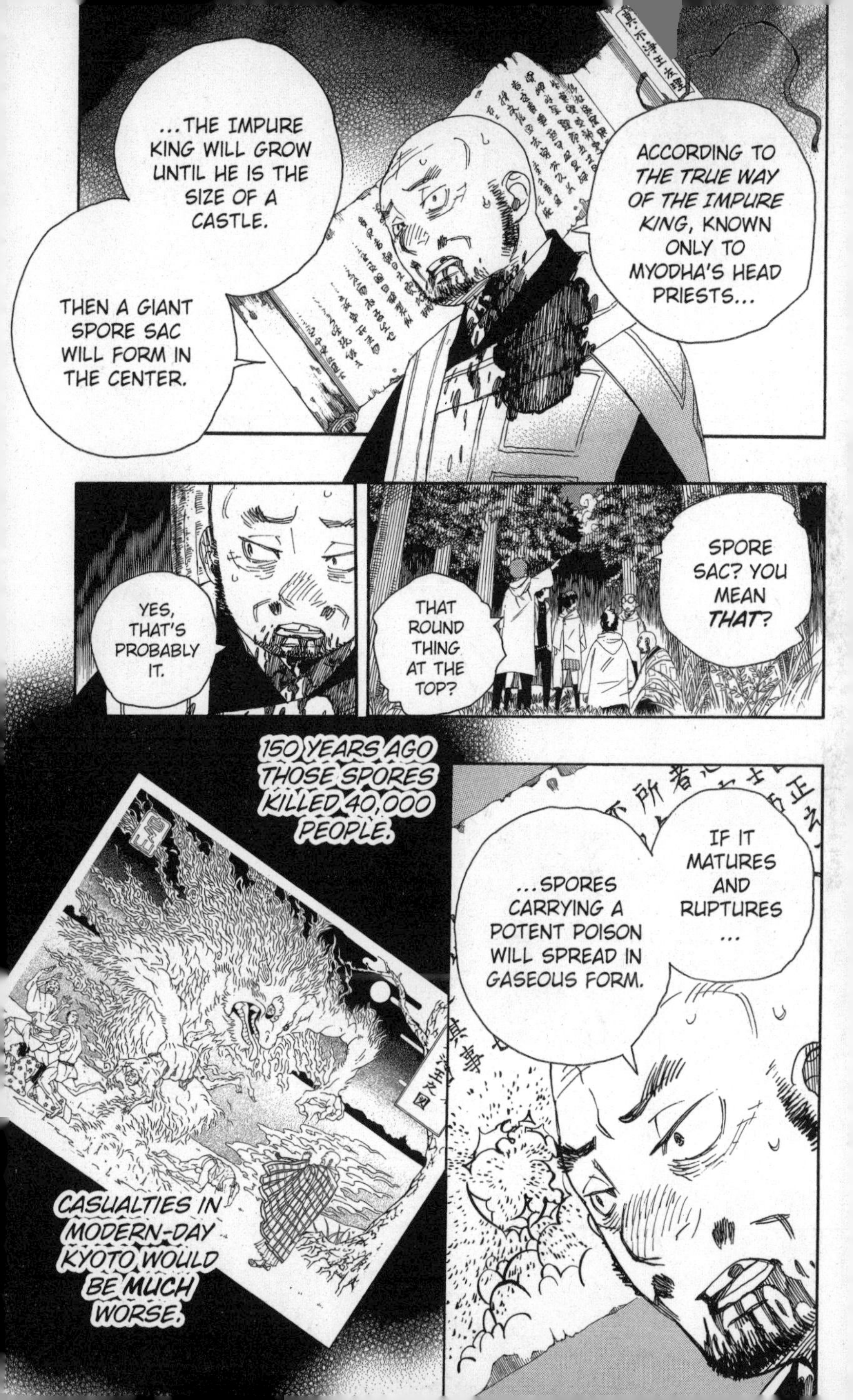

ACCORDING TO THE TRUE WAY OF THE IMPURE KING, KNOWN ONLY TO MYODHA'S HEAD PRIESTS...
...THE IMPURE KING WILL GROW UNTIL HE IS THE SIZE OF A CASTLE.
THEN A GIANT SPORE SAC WILL FORM IN THE CENTER.
SPORE SAC? YOU MEAN THAT?
THAT ROUND THING AT THE TOP?
YES, THAT'S PROBABLY IT.
IF IT MATURES AND RUPTURES...
...SPORES CARRYING A POTENT POISON WILL SPREAD IN GASEOUS FORM.
150 YEARS AGO THOSE SPORES KILLED 40,000 PEOPLE.
CASUALTIES IN MODERN-DAY KYOTO WOULD BE MUCH WORSE.

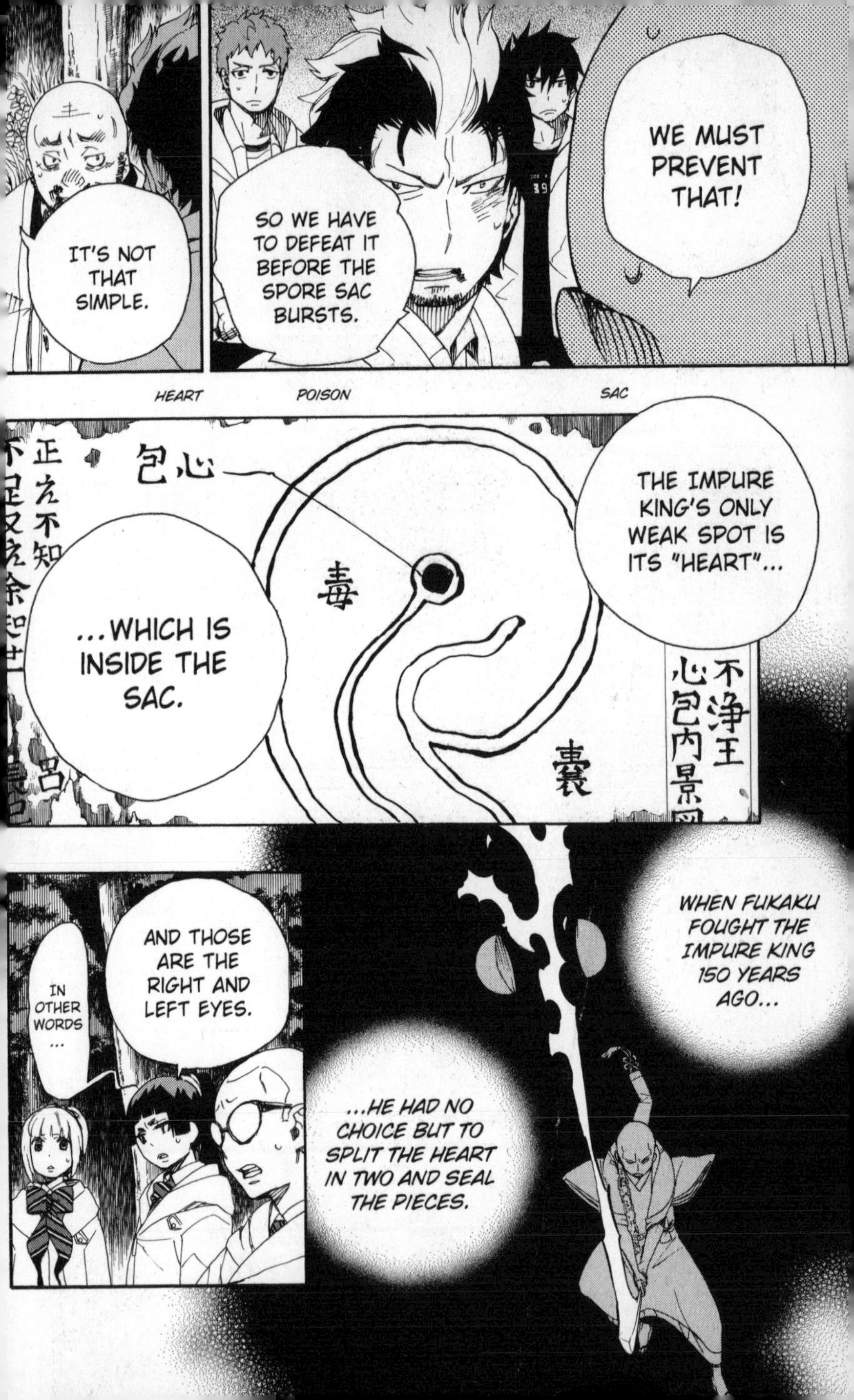
WE MUST PREVENT THAT!
SO WE HAVE TO DEFEAT IT BEFORE THE SPORE SAC BURSTS.
IT'S NOT THAT SIMPLE.
HEART
POISON
SAC
不浄王心包内景図
包心
毒
嚢
THE IMPURE KING'S ONLY WEAK SPOT IS ITS "HEART"...
...WHICH IS INSIDE THE SAC.
WHEN FUKAKU FOUGHT THE IMPURE KING 150 YEARS AGO...
...HE HAD NO CHOICE BUT TO SPLIT THE HEART IN TWO AND SEAL THE PIECES.
AND THOSE ARE THE RIGHT AND LEFT EYES.
IN OTHER WORDS...

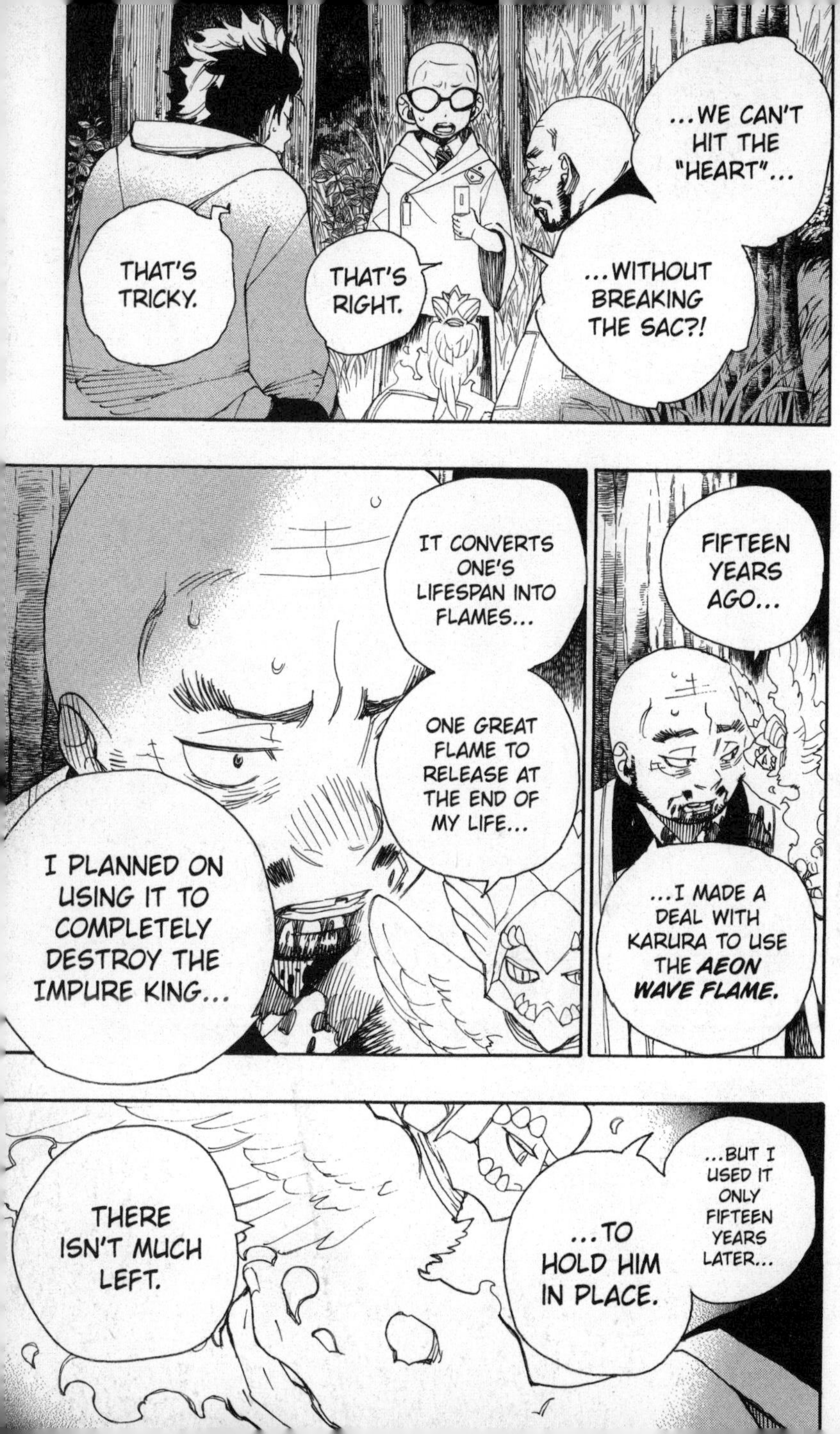
...WE CAN'T HIT THE "HEART"...
...WITHOUT BREAKING THE SAC?!
THAT'S RIGHT.
THAT'S TRICKY.
FIFTEEN YEARS AGO...
...I MADE A DEAL WITH KARURA TO USE THE *AEON WAVE FLAME.*
IT CONVERTS ONE'S LIFESPAN INTO FLAMES...
ONE GREAT FLAME TO RELEASE AT THE END OF MY LIFE...
I PLANNED ON USING IT TO COMPLETELY DESTROY THE IMPURE KING...
...BUT I USED IT ONLY FIFTEEN YEARS LATER...
...TO HOLD HIM IN PLACE.
THERE ISN'T MUCH LEFT.

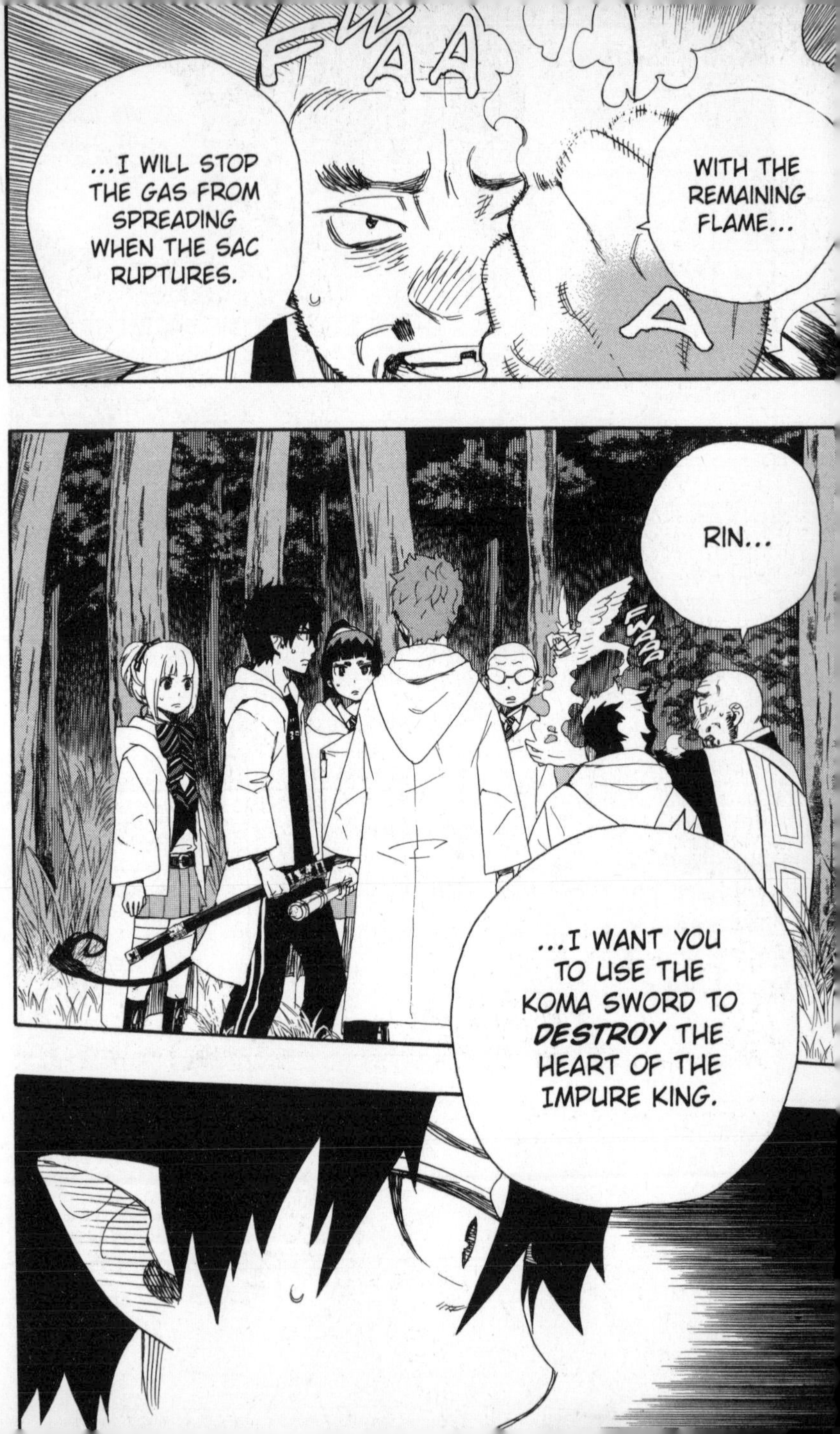
FWAA
WITH THE REMAINING FLAME...
...I WILL STOP THE GAS FROM SPREADING WHEN THE SAC RUPTURES.
RIN...
...I WANT YOU TO USE THE KOMA SWORD TO DESTROY THE HEART OF THE IMPURE KING.

I KNOW...

...YOU COULD DIE, BUT—

I'M SORRY, BUT...

K CHA

HUH?!

HUH? NO...I MEAN, I CAN'T DRAW MY SWORD.

ARE YOU SERIOUS?!

I DON'T KNOW. IT'S SOME KIND OF MENTAL HANG-UP.

WHY NOT?!

HUH ?!

I'VE BEEN TRYING, BUT I CAN'T DO IT.

SORRY, POPS!

EVEN I GET WORRIED SOMETIMES!! SO I'M NO USE RIGHT NOW!

I SEE. THAT *IS* A PROBLEM...

OSSAMA!!

UNGH...

YOU MUST NOT, TATSUMA.

YOU HAVE LOST TOO MUCH BLOOD.

...BUT I CAN AT LEAST...

...PUT UP THE BARRIER!!

NO, I'M—

I HEALED YOUR WOUNDS, BUT YOU NEARLY BLED TO DEATH.

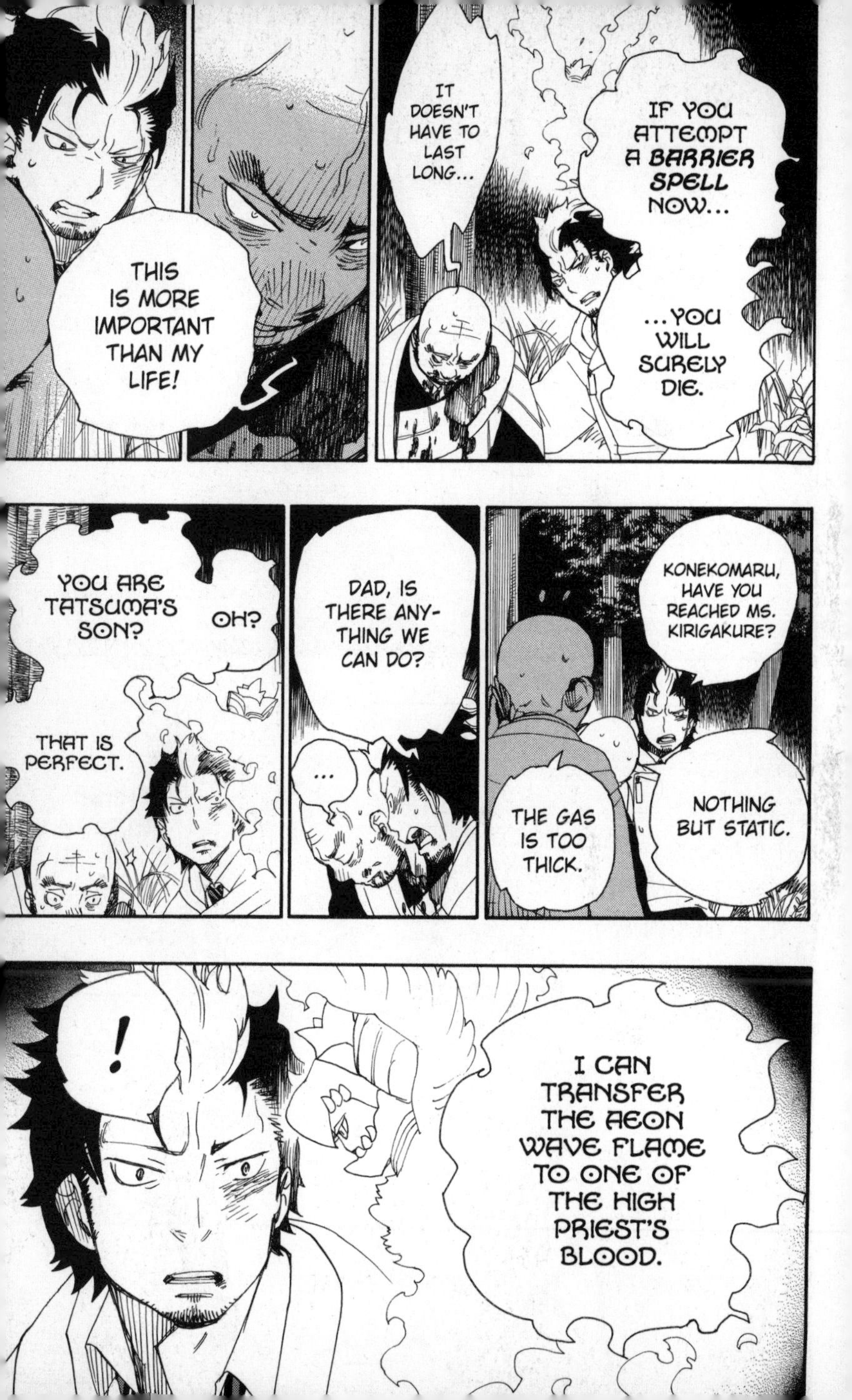
IF YOU ATTEMPT A **BARRIER SPELL** NOW...
...YOU WILL SURELY DIE.
IT DOESN'T HAVE TO LAST LONG...
THIS IS MORE IMPORTANT THAN MY LIFE!
KONEKOMARU, HAVE YOU REACHED MS. KIRIGAKURE?
NOTHING BUT STATIC.
THE GAS IS TOO THICK.
DAD, IS THERE ANY-THING WE CAN DO?
...
OH?
YOU ARE TATSUMA'S SON?
THAT IS PERFECT.
I CAN TRANSFER THE AEON WAVE FLAME TO ONE OF THE HIGH PRIEST'S BLOOD.
!

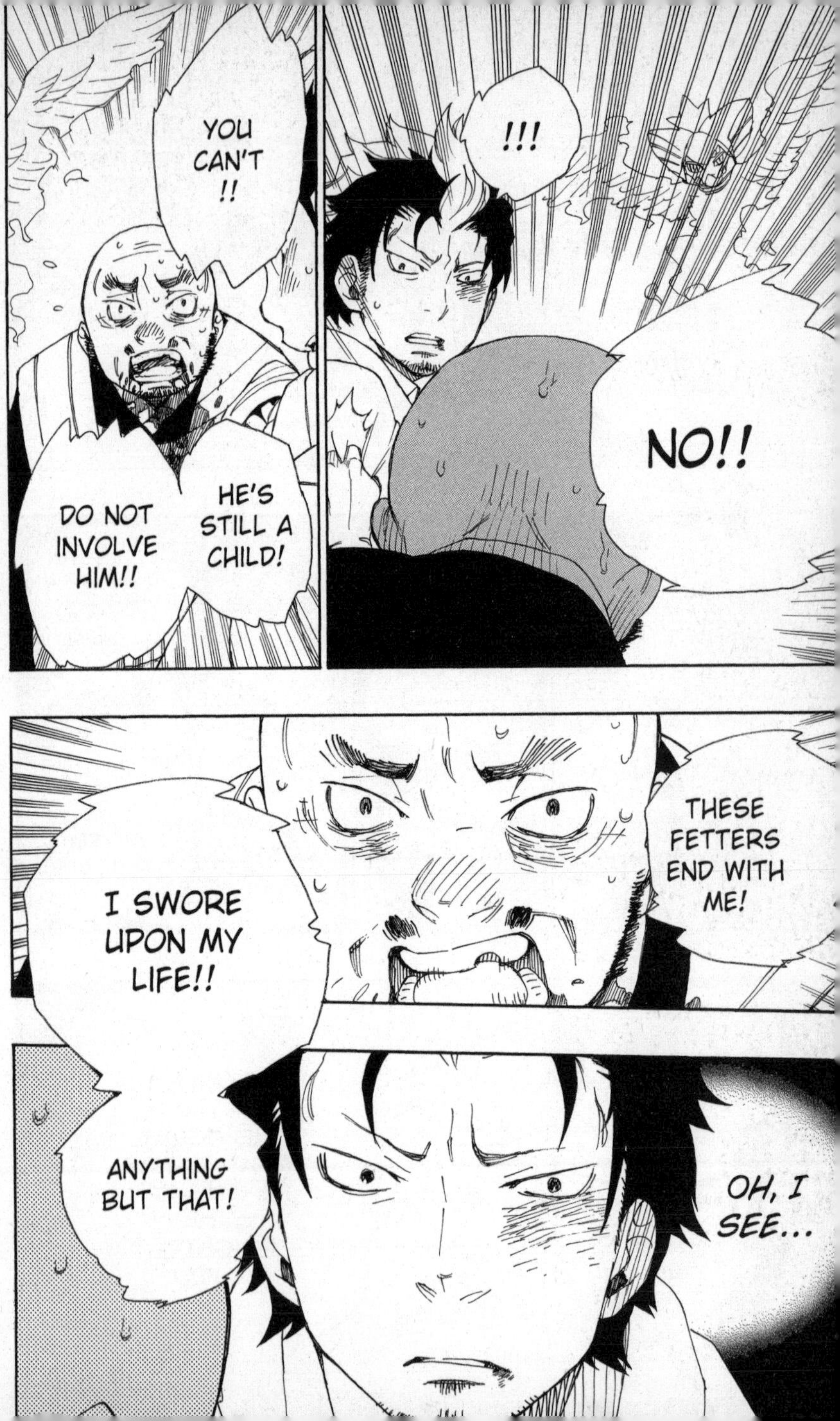
!!!
NO!!
YOU CAN'T!!
HE'S STILL A CHILD!
DO NOT INVOLVE HIM!!
THESE FETTERS END WITH ME!
I SWORE UPON MY LIFE!!
ANYTHING BUT THAT!
OH, I SEE...

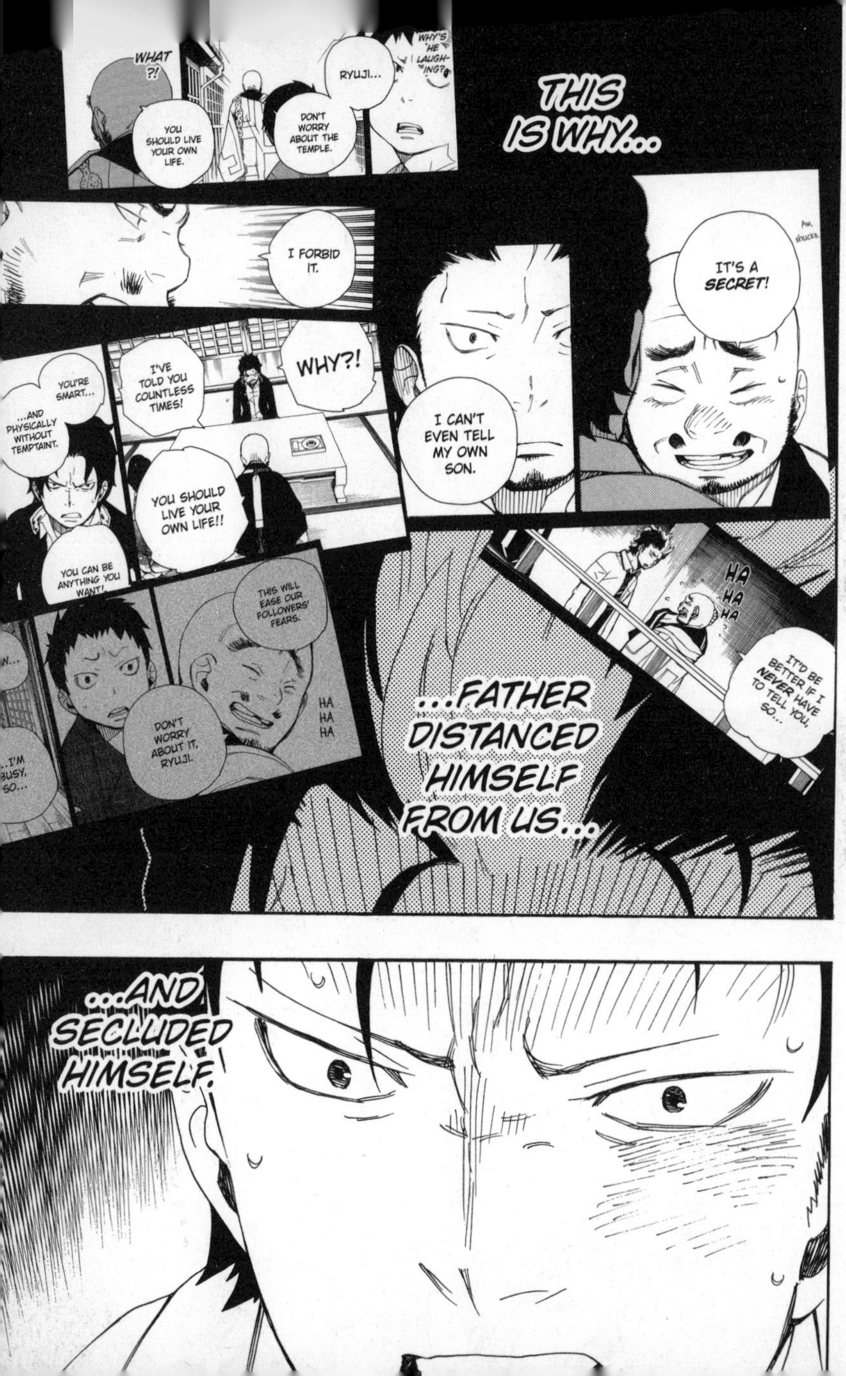
THIS IS WHY...
WHY'S HE LAUGHING?
RYUJI...
DON'T WORRY ABOUT THE TEMPLE.
WHAT?!
YOU SHOULD LIVE YOUR OWN LIFE.
IT'S A SECRET!
Aw, shucks.
I CAN'T EVEN TELL MY OWN SON.
I FORBID IT.
WHY?!
I'VE TOLD YOU COUNTLESS TIMES!
YOU SHOULD LIVE YOUR OWN LIFE!!
YOU'RE SMART...
...AND PHYSICALLY WITHOUT TEMPTAINT.
YOU CAN BE ANYTHING YOU WANT!
HA HA HA
IT'D BE BETTER IF I NEVER HAVE TO TELL YOU, SO...
...FATHER DISTANCED HIMSELF FROM US...
THIS WILL EASE OUR FOLLOWERS' FEARS.
HA HA HA
DON'T WORRY ABOUT IT, RYUJI.
...I'M BUSY, SO...
...AND SECLUDED HIMSELF.

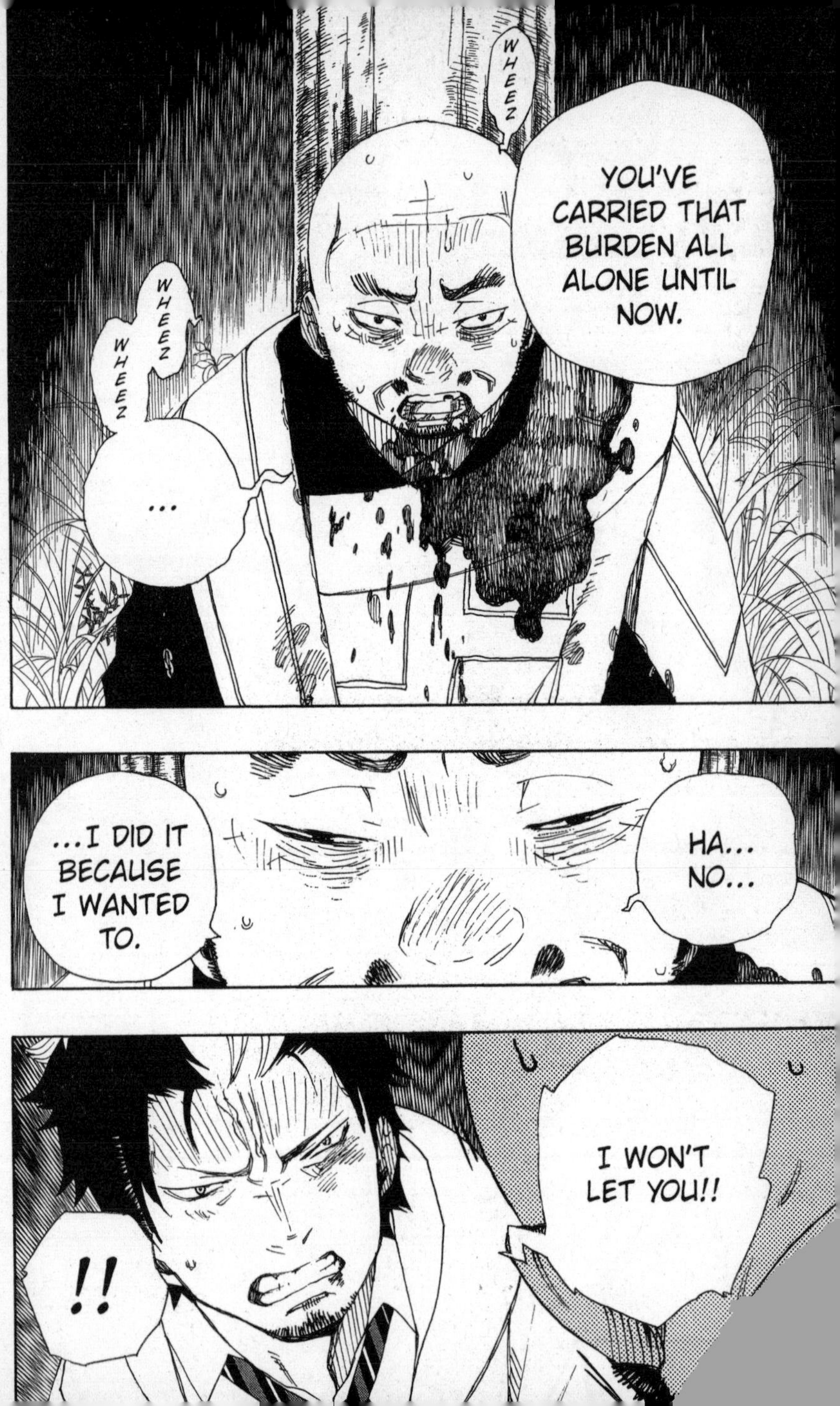
WHEEZ
YOU'VE CARRIED THAT BURDEN ALL ALONE UNTIL NOW.
WHEEZ WHEEZ
...
HA... NO...
...I DID IT BECAUSE I WANTED TO.
I WON'T LET YOU!!
!!

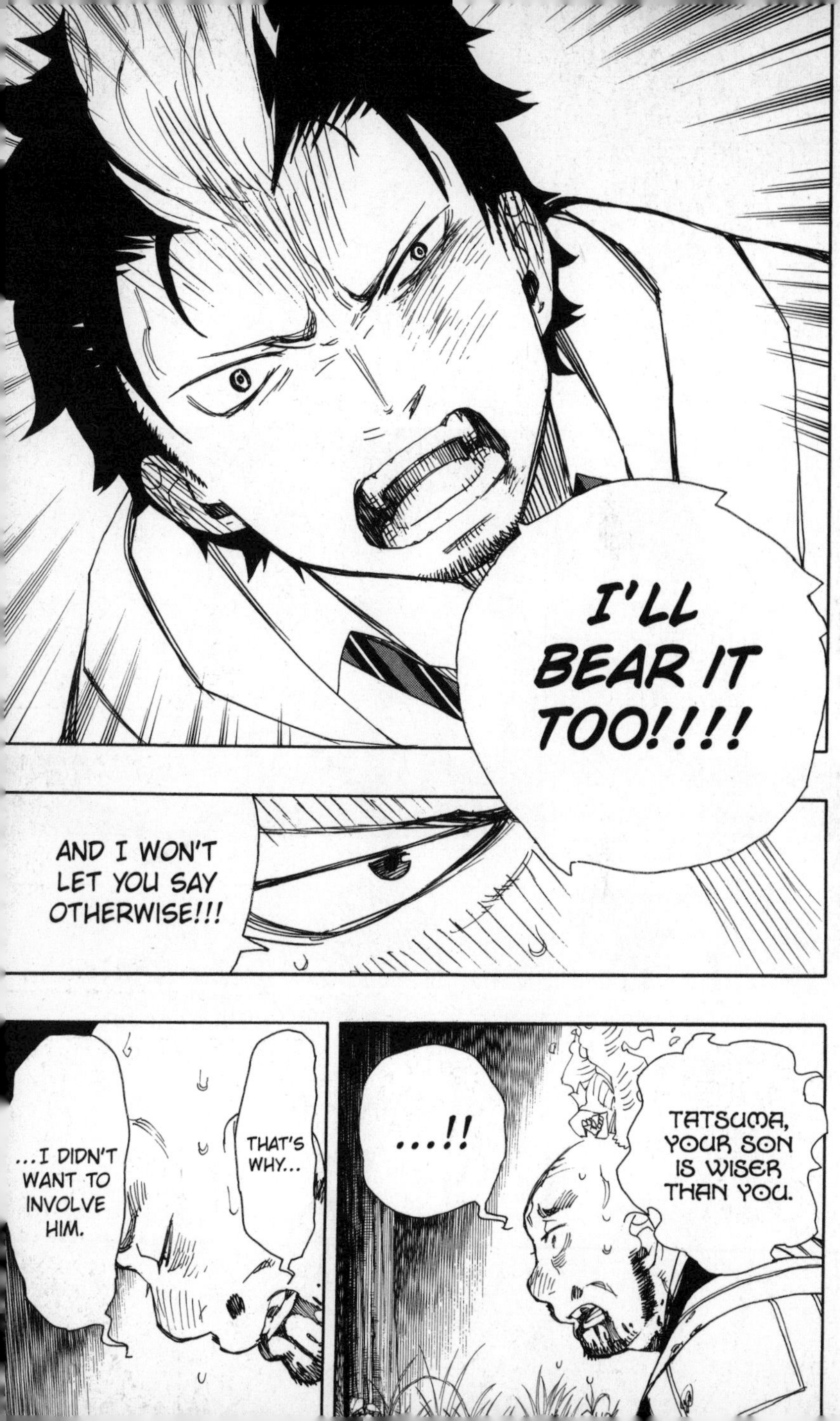
I'LL BEAR IT TOO!!!!
AND I WON'T LET YOU SAY OTHERWISE!!!
TATSUMA, YOUR SON IS WISER THAN YOU.
...!!
THAT'S WHY...
...I DIDN'T WANT TO INVOLVE HIM.

I WILL NOW TRANSFER THE AEON WAVE FLAME.

FLASH

IF YOU ARE INDEED THE CHILD OF TATSUMA SUGURO...

...PROVE YOUR BLOOD.

ZIK

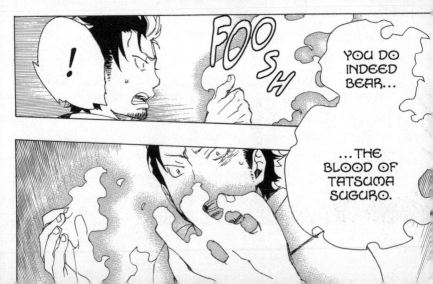

FOOSH

YOU DO INDEED BEAR...

...THE BLOOD OF TATSUMA SUGURO.

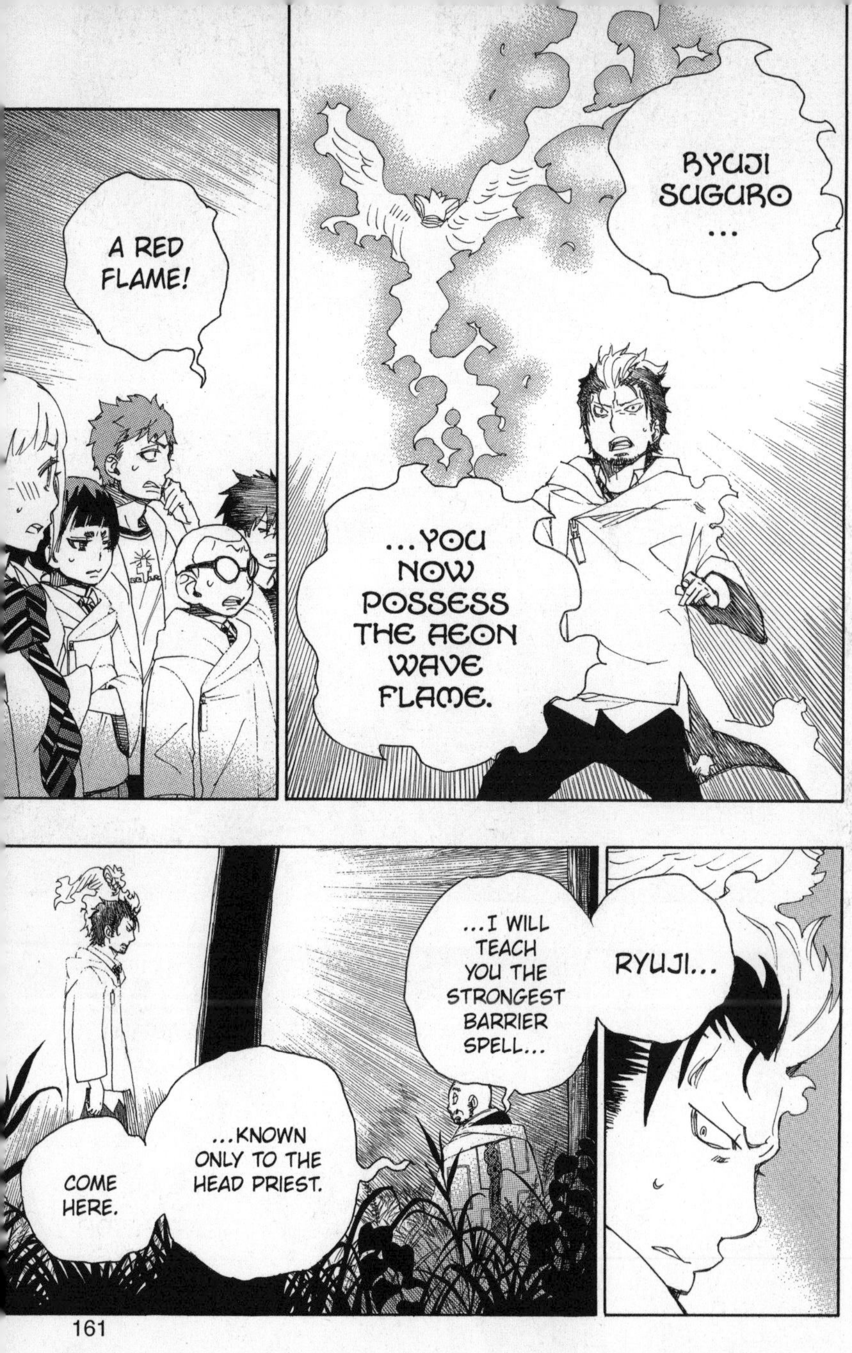
RYUJI SUGURO ...
...YOU NOW POSSESS THE AEON WAVE FLAME.
A RED FLAME!
RYUJI...
...I WILL TEACH YOU THE STRONGEST BARRIER SPELL...
...KNOWN ONLY TO THE HEAD PRIEST.
COME HERE.

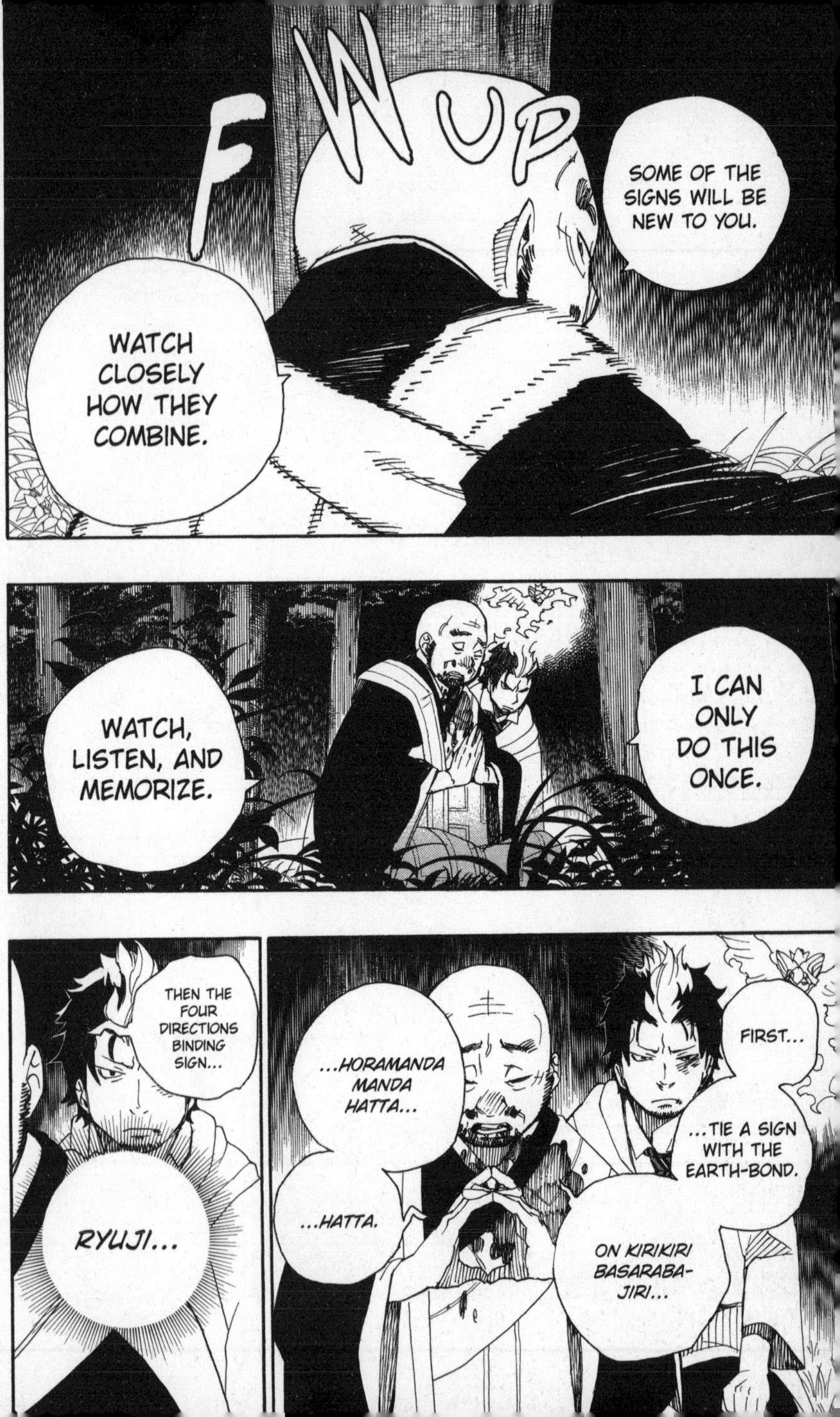
FWUP
SOME OF THE SIGNS WILL BE NEW TO YOU.
WATCH CLOSELY HOW THEY COMBINE.
I CAN ONLY DO THIS ONCE.
WATCH, LISTEN, AND MEMORIZE.
FIRST...
...TIE A SIGN WITH THE EARTH-BOND.
ON KIRIKIRI BASARABA-JIRI...
...HORAMANDA MANDA HATTA...
...HATTA.
THEN THE FOUR DIRECTIONS BINDING SIGN...
RYUJI...

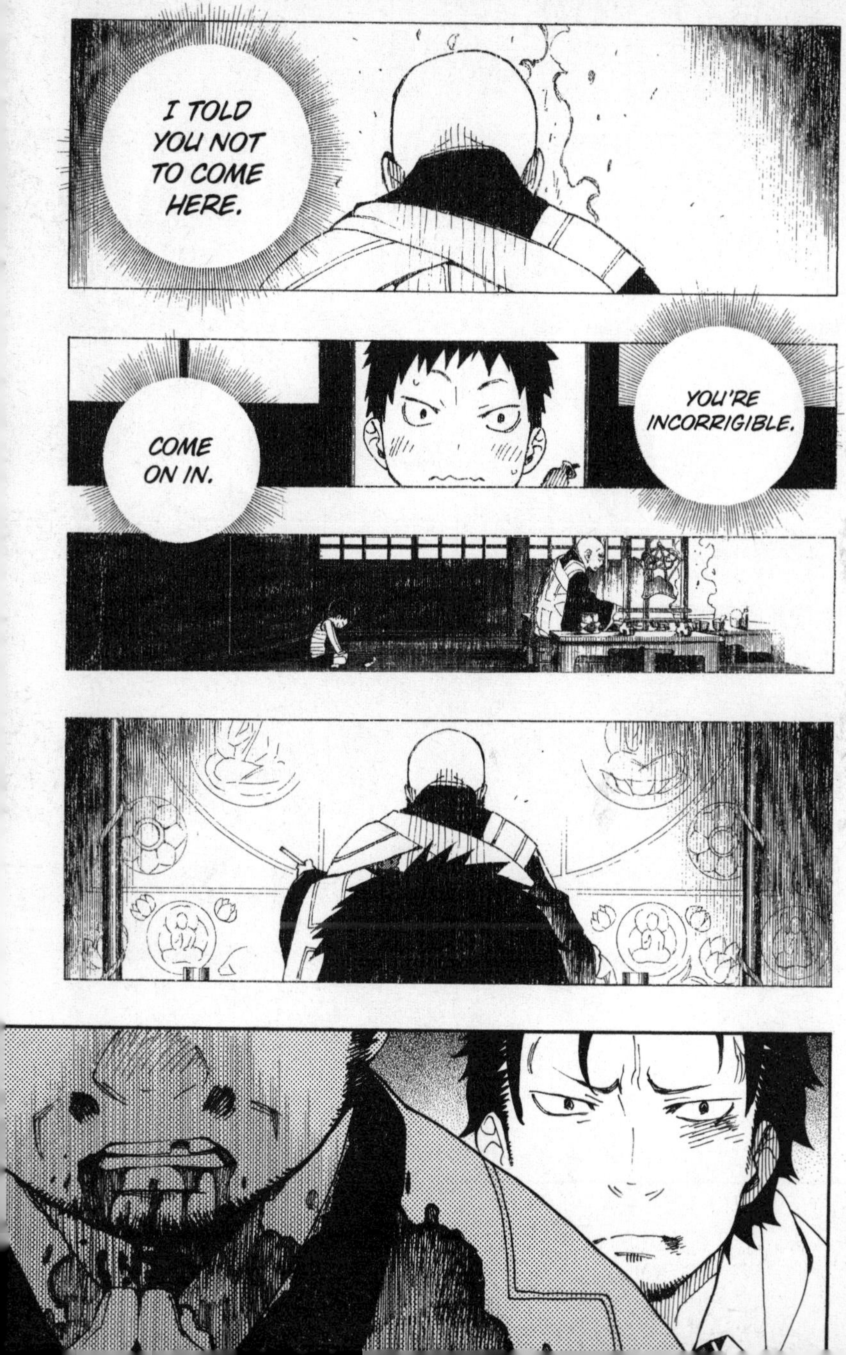
I TOLD YOU NOT TO COME HERE.
YOU'RE INCORRIGIBLE.
COME ON IN.

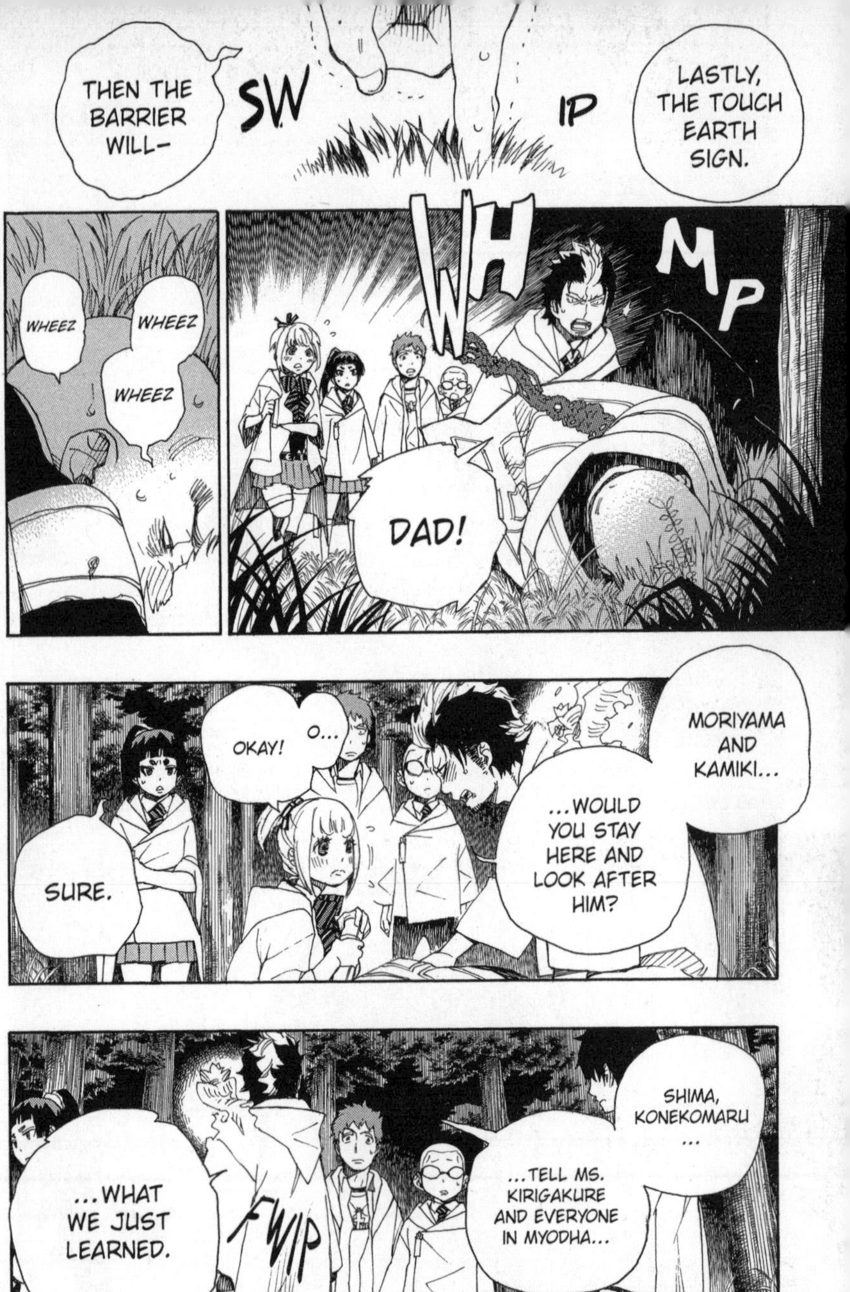
LASTLY, THE TOUCH EARTH SIGN.
SWIP
THEN THE BARRIER WILL-
WHMP
DAD!
WHEEZ
WHEEZ
WHEEZ
MORIYAMA AND KAMIKI...
...WOULD YOU STAY HERE AND LOOK AFTER HIM?
O...
OKAY!
SURE.
SHIMA, KONEKOMARU...
...TELL MS. KIRIGAKURE AND EVERYONE IN MYODHA...
FWIP
...WHAT WE JUST LEARNED.

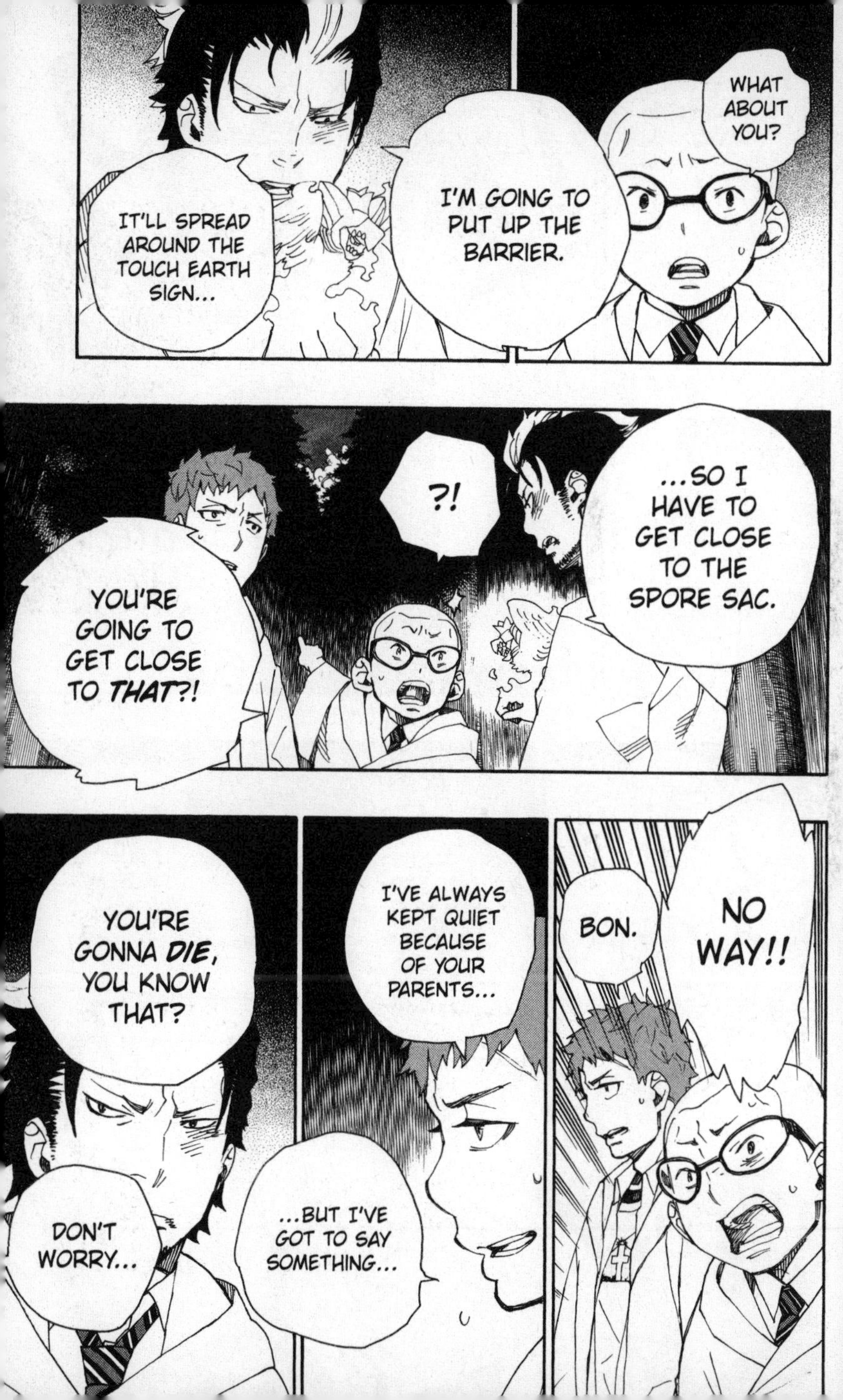
WHAT ABOUT YOU?
I'M GOING TO PUT UP THE BARRIER.
IT'LL SPREAD AROUND THE TOUCH EARTH SIGN...
...SO I HAVE TO GET CLOSE TO THE SPORE SAC.
?!
YOU'RE GOING TO GET CLOSE TO *THAT*?!
NO WAY!!
BON.
I'VE ALWAYS KEPT QUIET BECAUSE OF YOUR PARENTS...
...BUT I'VE GOT TO SAY SOMETHING...
YOU'RE GONNA *DIE*, YOU KNOW THAT?
DON'T WORRY...

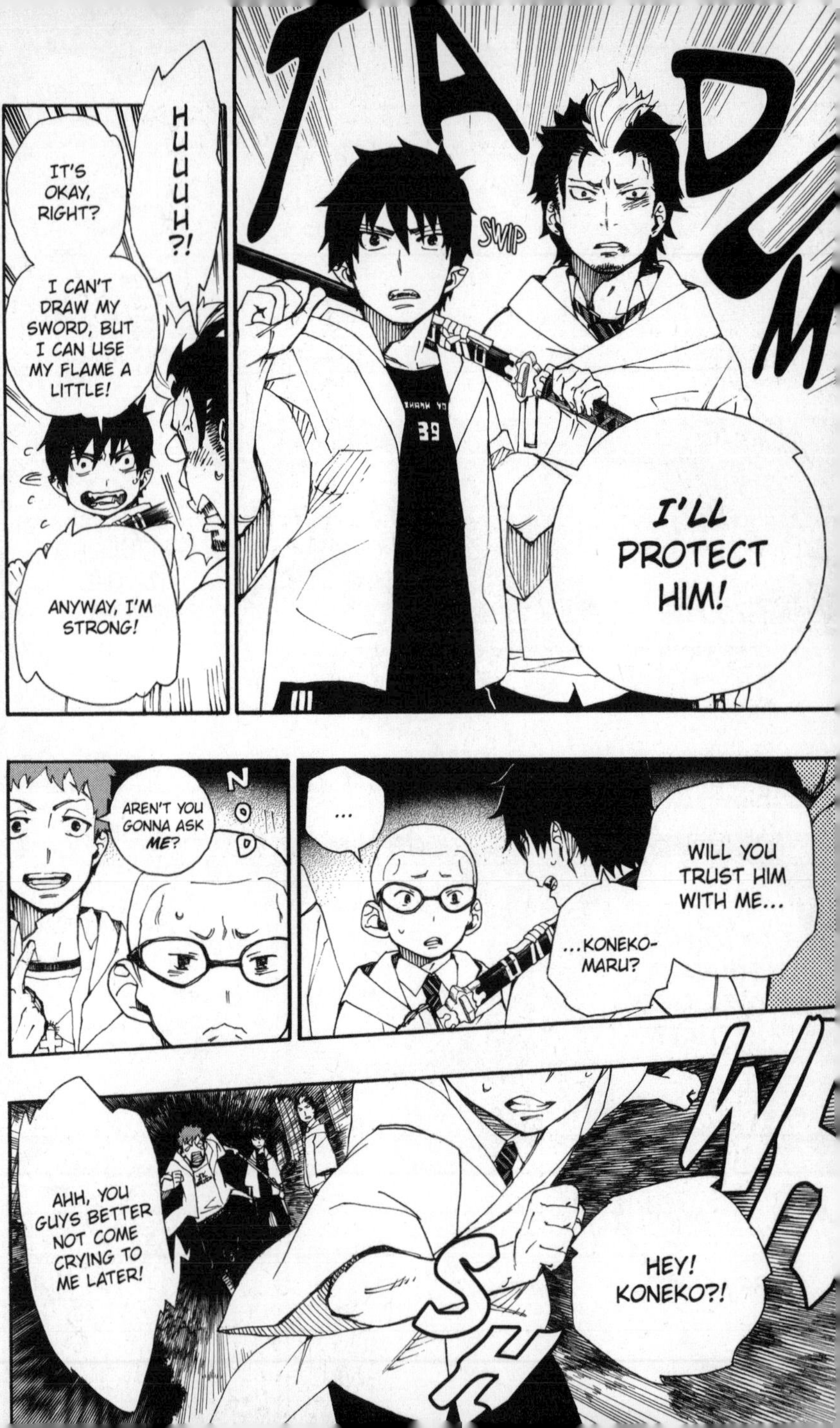
TADUM
SWIP
I'LL PROTECT HIM!
HUUUH?!
IT'S OKAY, RIGHT?
I CAN'T DRAW MY SWORD, BUT I CAN USE MY FLAME A LITTLE!
ANYWAY, I'M STRONG!
WILL YOU TRUST HIM WITH ME...
...KONEKO-MARU?
...
NOD
AREN'T YOU GONNA ASK ME?
HEY! KONEKO?!
AHH, YOU GUYS BETTER NOT COME CRYING TO ME LATER!

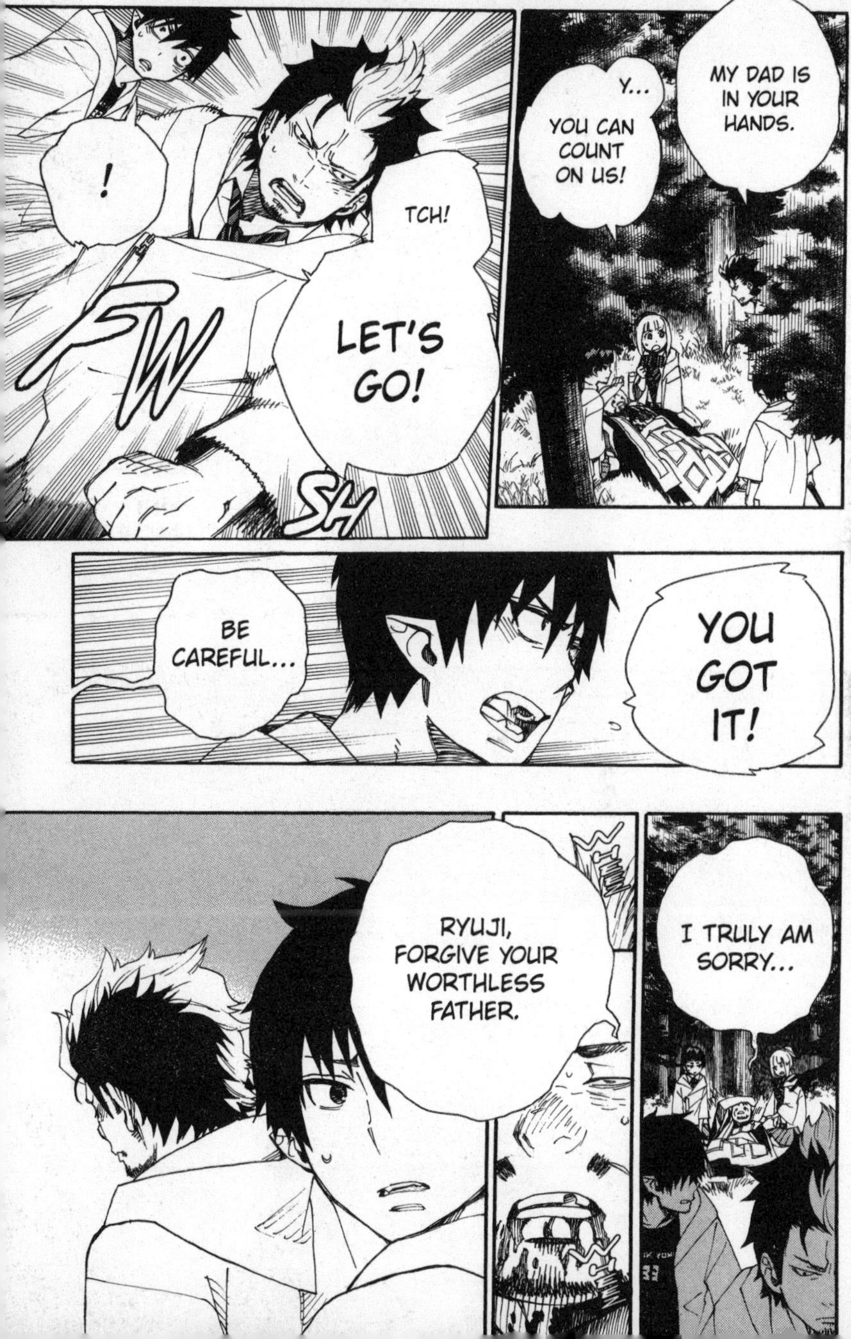
MY DAD IS IN YOUR HANDS.
Y...
YOU CAN COUNT ON US!
TCH!
LET'S GO!
!
FW
SH
YOU GOT IT!
BE CAREFUL...
I TRULY AM SORRY...
RYUJI, FORGIVE YOUR WORTHLESS FATHER.

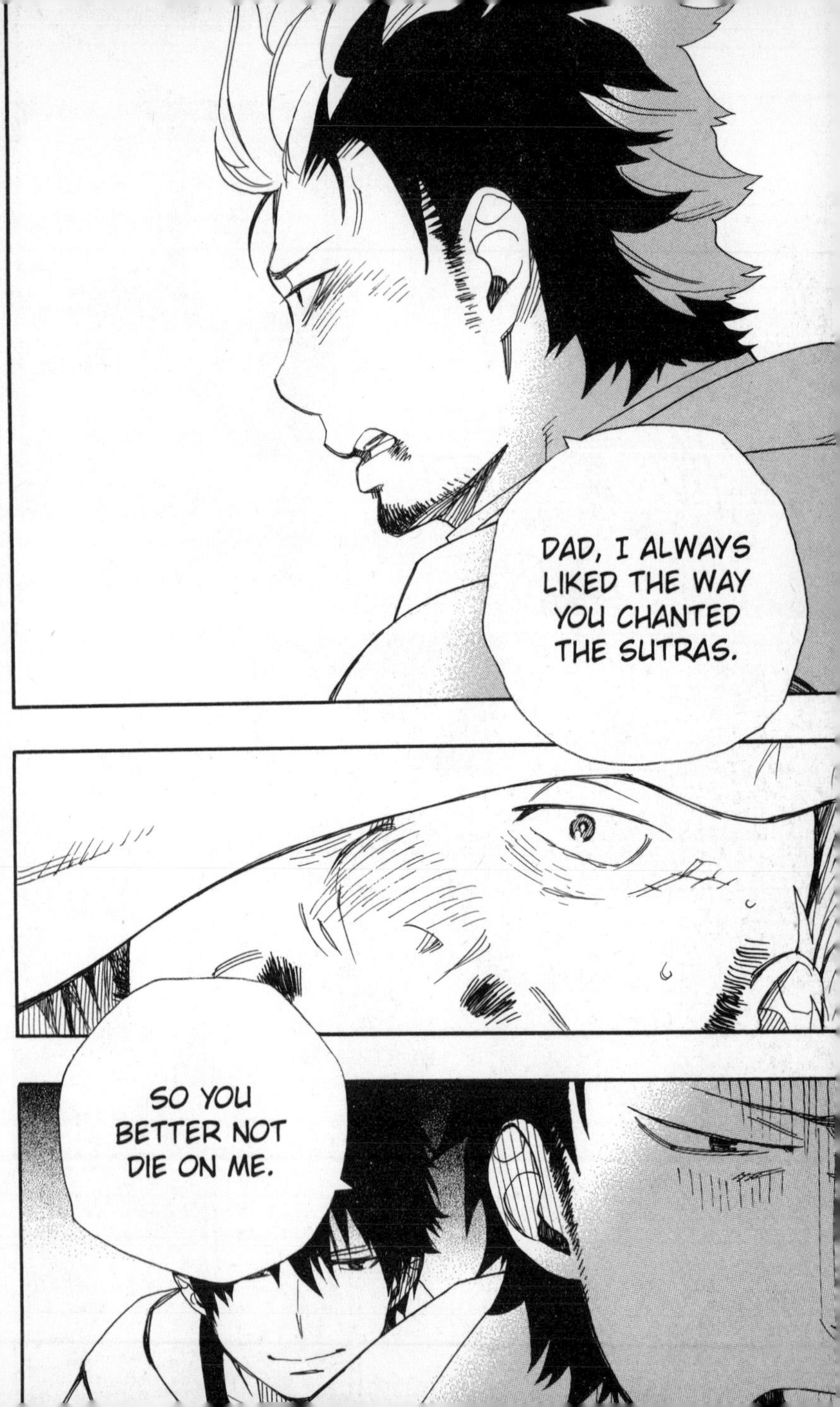
DAD, I ALWAYS LIKED THE WAY YOU CHANTED THE SUTRAS.
SO YOU BETTER NOT DIE ON ME.

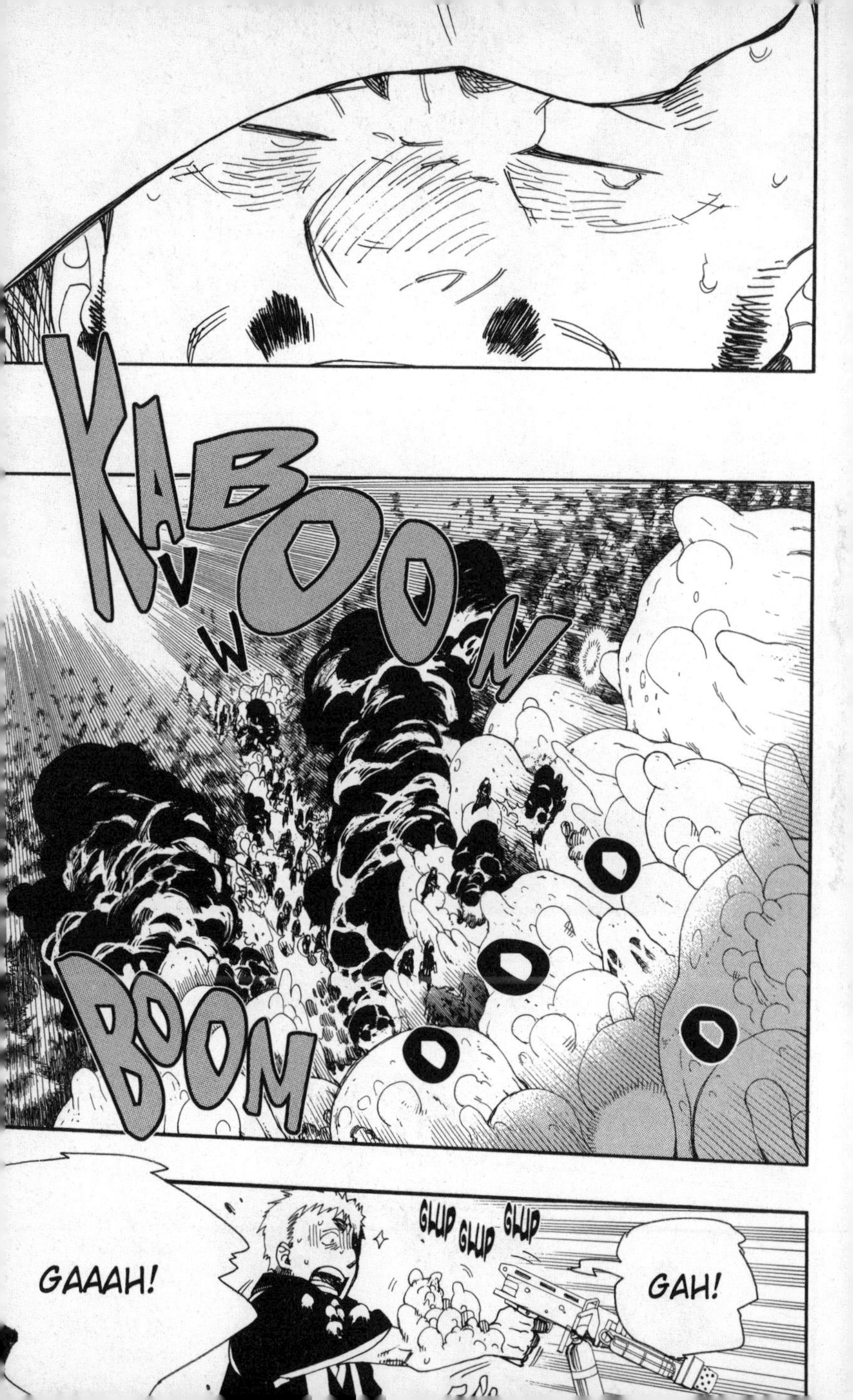
KABOOM
BOOM
OOOO
GAH!
GLUP GLUP GLUP
GAAAH!

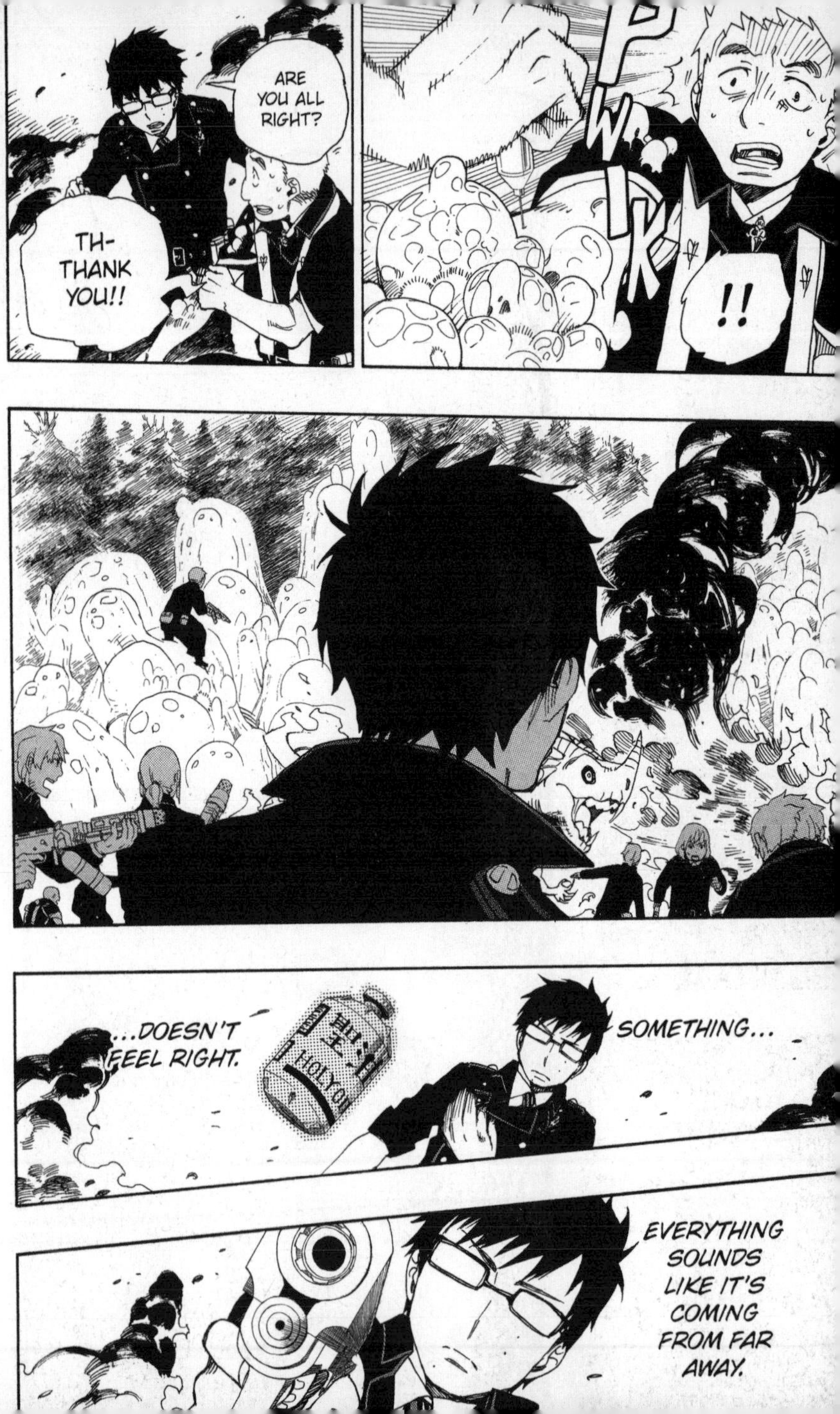
PWKK
!!
ARE YOU ALL RIGHT?
TH-THANK YOU!!
SOMETHING...
...DOESN'T FEEL RIGHT.
EVERYTHING SOUNDS LIKE IT'S COMING FROM FAR AWAY.

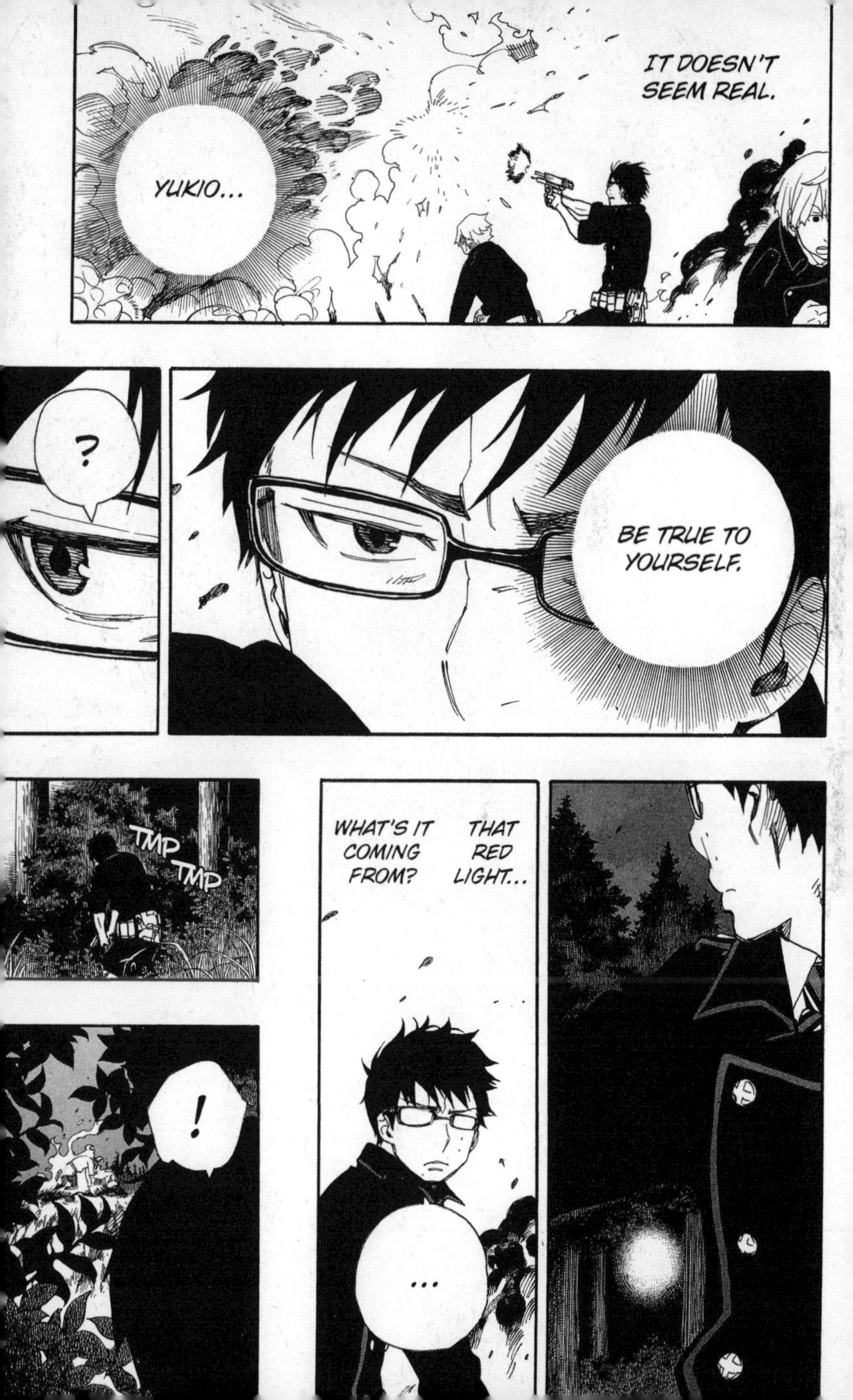
IT DOESN'T SEEM REAL.
YUKIO...
BE TRUE TO YOURSELF.
?
THAT RED LIGHT...
WHAT'S IT COMING FROM?
...
TMP TMP
!

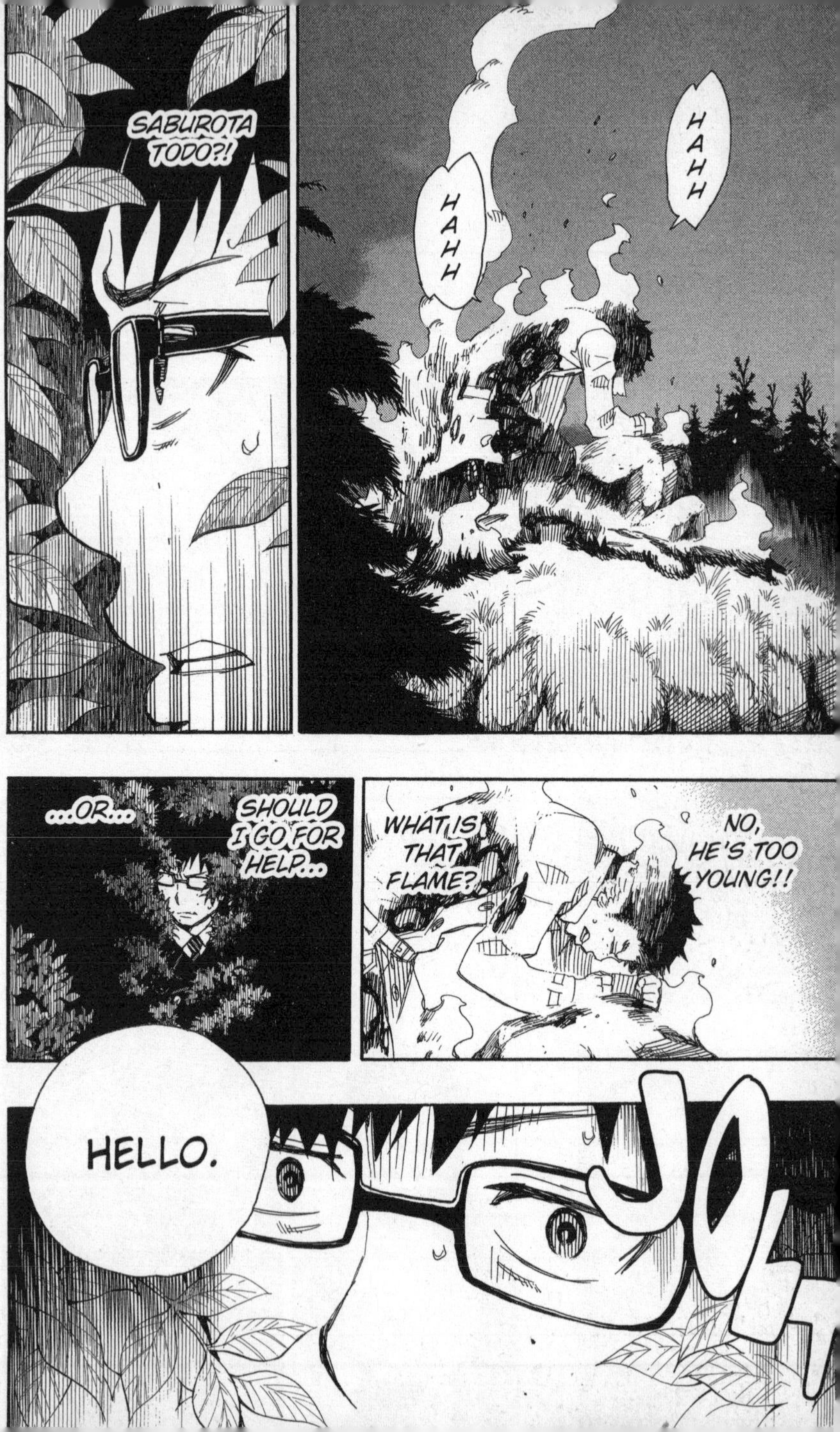
HAHH
HAHH
SABUROTA TODO?!
NO, HE'S TOO YOUNG!!
WHAT IS THAT FLAME?
SHOULD I GO FOR HELP...
...OR...
HELLO.

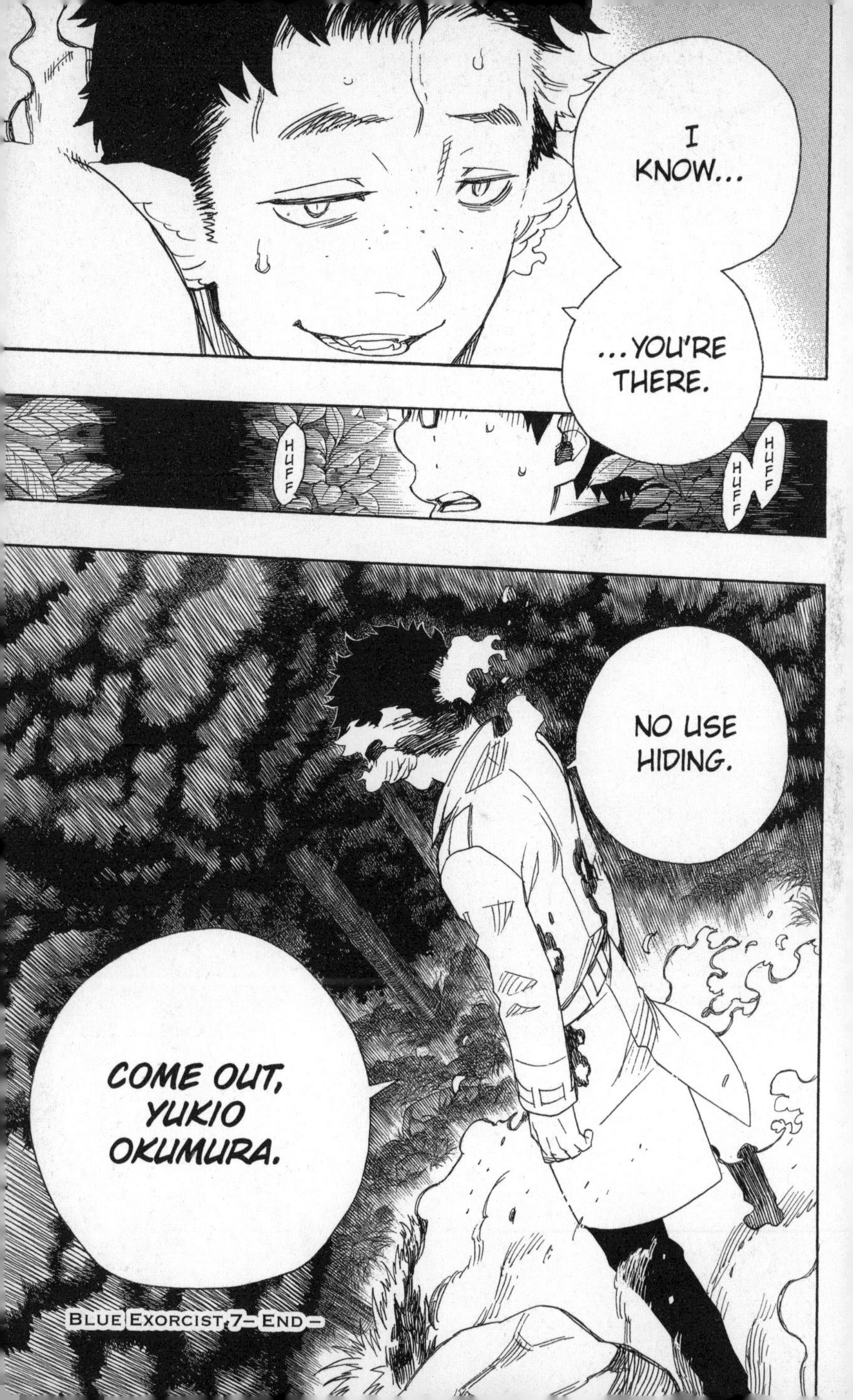
I KNOW...
...YOU'RE THERE.
HUFF HUFF
HUFF
NO USE HIDING.
COME OUT, YUKIO OKUMURA.
BLUE EXORCIST 7 – END –

Blue Exorcist Chapter 27 Battle at Kongo-Shinzan!

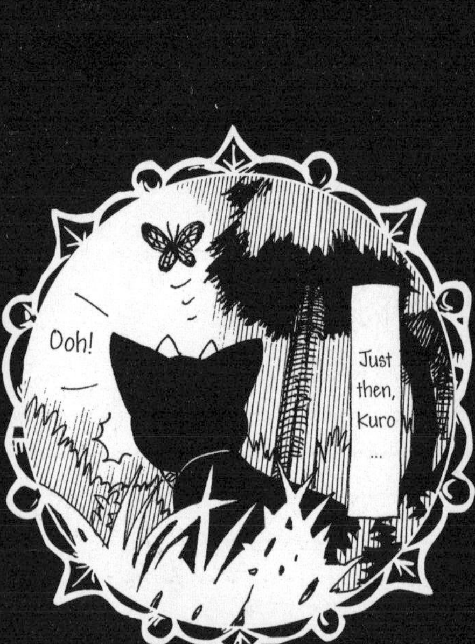

Just then, Kuro ...
Ooh!

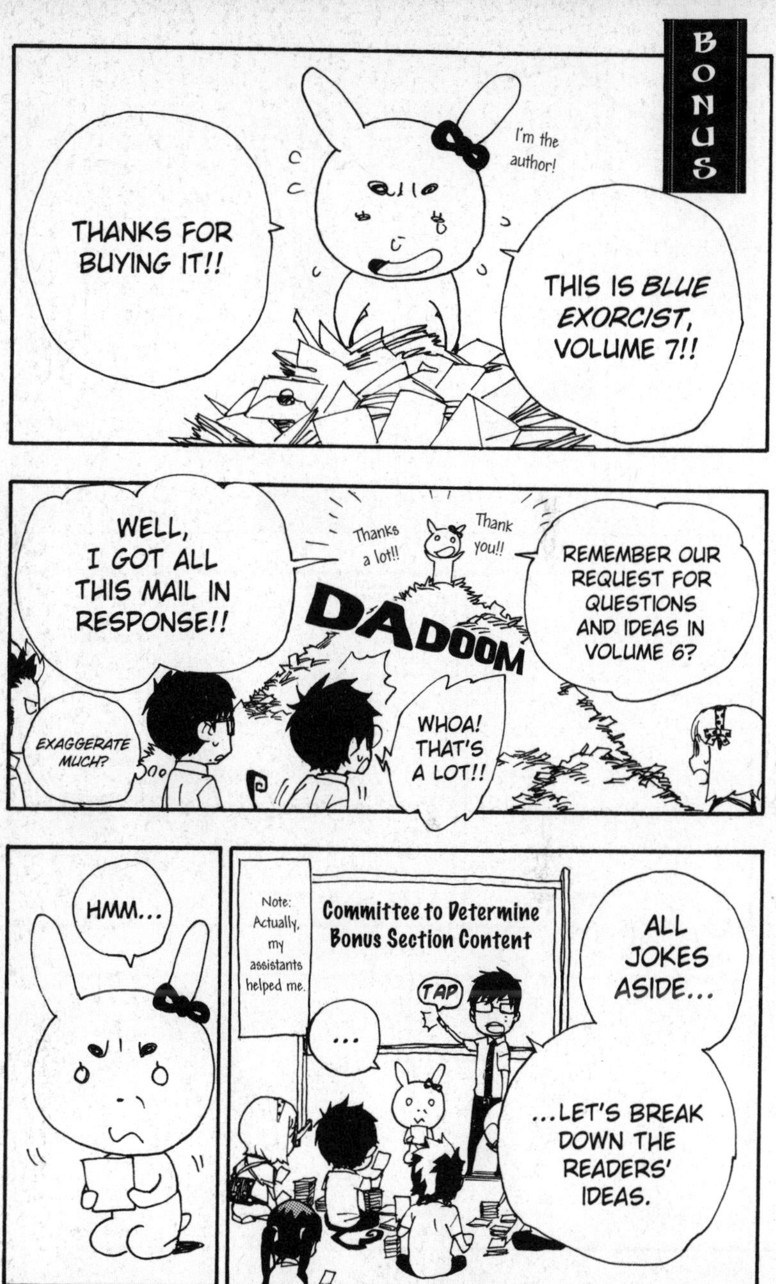
BONUS
THIS IS *BLUE EXORCIST*, VOLUME 7!!
I'm the author!
THANKS FOR BUYING IT!!
REMEMBER OUR REQUEST FOR QUESTIONS AND IDEAS IN VOLUME 6?
Thank you!!
Thanks a lot!!
DADOOM
WELL, I GOT ALL THIS MAIL IN RESPONSE!!
WHOA! THAT'S A LOT!!
EXAGGERATE MUCH?
Committee to Determine Bonus Section Content
Note: Actually, my assistants helped me.
ALL JOKES ASIDE...
TAP
...
...LET'S BREAK DOWN THE READERS' IDEAS.
HMM...

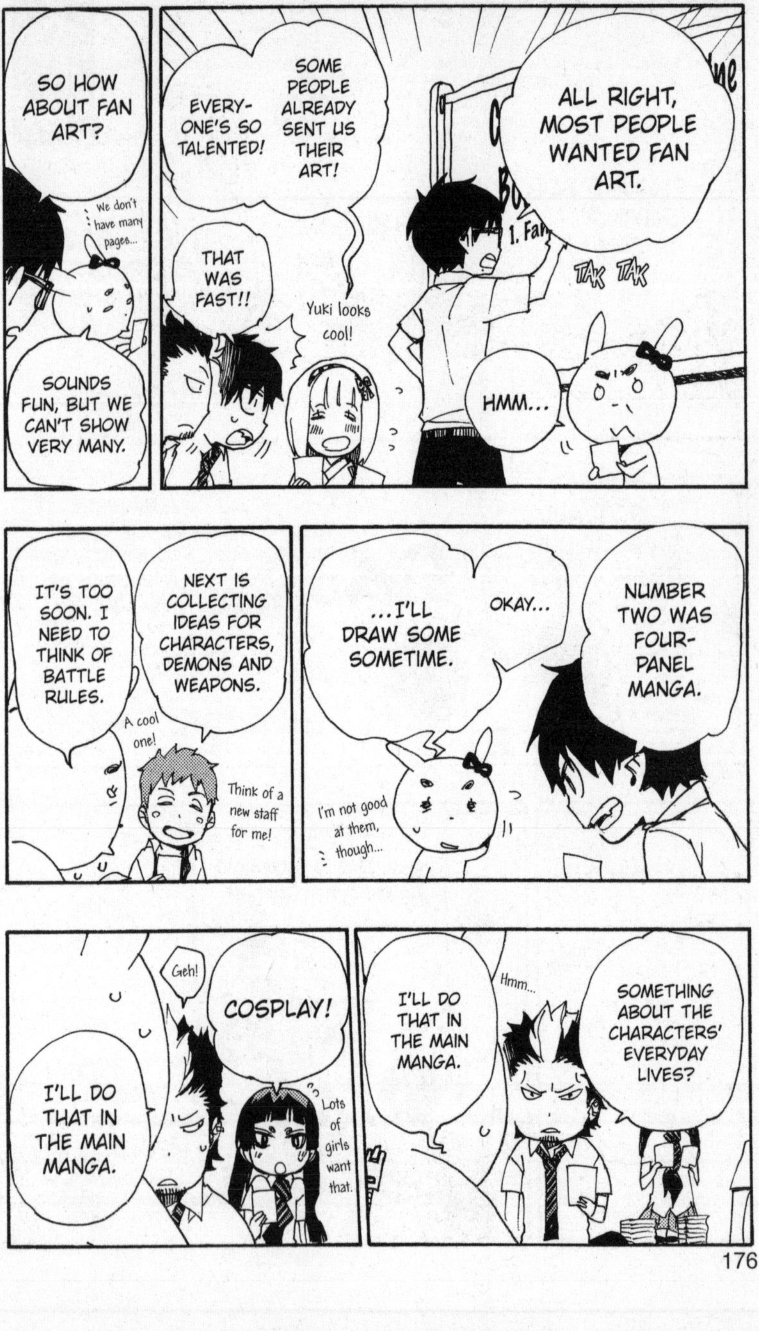
ALL RIGHT, MOST PEOPLE WANTED FAN ART.
TAK TAK
SOME PEOPLE ALREADY SENT US THEIR ART!
EVERY-ONE'S SO TALENTED!
HMM...
Yuki looks cool!
THAT WAS FAST!!
SO HOW ABOUT FAN ART?
We don't have many pages...
SOUNDS FUN, BUT WE CAN'T SHOW VERY MANY.
NUMBER TWO WAS FOUR-PANEL MANGA.
OKAY...
...I'LL DRAW SOME SOMETIME.
I'm not good at them, though...
NEXT IS COLLECTING IDEAS FOR CHARACTERS, DEMONS AND WEAPONS.
IT'S TOO SOON. I NEED TO THINK OF BATTLE RULES.
Think of a new staff for me!
A cool one!
SOMETHING ABOUT THE CHARACTERS' EVERYDAY LIVES?
Hmm...
I'LL DO THAT IN THE MAIN MANGA.
COSPLAY!
Geh!
Lots of girls want that.
I'LL DO THAT IN THE MAIN MANGA.

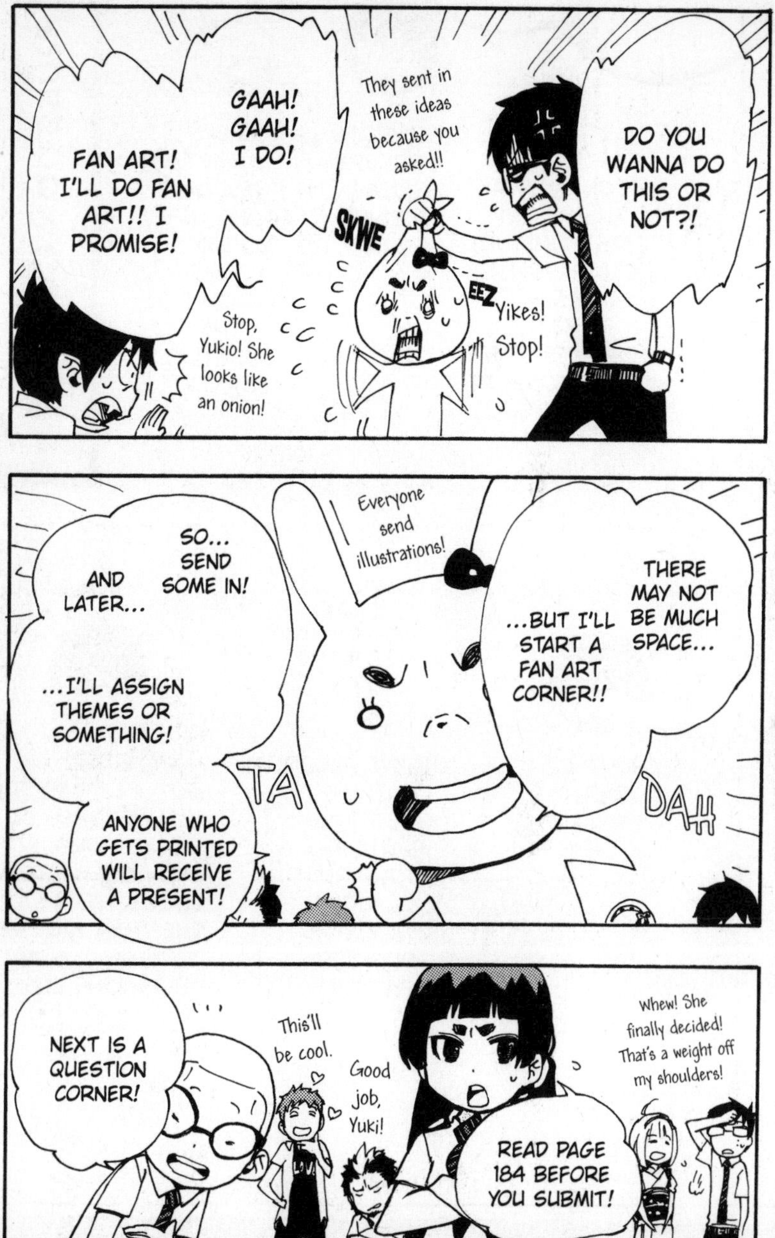
DO YOU WANNA DO THIS OR NOT?!
They sent in these ideas because you asked!!
SKWEEZ
Yikes! Stop!
GAAH! GAAH! I DO!
FAN ART! I'LL DO FAN ART!! I PROMISE!
Stop, Yukio! She looks like an onion!
THERE MAY NOT BE MUCH SPACE...
...BUT I'LL START A FAN ART CORNER!!
Everyone send illustrations!
SO... SEND SOME IN!
AND LATER...
...I'LL ASSIGN THEMES OR SOMETHING!
TA DAH
ANYONE WHO GETS PRINTED WILL RECEIVE A PRESENT!
Whew! She finally decided! That's a weight off my shoulders!
READ PAGE 184 BEFORE YOU SUBMIT!
Good job, Yuki!
This'll be cool.
NEXT IS A QUESTION CORNER!

QUESTION CORNER α

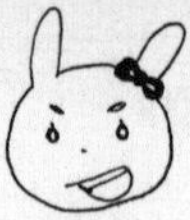

THERE AREN'T MANY PAGES LEFT, SO LET'S JUMP RIGHT INTO THE QUESTION CORNER!

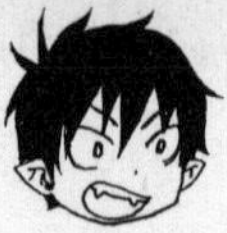

QUESTION CORNER? COOL! SOUNDS SMART!

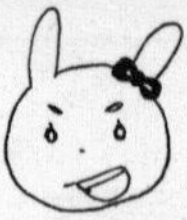

IT'S NOT PARTICULARLY COOL. ANYWAY, THIS IS OUR FIRST TIME, SO I'LL HAVE THE CRAM SCHOOL STUDENTS ANSWER THE MOST COMMON QUESTIONS.

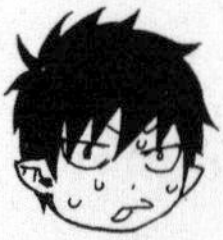

UM, ERRR...WE GOT A LOT OF THE SAME TYPES OF QUESTIONS, SO ONLY ONE PERSON WHO SENT IN EACH QUESTION WILL GET A PRESENT. SORRY, EVERYONE ELSE!

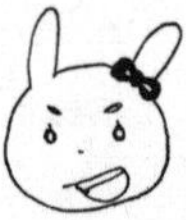

AND WE RULED OUT ANY QUESTIONS ABOUT THE FUTURE PLOT. ALL RIGHT, RIN, YOU'RE OUR TOP BATTER!

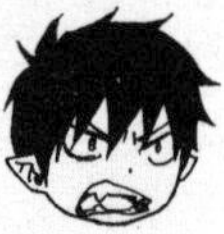

HUH? ALL RIGHT, BRING IT ON!!

HAPPY QUESTION CORNER!

MY QUESTION IS FOR RIN! YOU'RE GOOD AT COOKING, RIGHT? SO HERE'S THE QUESTION... WHAT FOOD ARE YOU BEST AT MAKING?
URUBOTATA-SAN (25), AICHI PREFECTURE

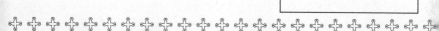

WHAT I'M BEST AT COOKING?!

THIS WAS THE MOST COMMON QUESTION. LOTS WERE ABOUT FOOD.

HMM. SUKIYAKI!

ISN'T THAT JUST YOUR ***FAVORITE*** FOOD?!

NO! MY OWN SUKIYAKI IS THE BEST! I'M SURE OF IT. I'VE GOT A WHOLE REPERTOIRE OF ONE-POT DISHES! THE MONASTERY WAS A BIG FAMILY, SO THAT WAS EASIEST.

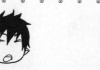

I'M ALSO GOOD AT JAPANESE-STYLE ROLLED OMELET. I'M THE TYPE WHO PUTS IN ONION.

THAT'S A PRETTY ***NORMAL*** ANSWER.

WHEN IT COMES TO FOOD, RIN CAN CARRY ON A CONVERSATION LIKE A NORMAL PERSON.

WHAT?!

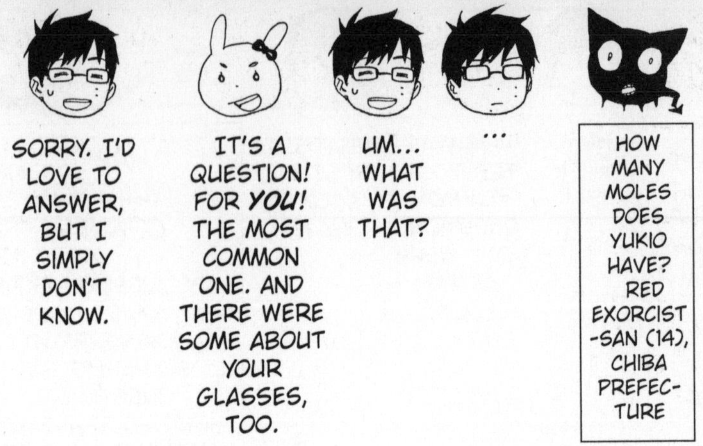
HOW MANY MOLES DOES YUKIO HAVE? RED EXORCIST-SAN (14), CHIBA PREFECTURE
...
UM... WHAT WAS THAT?
IT'S A QUESTION! FOR *YOU*! THE MOST COMMON ONE. AND THERE WERE SOME ABOUT YOUR GLASSES, TOO.
SORRY. I'D LOVE TO ANSWER, BUT I SIMPLY DON'T KNOW.

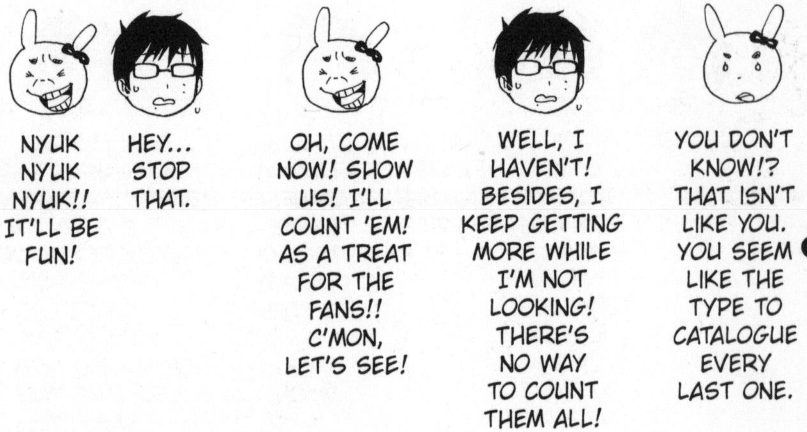
YOU DON'T KNOW!? THAT ISN'T LIKE YOU. YOU SEEM LIKE THE TYPE TO CATALOGUE EVERY LAST ONE.
WELL, I HAVEN'T! BESIDES, I KEEP GETTING MORE WHILE I'M NOT LOOKING! THERE'S NO WAY TO COUNT THEM ALL!
OH, COME NOW! SHOW US! I'LL COUNT 'EM! AS A TREAT FOR THE FANS!! C'MON, LET'S SEE!
HEY... STOP THAT.
NYUK NYUK NYUK!! IT'LL BE FUN!

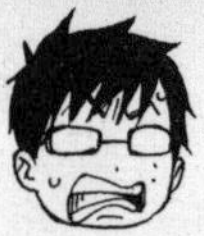

KNOCK IT OFF ALREADY!! DON'T SAY ANOTHER WORD ABOUT MY MOLES!!

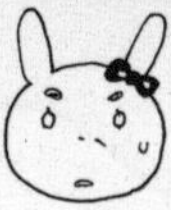

!!!

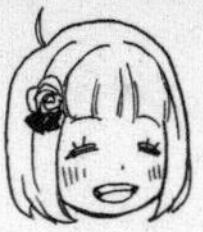

MOLES? I LIKE YUKIO'S MOLES!

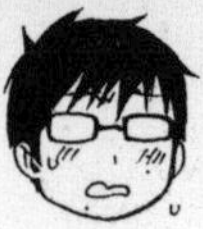

SH-SHIEMI...

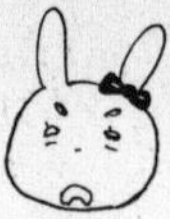

FINE. MOVING ON...

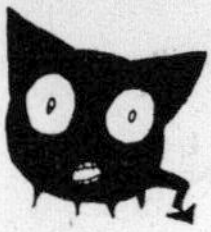

● WHY DOES SHIEMI CALL THINGS BY WEIRD NAMES LIKE SANCHO AND OONI-OONI? TOMOMARU-SAN (14), FUKUI PREFECTURE

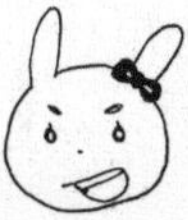

A LOT OF PEOPLE ASKED WHERE SHIEMI GETS THOSE NAMES FROM. BUT...I DON'T REMEMBER *OONI-OONI!!*

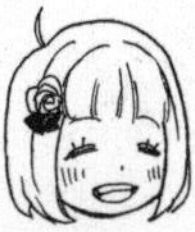

MAYBE THAT'S SUPPOSED TO BE OONA-OONA. BUT OONI-OONI IS CUTE, TOO! IT'S SOMETHING I'VE DONE EVER SINCE I WAS LITTLE. I JUST COME UP WITH THOSE SOUNDS BASED ON HOW THEY LOOK.

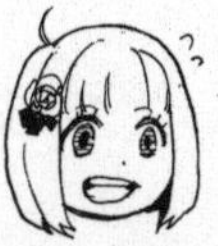

FOR PLANTS THAT LOOK STRONG AGAINST THE HEAT, LIKE ALOE, I TEND TO GIVE THEM VAGUELY LATIN-SOUNDING NAMES. LIKE SERGIO AND ESMERALDA. BUT NOW THAT I'M ATTENDING THE CRAM SCHOOL, I SHOULD LEARN THEIR REAL NAMES!

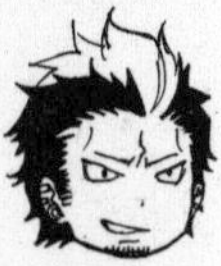

● STUDYING IS IMPORTANT!

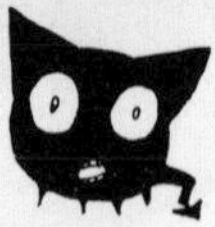

I'VE GOT A QUESTION!! WHY IS SHIMA'S HAIR PINK?

KAMOSHIKA-SAN (13), CHIBA PREFECTURE

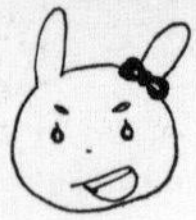

SUGURO GOT LOTS OF QUESTIONS ABOUT HIS HAIRSTYLE. HERE'S A SIMILAR QUESTION.

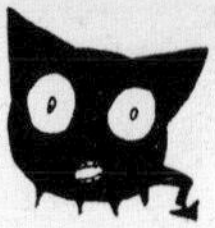

I'VE ALWAYS WONDERED, DOES SUGURO ONLY DYE HIS HAIR IN THE CENTER? IN VOLUME 5, HE SAID IT SHOWED HIS DEDICATION, BUT WHY DIDN'T HE DYE ALL HIS HAIR? PLEASE TELL ME.
ANONYMOUS-SAN (17), YAMAGATA PREFECTURE

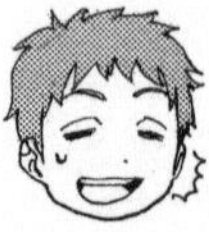

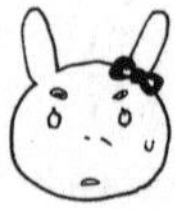

WHOOEE...

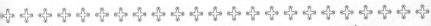

WHAT'S "WHOOEE" SUPPOSED TO MEAN?!

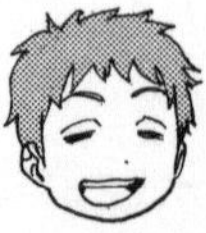

BON, IF YOU AREN'T NICER, GIRLS WON'T LIKE YOU. AND THE LOOK ON YOUR FACE IS ALWAYS SO SCARY! MY HAIR'S PINK BECAUSE GIRLS LIKE PINK. THAT'S WHY!

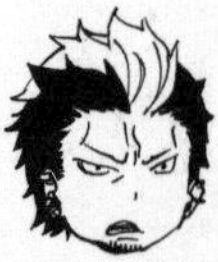

MY HAIRSTYLE IS A SLIGHTLY LONG AND SOFT MOHAWK. I CHANGED THE COLOR TO EMPHASIZE THE MOHAWK PART. IF I DYED THE WHOLE THING, IT WOULDN'T WORK.

NO, I BET THAT'S YOUR NATURAL HAIR COLOR. YOUR HEAD IS PINK INSIDE, SO YOUR HAIR GREW THAT WAY.

NUH-UH! I'M SERIOUS SOMETIMES! LIKE A RATIO OF 8:2.

SHIMA, I WOULDN'T CALL THAT SERIOUS...

HOW BAD IS KONEKOMARU'S EYESIGHT? MOMOOGATA (10), MIYAGI PREFECTURE

WELL, WITHOUT GLASSES, IT'S ABOUT 0.07. WITH GLASSES ON, IT'S ABOUT 1.0. WITHOUT MY GLASSES, I CAN'T QUITE MAKE OUT FACIAL EXPRESSIONS.

THAT'S ROUGH! I'VE GOT GOOD EYES, SO I CAN'T REALLY RELATE.

I HEARD THAT PEOPLE WITH GOOD EYES LOSE THEIR EYESIGHT QUICKER WITH AGE.

!!!!

IN VOLUME 6, IZUMO USED BABY TALK WITH KURO. DOES IZUMO LIKE CATS? ANRI-SAN (13), FUKUI PREFECTURE

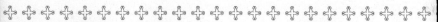

BWUH?! WHAT?! BABYTALK?! WH-WH-WH-WH-WHAT'RE YOU TALKING ABOUT?! (HEY! HOW DID YOU KNOW?!)

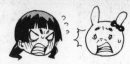

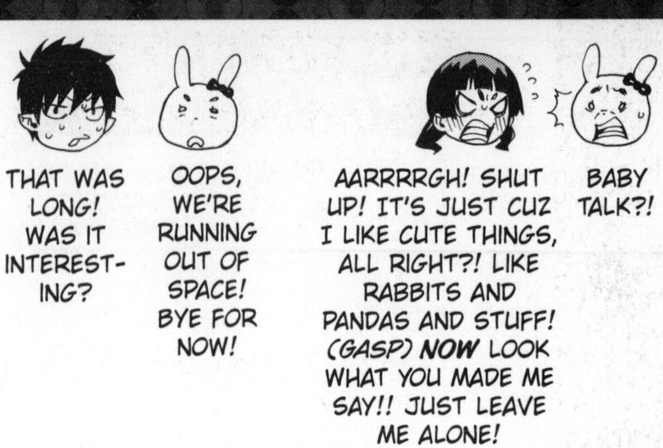

BABY TALK?!
AARRRRGH! SHUT UP! IT'S JUST CUZ I LIKE CUTE THINGS, ALL RIGHT?! LIKE RABBITS AND PANDAS AND STUFF! (GASP) **NOW** LOOK WHAT YOU MADE ME SAY!! JUST LEAVE ME ALONE!
OOPS, WE'RE RUNNING OUT OF SPACE! BYE FOR NOW!
THAT WAS LONG! WAS IT INTEREST-ING?

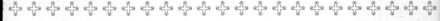

BONUS PAGE GUIDELINES

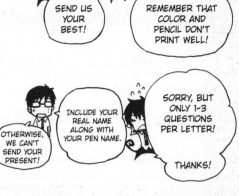

PLEASE DRAW CLEARLY IN BLACK AND WHITE!
REMEMBER THAT COLOR AND PENCIL DON'T PRINT WELL!
SEND US YOUR BEST!
SORRY, BUT ONLY 1-3 QUESTIONS PER LETTER!
THANKS!
INCLUDE YOUR REAL NAME ALONG WITH YOUR PEN NAME.
OTHERWISE, WE CAN'T SEND YOUR PRESENT!
LOTS OF PEOPLE ASKED WHERE TO SEND FAN LETTERS.
THE ADDRESS IS THE SAME!! LET ME KNOW YOUR THOUGHTS!!

SEND YOUR LETTERS, QUESTIONS AND FAN ART TO:

BLUE EXORCIST EDITOR
C/O VIZ MEDIA
295 BAY ST.
SAN FRANCISCO, CA
94133

TO BE CONSIDERED FOR PUBLICATION, FAN ART MUST BE ACCOMPANIED BY A SIGNED RELEASE FORM WHICH CAN BE FOUND ONLINE AT:

SHONENJUMP.VIZ.COM/FANART

FAN ART SUBMISSIONS WILL NOT BE RETURNED.

BLUE EXORCIST 7

Art Assistants:

 YOU'RE DOING GOOD! — **Shibu-tama**

 UH, NO THANKS! — **Uemura-san**

 NO, MORE LIKE THIS... — **Kimura-kun**

 I'LL PASS. — **Hayashi-kun**

 I'M GONNA MOVE!! — **Kawamura-san**

 I HAD A BABY! — **Goro-chin**

 GIRAFFES ARE CUTE! — **Fukushi-san**

 VEGETABLES! — **Yamanaka-san**

 IT BECAME A BOOK! — **Araki-san**

 LIKE A ZOMBIE! — **Kaneko-san**

 HUH?! — **Takeda-kun**

 SHALL WE DO IT? — **Mino-mino**

Composition Assistant:

 OOH, THIS IS HARD! — **Minoru Sasaki**

Editor

 I GOT AN AWARD! — **Shihei Rin**

Graphic Novel Editor:

 THE COVER'S NOT TATSUMA?! — **Ryusuke Kuroki**

Graphic Novel Design:

THANKS FOR THE FAST AND GREAT DESIGNS! — **Shimada Hideaki**
Masaaki Tsunoda
(L.S.D.)

Manga:

 THE ANIME'S ENDING! — **Kazue Kato**

(in no particular order)
(Note: The caricatures and statements are from memory!)

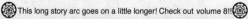 This long story arc goes on a little longer! Check out volume 8!!

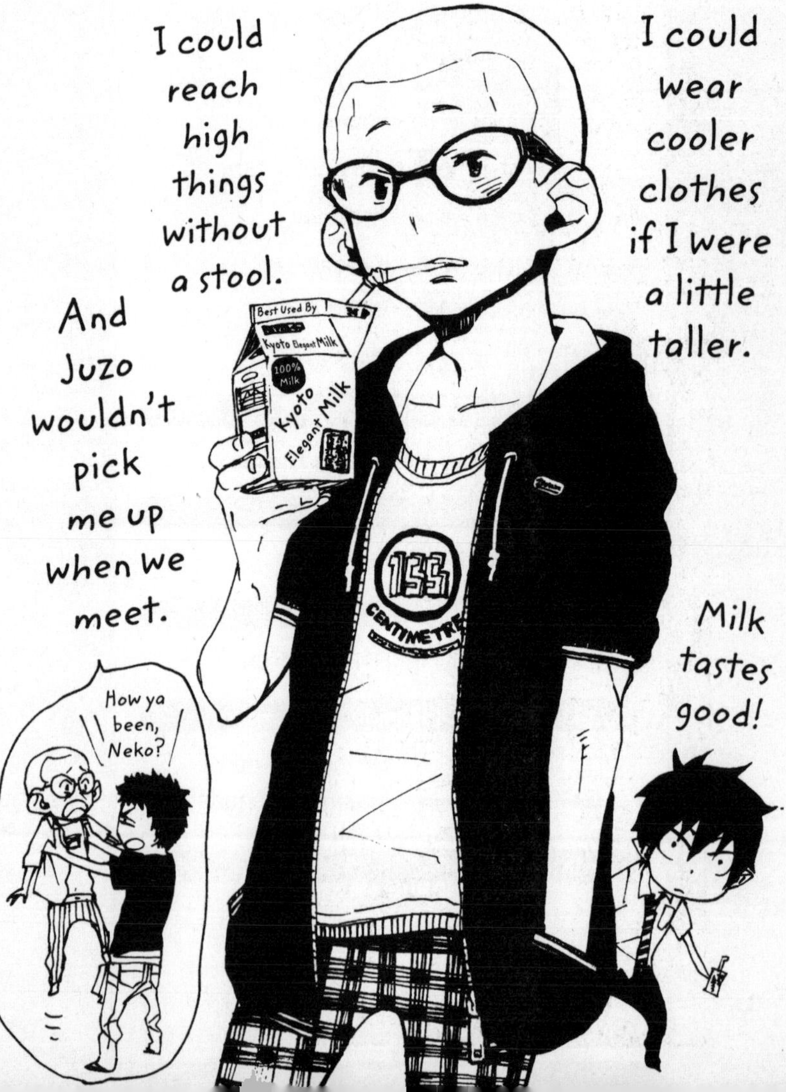
I could wear cooler clothes if I were a little taller.
I could reach high things without a stool.
And Juzo wouldn't pick me up when we meet.
Milk tastes good!
How ya been, Neko?
Best Used By
Kyoto Elegant Milk
100% Milk
Kyoto Elegant Milk
155
CENTIMETRE

A Sensitive Situation

(Note: In the elevator.) →

VRRRR RRRRRRRRR
What is it with 15-year-olds today?
VRRRR RRRRRRRRR
Are you all models or descended from giants?
VRRRR RRRRRRRRR
You're an exception, though. Ha ha!
PAT
SMACK
I KNOW!!!
WHOA
WHOA
WHOA

Not yet?

Huh?

KAZUE KATO

UH, WHAT? THIS LONG STORY ARC WAS
SUPPOSED TO END IN VOLUME 7, BUT
IT'S GOING TO CONTINUE IN VOLUME 8!!

I GUESS THIS KIND OF THING HAPPENS!
IT'S HARD SOMETIMES, BUT I'M DOING
JUST FINE.

HERE'S VOLUME 7!

BLUE EXORCIST

BLUE EXORCIST VOL. 7
SHONEN JUMP ADVANCED Manga Edition

STORY & ART BY KAZUE KATO

Translation & English Adaptation/John Werry
Touch-up Art & Lettering/John Hunt, Primary Graphix
Cover & Interior Design/Sam Elzway
Editor/Mike Montesa

Published by VIZ Media, LLC
P.O. Box 77010
San Francisco, CA 94107

10 9 8 7 6 5 4 3
First printing, April 2012
Third printing, March 2015

www.viz.com

In the next volume...

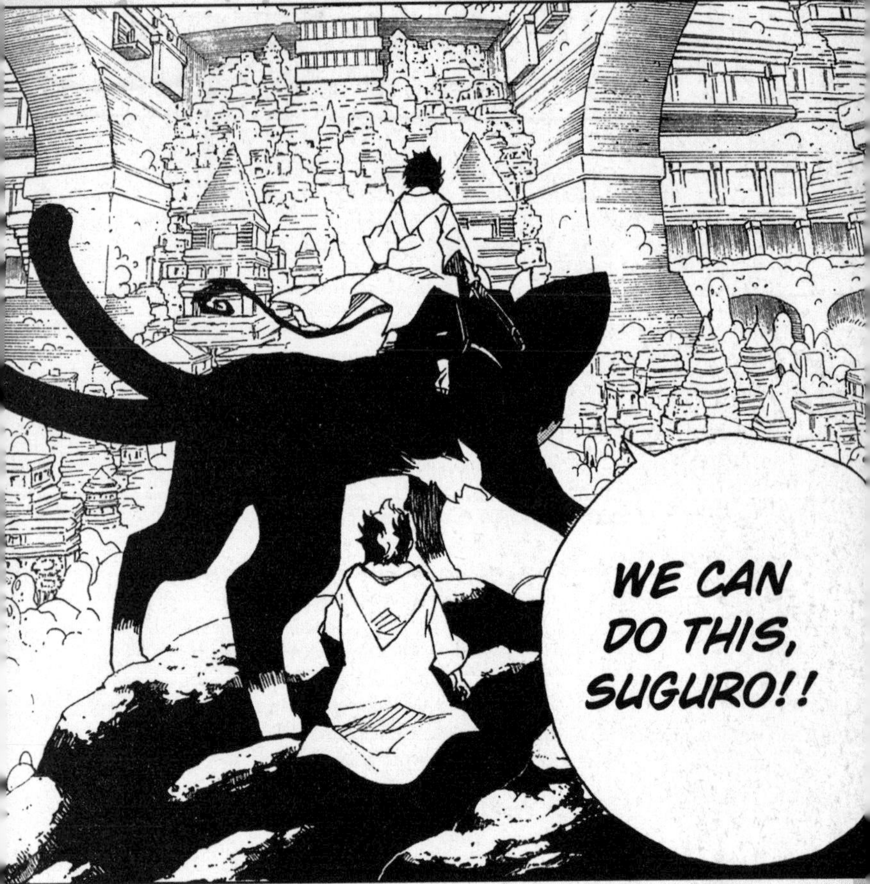
WE CAN DO THIS, SUGURO!!

Awakened by the traitor Saburota Todo, the Impure King's massive form threatens to engulf the city of Kyoto. As the Exorcists of the Tokyo Branch and the monks of the Myodha temple do all they can to contain the demon, Rin and his friends find themselves separated and facing their own battles. While Rin and Ryuji race to confront the full might of the Impure King, Yukio takes on Todo single-handed and discovers that his memories may be his own worst enemy!

Available now!

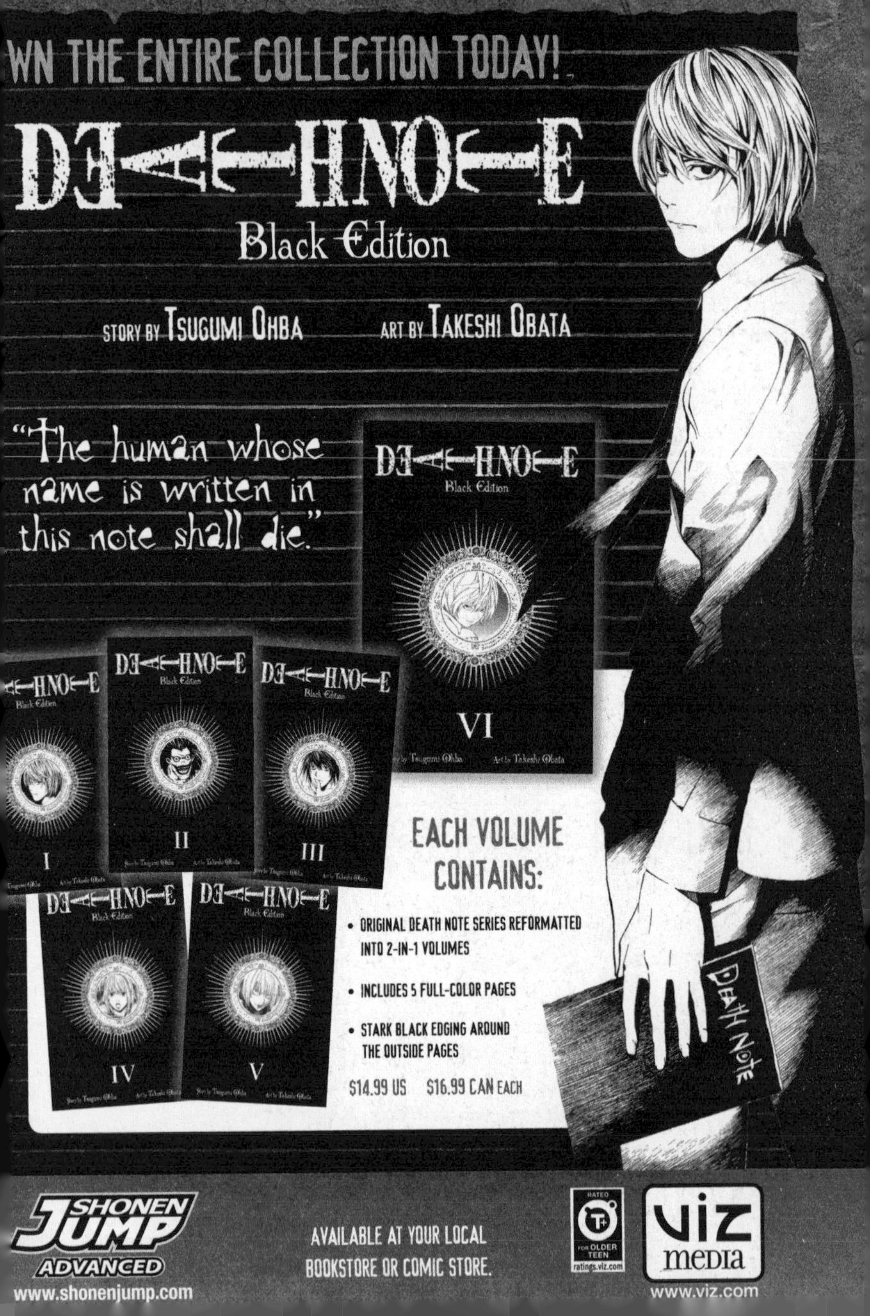
WN THE ENTIRE COLLECTION TODAY!
DEATH NOTE
Black Edition
STORY BY TSUGUMI OHBA
ART BY TAKESHI OBATA
"The human whose name is written in this note shall die."
DEATH NOTE Black Edition VI
I
II
III
IV
V
EACH VOLUME CONTAINS:
• ORIGINAL DEATH NOTE SERIES REFORMATTED INTO 2-IN-1 VOLUMES
• INCLUDES 5 FULL-COLOR PAGES
• STARK BLACK EDGING AROUND THE OUTSIDE PAGES
$14.99 US $16.99 CAN EACH
DEATH NOTE
SHONEN JUMP ADVANCED
www.shonenjump.com
AVAILABLE AT YOUR LOCAL BOOKSTORE OR COMIC STORE.
RATED T+ FOR OLDER TEEN
ratings.viz.com
VIZ media
www.viz.com

You're Reading in the Wrong Direction!!

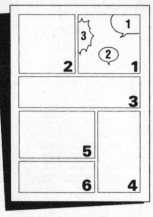

Whoops! Guess what? You're starting at the wrong end of the comic!

…It's true! In keeping with the original Japanese format, **Blue Exorcist** is meant to be read from right to left, starting in the upper-right corner.

Unlike English, which is read from left to right, Japanese is read from right to left, meaning that action, sound effects and word-balloon order are completely reversed… something which can make readers unfamiliar with Japanese feel pretty backwards themselves. For this reason, manga or Japanese comics published in the U.S. in English have sometimes been published "flopped"—that is, printed in exact reverse order, as though seen from the other side of a mirror.

By flopping pages, U.S. publishers can avoid confusing readers, but the compromise is not without its downside. For one thing, a character in a flopped manga series who once wore in the original Japanese version a T-shirt emblazoned with "M A Y" (as in "the merry month of") now wears one which reads "Y A M"! Additionally, many manga creators in Japan are themselves unhappy with the process, as some feel the mirror-imaging of their art skews their original intentions.

We are proud to bring you Kazue Kato's **Blue Exorcist** in the original unflopped format. For now, though, turn to the other side of the book and let the adventure begin…!

—Editor